The Protestant Ethic and the Spirit of Sport

The Protestant Ethic and the Spirit of Sport

How Calvinism and Capitalism Shaped America's Games

STEVEN J. OVERMAN

MERCER UNIVERSITY PRESS
MACON, GEORGIA

MUP/P419

First Edition.

Books published by Mercer University Press are printed on acid free paper that meets the requirements of American National Standard for Information Sciences—Permanence of Paper for Printed Library Materials.

Mercer University Press is a member of Green Press initiative (greenpressinitiative.org), a nonprofit organization working to help publishers and printers increase their use of recycled paper and decrease their use of fiber derived from endangered forests. This book is printed on recycled paper.

Library of Congress Cataloging-in-Publication Data

Overman, Steven J.
The Protestant ethic and the spirit of sport : how Calvinism and capitalism shaped America's games / Steven J. Overman. -- 1st ed.
p. cm.
Includes bibliographical references and index.
ISBN 978-0-88146-226-5 (pbk. : alk. paper)
1. Sports—Religious aspects—Protestant churches. 2. Capitalism—Religious aspects—Protestant churches. 3. Sports—Social aspects—United States. 4. Protestantism—United States. 5. Capitalism—United States. 6. Puritan movements—United States.
I. Title.
GV706.42.O94 2011
796.01—dc22
2011000922

Table of Contents

PREFACE

Most American youngsters grow up playing sandlot ball and join in backyard pick-up games. Many go on to compete in school, church-league, or municipal-league sports. As they make this transition, they are introduced to the rationalized conventions, competitive ethos, and status rituals of organized sports. American sports fans are exposed to the rampant commercialism, celebrity culture, and careerism that increasingly define spectator sports. I have shared these experiences through the course of my life. As I pursued my graduate education, I mulled over the sway of cultural values on sport.

I began reading on the Protestant ethic, having returned to graduate school to complete a Master of Arts degree with an emphasis in sport sociology, while on the faculty at Jackson State University. Among the scholarly works I encountered was Professor Allen Guttmann's *From Ritual to Record: The Nature of Modern Sports*. Guttmann opened my eyes to the influences of industrial capitalism on modern sport and peaked my interest in Max Weber's Protestant ethic thesis. The intellectual force of this concise book induced me to attempt an in-depth study of the relationship between the Protestant ethic, capitalism, and modern sport.

The present book appears more than a decade following the publication of my scholarly monograph titled, *The Influence of the Protestant Ethic on Sport and Recreation*. This rather broad study incorporated physical recreation and the use of leisure time, and extended the Protestant ethic thesis to other nations in the context of the Modern Olympics. I felt the need to hone and further develop my ideas within the parameters of American sport. In the interim, sport has changed significantly, and I have been able to mine the more recent literature in re-forming my thesis. My updated reading included numerous auto/biographies of American athletes ranging from the legendary Ty Cobb and Babe Didrikson to Tiger Woods and Danica Patrick. These personal narratives provided a valuable complement to the analysis of social theorists who explicate cultural influences on sport.

The Protestant Ethic and the Spirit of Sport follows sport from the contentious scenes of the English Reformation to Colonial America steeped in Puritanism, through the Industrial Age and the Progressive Era into the throes of modern corporate capitalism and the pervasive electronic media. This study offers readers a broad examination of American sport that includes the institutionalization of children's sport, the professionalization of college sport, the commercialization of participant sport, and media exploitation of professional sport. The later chapters examine the components of a secular Protestant ethic that have shaped modern sport: asceticism, rationalization, the work ethic, goal-directedness, individualism, competitiveness, and the need for achieved status. The book concludes with a brief statement of what should be made of these sundry influences.

This study in historical sociology elucidates the relationship between American sport and a culture infused with residual Puritanism and shaped by evolving capitalism. As such, I believe it makes a valuable contribution to the scholarly literature. I hope the book will interest both academics and the more reflective sports aficionados who care about the direction of contemporary sport.

I am grateful to Sports and Religion Series editor, Joe Price, Professor of Religious Studies at Whittier College, baseball writer and fan, whose understanding of American religion and sport informed my writing on the subject. I also extend my thanks to Marsha Luttrell, Publishing Assistant at Mercer University Press, and her staff for their careful editing and assistance in compiling the index. I take full responsibility for any errors or misinterpretations that remain. Finally, I wish to thank my wife, Elizabeth, whose encouragement motivated me throughout this extensive project.

Part I

The Protestant Ethic

1

Introduction

Sport, Culture, and Religious Values

It is a fact of civilization that each society creates the games it wants to play
and rejects those it regards as irrelevant.
—Gore Vidal

Americans have transformed virtually every game and recreational activity
from Frisbee to football into highly competitive contests. Pickup games and
sandlot play inevitably give way to organized leagues, local, regional, and
national tournaments. Sophisticated strategies and technologies are applied
to the problems of how to throw or hit a ball, to run faster or jump higher.
Meanwhile, sports aficionados compile statistics on every arcane indicator
of athletic performance. We pay professional athletes as much as corporate
executives and charge admission to watch them perform. America's colleges
sponsor teams of quasi-professionals at the risk of jeopardizing their
academic integrity. Middle-aged Americans train with the intensity of
Olympic athletes to compete in marathons and triathlons. Parents employ
coaches to mold children into highly skilled performers and arrange the
family schedule around their games. Sports fans routinely berate coaches
and officials for failing to perform to expectations. Local communities bask
in the victories of athletes and teams with whom they identify.

How does one explain these attitudes and behaviors? Four fundamental
questions lie at the heart of the matter. Why do Americans feel guilty when
they play for the fun of it? Why must we infuse games with high moral
purpose? Why have we turned sports into rational, goal-directed, work-
infused activities? And why is winning so important? A related inquiry
addresses why and how American sport has been transformed into a
factotum of consumer capitalism.

I searched for the answers to these questions beginning with the
writings of the German economist and sociologist Max Weber (1864–1920).
At the turn of the twentieth century, Weber presented his theory that
described a relationship between the Protestant ethic and a form of

economic achievement behavior that he labeled "the spirit of capitalism." At the same time, Weber conceptualized the Protestant ethic as a cultural force that exerted a general influence upon a wide realm of social behaviors and institutions beyond those directly concerned with economic activity.[1] The present book extends Weber's thesis into leisure behavior. My basic premise is that the Protestant ethic became the dominant social and cultural force that influenced American values and shaped the nation's institutions— including sport, the focus of this book. The derivative spirit of capitalism, in turn, inspired economic attitudes and habits that impinged on both work and leisure. Together, these cultural and economic forces formed the spirit of American sport.

By employing the theoretical perspective of sociology and the narrative of social history, I shall attempt to establish the connection between modern sport and the Protestant ethic. The roots of the ethic extend back to the Protestant Reformation. This discourse takes us on a retrospective journey. The itinerary includes a brief excursion into historical Calvinism prior to analyzing the basic Protestant values within the context of modern secular culture. The book chronicles the American experience beginning with the Colonial period. A discussion of the Puritans' struggle with uses of leisure is followed by an investigation of the rise of organized sport during the nineteenth century, which in turn leads us to the evolving structures and values of modern sport. The exploration of the relationship between the Protestant ethic and the spirit of sport unfolds chronologically and encompasses the link between sport and capitalism.

The book doesn't attempt to provide a broad history of American sport, which can be found elsewhere. Instead, it borrows examples from various periods of history in order to make specific points about the relationship of sport with the Protestant ethic. The reader will discern that the second half of the nineteenth century is discussed in disproportion. This era witnessed the rise of sport during the onset of industrial capitalism and the concurrent Progressive campaigns to reform recreation and the uses of leisure. Indeed, many of our social and cultural institutions are Victorian inventions. What occurred during this seminal period has exerted an enduring influence on the structures and ethos of American sport and popular culture.

Every society cultivates its own distinct ideology and value system. This collection of ideals and values is what holds a society together. It provides the cultural criteria that make up the basis for judging people and institutions as to their morality or merit. Even where cultural diversity exists, basic values are assimilated by the population. Children are taught the prevailing cultural values through parents and in contact with socializing agencies including schools, youth groups, and churches. Consequently, values tend to endure across groups and across generations. The virtues I was taught in scouting were the same ones instilled in my sons and grandsons when they joined Boy Scouts and in my daughter and granddaughters when they became Girl Scouts. This carryover is equally evident in the creed taught in youth sports programs. My father learned these lessons playing basketball in YMCA gymnasiums, as did I a generation later.

A common means of justifying social values and prioritizing them has been to link them to a shared religious heritage. This connection with religion carries conviction because religion traditionally has expressed the ultimate values that endow human activity with meaning. It follows that religious values find many outlets and expressions within a society. They live on in economics, politics, morals, and in leisure culture. Each of the major world religions has had its own distinctive orientation to individual human behavior and to social and cultural institutions. Values tend to be stable over time, short of an outright revolution. We recognize Reformed Protestantism as a strain of Christianity that has emphasized purity and control. The English Calvinists were labeled "Puritans" for their attempts to purify the English Church, the world around them, and their own lives. The Puritans who migrated to New England carried with them these and other values that shaped America's moral and cultural framework.

Max Weber understood that religious values and ideas influenced a wide range of social conduct. However, he didn't believe that religion functioned unilaterally as a causal factor in most circumstances. Weber conceded a certain level of reciprocity. He observed, "If we look at the causal lines, we see them run, at one time, from technical to economic and political matters, at another from political to religious and economic ones, etc. There is no resting point."[2] Ideas shape and, in turn, are shaped by our interests and actions. Ultimately, interests are what directly govern human lives. Interests are influenced by world images that have been created by ideas that determine the tracks along which actions are pushed.[3]

Particular social classes or groups with special material interests adopt controlling ideas and are influenced by them. These ideas often are based on or buttressed by religious beliefs. In the historical case of the Protestant business classes, their capitalistic activity received a unique sanction from

Reformation religion.[4] Weber demonstrated that for this class, the ideological influence of religion operated as an agent of social change. His research and writings brought the relationship between religious values and social action into the framework of sociological analysis.

Weber also recognized the crucial role the historic process of secularization played in the linking of religious values and a broad range of social action in Protestant culture. Post-Reformation religion was concerned with the world and inserted its authority and influence into the life of the community. Over time, mundane concerns gradually superseded a preoccupation with the supernatural. In the process, sources of human meaning and obligation were redistributed from one all-encompassing, essentially religious view to a variety of outlooks—some religious and some not. In turn, this led to the modification in basic social institutions like schools and government agencies that took over functions carried out traditionally by the church. This transformation modified individual behaviors, both prescriptive (obligatory) and elective (discretionary). For example, traditional obligations on the Sabbath vied with emerging interests in recreational activities. Generally, culture shifted from institutionalized traditions to the institutionalization of change. Fewer and fewer social actions remained under direct religious control as Protestant religious values became secularized.[5]

Calvinism provided the thought system that was central to the continuing secularization of Western culture. Combined with the worldly emphasis of Enlightenment thought, Calvinism led to a pronounced rationalization of behavior. Although religious values were still included within this new framework, the sources of human meaning and obligation now included both the religious and nonreligious. Secularized religious values began to influence a wider range of social action as human attitudes and behaviors were liberalized. The process of secularization led to social action being less prescriptive, more elective.[6] While religion no longer had a monopoly on the definition of reality or the formation of personality, religious values continued to underlay systems of meaning and continued to shape human action. People still turned to religion to justify personal behavior. Significantly, ethical behavior in daily activities became as important as religious doctrine. The mundane endeavors of work, the state, and the family were glorified as never before.[7]

When social and cultural institutions are interdependent, the interests, motivations, and behaviors established in the one sphere influence interests, motivations, and behaviors obtained in others. For instance, religious values assist individuals struggling with life decisions and in forming goals. In the process, goals are attached to deeper levels of motivation and are integrated with meaningful definitions of the situation; in other words, they are institutionalized. Various human goals and interests, both economic and non-economic, are susceptible to the influence of religious ideologies.[8] Sociologists attempt to identify what values are inherent in various social institutions, the patterns of activity, and the features of social structure that tend to change or persist as a result of these institutionalized values.[9]

Are America's cultural goals and values reflected in the nation's sports? Baseball historian Leonard Koppett argues that sport constitutes an important element in community and national consciousness. Sport reinforces values through the elements of rooting interest, hero worship, nostalgia, participation in mass activity, and as a medium for common discourse, from talk radio to the barbershop.[10] Notwithstanding, some of the intrinsic values evident in sport conflict with values found elsewhere in the social order. The recent epidemic of performance-enhancing drugs is a prime example. At the same time, sport's ideology is appropriated for extrinsic purposes: commercialism, patriotism, alumni loyalty, etc. Politicians routinely exploit sports champions for photo opportunities; merchandisers employ sporting images to advertise their products.

Robert K. Merton noted that separate institutional spheres are partially autonomous, but only after a prolonged development do they acquire any significant degree of autonomy.[11] Relatively young institutions such as organized sport reveal a susceptibility to outside influences from other, more established institutional spheres, particularly during the formative years. Thorstein Veblen coined the term "instinct of sportsmanship" and noted that it was more recent and more unstable than the "instinct of workmanship," and that this accounted for the infusion of work-like attitudes into sport.[12]

Weber's seminal thesis encouraged social scientists to set about the task of searching for Protestant values within various social and cultural developments. Merton applied Weber's thesis to demonstrate that religious ideas derived from the Protestant Reformation had a notable effect upon the development of rational science in the seventeenth century.[13] David McClelland, in his classic study of achievement, posited that Weber's hypothesis represented a special case of a more general relationship with the need for achievement, one that he felt should be fully investigated.[14] The present book argues that institutionalized values of secular Protestantism have exerted a profound influence on organized sport. There are compelling reasons to extend Weber's thesis to sporting behavior. Scholars interested in the Protestant ethic thesis have given more attention to its influence on human labor and economic activity than to noneconomic attitudes and behaviors. This omission appears significant, for religious values have framed our basic ideas of leisure as well as work. Neulinger points out that religion is "most intimately related to work *and leisure* [emphasis mine] attitudes. One might even say that, for some...leisure *is* their religion. We speak here of religion, not in the formal sense, but as a basic belief that determines one's life style. But even if we think of religion in a narrower sense, it is certainly true that religious dogma had a great impact on...leisure habits."[15] Neulinger singled out the Protestant ethic as having had a profound influence on present-day thinking in regard to matters of both work and leisure.

Contemporary social scientists have recognized sport as a leisure institution in which religious values and physical culture meet. Harry Edwards observed that "the socially significant secular values infused into sports activities typically have their roots in large part in the religious and moral heritages of the societies in which these activities are pursued."[16] Lueschen argued that Weber's findings about the relationship between the Protestant ethic and the spirit of capitalism might well be extended to conceptualize a "spirit" of sport.[17] Such a relationship was postulated by sport sociologists Eitzen and Sage when they expressed what is the basic premise for this book: that the value orientations underlying competitive sports in America are "...more or less, secularized versions of the core values of Protestantism which has been the dominant belief system throughout American history."[18]

Before exploring the specific influence of the Protestant ethic on American sport, it is helpful to take a brief look at the general relationship between sport and religion as conceptualized by social scientists and religious scholars. The following section discusses religious forms and values apparent in sport.

Sport as Religion

> Baseball may be a religion full of magic, cosmic truth, and the fundamental
> ontological riddles of our time, but it's also a job.
> —Annie Savoy, *Bull Durham*

Sport, like religion, can serve as a model *for* and model *of* reality. Both traditions have their own cultural symbols (icons, liturgy), established moods and motivations (adulation, reverence), and conceptions of the world ("Life is a game." "The body is a temple."). In addition, sport and religion each perform functions required by society. They socialize novices into the group, reinforce behaviors, and reaffirm cultural values. Moreover, sporting events can assume the character of rituals and, like the rituals of religion, reinforce feelings of commitment within a community. Sociologists have identified several similarities between "religious systems of meaning" and the spirit of modern sport. The overlap in the meanings of sport and religion doesn't imply necessarily that sport is a *form* of religion, although this thesis has been explored at some length (see below). The present book's thesis is based on the idea that sport can act as a *functional equivalent* of religion.[19]

The religious dimensions of sport were particularly salient in its historical contexts. Under the "sacred canopy" of tribal societies, games were replete with religious forms and meanings. To a great extent, preliterate people expressed their religion through play and dance.[20] Students of sport still find remnants of religious forms in modern games and contests. Speaking metaphorically, sports have their gods, saints, scribes, and houses of worship. In his caricature of American football, Linwood Fredericksen observed that the modern sporting event has all the trappings of an ancient religious festival. He suggested that what a person from a preliterate culture would perceive at a contemporary football stadium is a large congregation gathered together to witness a ritual combat conducted according to prescribed rules. The participants in the ritual are dressed in identifiable costumes, with one side representing good and the other evil— depending upon the viewpoint of the audience. Leading the congregation are priestesses/cheerleaders dressed in distinct garb, performing ritualistic dances and chanting various formulas that are deemed efficacious. Through sympathetic magic, they attempt to transfer the enthusiasm of the crowd to the appropriate combatants.[21] Indeed, modern sport spectacles have incorporated a variety of ceremonies and rituals such as the singing of anthems, coin tossing to begin the contest, elaborate halftime events, and post-game locker-room celebrations. These elaborate rites place the events surrounding competition in a traditional and orderly context and give the occasion meaning.

Sport, like religion, offers its followers a grouping of myths and symbols that facilitate the total experience. It serves the function of religious dramatization in that it feeds a deep human hunger, placing humans in touch with features of human life within the cosmos. Sport can be a dramatization of life, a type of "deep play" that has sacred overtones. Sport may provide an answer to the discontent that humans feel, a response to the feeling that life isn't all that it should be. The religious impulse within sport is expressed in various ways: through asceticism, comradeship, by a sense of fate and destiny, and by a feeling of participation in the rhythms of nature. Humans find it difficult to live without rituals to judge from history. Public sport rituals convey the struggle of the human spirit to prevail.[22]

In this sense, sport constitutes what Novak calls a "natural religion." By this label, he means that sport flows outward into action from deep natural impulses that are in a sense "religious." Sport represents a desire for freedom, a zest for symbolic meaning, and a longing for perfection. Sport provides a way to exhilarate the human body, to fulfill an aesthetic sense of beauty and a feeling of oneness with the universe. The chants and songs, the rhythm of bodies in unison, and the willing of one thing by many who are members of a single body are all features of this natural religion. Sport harbors religious qualities in its powers to exhilarate or depress. Winning can be a rebirth—losing, a kind of symbolic death.[23]

In performing the above "religious" functions, sport doesn't necessarily replace religion but supplements it. Veblen recognized that the same temperament that inclined individuals to religious observances also inclined them to sport. He noted that the "sporting character" shaded off into that of a religious devotee. The professor detected that among his college students, it was the athletes especially who were given to devout observances. Three generations later, Soell observed that the Christian and the athlete were very close in the qualities fundamental to their shared ethos.[24] Based upon these observations, it isn't surprising that a belief in traditional religious precepts has been encouraged in American athletes and perpetuated by sports organizations like Fellowship of Christian Athletes and Campus Crusade for Christ (see chapter 7).

Sport can act as a substitute for, as well as a reinforcer of, religious tendencies. The experience of a contemporary science writer exemplifies this point. *Skeptic* magazine editor Michael Shermer described himself as a "fundamentalist Christian" while enrolled in undergraduate studies at Pepperdine University in California. Subsequently, he became a religious agnostic and developed an intense devotion to endurance sports. The adult Shermer became an avid runner and cycling enthusiast. He competed in the LA Marathon, the Hawaiian Ironman triathlon (which involves running a marathon after swimming 2.4 miles and riding a bike 112 miles), and in the Race Across America, a coast-to-coast marathon bicycle race of some 3,000 miles.[25] It is axiomatic that athletes like Shermer who compete in these grueling endurance events must train "religiously." Sport, like religion, can inspire resolute dedication and ascetic discipline.

This supplanting of sport for religion, evident in individual lives, also occurs on a broad cultural level. In a secular society where sport often acts as—or transmits—a form of civil religion, public sports ceremonies increasingly displace religious ones. Arguably, the dates on the American ceremonial calendar are becoming less concerned with religious observances than with sporting events and spectacles. Memorial Day in the state of Indiana, where I spent my youth, was a day devoted to the Indianapolis 500 auto race as much as to visiting cemeteries to honor the war dead. Autumn Sundays increasingly are dedicated to watching football as much as to attending church services. The Christmas and New Year holidays are filled with televised football bowl games, culminating with the mid-winter staging of the Super Bowl, an event that has all the trappings of civil religion.[26]

Despite the remnants of religious forms in the stadium, most scholars have emphasized the secular milieu of contemporary sport. Huizinga observed that modern sport had severed its organic connection with the religious structure in society that once was evident.[27] Likewise, Higgs asserts that contemporary sport may provide aesthetic pleasure, natural delight, and rest for the mind and soul, but not a religious experience.[28] Guttmann identified seven definitive characteristics of modern sport— secularism, equality, rationalization, specialization, bureaucracy, quantified achievement, and record keeping—all indicative of its break from the sacred and festive.[29] Consistent with these observations, one notes that the ritualistic and festive elements of sport increasingly are relegated to the pre-game, post-game, and intermissions.

Consistent with the secularization thesis, the focus of this book is not on sport as a form of religion but the ways in which modern sport reaffirms, reinforces, and disseminates values that have their origins in religion. This approach to sport is dependent upon a particular theoretical model (or models) of analysis. The following section explores three sociological/philosophical points of view as they have informed the present effort.

Competing Models of Sport: Marxism, Functionalism, and Idealism

It is more important for a hypothesis to be useful than for it to be true.
—Alfred North Whitehead

The metaphors employed to describe the relationship between sport and culture are numerous and inventive. It has been suggested that sport functions as a two-way mirror that both absorbs and reflects culture, that sport is a cauldron where culture is distilled, a laboratory in which cultural values can be observed in their simplified form. Sport can be viewed as a vehicle for the transmission of cultural values and ideas. Indeed, figures of speech borrowed from sport punctuate the popular idiom. We refer to "dark horses," "political footballs," and "Monday-morning quarterbacks" in a wide range of contexts. At the same time, the nation's culture permeates sporting events, as noted in the above section regarding pre-game and halftime festivities. But to fully understand the relationship between sport and culture, it is necessary to move beyond metaphors to more sophisticated explanations.

Several models have been proposed to explain the nature of modern sport within its cultural settings. One of the more prominent viewpoints competing with Weber's view of sport was that of the Marxists. Karl Marx (1818–1883) and his disciples built an impressive amount of theory to explain social action and institutional behaviors. Marxist sociology focuses on class struggle and class consciousness. Thus, the emphasis is on conflict rather than social cohesion. From this perspective, the state is viewed as an instrument of the ruling classes. This model explained, among other things, the promotion of capitalism. A dominant class of capitalists is seen as controlling the ideology of the nation, influencing the way people think, their conception of reality, and their values. The Marxist perspective frames sport as little more than a byproduct of capitalist consciousness and institutions.[30] This consciousness carries over into leisure culture. For the working classes, filling of time away from the job becomes dependent on the artifacts of capitalism. Leisure under capitalism becomes an extension of work. Amusements and recreation are incorporated into the market. Professional sport becomes part of the production process for the accumulation of capital. Both spectator sports and participant sports are commercialized and commodified—transformed into little more than "products" to purchase.[31]

The Marxist model has had its share of revisionists and critics. Writing from a conflict perspective, Gruneau suggests that industrialization per se does not explain enough and no longer seems pivotal to the understanding of organized sport. He proposes instead a reapplication of conflict theory focusing on class divisions to explain sport.[32] Weber, for his part, played down the role of materialistic factors and institutional conflict in the chain of causation. Responding to the Marxist emphasis on the forces of production, Weber counters, "The view that the economic is in some sense the ultimate point in the chain of causes is completely finished as a scientific proposition."[33] In contrast with the conflict model, Weber saw in the microcosm of sport the characteristics of the macrocosm. Essentially, this model provides a functionalist view of sport, one that understands society as being based primarily upon value consensus and organized as a system in which the parts are interrelated to each other. This view emphasizes "spill over" of general cultural values into specific areas like sport. These receptive institutions then mirror and reinforce the general cultural values.[34] Weber influenced a large number of contemporary scholars. Guttmann, for one, views the functionalist model as a distinct improvement over the Marxists' heavy reliance on conflict and economic factors to explain sport.[35]

The historian and social critic Christopher Lasch proffers a modification of Weber's model. He notes that while sport reflects external social values, it also contains its own forms and traditions that are passed from generation to generation unaltered.[36] A similar view is held by Heinz Meyer in his discussion of Puritanism's influence upon sport. He suggests that only a certain sector of motivations derived from the "spirit of Puritanism" is carried over into sport, but that sport remains impervious to other puritanical elements.[37] Sociologist George Sage and economist John McMurtry independently highlight the reciprocal relationship between sport and cultural values, noting that American sport promotes and reinforces the national value system as well as reflects it.[38] McMurtry asserts, "The logic of major spectator sports does not merely *mirror* the social order in which they occur, but more importantly, *causes this order to be maintained intact* by evangelizing in popular forms its essential structure of action."[39] These reciprocal affinities between sport and the larger social order are analogous to what Weber observed occurring between the Protestant ethic and the spirit of capitalism.[40]

In contrast to the Marxist and functionalist models, the idealists conceptualize sport as a relatively autonomous realm of human activity with its own sense of time and space, and resistant to outside influences. Catholic philosopher Michael Novak envisions sport as a form of play with its own transcendent myths and rituals. He argues that sport flows outward into action from a deep natural impulse, an impulse of freedom, respect for ritual limits, a zest for symbolic meaning, and a longing for perfection. To the extent that sport develops its own lasting traditions, he considers it "sacred." In this sense of being revered, its forms and structures are—or should be—relatively impervious to manipulation and revision.[41] Such idealism is reflected in the sentiments of the purists who react negatively to the altering of the traditions and rules of sport. When the American League replaced the pitcher in the batting order with a designated hitter, many baseball fans considered this change tantamount to a sacrilege. Novak, for his part, views the commercial intrusions and instrumental uses of sport as a debasement of its underlying spirit.

The British social scientist Brian Martin encapsulates the idealist framing of sport as an autonomous realm in an article on the modern Olympic games:

> One of the important characteristics of games is that they are worlds unto themselves, with rules to define behaviour and an explicit separation from outside concerns. To be sure, many games in practice are marked by...other social dynamics. But the ideal of the game involves a bracketing or exclusion of these factors, with all attention on abiding by the artificial reality of the game itself. It is this that makes games such a valuable escape from the oppressive realities of people's lives. Participants and spectators alike can concentrate on performances and dramas in a miniature social world in which talent, effort and luck combine to produce outcomes.[42]

Martin acknowledges that, "because games are experienced as separate realities, they are ideal for exploitation by groups that would like to use them for their own purposes."[43] In fact, the Olympics games have proved less than impermeable to outside influences, most notably nationalism and commercialism (see chapter 11). The French aristocrat Baron Pierre de Coubertin, founder of the modern Olympics, was an idealist, but he was not averse to appropriating the games for political and cultural ends. His Olympic model incorporated historical, philosophical, and educational rationales. Notably, the baron was influenced by British and American school sports programs with their salient pedagogical goal of building character.[44]

Coubertin's goal was to promote the unification of mind and body in a spirit that he labeled "Olympianism." This spirit was supposed to bring about the brotherhood of humankind and world peace. He wished to create an international reconciliation through sport, to substitute a healthy form of patriotism for what he saw as destructive nationalism. (Coubertin may have had in mind Frederick Jahn's militaristic gymnastics and the German Turner Movement.) The Olympic games were projected to be an event of worldwide significance framed within a set of classicist ideals borrowed from the ancient Greek games. Thus, the modern games were framed in a highly idealized context, and at the same time exploited as a means to an end. On the hundredth anniversary of the baron's birth, Avery Brundage, then President of the International Olympic Committee, declared that de Coubertin had founded a religion of the twentieth century.[45]

If Coubertin did indeed establish a religion, it was an evangelical one that had arisen in the wake of a new "Reformation." The Olympic games were revived at a time when sport was being promoted by an array of reformers for worthy purposes and enterprises. The various agendas imposed upon sport recall the Puritan uneasiness with recreation without moral purpose. The Victorians proclaimed that sport builds character and that its intrinsic values carry over into life. They were fond of quoting a statement attributed (erroneously) to the Duke of Wellington that "[t]he battle of Waterloo was won on the playing fields of Eton." Characteristically, the early twentieth-century philosopher John Dewey promoted play and sport as a medium for learning. Thus did Victorian idealism incorporate elements of instrumentalism. The appropriation of sport for political and pedagogical ends illustrates Weber's assertion that it is ideas that shape social institutions. In opposition to this view, the Marxists would argue that the highly commercialized Olympic games of the modern era are little more than a byproduct of industrial (and post-industrial) capitalism. The Olympic movement may be visualized as a vehicle for the transmission of cultural values, but clearly the transfer of values hasn't been a one-way street.

Arguably, sport manifests intrinsic meaning and a natural spirit, but its forms and ethos are mediated through complex articulations with cultural and social forces. Sport, in practice, routinely incorporates political, technical, religious, and economic meanings. The modern Olympic movement provides but one example. An equally compelling case could be made for British school sport, American college athletics, and even global soccer. Certainly, sport transcends specific cultures; it can promote social and cultural integration on both the national and international levels. However, the import of sport carries beyond its integrative functions. Sport can offer an interpretation of social reality and, at the same time, be a significant symbol of and a key to understanding the components of culture.[46] Sport is indeed a two-way mirror.

This book focuses on the values, meanings, and spirit of American sport and games within the context of secular Protestant culture. It employs an eclectic approach that borrows heavily from Weber and the functionalists in placing an emphasis on the interdependence of social institutions. However, the book also makes use of the theories of Marx and the economic determinists when these models seem to have explanatory value. The conflict paradigm lends a valuable perspective to understanding sports labor relations in the discussion of capitalism and sport.

The overall purpose of this book is to argue that the ethos of American sport is best explained as a derivative of secularized Protestant values operating within the milieu of industrial (and now post-industrial) capitalism. The book doesn't attempt to address the common characteristics of sport as religion or the infusion of religion into sport, as this can be found elsewhere.[47] Instead, the focus is on the legacy of a religious ethic as the source of the prevailing spirit of sport. The present effort builds on the work of previous sport sociologists who have attempted to describe the characteristics of modern sport and to identify an American sports creed.[48] We begin this endeavor with a narrative of Calvinism and Puritanism in their European and American settings, as these historical forces influenced the meanings and uses of leisure time.

2

The Legacy of Puritanism

The Protestant Reformation

> The Reformation provided the hinge upon which all modern history turns.
> —James Froude

What began with Martin Luther nailing his theses to the door of the church in Wittenberg resounded in a crescendo of new ideologies and social structures that revolutionized Europe and broadly influenced American culture. In many ways, the Protestant Reformation was as momentous as the Fall of Rome. This was one of those points in history when societies acquire a new texture and subsequent events form as patterns within that texture. The Reformation reshaped communities, transformed social institutions, and redefined the individual. It brought forth a new consciousness that affected the way people came to view such fundamental human activities as work and play.[49]

The break from Catholicism profoundly influenced personal values and behaviors. The Protestant's approach to life was distinguished by an "inner-worldly" asceticism. It was as if the ascetic discipline previously reserved for clerics became obligatory for everyone. This ethic imposed a standard of human conduct that compelled laypersons to lead constant, disciplined lives. The Protestant was obliged to save his own soul and at the same time construct a "city on the hill." This dual imperative derived from a profound belief in the extent to which human will could shape the human condition. It was a conviction that accentuated individual responsibility and thus spurred social and political activism.[50]

Protestantism was less a coherent intellectual system than a collection of related themes. In the absence of a structured canon, individual actions for Protestants took on a distinct value in and of themselves. This emerging activism contrasted sharply with the more ritualistic and traditional Roman Catholicism. Post-Reformation religion attached no particular significance to ritual acts and traditions. The Protestant temperament tended toward the rational rather than the symbolic, toward the juridical rather than the sacramental, and toward an emphasis on public acts rather than upon communal rituals. Ethical acts implied control over oneself and the world through a judicious organizing of life. In the process of carrying out this agenda, individual behavior became progressively rationalized as religious practice was secularized.[51]

As the Protestants attained salvation through their actions in the world, the church acted less as a sacramental order than a disciplinary agent. Religious activity focused on the congregational level. Beyond the obligatory religious devotions, Protestants participated actively in the life, witness, and charitable functions of the community. The citizen-pastor, who supplanted the celibate priest, set a concrete example for community activism. Because Protestants performed individual acts more easily outside the church, their values secreted themselves into every aspect of social and cultural life: the activities of business organizations, town councils, schools, and the other conventionalized structures of community life. Protestant activism exerted its influence upon labor *and leisure*. This activism was most apparent among the emerging middle class, who imposed their agenda upon the mundane features of daily existence.[52]

Among the various Protestant sects, the Calvinists were conspicuous in their devotion to an activist religion based on inner-worldly asceticism. It is this strain of Protestantism that profoundly influenced the culture of British North America and the one to which we shall now turn our attention.

The Moral Imperatives of Calvinism

> In this world, the last word always belongs to the worldlings and not to the
> saints. It is a complacent word and it comes when salvation, in all its
> meanings, is no longer a problem. But the saints have what is more
> interesting: the first word. They set the stage of history for the new order.
> —Michael Walzer

John Calvin (1509–1564) was the real revolutionary among the Protestant reformers, the one who completed the break with the Catholic Church. Calvin was not only an outstanding theologian but also the great systemizer of the doctrine, faith, and practical politics of Protestantism. The second edition of his *Institutes* has remained the essential textbook of practical theology in the Reformed churches for more than three centuries.

More broadly, its rules of conduct have influenced the morals and social mores of generations of American Protestants.[53]

Given that Calvinism came to be known for its rigid moralism, Calvin's personal habits and statements are instructive. The great reformer's adult life represented the stance of sobriety, a compromise between extreme asceticism and natural enjoyment. The mature Calvin's statement that "[w]e are not forbidden to laugh or to drink wine" suggests that he had renounced the rather austere discipline of his youth. He was known to engage occasionally in a game of quoits, and John Knox once found his teacher playing "bowls" on the Sabbath. However, such indulgences in recreation must have been exceptional. Although not ascetic at this point in his life, Calvin remained stern with himself in practice. Moreover, chronic health problems rendered him an invalid for much of his adult life and necessitated self-restraint. His stance of sobriety and his personal habits, however, stand in contrast to the tone of Calvinism that succeeded him. [54]

Calvin's disciples chose to downplay the elements of moderation, instead delineating the moral life as one of rigorous restraint. John Knox, the Scottish reformer, reworked Calvin's original doctrines so that their most notable aspects were a harsh ascetic discipline, an extreme legalism, an acutely rationalized theory of action, and an intensified mood for work. With few exceptions, the prevailing mood of Calvinism after its founder's death was toward more severe doctrines and practices.[55]

The basic tenets of mature Calvinism were presented in the Articles of the Synod of Dort (1618–1619). They included the doctrine of election (i.e., salvation) of the few by predestination, the doctrine of individual conscience, the doctrine of binding sin (inborn sinfulness of humans and the world), and that of salvation through work in one's calling. Of these doctrines, the one concerning predestination was the most basic. All other formal doctrines and consequences of Calvinism were derivative and subordinate to it. Predestination placed an enormous emphasis upon original sin and what the scripture pronounced "works of the flesh." The major effect of this doctrine was to cause the fear of damnation to weigh heavily upon the personal conscience. The uncompromising view of human nature as depraved would exert a portentous influence over individuals and institutions.[56]

A fundamental dilemma was created by the two contradictory tenets of predestination and free will. To wit, how could humans exercise free will if their salvation or damnation was predetermined by God? Theologians attempted to resolve this incongruity, but their rationalizations were never completely convincing. Thus the individual Calvinist, ever anxious about his place among the elect, was steered by incompatible beliefs in attempting to walk the straight and narrow path toward salvation. Clearly, the authority of the doctrine of predestination was psychological rather than logical; its primary effect was on the level of the emotions.[57]

Psychological pressures were fueled by the uncertainties of personal salvation. As the sociologist of religion Talcott Parsons noted,

> The strict construction of the doctrine of predestination was that election was to be recognized by no external signs whatsoever. However, the problem of knowing one's state of grace brought out the more specific consequences of predestination for conduct. Since man's acts could not influence his eternal fate, the whole pressure of his religious interest was to *know* whether he was saved or damned.[58]

The faithful sought out concrete means by which they could resolve the question of their individual fates, but the pressures created by the Calvinist scheme of salvation proved too great. The strict view of salvation gave way. A revised doctrine emerged implying that good works could be interpreted as signs of grace. Since the chosen were blessed by the success of their labors, indications of success were seen as the mark of God's blessing. In this way, some assurance of grace could be acquired. This revision in the doctrine had dramatic consequences. When tied to Martin Luther's concept of the calling, the scheme of salvation defined the fundamental meaning of social action in Protestant culture.[59]

No concept in the history of Protestantism has played a more enduring role in shaping attitudes toward human conduct than that of the calling. Martin Luther broke with Catholic tradition that had exalted labor primarily as a monastic discipline; instead he taught that each individual was to fulfill his God-appointed task—not in the religious sphere but in everyday life. Although the Lutheran concept of the calling emphasized vocation, there was no particular emphasis on labor beyond what was required for one's daily bread. In this sense, the Lutheran calling wasn't a complete break from the Catholic view of labor.[60]

The Calvinists completed the transformation of the calling by emphasizing relentless, disciplined labor. The calling formed an exacting enterprise chosen by each individual to be pursued with religious responsibility. As noted above, this belief derived from the idea that success in one's worldly labors was to be regarded as the sign of grace.[61] In the *Institutes* (1536), Calvin defined the role of "[t]he Christian in his vocation." He noted that God has prescribed appointed duties to men and has styled such as vocations or callings. Every individual's line of life is a post assigned to him so he may not wander about in uncertainty all his days. And so necessary is this distinction that in God's sight all our actions are estimated according to it.[62]

Calvinists distinguished two callings: (1) to serve God, and (2) to engage in a particular employment by which one's usefulness is determined. This distinction followed scripture, which had spoken of the *general* calling wherewith God called men to the faith and the *particular* calling wherewith God directed men to some special course. The Puritan minister Cotton Mather (1701) described the obligations of the personal calling as "some *special business*, and some *settled business*, wherein a Christian should for the most part spend the most of his time; so he may glorify God by doing good for himself." Mather admonished that it wasn't lawful ordinarily to live without some calling, for men will fall into "horrible snares and infinite sins."[63] This idea has maintained its authority throughout the history of Protestantism. Three centuries after John Calvin's death, Thomas Carlyle would proclaim, "The latest Gospel in this world is, 'know thy work and do it.'" The only true faith for Calvinists was that which produced works. It became impossible to sustain the belief that one's faith was genuine in the absence of the "fruits" of labor. The Calvinists' God judged men by asking not only, "Do you believe?" but also "Were you doers?" The metaphors employed are telling. Calvinists refer to man as an instrument of divine will and the relationship between God and man as that of master and apprentice.[64]

The evidence of good works gave the individual some assurance that he was indeed saved. However, as an indication of salvation, the necessity for evidence of good works required unceasing commitment to one's calling without lapse. At the same time, Calvinists had to remind themselves that the aim of all this activity was neither material happiness nor the enjoyment of any profits reaped from their labors. Although the rapid increase in productivity made Calvinism a religion of the economically prosperous, any sign of opulence was greatly mistrusted. The individual was to obtain nothing from accumulated material wealth except the reassuring sense of a job well done. The effort wasn't for the sake of the object of all that industry; work was done for no other reason than God commanded it.[65]

Despite revisions in the strict doctrine of salvation, the above scheme never completely alleviated the Calvinist's anxiety. Work in one's calling invariably failed to provide an assured road to salvation for those who believed literally in eternal hellfire. The followers of Calvin sought to salve the intense feelings of insecurity about their state of grace by constantly seeking some further indication of the direction of divine will. However, individuals couldn't know for certain to whom the grace of salvation had been extended through God's inscrutable plan. Wracked by doubts, the Calvinists continued to labor conscientiously at their calling, though technically works couldn't purchase salvation but only demonstrate it. It's fair to say that the godly life didn't so much procure assurance of salvation as alleviate the fear of damnation. The critical question for the individual has been how in everyday life to rid oneself of these doubts by finding one's calling and then constantly striving toward perfection in it. Failure was most assuredly evidence that the individual was cast among the damned.[66]

One thing was certain: proof of grace implied constancy. Work could be taken as a sign of grace only if believers applied themselves with diligence to their calling. Caught in a relentless spiral of obligations to accumulate the assurance of salvation, Calvinists were ever seeking new tasks and then carrying them out carefully and systematically. The individual at his calling would be up early in the morning and about his craft or business, working without distraction until the sun went down. It made no difference what type of work a person identified as his calling; before God, all moral callings were equal. A calling could include the intellectual work of a scholar as well as the manual labor of a field hand. Quite simply, individuals were to do their best at whatever station God had assigned them in life.[67] In this regard, the *Institutes* counseled, "[L]et us not cease to strive...nor let us despair on account of the smallness of our success, for however our success may not correspond to our wishes, yet our labor is not lost...provided that, with sincere simplicity, we keep our end in view, and press forward to the goal."[68] All righteous activity was in accord with the divine plan.

Man's particular calling extended to stewardship and commitment to the community. Protestants have a mission to master nature, to mold a better society, and to create a new world order—and the task is never complete. They approached life as an unending series of problems to be solved. As a group, they demonstrated a great genius for creating social and political associations to carry out this agenda. They became organizers and "do-gooders," perpetually engaged in public activity. There was a constant striving to create a New Jerusalem.[69]

The span of life was infinitely short in which to assure personal salvation and to build a new society. Thus, Calvinists spurned the present while "saving up for a perpetually receding future."[70] John Bunyan had instructed the readers of *Pilgrim's Progress* that "it is not best to covet things that are now, but to wait for things to come."[71] Bunyan's pilgrims were consumed with the idea of progress, the progress of their own souls and in building the community of the elect. The unrelenting quest for personal and communal salvation created a sect of instrumentalists with a singular, goal-directed approach to life.

As there was always work to be done, no slackers were tolerated. Sloth was among the deadliest of sins, harmful to the individual's soul and to the community. The dangers of sloth were on every side. A great concern prevailed in that individuals might be tempted by indolence through personal wealth. While success was an indication of salvation, the wealth that accompanied it was to be distrusted as a temptation to idleness and the sinful enjoyment of life. The wealthy individual was expected to distribute his bounty to worthy causes in the community, not use it to indulge in a life of leisure or ostentation.[72]

The preoccupation with salvation also led to a morally charged obsession with control over oneself and one's neighbors. Calvinists multiplied rules and strictures upon conduct to an extraordinary number of offenses so as to assure that the common people didn't stray from the straight and narrow path. Calvin's Geneva was a bastion of regulation and control that stood in stark contrast to life in the medieval cities of Catholic Europe. Tawney labeled Geneva a "city of glass houses" in which few dared to throw stones. He noted the military-like discipline imposed upon its citizens from which even children were not spared. The authorities were preoccupied with the minutiae of human conduct and were forever expanding the list of scandalous and notorious sins.[73]

Control of various "recreations" was evident within this regulated climate. Dancing with the opposite sex was considered an incitement to lust and was forbidden outright. Games of chance, like betting on shuffleboard, were prosecuted with less severity; even card playing was tolerated. The Puritans expressed more concern with recreations that led to disorderly conduct. Calvinists had always been apprehensive about too much idleness. This was reflected in the vacation schedule of Geneva's schools—a marked reduction from the relaxed medieval holiday calendar. School children were allowed only supervised recreation, as free play was mistrusted.[74] Though the early Calvinists cannot be accused of a systematic repression of all sports and recreation, their efforts to control simple pleasures and limit idleness appear stern by both medieval and modern standards.

Ethical human action implied control over oneself, and strict standards of self-discipline reinforced community sanctions. The strong emphasis upon individual responsibility led to a narrowly conceived view of human purpose and action. Little tolerance existed for self-expression or communal expression within formal religion or beyond. The Calvinist was hesitant to show emotion publicly or to form casual intimacies. Individual relations became impersonal and instrumental.[75] Calvinists demonstrated a negative attitude toward anything that had no direct use for achieving salvation. They seemed to reach a state of grace through a process of subtraction. The Calvinists not only eliminated salvation through the church and its sacraments, they also eliminated religious ceremony from the world and stifled the sensuous and emotional elements in culture. Religious rituals and traditions were viewed as akin to idolatry. The result was a cold, rational social climate marked by unprecedented austerity.[76]

In short, Calvinists rejected ritual, held an aversion to pleasures of the flesh, condemned sloth, and were suspicious of personal wealth. The individual was to serve God by diligence in his calling, by constant control over his life, by acting rationally and taking individual responsibility for personal actions, by not wasting time, and by focusing on the future. Calvinism was a religion characterized by the unrelenting application of a strict system of moral asceticism.[77]

The constant striving to control personal conduct and that of one's neighbors, both public and private, can best be understood as a preoccupation with purity. Calvinists were "puritans" in the sense that they felt contaminated by anything nonscriptural. Their great concern was that the community of the elect not be contaminated by the presence of immoral and slothful individuals. Even those among them who were diligent in their duties might be tempted by their association with reprobates. If the impure couldn't be removed from their community, then the elect would migrate from Sodom. These were the sole options of a people obliged to practice their beliefs in a world beset by sin.[78]

Historically, the term "Puritan" came to refer to the Calvinist strain of Protestantism that predominated among English-speaking peoples.[79] While

John Knox brought Reformed Protestantism to Scotland in 1560, the English Church, which had been Roman, became Protestant during the reign of Henry VIII (1509–1547). The Anglican Church of England continued to be challenged "from the left" by Reformed Protestants labeled Puritans. Under this banner gathered a variety of nonconforming Calvinists including the more radical Separatists. The Puritans were made up of independent yeomen, small merchants, artisans, and householders, as well as common lawyers and magistrates. Puritanism had special appeal to the middle and working classes, and to the rural English who were moving into the cities to seek work. The city of Exeter in the heart of the textile region and the London metropolitan area both became centers of Puritan influence.[80]

Puritanism was not just a set of personal beliefs but a measuring rod for political and social attitudes. The Puritan agenda included purifying policies and practices of the English Church along with those aspects of the broader society to which they objected. Ultimately, the uncompromising moralism of the Puritans led to open conflict with the English Crown. The Puritans attempted too many social changes, made too many political waves, and consequently suffered political and religious persecution. These trials and tribulations did nothing to ameliorate the Puritans' characteristic lack of tolerance or their heavy-handed moralism.

The Puritan as "Moral Athlete"

> [A] moral nature burdened and over-strung, and a critical
> faculty fearless but helplessly subjective.
> —George Santayana, *The Last Puritan*

The excesses of inner-worldly asceticism were concentrated in the Puritan. The ascetic treats the will like a muscle that can be strengthened by a moral "daily dozen," what the American philosopher Ralph Barton Perry labeled "moral athleticism." It was a will that took pride in negating itself before the world. Deprived of natural delights, the Puritan retaliated by affecting to despise them. The saving grace of this Puritan rigor was that it instilled individuals with courage, self-reliance, and sobriety. Such are the qualities of champion athletes—and of ascetics. Perry refers to Cotton Mather and Jonathan Edwards as "moral athletes" who compare to modern Olympic athletes in their devotion to disciplined lives.[81]

Puritan character was shaped by two forces, an exacting and uncompromising set of theological premises and the challenge of adhering to these precepts in daily life. Herein lay the classic Puritan dilemma: how to live as a saint in a sinful world. It was a dilemma replete with internal and external conflicts. The clash of impulses extended beyond the confines of the church. They were tied inexorably to the larger society through the obligations of one's calling. The early nineteenth-century itinerant preacher Lorenzo Dow encapsulated the essence of the Puritan's predicament with this sarcastic rhyme: "You can and you can't... You will and you won't... You will be damned if you do [a]nd you will be damned if you don't."[82]

The conflicts, both internal and external, were brought on by the unrealistically high standards for moral conduct. The relentless demands for personal discipline and technical perfection led to constant introspection and self scrutiny. The Puritan was judged by personal motives and governed by an intense rationality. One could never be self-satisfied, for there was no assurance of forgiveness comparable to what Catholics received through confession. Penance, not penitence, was all that was available, a constant, vigilant, working penance. Only through the fruits of labor could individuals demonstrate that they were "chosen." Thus, vocation became a compelling part of the Puritan's emotional life.[83]

One is struck by the radically uncompromising view of human purpose and conduct inherent in Puritanism. The effort to live within its doctrines took its toll upon the collective psyche. If a culture can manifest characteristics of neuroses, then Puritanism was defined by repression and obsession/compulsion. To be a Puritan was to repress oneself and others, to be obsessed with salvation, obsessed with control, and obsessed with right and wrong. Puritans were compulsive in their ordered lives and in their vocations. The classic symptom of the Puritan neurosis was anxiety about one's ability to control natural impulses, and ultimately about salvation. If the precepts of Puritan doctrine were the cause of this anxiety, the only escape was through the successful exercise of self-control and immersion in one's work.[84]

The obsession with control was fed by the pervasive climate of moralism. The core of Puritanism, once the theological husks were stripped away, was its intense moral zeal. The Puritan's God was a judge, and all ponderable values were cast in terms of right and wrong. Puritans were radical exponents of rigorous justice who relished the earthly roles of judge and policeman. They were intolerant of opposition and displayed a relentless lust for persecution. The extent of their moral zeal often suggested an innate hostility to civilization. Calvin's counsel for a degree of moderation in preventing the rise of extreme legalism had been forgotten. Colonial Massachusetts was characterized as "an over governed society with every tenth man an official." Control was pervasive; no realm of life was exempt. The Puritans legislated every aspect of daily living, public and private. The law was believed to be a great teacher, and the Puritans weren't shy about multiplying laws.[85]

Control of self was centered in the family, where attention was lavished upon the problem of human conduct. The Puritan family was, above all, an institution for the repressing and disciplining of rebellious children. The father operated as an absolute sovereign and, along with the elders of the church, continuously watched for children on the devious path to sin. The inherent fear of disorder and concern with maintaining control extended to one's neighbors. The Puritan community implied a covenant in which all individuals were in compact with each other, and the sins of any individual imperiled the entire group. The conduct of fellow citizens was judged publicly by those with whom they had freely entered into association. One had to prove himself not only before God but before man. Puritans enforced their creed upon others through constant scrutiny; everyone was made aware of his or her sins. Public vices were condemned more harshly than private ones. While it was desirable that vice shouldn't occur, it became essential that it shouldn't be seen to occur.[86]

The Puritans' approach to controlling behavior was to impose a set of elevated ideals with the assumption that most individuals would miss the mark. Moral standards were implemented through laws and regulations that were enforced by disciplinary measures. If the early Puritans had been skeptical of corporal punishment, they were great believers in the value of humiliation. A system of social control by gossip, shaming, public confession, and repentance became the effective means of controlling individual conduct. Puritans also believed in instruction, admonition, and the imposition of penance for sins—and failing these, expulsion from the community. Discipline usually began with admonition or censure. As for instruction, much store was set in preaching. Expulsion followed if the person wasn't repentant. Heresy or misconduct constituted the usual grounds for ejection, and it wasn't unusual for Puritans to impose this measure upon their brothers and sisters. The distinction between saints and sinners was absolute; no halfway measures were countenanced regarding the state of grace.[87]

The church was, above all, an institution to control human corruption and heresy. This institution enforced uniformity in belief and practice and required an internal experiential test for membership. Only those who could give credible evidence that they had inwardly experienced God's call were to be admitted. The elect would stand at the church door to determine whom to admit and to deny admission. The purity of the church had to be maintained either by purifying the impure, expelling the impure, or by the withdrawal of the pure. In this sense, the Puritans were truly separatists and elitists.[88]

Within this strict Separatist climate, a strain of Protestantism emerged that took a more moderate position on grace. This relaxation of the strict Calvinist tenets allowed for the growing conviction of the worth and possibility of human improvement. For these moderates, conversion was a process of gradual infusion of grace rather than an abrupt transformation. The so-called Armenian Compromise (after seventeenth-century theologian James Arminius) on the doctrine of predestination allowed that salvation was the result of individual choice and behavior. As Armenianism emphasized free will, its adherents embraced the idea that conduct could shape moral character. Whether this revised position on grace was a reflection of the ambivalence that ran through the lives of those who doubted their own sufficient piety and virtue or a concession to the stirrings of democratic egalitarianism is an issue beyond the scope of this study.[89]

This compromise didn't prevail among the Puritans (though it found support in the following century among Methodists), but it would have significance in justifying such practices as compulsory training and education. Countering these Armenian tendencies was the predominate concern for maintaining the purity of the elect. It was the latter view that prevailed, and that led to elitism. Following the first few years in the New World, Puritans gradually made their peace with class distinctions, while supporting the principle of open access to all positions for believers.[90] John Winthrop announced that "in all times some must be rich, some poor; some high and eminent in power and dignity; others, mean and in subjection."[91] The idea of a "visible elect" was tied to the Puritan belief that a relationship existed here on Earth between good behavior and just desserts. These elitist inclinations would remain in constant tension with the egalitarian principles of an emergent democracy.

The self righteousness of the elite was tempered by fundamental elements within the Calvinist scheme of salvation, for even though an individual reached a stage of some assurance, personal doubts were expected to continue. If doubts ceased, that in itself would be a sign that one never had faith to begin with but was simply deluded. The surest earthly sign of a saint, beyond worldly success, was a personal feeling of uncertainty, and the surest sign of a damned soul was smug assurance. In this sense, anxiety about one's election wasn't only normal but obligatory. The Puritan felt the compelling need to engage in constant self-examination.[92]

Colonial Puritanism remained severe and uncompromising. Those who migrated to New England settled in a harsh, isolated environment with the sea behind, the untamed wilderness ahead, and a cloud of human enemies on either hand. The New Englanders were cut off from immediate intercourse with other points of view that might have mitigated the severity of their opinions. They behaved like soldiers in hostile territory, and both body and soul were hardened by the experience. In this milieu, simply sustaining the machinery of life became a kind of end in itself. Early Americans embraced the view that whatever wasn't in some way materially necessary was somehow wrong. This idea retained its moral force long after the need for such strident austerity had passed.[93]

Striving for survival in a harsh environment reinforced the activism that had always distinguished Calvinist religion. Puritans flung themselves into practical matters with a demonic energy—tempered only by a compelling need for order. Life was organized into a highly regimented discipline with all the natural tensions this presented. To be a Puritan was to be plagued by a "strange unsettledness," a constant tension. The Puritan temperament was like a steel spring compressed by inner force that could shatter every obstacle by its rebound.[94]

Though they were compulsive moralists, the Puritans weren't moral introverts; they sailed their ship in the open seas. The common man exalted experience above theory. What emerged from this impulse was a pietistic volunteerism with an acute emphasis upon the practical. The Puritans emphasized good works over faith, as the idea of the calling underwent significant changes during the course of the seventeenth century. They tended to de-emphasize the satisfaction of creative work experience to the point that even drudgery became a means of attaining grace. Constant work provided them with a defense against dissipation and a palliative for religious doubts.[95]

The Puritans developed a set of moral attributes and virtues that insured material success for those who practiced them. Among these virtues were industry, sobriety, frugality, reliability, temperance, and simplicity of living. Broadly characterized, the Puritans were patient, grave to sternness, earnest, zealous, scornful of delights, perpetual in labor, constant in prayer, thrifty and thriving, filled with pride in self and calling, and assured of the worth of strenuous toil.[96] Meyer encapsulated the essence of the Puritan character as "leading a pious life in evangelic purity with a distinctly reformational tendency against worldly pleasure, combined with strict self-discipline and rational control of carnal desires, all this leading to the restraint of pleasure and, together with the belief in predestination, to the sanctification of professional work."[97]

The Puritan character type didn't disappear with the demise of the Colonial era. Just as there had been Puritans before the name was invented, there would continue to be Puritans long after the term has ceased to be a common epithet. Indeed, nineteenth- century America was as Calvinistically Protestant as the Middle Ages were Catholic. The descendents of Colonial Americans have divulged their Puritan heritage in sundry ways. They remain impersonal, legalistic, and moralistic with a strong interest in reform. The neo-Puritan is decisive, rational to a fault, a stickler for the truth, and harbors an overwrought concern for governing one's own conduct and that of others. In addition, latter-day Puritans are characterized by their desire to legislate simplistic moral codes, a need to conform, an intolerance of outsiders, and a tendency to intermingle religion and politics.[98]

Puritanism's imprint on the individual personality was matched by its influence on social institutions, among them the family, the schools, and most importantly in the present context, sport and recreation. Puritans had taken a particular interest in popular culture. Because of their exaggerated sense of morality, the leisure activities of men, women, and children were an area of human conduct that caused them great concern. The Puritans engaged in a long struggle against those playful forms of human behavior that kept spurting forth whenever the sentinels of morality were momentarily withdrawn from the wall that protected the New Jerusalem from the recurring waves of natural impulse.

The Puritan objection to much of play and recreation resides in the following trait. They could offer their allegiance to the structure, the artifact, or the style but not to the pleasure of the act. The unlawfulness of an act lay in the inordinate fondness produced by it. Puritans tended to feel guilt in enjoyment for they were obliged to constantly engage in serious and useful activities. Thus, the Puritans bared every natural human act to moral scrutiny to prohibit their brethren from sinking into unlawfulness due to misconduct.[99] Geldbach commented upon how often in Puritan literature the words "sports," "games," and "recreation" were accompanied by such adjectives as "lawful," "unlawful," "honest," "good," "moderate," "harmless," "indifferent," and even "Christian."[100] Before sport and recreation could take their natural place in society, they had to escape the deep-seated mistrust toward amusements and unrestrained human movement inherent in moral asceticism.

The following section presents a brief history of sport and recreation among the Puritans in England and New England. The reader can find more complete accounts elsewhere. Brailsford has written broadly on sport and Protestantism in England. Struna provides detailed examinations of sport in Colonial Puritan society. For those who read German, Geldbach offers a chapter on Puritanism and sport in his *Sport und Protestantismus*.[101]

The English Puritans and Sport

> The puritan hated bear-baiting, not because it gave pain to the bear, but
> because it gave pleasure to the spectators.
> —Thomas Babington Macaulay

If the Puritans developed a hostile attitude toward most sport and recreation in England, it wasn't based on a negative view of physical exercise and training per se. The English Puritans had tempered the traditional Christian antagonism to man's physical nature that was evident in the writings of the early Church fathers—as well as that of Martin Luther. John Milton (1608–1674) iterated the prevailing view in noting that physical strength is worthy when, "like Sampson's, it is used to good purpose."[102] For Puritans, physical exercise constituted a duty to preserve health and strength and to make one fit for serving God. It followed that they should choose and engage in appropriate exercises. Puritan education in the seventeenth century reflected this position. Milton's plan for an academy for young men included an hour of physical education in the curriculum.[103]

Natural acts such as those occurring in sport and recreation were neither imperative nor forbidden outright but fell within the category of the indifferent. The good or evil in an act resided not in the act itself but in its consequences—that is to say, its utility. The seventeenth-century Puritan minister William Perkins expressed this opinion in his advice that "all Christians may freely without Scruple of conscience, use all things indifferent, so it be, the manner of using them be good."[104] Sport and physical recreation put to good purpose were quite acceptable. On the other hand, activities that were a frivolous waste of time or encouraged intemperance, or other social vices, were frowned upon.

The moderate attitude toward physical recreation was presented in Richard Baxter's *Christian Directory* (1678), a popular book representing the culmination of English Puritan thought at that time. Baxter spoke of sports serving a higher end consonant with the moral upbringing of the person to become a responsible Christian. He based his views on the doctrinal belief that vice begins where physical gratification is sought for its own sake and not to further a higher end. This topic was discussed at some length in his chapter on "The Government of the Body," with its "Directions about Sports and Recreations." Here, Baxter suggested no absolute ban on sporting activities, but rather, firm control. Among the dozen or so restrictions Baxter placed on recreation was the admonition that one shouldn't overexert his body but know his own limitations and play accordingly.[105]

Temperance was one gauge for Puritans in determining acceptable forms of sports participation. The minister Richard Byfield had written in 1630 that "young men are especially to looke to Temperance that they be sober minded. This it delivers from all excesse, in recreation."[106] Moderate physical recreation was seen to have a compensatory function against the passions, desires, and evil inclinations of humans. Likewise, the Puritans accepted the health benefits of moderate physical recreation as an instrument to facilitate hard work. Thomas Gouge admonished, "Now Recreation [should take up] no more time...than doth conduce to the better fitting us for the duties of our general and particular callings."[107] Notwithstanding these concessions, Puritans always considered recreation but a poor substitute for productive work.

Baxter and the other moderates didn't speak for everyone. The harsher Puritan view projected a simple continuum with hard work at one end and necessary rest at the other. Anything between these polarities tended to be condemned as sinful idleness. The strong appeal of physical pursuits with the accompanying sin of pride in physical prowess was well understood. Moreover, those who equated pleasures of the body with sin argued against physical recreation as personally damning and socially damaging. Even where the deeper sins of lust or pride were avoided, there remained the danger of wasting time, and the foremost duty of a Christian was to make the most of his or her time. Play, in general, became equated with time-wasting. Playing cards and dice were singled out as senseless dissipation. An excessive indulgence in any sport, including hunting, was viewed as a waste of time. Even if sports weren't inherently sinful, the precious hours spent at them could be used more constructively.[108]

Recreations that proved costly were considered unlawful. A Christian steward had to be accountable to God for all he had, and thus, it was sinful to spend money needlessly on sports and recreations. Activities necessary for one's physical healing might be allowed only if the expenditure was not above their worth. Baxter was critical of hunting with dogs for both the expense for the animals and the inordinate time involved. He accepted betting on horse and dog races as long as the wager was modest. He approved of bowling, running, and shooting for money if they avoided dishonesty, if the betting was congenial and appropriate, and they weren't pursued for covetness.[109] Sport and recreation were thus moral issues with which Baxter's more severe contemporaries were inclined to find fault. They denounced dancing by partners of different sexes as tempting lust (though folk dancing and social dancing with same-sex partners met with less objection); they attacked the primitive forms of football for their violence; they opposed the Florian May games as not being Christianized; and they rejected the bloody spectacles of bull and bear baiting as a cruel and vulgar amusement. There may have been some winking at polite sport in private, but the bounds of tolerance did not stretch to public amusements.[110]

The English Puritans' ambivalence toward sports and recreation of their era owed as much to the corrupt nature of upper-class sport as to their mistrust of natural acts. They found reason to object to a great deal of the behaviors of the leisure class at their popular sports. Admittedly, much of English sport and recreation in the seventeenth century was less than commendable. Spectacles like bull and bear baiting were inherently corrupt and often accompanied by gambling, drinking, and rioting. It was the degrading nature of the sporting elements—not the physical activity—that garnered the crux of objections. Because of the depraved nature of much English sport, the Puritan perceptions of play and the body's vices tended to fuse without distinction. Their attitudes toward sport came to be more antagonistic than an exacting interpretation of Calvinist doctrine required.[111]

The Puritan criticism of leisure-class sport was exacerbated by class antagonism, and they weren't above amending their view of sport to bolster this enmity. The working-class prejudice toward the upper classes and their amusements carried back to John Wycliffe and the Lollards, who had rebelled against the Anglican Church in the fourteenth century. The seventeenth-century Puritans found themselves in much the same frame of mind. Their disapproval of the moral laxity of the leisure class became increasingly scornful as they struggled, with limited success, to bring about reforms. Eventually, their views hardened into outright disapproval of most upper-class diversions.[112]

The hostility between Puritans and the English establishment came to a head over the issue of sport on the Sabbath and the *Book of Sports*, published in 1618.[113] In the previous century, opposition against Sunday sports had been widespread even among the gentry and Anglican clergymen, but the opposition by the establishment declined by the end of the century. As religious observances on the Sabbath deteriorated, however, Puritan magistrates reasserted the need for banning Sunday sports in an ordinance in 1616. The unsympathetic James I reacted to the ordinance with the *Book of Sports*. The book's own ordinances permitted certain popular amusements on Sunday after church hour, and were accompanied by threats of punishment from the king for any attack upon the legality of these sports. The book was most odious to the Puritans' strict Sabbatarian views and became a longstanding point of contention. During the Long Parliament (1643) when the Puritans came into power, they had the *Book of Sports* publicly burned by the hangman. Although the struggle over the *Book of Sports* had political and class overtones (and primarily concerned Sabbatarian practices), it can be seen as a focal point for the uncompromising attitude toward popular sport held by many English Puritans.[114]

Thus, two strains of Puritanism were apparent in the English experience. Many Puritans were severe and uncompromising in their attitudes toward sport and recreation. This severity was fueled by strict Sabbatarian views, class antagonism, and a reaction to the rather decadent nature of English upper-class sport. Yet, within the generally harsh assessment of popular recreations, moderate voices like Richard Baxter's and John Milton's could be heard to support temperate physical activity put to a good purpose. The strain of Puritanism that carried to the New World would shape the early sporting culture of a nation.

Sport and Recreation in Colonial North America

Avoid all impertinent avocations. Laudable recreation be used
for *sauce* but not for *meat.*
—Cotton Mather

The religious conflicts in England and on the European continent occasioned what was to become the largest transoceanic migration the world had ever seen. In the thirty-year period from 1611 when Sir Thomas Dale brought a Puritan influence to Jamestown, Virginia, several covenant communities established themselves on the North American continent. Some 20,000 Puritans and Puritan sympathizers had arrived in Massachusetts by 1640. At the end of the seventeenth century, Massachusetts Bay, Connecticut, New Haven, and Rhode Island all could be claimed as colonies with a strong Puritan influence. During this same period Scotch Presbyterians were settling the middle and Southern colonies, while the Reformed Dutch Calvinists inhabited New York. Even in Catholic Maryland, Protestants constituted a numerical majority. The American colonies were on their way to becoming "the most thoroughly Protestant, Reformed, and Puritan commonwealths in the world."[115]

The Puritans who migrated to the New World were among the least moderate of the fold. They carried with them not only a prejudice against the activities of the English leisure class but a profound distrust of any form of idleness. Though they found no social system in the New World to rekindle their innate class antagonism, the harsh realities that awaited them on the North American continent did nothing to ameliorate their severity. As Olmstead noted, the Colonial Puritans literally hurled themselves into the task of building the kingdom of God.[116] In a setting where the effort to survive could be overwhelming, idleness and frivolity became anathema. The New England colonies tolerated no pagan festivals, plays, and spectacles, no violations of the Sabbath, or other dissipations of a leisure class. Suppression of such entertainments was rationalized as a necessary measure.[117]

Beginning with the earliest English colonization, moral sanctions and laws enforced mandatory labor and restricted sports and recreation. In the settlement at Jamestown, offenders of compulsory work laws were dealt with severely. Tradesmen who were found to be negligent in carrying out their daily occupations were threatened with three-year jail sentences. The

Colonial Virginian Assembly in 1619 decreed that any person found idle should be bound over to compulsory work. As for recreation, the assembly prohibited bowling, dice, and cards, strictly regulated drinking, and rigidly enforced Sabbath observances.[118]

Intolerance of idleness and amusements were just as characteristic of the settlers in New England. Massachusetts and Connecticut banned dice, cards, quoits, bowls, shuffleboard, nine pins, and other "unlawful" games both private and public. On Christmas Day 1621, Plymouth's Governor Bradford took away all sporting implements because citizens were openly playing at stool ball (a variety of cricket) and other sports. Governor John Endecott of the Massachusetts Bay colony cut down the maypole at Merry Mount in 1629 with a stern warning to revelers. He vigorously enforced the general court's law that no one should spend time idly or unprofitably, under threat of punishment. The constables were ordered to search for all manner of gaming, singing, and mixed dancing. The Sabbath was to be wholly devoted to pious reflection with no tolerance of recreation. In Boston, King James's *Book of Sports* was publicly burned for good measure. The New England magistrates would persist in suppressing recreation even when the practical justifications seemed to have diminished.[119]

The Puritans were particularly alert to restrict activities that detracted from economic endeavors or threatened social control, but they saved the brunt of their disapproval for those that wasted time, tempted lust, or facilitated gambling. For these reasons and others, the inns and commonhouses were singled out for particular scrutiny by the magistrates. These establishments stood condemned as places where time was misspent. Gaming at shuffleboard and bowling were held up as two of the more notorious and nonproductive activities taking place at inns and were outlawed. The enforcement against gaming in public houses extended to private residences. The heads of families were ordered to prevent such sports from occurring within their purview.[120]

The Reformed Dutch who settled New Netherlands (now New York) in the seventeenth century revealed a similar ambivalence toward sport and an intolerance of idleness. In Washington Irving's *Diedrich Knickerbocker's History of New-York* (1809), and in his short stories, the author (whose father was a Scotch Covenanter) relates his impressions of the Dutch Protestants in the New World. His accounts provide an informative parallel to the lives of the New England Puritans. Although the record indicates that the Dutch played at bowls and skated on the wintry ice, it is quite clear in

Irving's story "Rip Van Winkle" that the New Netherlanders took the work ethic seriously and frowned upon idleness and excess frivolity. Rip is discredited by his fellow villagers because of his aversion to labor and his inability to keep his personal affairs in order. He and his ne'er-do-well cronies found it necessary to retreat into the secluded foothills of the Catskills in order to play at bowling and imbibe alcohol undisturbed.[121]

Thus did the transplanted Calvinists diligently strive to limit unlawful sports and amusements particularly during their first two decades in North America. Yet, we must not overstate their intent or overestimate their success in enforcement. The New England scene never was wholly devoid of recreation, as has been implied by some historians. One mitigating factor in enforcement was that many early settlers weren't Puritans. The first party of Pilgrims that landed in 1620 at Plymouth was made up of a collection of both the religious and the nonreligious (notably Miles Standish among the latter). The settlement at Plymouth was hardly a bastion of Puritan orthodoxy. During the Great Migration between 1630 and 1640, only some 4,000 out of 16,000 arrivals in Massachusetts Bay were actual church members. Moreover, Puritans enjoyed mixed success in controlling their own flock. Church membership actually declined among second-generation Puritans, and nonmembers were especially recalcitrant toward attempts at social control.[122]

Whether we focus on the English Puritans or the Reformed Dutch, the fact is that a gap existed between the professed ideals reflected in the laws and regulations, and the actual behaviors of the populace. Though the New England Puritans had signed a covenant that committed them to an exemplary life, no one could live constantly at the pitch of intensity implicit in that covenant. Predictably, a life of stern discipline occasionally gave way to springs of impulse, including the impulse to play. The Puritan preacher might rail against the vanities of human nature but found it more and more difficult to enforce the unforgiving rules that had been laid down. The magistrates were never able to entirely repress sporting behavior, and it increased in frequency and variety through the course of the seventeenth century. Although the undaunted elders continued to pass laws, effective control of forbidden recreational activities proved increasingly problematic.[123]

In fact, the residents of New England had become conditioned to many unenforced laws, including the lax enforcement of regulations governing sport and recreation. By the late seventeenth century, laws regulating sports were republished with provisions for additional punishment for second offenders, suggesting they were being ignored. A general erosion of control continued as the tightly knit Puritan communities grew into midsized towns. Typical was the city of Boston where upright citizens complained that children routinely engaged in unsupervised free play right under the disapproving brows of their elders. Gradually, concessions were made. By 1714, Boston had a bowling green, and third-generation New Englanders were merchandising sporting goods or offering themselves as dancing teachers. Harvard College, whose main mission was the training of clergymen, designated land for recreation in order to permit sports on campus where they could be controlled, rather than force students to venture off campus to play unsupervised.[124]

Seventeenth-century property owners generally were allowed to engage in fishing and fowling for sport, as well as for their livelihood. Military companies, organized as early as the 1630s, staged athletic contests for training purposes. A minister observing one of these training sessions is reported to have cajoled the recruits to "play like men and not like boys."[125] Thus, allowances were made for what were deemed worthwhile sports and purposeful recreations. In general, Colonial ministers and magistrates—like their predecessors in England—accepted sport if it contributed in some way to a higher end. For instance, sport might be justified as a form of physical training that served the purpose of introducing people to social labor, or as a way to control physical desires to lead them away from sin. Worthy sport could maintain military preparedness, promote education or health, instill the values of discipline, socialization, cooperation, and equitable competition, or reinforce the will to struggle.[126]

Physical activities also could be justified if they promoted "re-creation," meaning refreshment from the drudgery in work preparatory to returning to one's labors. The Calvinist mindset was that individuals did not work in order that they might play, but that play renewed a person for work. Even the austere John Winthrop admitted the need to seek refreshment from his duties by engaging in innocent recreation on occasion. On the other hand, those forms of sport and recreation inadaptable to higher ends continued to be stigmatized long after the Colonial theocracies gave way. Over time, three important principles endured: that sport not be conducted on Sunday, that sport be put to a good purpose, and that the participants in sport avoid excess.[127]

As the Puritans recognized the impossibility of controlling sport and recreation entirely, accommodations appeared as a tack for dealing with these activities. From the very beginning, some relaxation had been evident in references to "lawful sports and recreations." Lawful sports referred to avocations of upstanding members of the Puritan community and were subject to the same criteria that governed their vocations. This isn't to say that avocations were placed on the same level as vocational callings; they were still the "sauce" and not the "meat." By the early eighteenth century, Increase Mather was offering advice that distinguished between "lawful" and "indulgent" sport. At this point, one could look back on a century of social practice in the Puritan colonies and detect signs of irreversible change. Sports and recreation were increasingly accommodated by the descendants of Puritan immigrants as they adjusted to a heterogeneous and rapidly changing world.[128] However, an ambivalence toward use of leisure persisted among the Puritans as evident in the oxymoronic concept of "sober mirth" employed by Mather's contemporary Reverend Benjamin Colman in his book-length tract *The Government and Improvement of Mirth, According to the Laws of Christianity, in Three Sermons* (1707).[129]

We can conclude that at no time were the Puritans wholly comfortable with sport or successful in eliminating objectionable forms of recreation. The reasons for this are fairly clear. The most salient one is that no monolithic attitude toward sport and recreation existed among Puritans. Brailsford's comment that the mission of the Puritans was "to erase all sport and play in men's lives" refers to the agenda of a select group at one point in time.[130] Geldbach, on the other hand, tends to overstate the positive influence of Puritanism on sport.[131] Jable seems more accurate in his assessment that antagonism to sport was characteristic of only a certain faction of the Puritans.[132] Over the course of Anglo-American history, attitudes and practices relating to sport and recreation varied, from the more moderate views of John Milton and Richard Baxter to the extreme doctrines of the English Long Parliament and those of the early governors of the New England colonies. In addition, the enforcement of regulations concerning sport and recreation remained inconsistent and ineffective. As a consequence, various forms of physical recreation persisted in England and in the colonies of the New World.

Americans at Play: The Puritan Legacy

> Americans play many roles and believe many different things. But after
> more than three and a half centuries—for better and for worse—
> we remain Puritans all.
> –James A. Morone

The reputation of Puritanism is somewhat worse than the reality. Its legacy has not been the suppression of sporting behavior. Indeed, the Puritans never condemned all forms of physical recreation, as evident from the above discussion. Furthermore, the spiritual descendants of Puritans gradually lost control over manners and mores amidst the emerging secularization of culture in the eighteenth and nineteenth centuries. Their response to these social forces reflected the general tendency of Western religion to first reject outright those independent developments that cannot be controlled, only to eventually accommodate or appropriate such developments for its own ends. (Such had been the response of the Church to the scientific discoveries of the Enlightenment.) This familiar pattern provided America's mainstream religions a strategy to deal with the increasing popularity of sporting activities. When the establishment cannot morally justify certain practices, it must either change its morality or change the practice—a sort of moral revisionism. In the case of religion and sport, it was a matter of both changing the practice to fit the morality and a relaxing of moral standards.

Worldly asceticism by its very nature required confrontation with human nature and the real world. The Puritan saints had to find ways to accommodate the sporting impulse. They no longer had the option of withdrawing from a society that harbored increasingly popular forms of physical recreation. Indeed, they had to make peace with these disconcerting developments. In the process of accommodation, the values of moral asceticism encroached upon a wide range of sporting behaviors; what originally were playful activities would evolve into more serious endeavors. Messenger succinctly summarized the changing status of play and sport in Protestant America:

> America traditionally denied play in the name of seriousness or absorbed play in the name of seriousness. The ingrained moral objection to play in the seventeenth century became the material seduction of play...after the Civil War. In each case, the pressures of society were matched against play's freedom as the theological

proscription against play shifted to a secular imperative to play in concert with others for external reward.[133]

Protestant churches made one last attempt to assemble the forces of moralism against the freedom of play. A new generation of spiritual leaders "took up arms" against sport and sundry amusements. They preached a fierce intolerance of the sinfulness of idle pleasures. This jeremiad followed a wave of Pietism that washed upon the American shore with the great migration from the continent in the 1840s. Baptists, Presbyterians, and Methodists reimposed many of the prohibitions of the Colonial period. The resounding admonitions from the pulpits would have some effect upon public attitudes toward sport and recreation through the middle decades of the century. However, the rejuvenated moralism failed to carry the day and proved little more than a rearguard action.[134]

The reactionary tendencies to prohibit sport and recreation outright were diluted in the sea of change within mainstream religion that found ways to accommodate these problematic activities. In the classic Calvinist tradition, play was absorbed in the name of seriousness. The Protestant at play wasn't to drop all inhibitions and "disport" but maintain control of the emotions and the body on the playing fields. The prudent athlete didn't overindulge in sport but took it seriously as a way to improve oneself. The phrase "soap-swimming Presbyterians" implied that recreational bathers took a cake of soap along so as not to waste an opportunity. Eventually, even bowling and shuffleboard— neither featuring hygienic prospects— were to be tolerated as rather harmless recreations.

The Puritans had always been less concerned in theology per se than in its application to everyday life and society. The main thrust of their influence was upon secular institutions. They practiced a pragmatic and worldly form of religion that required occasional, if reluctant, compromises. When the clergy realized they could no longer successfully enforce restrictions against many forms of sport and recreation, they began adapting these activities to their own ends. They attempted to purify sport, as they had other social institutions. With this goal, the New England saints left their mark indelibly impressed upon American sport and recreation. Calvin's ghost still haunts the sports arenas and the playgrounds. The following chapters will explore this legacy.

3

The Protestant Ethic and the Spirit
of American Capitalism

The Protestant Ethic Thesis

> Such is Weber's methodological achievement and so impressive is the scope
> of his comparative sociology, that his Protestant ethic thesis "must" stand.
> —Gordon Marshall

During the Reformation such virtues as hard work, thrift, and efficiency in one's vocation were infused with moral overtones. For Protestants these personal attributes, attended by visible signs of prosperity, constituted indirect evidence of salvation. The German economist and sociologist Max Weber, in his essay *Die Protestantische Ethik und der Geist des Kapitalismus,* 1904–1905 (translated as *The Protestant Ethic and the Spirit of Capitalism,* revised edition 1958), referred to this set of virtues as the Protestant ethic. He argued that this ethic was an important factor in the economic success of Protestants in the early stages of European capitalism, kindling revolutionary change not only in Protestant Europe but in the developing nations of the post-Reformation West.[135] With this thesis, Weber provided a forceful alternative to Karl Marx's model of ideas and ideologies as the mere reflection of material conditions. Weber perceived ideas as independent forces that transformed a wide range of modern economic and social institutions.[136]

Weber's thesis proved seminal in Western social science. His assertion that a specific ideological and psychological complex existed in association with this ethic has become a fundamental part of the general literature of sociology. Although the Protestant ethic thesis has had its critics (e.g., Werner Sombart and Pitirim Sorokin), Weber's main argument has retained its integrity and continues to interest a wide range of social scientists. Prominent defenders of the thesis include Gordon Marshall among others.[137] I am persuaded that Weber made a convincing case for the Protestant ethic thesis, and that it has explanatory power that deepens the understanding of social actions and institutions, including those related to sport.

Weber's thesis about the relationship between the Protestant ethic and capitalism was born in his observations of differences in certain types of social behavior among Protestants and Catholics in post-Reformation Germany. He inquired as to what kind of historical processes would account for the fact that the Protestant sections of Germany were more industrialized, that they constituted a disproportionate number of the industrial affluent, and that they were more likely to attend the types of schools that would equip them for business enterprises. These developments encompassed essential patterns for success under capitalism.[138]

After searching for the historical processes that accounted for these developments, Weber recognized the pivotal nature of Martin Luther's idea of the calling, ultimately refined by the Calvinists. Weber focused on two elements of this idea: a code of ethics for the conduct of everyday life and a sanction that would compel the faithful to adhere to a set of ethical maxims. This focus brought Weber to the central point of his thesis: that the Reformed Protestant belief in predestination manifesting itself in the performance of good works was the driving force behind the spirit of capitalism. Consistent with this notion, the individual Protestant was expected to practice a type of inner-worldly rational asceticism in which meticulous attention must be paid to the affairs of everyday life as proof of election (i.e., personal salvation).[139]

Weber explored the influence of worldly asceticism on men like John Wesley and Benjamin Franklin, whose maxims served as guides to a moral life for Protestants. Among the lessons to be learned were that pleasures and amusements should be restrained and controlled in deference to mental and physical labor. Wesley's dictum, "He who plays as a boy will play as a man," is typical of these moral lessons. Indeed, an unwillingness to work denoted the absence of a state of grace. Franklin offered, "As we must account for every idle word, so must we account for every idle silence." This mindset extolling work and condemning idleness came to be known as the Protestant work ethic. Weber's argument about the nature and consequences of this attitude would remain the most straightforward, demonstrable part of his thesis.[140]

Although the foundation for the Protestant ethic resided in religious teachings, Weber realized that this ethic "once in the saddle" (his metaphor) no longer required religious motives to spur its imprint upon individuals or institutions. Indeed, the ethic would exert an influence on social behavior far beyond the confines of the Protestant theocracies of the sixteenth and seventeenth centuries. The ethic endured as a secular force that continued to shape cultural values and social actions well into the twentieth century. It had its most notable effect in America. Weber's character type, the "secular Puritan," can be recognized as a prominent persona that existed during the early national experience. Benjamin Franklin's values represented the essence of the Protestant ethic shorn of its religious trappings. Franklin's brand of rational asceticism would provide the model not only for economic life but for the "whole cloth" of human existence in American Protestant culture.[141]

The present chapter addresses the second part of Weber's thesis: that Protestantism played a preponderant role in creating a moral and political spirit favoring capitalist enterprise. A "spirit of capitalism" bestowed the necessary (though not sufficient) conditions for the emerging capitalist economic system that formed in the West. The relationship between Protestantism and capitalism was more of a mutual influence than a causal one. Weber labeled the relationship an "elective affinity," implying that people didn't become capitalists simply because they were Protestants or vice versa. This connection was rooted in Protestant doctrine that supported and reinforced the emerging capitalist tendencies in post-Reformation economies.[142] Following Weber, Michael Walzer proposed that the moral discipline of the Puritan saints could be interpreted as the historical conditioning of the "capitalist man."[143] In Puritan England and America, the ethic would have a particularly strong effect upon the rising middle class who used it to justify their material interests.

The tie between capitalist enterprise and morality was part and parcel of a religion whose primary function was to legitimize life in the world. The Protestant not only had to prove himself before God, but also before his neighbors in the sense of holding his own in the community. Economic success served as a necessary sign of salvation. This association reinforced the revolutionary idea of "economic virtue" which provided the moral legitimation for capitalism. To the extent that material success and virtue were interwoven, the worth of social actions was judged increasingly by economic criteria.[144]

This basic outline of Weber's Protestant ethic thesis is followed by an overview of the development of capitalism through its various stages over the course of the last 400 years. This chronicle is prefatory to discussing the evolving relationship between Protestantism and economic behaviors that culminated in the distinct American spirit of capitalism.

Capitalism: A Brief Overview

> While the miser is merely a capitalist gone mad, the
> capitalist is a rational miser.
> Karl Marx

Capitalism essentially is the investment of money in the expectation of making a profit. This economic strategy was systematized in areas of Europe during the Reformation. The capitalist system that developed is characterized by: (1) a wage-earning labor force separate from ownership of the means of production, (2) free labor acting rationally, and (3) the emergence of a competitive market. Capitalism became the dominant economic system in the West following the decline of feudalism. Its rise brought about radical changes in society. In the pre-capitalist era, wealth typically derived from the ownership of land, such as the immense feudal estates of medieval Europe—the other lucrative source of income being reward for government service. When capitalism emerged, the basis of wealth shifted from the ownership of land to that of creating, producing, and distributing new products or offering new services like milling and shipping.[145]

Under early capitalism the economic mechanisms of market transactions, capital accumulation, and wage labor gradually replaced bureaucratic feudalism. Following the demise of feudalism, capitalism evolved in three stages. The first stage was merchant capitalism, followed by capitalist production (accompanied by the onset of consumer capitalism), and finally, financial capitalism. The first stage was flourishing in Northern Europe by the mid seventeenth-century, as merchants began financing the heavy capital investments required for long distance trade by forming joint-stock companies. Stock exchanges opened in both Amsterdam and London during this century. Merchants further reduced their risks by attempting to control markets and/or by forming monopolies. These features of capitalism carried into the modern era.[146]

The initial phase of capitalism was augmented by industrialization in Britain beginning in the late eighteenth century. This phase was characterized by an emphasis on production, standardization of work, and the supervision and control of workers. Industrial capitalism would enhance the economic status of laborers over time, but this form of capitalism incorporated a built-in tendency to overproduce. The inherent instability led to a vicious cycle of lower wages and layoffs followed by reduced consumption. Workers were coerced into accepting the stark realities of the system by their economic dependence on employment. In times of prosperity, industrial capitalism provided a steady income for workers, while creating a sharp distinction between work time and leisure time. As workers acquired more discretionary time and income, the conditions were ripe for the emergence of consumer capitalism.[147] One consequence of an expanding consumer market was the commercialization of leisure, including the growth of spectator sports charging admission to the public. Commercial sports were but one of many cultural institutions that shaped, and were shaped by, industrial capitalism. These expanding enterprises would prove equally adept at adjusting to the emerging stage of financial capitalism.[148]

The economic innovations of industrial and merchant capitalism, particularly the creation of bills of exchange, instigated financial capitalism. In this stage, markets and financial institutions emerged that allowed assets of various kinds, including property, to be converted into capital. Financial markets formed anywhere goods and services could be bought and sold. Capital accumulated in trading adventures enabled the growth of world markets. Markets existed for labor, money (currency markets), and capital itself—for example, ownership of companies bought and sold on stock exchanges. Because capitalist markets are inherently unstable, speculation became a definitive feature of financial capitalism. Early on, this type of capitalism remained relatively unregulated; however, by the second half of the nineteenth century an impetus toward state intervention, or "managed capitalism," emerged.[149]

A classic instance of government regulation was the anti-trust movement that arose in the United States during the late nineteenth century, culminating in the Sherman Anti-Trust Act of 1890. In the 1930s when the collapse of world markets threatened to obliterate capitalism, federal intervention became even more aggressive. The government-managed capitalism of President Franklin Roosevelt's New Deal was an example of regulation that would endure into the late twentieth century. What emerged was "mixed capitalism," an amalgamation of market capitalism and managed capitalism that became the paradigm for the contemporary corporate economy.[150] It is germane to point out that this form of corporate capitalism shaped the structure of professional sport franchises.

The corporation, as a distinct entity, evolved from the partnership.

Partnerships were relatively small groups of individuals who pooled their resources and set up a business they ran as well as owned. Significantly, the corporation separated ownership (by individual stockholders collectively) from management. American railroad barons were the true creators of the modern corporation in the post-Civil War era. Early on, the prominent companies tended to be family owned (e.g., the Goulds, Rockefellers). Shares, if they existed at all, were traded on a person-to-person basis. However, by the 1890s, the corporation underwent a revolutionary transformation. Because of changes in state laws, many of the existing small corporations were merged into larger ones. The public corporation with numerous shareholders soon eclipsed the family-owned business. Today, practically all economic activity is carried on under the corporate form.[151]

However, there remained an individualist facet of capitalism, one that was most salient in the United States during the nineteenth century. Strong profit motives coupled with a ready supply of investment capital created a climate supportive of entrepreneurship, what de Tocqueville referred to as "l'esprit de l'enterprise."[152] The entrepreneur was a major catalyst for economic development, as profits generally were created by engaging in innovative activities and by discovering new investment tactics and schemes. The essence of entrepreneurial behavior can be viewed as a rationally ascetic temperament applied to economic development. Specific characteristics of entrepreneurial behavior include decisiveness along with moderate risk taking, energetic pursuit of instrumental activity, a sense of individual responsibility, profit as the criterion for judging results of decision making, anticipation of future possibilities, and organizational skills.[153] This list provides a template for the convergence of Protestant rationalism and capitalist economic behavior, the keystone of the spirit of capitalism.

In summary, the capitalist spirit constituted a set of values that imparted meaning to human existence while inspiring a relentless drive in those committed to it. Significantly, this spirit shaped not only individual economic behaviors and modern economic institutions, but broadly influenced Western culture. It would transform the legal system, the political structure, science, and technology. In the broadest sense, the entire social and cultural structure governing individuals and group behavior was influenced by this spirit.[154]

Protestantism and Capitalism

> As long as I am getting rich, I feel well. It is my Presbyterian blood.
> —Walker Percy

Capitalism flourished in the regions of Europe where Protestantism became the dominant religion. Here the prevailing religious ethic reinforced behaviors that led to economic prosperity. Political economist R. H. Tawney observed, "By a fortunate dispensation, the Protestant virtues of diligence, moderation, sobriety, and thrift were the very qualities most conducive to commercial success."[155] Tawney's observation calls to mind Max Weber's premise that the essence of the spirit of capitalism is rational asceticism applied to economic activity. As noted above, Weber wasn't proposing that the Protestant ethic is the direct *cause* of capitalism but that an affinity existed between the ethic and the spirit of capitalism.[156] Effectively, the values and behaviors inherent in these two historical forces buttressed each other.

The attitude toward economic behavior that evolved under Protestantism was radically different from that which had existed in Europe prior to the Reformation. Medieval Catholics had considered profit-seeking a form of avarice—and avarice was one of the Seven Deadly Sins. The change in attitude toward making money began with Martin Luther. Although no great supporter of commerce, Luther took a relatively liberal view on the charging of interest by merchants. Following Luther, John Calvin condoned interest on money with qualifications. As a hardheaded lawyer, Calvin argued that usury shouldn't be condemned as theft, but that payment of interest for capital was as reasonable as payment of rent for land. Loan interest became a matter of fixing a fair rate. Most of Calvin's followers endorsed this view. The revised attitude toward interest earnings was but one instance of the greater acceptance of capitalist activities. Money making, in general, was brought into the realm of moral behavior.[157]

Thus, the duties of religion and the expediencies of business ended their long estrangement in an unprecedented reconciliation. The erstwhile implications of business as mischief and impertinence gave way to the more positive connotations of diligence and systematic activity. Economic motive was no longer an enemy but an ally. The Puritan intellectual Richard Baxter (1615–1691) attempted to formulate a casuistry of economic conduct. The pragmatic Calvinist inquired, "When duty was so profitable, might not profit-making be a duty?" The affirmative response led to trade being pursued with "religious" zeal. Protestant business entrepreneurs directed their efforts at limitless increase and expansion, as profit became the supreme standard for measuring success.[158]

The English Puritans proved to be particularly adept at putting capitalist principles into practice. They liberalized the guidelines for the employment of money with dramatic results. By the end of the English Civil War (1651), most of the traditional restrictions on economic activity had disappeared. Tawney observed, "The storm and fury of the Puritan revolution [was] followed by a dazzling outburst of economic enterprise."[159] The changes in economic behavior reflected the new ethos, a spirit that was to set the tone for life in Protestant societies. The elements of rational asceticism were wedded to the capitalist spirit, and together they infused economic enterprise with an earnestness that placed it at the center of life and endowed it with an intrinsic dignity.

The spirit of capitalism didn't imply a greater love of money; its real import was in the drive to acquire money and the moral value attached to its acquisition. Economic gain was pursued relentlessly, often beyond reason, heedless of either one's actual needs or standard of living. If the pursuit of money seemed irrational at times, the methods remained highly rationalized. As capitalism matured, the importance placed on money dramatically influenced individual and societal values. Money-making became the chief aim of Protestant capitalism, its major preoccupation.[160] Contemporary media mogul and sports team owner Ted Turner famously professed, "Money is how we keep score."[161] This observation was as characteristic of his ancestors as his contemporaries.

Concurrently, Protestants invested the idea of economizing with unprecedented moral significance. Economizing became a test of inner resources and an affirmation of human worth. Coupled to the triad of rationalized efficiency, devotion to work, and the acquisition of capital, the practice of economizing led to the accumulation of individual fortunes. Increased wealth, in turn, financed the purchase of material goods. In a culture that also embraced asceticism, the coveting of material wealth generally was held suspect. It was always preferable to reinvest one's fortune than to spend it on possessions. The investor looked at everything in terms of balances and potential profitability, and persisted in taking calculated risks in order to exploit all he had to the end of making money. Calculated risk-taking served the double purpose of testing the individual and eliciting feelings of control. This practice of self-testing had obvious ties to moral asceticism.[162]

As society became more secular, the focus on self-examination, self-discipline, and work in one's calling continued to promote capitalist behaviors. These Protestant proclivities reinforced the dedication to systematic profits, reinvestment of earnings, and thrift. Weber was convinced that once the modern capitalist economy had established itself in the social order, the spirit of capitalism would become universalized and adherents of various religious orientations would no longer exhibit notable differences in economic behaviors. Nations with religiously and culturally diverse populations would provide a test for Weber's assertion. The United States offered the classic case. By the twentieth century, the disparities in American Protestant and Catholic economic behavior had become negligible. Once embedded within the national culture, the spirit of capitalism exerted a powerful influence as an idea, a social ethic, a set of moral attitudes, a complex of motives, and a set of maxims for the conduct of life.[163]

The essence of Protestant capitalism and its consequences can be summarized as:

1. The need to prove oneself by "holding one's own" economically in the community
2. The competitive market framed as a common "playing field"
3. Entrepreneurial behavior as the standard applied to a wide range of social action
4. Tradition subordinated to rational change
5. Rationalization and the work ethic applied to money making
6. Economic success as the criterion applied to personal and institutional behavior
7. Money-making dominating a wide range of human endeavors and shaping values
8. The intensive focus on making money resulting in the failure to recognize problems associated with this narrow outlook
9. The compelling need to make money interfering with the individual's ability to enjoy success
10. Equating of economic success with a sense of salvation.

This list provides the reader with a set of criteria by which to judge the extent to which individual Americans and their institutions, from corporate boards to sports clubs, acquired the values and strategies of capitalism. With this overview, we can turn to a discussion of the distinctive spirit of American capitalism as an influence upon social structure and cultural institutions.

The Spirit of American Capitalism

> America is the Canaan of capitalism, its promised land.
> —Werner Sombart

For Americans, capitalism has consisted of more than a system of ownership and distribution of economic goods; it is embraced as an ontological doctrine. Americans are inclined to believe that the production of economic goods and services is the pivotal activity upon which all other things are dependent. This American faith in capitalism constitutes a "disembodied spirit" expressing itself broadly in laws and social habits. John Kenneth Galbraith labeled the free-market economy the "totem of America's secular religion."[164] At the same time, American capitalism continued to convey religious connotations. The conservative publisher George Gilder would proclaim during the Reagan era, "Capitalism is the economic system that is consonant with Christianity."[165] Whether capitalism is framed as a secular or religious force, the emergent wealth derived from this economic system has been considered the source of all life's blessings in America. To find fault with the behavior of the capitalist market is both politically and theologically incorrect.

At times it seemed as though economic worth became the standard by which all other values were measured. As the journalist Thomas Low Nichols noted, an American "might be very unwilling to sell his dog; but he would be very likely to describe him as worth so many dollars." The same reckoning applied to the dog's master. Americans routinely speak of a successful individual—entrepreneur or professional athlete—as being worth so many millions of dollars. Indeed, virtually everything in American society would have an economic value placed upon it. The result has been that economic virtues often have eclipsed other virtues. Temperance, charity, and justice were made the servants of economic profit. Nichols lamented that "money is the great object and scruples are thrown to the wind." [166] The lives of Americans too often become a mere utility to profit. At its worst, an unchecked market economy can destroy family life, devastate neighborhoods, pollute the land and rivers, and disrupt folkways.

This mindset is capable of causing the deterioration of craft standards and the degradation of the arts.[167] Yet, the making of money seems to provide a sufficient compensation for these drawbacks. Americans have continued to look toward capitalism as the ultimate savior that eventually will rid them of most social evils.

This is not to say that the American spirit of capitalism has not provided notable benefits. The array of goods and services available to the working classes, and the disposable income to purchase such, has been unprecedented in world history. The capitalist system's encouragement of the entrepreneurial impulse, in tandem with a ready supply of investment capital, triggered a wide range of technological advances, created new jobs, and stimulated the economy. Consequently, the United States rapidly became the wealthiest economy on the planet. Like other economic systems (e.g., socialism, communism), though capitalism has been less a savior than a mixed blessing. The discussion of capitalism's influence on American sport in the closing chapters of the book illustrates this point. However, before we move ahead, it is worth taking a brief look at the history of American capitalism.

Capitalism arrived in North America along with the early immigrants fleeing religious and class persecution in Europe. Financial backers of the first settlements in the New World readily invested their money with an eye to making a profit. The Pilgrims who landed at Plymouth, Massachusetts, in 1620 obtained a subcontract of sorts with the group of investors who had made a similar contract earlier with the Virginia Company. In 1625, the Pilgrims negotiated to buy out the English shareholders. The purchase was completed by applying the proceeds of exports over the next seven years, and the Plymouth colony became an independent enterprise.[168] The Pilgrims' experience was a harbinger of the emergent nation's economic future.

A wave of commercial and financial expansion took hold in British America during the seventeenth century. The era was characterized by the three C's: companies, colonies, and capitalism. Various groups of gentlemen merchants like those of the Massachusetts Bay company organized under royal charters with the purpose of exploiting the immense North American continent. America was on its way to becoming a vast real estate development. These merchant companies were classic business enterprises. The London company, organized in 1609, had a governor, a council, and a general assembly of active shareholders. While providing a model for

Colonial governments, these fledgling enterprises also anticipated in many respects the modern American corporate structure.[169]

Capitalism, once implanted in the North American colonies, became a significant factor in the development of the way of life in the emerging nation. For over two centuries, the spirit of American capitalism thrived in the form of small businesses. The country towns became the centers for retail trade, and this preoccupation with trade shaped national sentiments and morals. Later on, big business would build on the ideals and traditions of this foundation. Farming was typical in its evolution from a self-sufficient way of life for individual families into modern agribusinesses with vast holdings. Likewise, craftsmen who organized into household industries were eventually absorbed by factories. Even the professions would adopt the corporate business model: medical doctors incorporated into physician's associations; lawyers banded together and formed law firms.[170]

As implied by these historical examples, American capitalism evolved in stages: first, a domestic form carried out in homes of wage workers; second, in the workshops where a technical division of labor was evident; and third, in factories and offices with large, organized labor forces. In its mature form, the typical capitalist unit came to be characterized by subordination of workers to managers, coordination of labor activities, and control of the entire enterprise through centralized accounting procedures. The early forms of open competitive capitalism were soon eclipsed by the highly structured, bureaucratic approaches to production and the shift to corporate organization.[171] These structural developments were to play an important role in shaping American attitudes toward both work and leisure (see chapter 6).

The spirit of capitalism was exemplified in the ingenuous faith in the virtues of profitable business. The very word "businessman" seems to have been American in its origin, dating from the 1830s, a decade of economic expansion. The emerging businessmen (and women) in the cities had much in common with their ancestors. They were the "Ben Franklins" of an expanding economic frontier. The entrepreneurial impetus was alive throughout the land and received a good deal of reinforcement in the subsequent era of economic growth in the late nineteenth century. The rewards went to the organizers, the persuaders, the discoverers of opportunities, the projectors, and the risk-takers. During the Gilded Age (1870s to 1890s), financial success was so common and so sudden that it was difficult to ascertain where fact ended and fable began. Fortunes were made and lost several times over. Spurred on by unprecedented success, money-making enterprises became a national phenomenon.[172]

Economic profit was a strong intoxicant. Van Wyck Brooks commented that the American businessman "cannot believe that he had gathered together enough money…but goes on making money in the honest conviction that it is necessary for him to do so."[173] As Peter Filene observed of businessmen in the 1920s, "Something in their work role was not quite right. Instead of making some thing, a man was making money."[174] Money-making developed into such a habit that the American continued to work at it as if he knew nothing else. Relentless profit-making became the national obsession as economic assertion took on the connotation of a moral obligation. Successful individuals found it traumatic to retire from business in order to enjoy their fortunes. Those forced to retire often became hypochondriacs; a few committed suicide.[175]

The spirit of American capitalism exerted an equally strong influence on the spending of money as it had on earning it. Economist Juliet Schor observed, "As people became accustomed to the material rewards of prosperity, the desire for leisure time was eclipsed by the aspiration to earn more discretionary income. Late capitalism is characterized by commodities, and Americans increasingly looked to consumption to give satisfaction, even meaning, to their lives." [176] Shopping appeared to be the primary recreational activity of the working classes. By the 1990s, the average person was consuming twice as much as he or she had in the 1950s. It was as if the American consumer was proclaiming, "I own, therefore I am."

Capitalism would transform the nation into a social system in which the pursuit of profit became the central enterprise. Education and government were brought under its sway; the American family was modified radically by this endeavor. Human relations increasingly were reshaped by economic relations. Economic privilege was held up as the highest prize, and the various classes defined themselves by economic symbols. A contemporary wag identified the indispensable upper-middle-class cachets as the largest house, the smallest cell phone, the thinnest laptop, and the thickest hiking boots. Not even American religion was exempt from the tropes of economic status. Characteristically, those called to the ministry interpret the offer of a large salary as a "loud call." In the same spirit, professional athletes measure their worth as much by their contracted salaries as their performance statistics. Economic status increasingly defines social status. Indeed, money is the way Americans kept score.[177]

The spirit of capitalism has continued to comprise a significant force in the shaping of American life and values. It reinforces—and is reinforced by—the national predisposition for achievement, competitiveness, and individualism. It has combined with the work ethic to define what constitutes success. The ambiance of capitalism pervades the entire culture. Not only America's economic institutions but a wide range of social and cultural institutions have adopted business methods and incorporated the values of efficiency, profitability, and productivity. The "operative values" in the management of corporate enterprises are inclined to become the values in the daily life of society.[178] Not only in the boardrooms of the large corporations but in nonprofit organizations and organized charities, the careful listener hears reference to "the bottom line" and "accountability." These also are values that influenced the emergent institutions of sport, as will become apparent in the following chapters.

4

The Seven Protestant Virtues

Distilling the Essence of the Protestant Ethic

Is it a world to hide virtues in?
—Twelfth Night 1.3.142

The Protestant ethic has transformed the behaviors of individuals and institutions. It has functioned as a general cultural influence, as a secular norm, and it has formed a personality type. The ethic has exerted an impact on a wide range of extra-economic, as well as economic, sectors of society. In America, where Protestantism remains the predominant religion of the establishment, the ethic has constituted a virtual hegemony. It has contributed broadly to the prevailing concept of reality through a set of values that are diffused throughout virtually every social and cultural institution, public and private. The Protestant ethic has decreed taste, morality, customs, ethical and political principles, and social relations.[179]

Given this breadth of influence, it is not surprising that the Protestant ethic has been a subject of interest to theologians, historians, and a wide range of social scientists. Following the publication of Weber's thesis, a large number of theoretical and empirical studies on the ethic were carried out. These efforts reflect the positivist bias that characterizes Western social and behavioral science. A number of contemporary psychologists and sociologists have applied empirical methodology to dimensions of the ethic. Mirels and Garrett framed the Protestant ethic as a dispositional variable and developed a widely used Protestant ethic scale as a measure. They found that the ethic correlates positively with occupations demanding concrete, pragmatic approaches to work.[180] MacDonald reported that valuation of the ethic correlated with ambition, self-control, and salvation, and that its valuation did not change as a function of aging or education.[181] In a series of studies, Greenberg observed that endorsement of the Protestant ethic correlated positively with rewarded performance and negatively with values toward pleasure. He further observed that those who endorsed the ethic tended to employ work-related behaviors beyond the workplace and to use nonwork time for doing work.[182] Chino concluded that the Protestant ethic was the basic value system underlying the American status structure, and that the ethic was internalized to the greatest degree by those persons whose fathers had high-status, white-collar occupations.[183]

As contemporary scholars operationally defined the Protestant ethic, a large collection of values, behaviors, and personality traits were assembled that characterize dimensions of the ethic. These include de-emphasis on ritual and traditionalism[184]; self-reliance, asceticism, rationality, and compulsive behavior toward work[185]; legalistic perfectionism[186]; a sense of responsibility for improving skills, excelling, and overcoming obstacles; repression of spontaneous impulses and of fleshly desires; motivation to face hardships, to enlarge opportunities, to reinvest a substantial share of one's income, and to curtail personal expenditures[187]; rugged individualism[188]; high achievement, deferred gratification, respect for property, self-reliance, control of emotions, rationality, and personableness[189]; the need to conform to the judgment of others (externally enforced discipline)[190]; sobriety, frugality, sexual restraint, and a forbidding attitude toward life[191]; anti-idleness, duty, pressure, status, production, gain, satisfaction, vitality, and identity[192]; persistence to work, resistance to fatigue, delayed gratification, and extension of work-related behaviors[193]; and striving and competing.[194]

We can distill this comprehensive and occasionally redundant collection into a concise set of constructs that reflect the essence of the Protestant ethic. The following list compiled by the author is labeled the "Seven Protestant virtues" (with apologies to Thomas Aquinas): (I) worldly asceticism, (II) rationalization, (III) goal-directed behavior, (IV) achieved status, (V) individualism, (VI) work ethic, and (VII) time ethic. The remainder of the chapter discusses each of these virtues at some length. We begin with what constitutes the hub of the Protestant ethic: an inner-worldly asceticism with roots carrying back to classical and religious strains in early Mediterranean and Middle-Eastern cultures, and subsequently acquiring its distinctive form in the wake of the Protestant Reformation.

I. Worldly Asceticism

> A man is not a man until he makes himself do with a smile
> whatever he hates most.
> –*The Independent*, ca. 1920

Something lurks within the human disposition that finds fulfillment in the denial of pleasure, that believes in the redeeming power of discomfort, and that revels in the rituals of self-discipline. Whether the goal is to purify the soul, to heal the body, or to propitiate the gods, these ascetic proclivities have provided a recurring theme in human history. Indeed, asceticism has appeared in both religious and secular settings. The ancient Hebrew sects fasted in order to experience the holy. The early Greeks undertook a regimen of severe physical discipline to prepare for battle. Medieval Christian monks eschewed the comforts of the world for the spiritual solitude of the desert. Following the Reformation, stiff-spined Puritans endured the rock-hard pews of freezing New England meeting halls to show their devotion to a stern and demanding God. Their descendants have taken their doses of cod liver oil or performed their "daily dozen" with the conviction that anything unpleasant is beneficial to body and soul. The essence of asceticism is the human need to give purpose to suffering. The Victorians encapsulated this conviction in admonishing, "You have to take your medicine like a man," and "Keep a stiff upper lip."

The asceticism that emerged in the context of Reformed Protestantism contained elements of earlier forms both secular and religious; thus, a brief historical account is in order. The Greek discipline of askesis, referring to the exercise of self-control and abstinence, was practiced by warriors and athletes to attain optimal bodily fitness and grace. The Dead Sea Scrolls revealed ascetic practices of the ancient Jewish sect of Essenes who took vows of abstinence to prepare for a holy war. Stoic philosophers disciplined their will against a life of sensual pleasure to attain spiritual goals. This latter form of spiritual asceticism was incorporated into European Christianity.[195]

Early Christians, influenced by Eastern concepts of good and evil, had treated the physical body as an obstacle to achieving spiritual goals. They pursued lives of solitude and contemplation with strict abstinence from all sensual pleasures. Monks reduced bodily movement to an extreme degree and inflicted their bodies with pain. Others subjected themselves to exhaustive exercises and hard labor, exposed themselves to extreme temperatures, fasted, abstained from sex, and mortified their flesh—all with the goal of obtaining an exalted spiritual state. For these "athletes of God," as they came to be known, pain, torment, and deprivation provided the path to salvation.[196]

Christian ascetics, inspired by the suffering of Christ, based their practices upon scriptural teachings. The writings of Paul of Tarsus were laced with metaphors to promote the ideal of the disciplined spiritual athlete seeking a state of ritual purity. Paul counseled in I Timothy 4:7–8, "Train yourself in godliness; for while bodily training is of some value, godliness is of value in every way...." Ascetic practices were then encoded and institutionalized within the medieval monasteries. The Order of Benedictines emphasized the discipline of physical labor, implicit in their motto: Laborare est orare, meaning "Labor is prayer." Various forms of ascetic doctrines and practices carried into the high Middle Ages.[197]

The early leaders of the Protestant Reformation may have rejected monastic practices, but the ascetic impulse wasn't easily extricated from Western religion. Distinct forms of asceticism began to appear especially among the Calvinist sects. However, the asceticism that emerged out of the Reformation revealed a dramatic shift in focus from that of medieval Catholicism. Protestants fulfilled their religious duties not by withdrawing from the world but by immersing themselves in the world and shaping it to divine ends.[198] Thus, Protestantism transported asceticism from the desert and the cloister to the larger world.

The secular focus of asceticism owed its rationale to the Protestant mission to affirm the world. "God made the world and it was good," the Protestant quoted from scripture. Protestants were to seek salvation in the life of the community. This change of focus began with Martin Luther's concept of the calling which meant for people to live the secular life religiously. The secular focus reflected the fact that Protestants were controlled less by the Church and were more easily "outside the church" than had been true of Catholics. The inner-worldly focus of Protestant asceticism thus worked to glorify mundane endeavors of laypeople.[199]

The contrast between Catholic and Protestant asceticism was evident in the metaphors employed by each. Medieval asceticism had implied a contemplative *possession* of the holy; Reformation asceticism represented devout *action*. The Catholic saw himself as a divine *vessel*; the worldly ascetic saw himself as a divine *tool*. One Protestant preacher sermonized,

"God moves all men…as the saw is moved by the hand of the craftsman."[200] The devout Catholic viewed action in the world as a danger to one's salvation, and turned to contemplation. The Protestant found assurance in mastery over the world and held contemplation to be a form of self-indulgence. Inward experience was eclipsed by an outwardly pious and active life. Protestants were compelled to engage in strenuous, protracted efforts to carry out God's purpose. This focus on mastery of the world gave birth to unprecedented activism.[201]

The drive toward action compelled each individual to constantly seek out tasks to perform and then carry them out carefully and systematically, in what Walzer termed the "asceticism of duty."[202] In its own way, worldly asceticism began to impose upon the Protestant layman a discipline every bit as severe as that of the Christian monk.[203] Jean Jacques Rousseau would observe that Calvinists lived like monks within the world. They felt compelled to discipline themselves constantly and rigorously and to submit their lives to the severest regulation and control. Poggi noted, "The Protestant sects require that a special quality and intensity of religious commitment be continuously sustained and affirmed by the members' exacting, exemplary practice of morality in all aspects of their private and public existence. To this end they subject members to a particularly searching and demanding discipline."[204] The Calvinists' need for constant discipline in their lives was revealed in their fondness for the military model. "God," said William Perkins, "is the general appointing to every man his particular calling." The English preacher Richard Sibbes commented, "An army is a beautiful thing, because of the order."[205] The Puritans fancied themselves as a "religious army" in defense of the cause. They often practiced military drill even when they weren't making war as a sort of moral calisthenics to bring discipline into their everyday lives.[206]

Protestant asceticism obliged each individual to exert will power and constancy in all aspects of life. As Poggi observed, the Protestant must avoid

> any tendency to engage in effort only in spurts, and then slacken; any complacent treatment of past attainments as ends in themselves; any spontaneous, unreflective attachment to familiar, comfortable, emotionally gratifying arrangements; any carefree enjoyment of the present for its own sake; any reliance for guidance in his conduct on unreflecting feeling or unexamined routine; any temptation to blame

his own failings on circumstances or fate rather than his own inadequacies.[207]

The great Protestant delusion was (and is) that human existence is shaped by human will.

However, a toll was to be paid for the inordinate emphasis on self-control and self-discipline, as it tended to destroy instinctive feelings and enjoyment of sensual pleasures. Protestant asceticism required not only mastery over the world but mastery of the flesh. Pleasures of the flesh were mistrusted above all else, and Puritans revealed an obsession with mastery of the flesh. Vice began where physical gratification was sought for its own sake. Appetite was conceived as a form of "possession" by an alien character, an enemy penetrating the individual to be repelled and disowned. Passions and appetites were subordinated to the dictates of reason and will. The Puritans sought a spiritual perfectionism that required abstinence from any activities that could provide pleasure. Suppression became a virtual fetish for a people who couldn't countenance worldly pleasure for themselves or for their neighbors. Puritan leaders preached of great moral peril in dancing, attending the theater, gambling, smoking, and drinking, as well as immodesty and sexual incontinence.[208]

Thus, while inner-worldly asceticism promoted an active life in the world, it inhibited worldly interests and satisfactions. This anomaly reflected an inherent dualism in Protestant theology. Although salvation was to be found in the world, the valuing of natural things constituted a form of idolatry. This aversion to the natural world led to a marked austerity in personal lives. Nothing ostentatious could be evident in social actions. Consequently, a marked sense of restraint pervaded the lives of Protestants. Austerity was reflected in their attire, the ambiance of their churches, and in their religious ceremonies.

Fear of indulging in worldly pleasures discouraged Protestants from consuming luxury. Consequently, they became compulsive savers. However, individual savings couldn't be savored because wealth itself was distrusted insofar as it became a temptation to idleness or sin. Even the laboring to acquire wealth was suspect if its ultimate purpose was to live merrily and without care. Wealth must not be allowed to distract a person from the pursuit of a righteous life. The limit on what was permissible was defined narrowly by the term "comfort." Any extravagance or excess beyond this standard was deemed sinful. The affluent Protestant was to desire no jewelry or other visible luxuries. Material possessions served the limited purpose of assuring the owner of personal salvation—nothing more.[209]

Inner-worldly asceticism taught the proper attitude toward failure just as it prescribed the proper demeanor to accompany success. Failure implied that the individual wasn't one of the elect, for he lacked the visible signs of salvation. Yet, the failed individual must not despair in his circumstances but must constantly maintain a stoic facade, to "keep his chin up" and "make the best of it"—a sanitary packaging of oneself. The stigma of failure led to conservatism in personal actions, an unwillingness to take unnecessary risks as well as to an exaggerated sense of privacy. The fear of failure, more than anything, reinforced the psychological drive in Protestants that impelled them to seek success, and thus salvation.[210]

The quest for salvation was framed as a trial, a lifelong effort (rather than a matter of sudden conversion). Consequently, Protestants became preoccupied with long-range goals that blocked out pleasures of the moment. The relentless pursuit of salvation led to a narrow focus on personal goals and duties. The emphasis placed on limitations, boundaries, and balances was reflected in their writings, which invoked images of containment, control, and order. The individual was admonished to stick to the "straight and narrow" and not venture too far off the "beaten path."

This severe discipline and repression of desires had its rewards in the context of the bargain struck between the Protestant and his God. It constituted what Walzer called "spiritual commercialism": for so much obedience there would be so much grace.[211] These tendencies were carried to extreme measures by the Calvinists, who practiced a system of moral bookkeeping that marked in indelible ink the credits and debits that had to be balanced before the final reckoning. Through sacrifice, the individual paid off the debts he or she had contracted by indulging in personal desires. Puritans tormented themselves and denied themselves in order to pay in advance for the spiritual happiness they were seeking.[212] The Puritan's deep fear of pleasure went beyond a rational belief in the efficacy of abstinence. The aversion to pleasure was deeply ingrained in the Puritan temperament and it endured across generations. George Santayana's title character in *The Last Puritan* proclaimed, "I hate pleasure. I hate what is called having a good time. I hate stimulants…while the pleasure lasts it's nothing but a sort of flurry more than half trouble. When it's over, there's just emptiness."[213]

Asceticism would endure beyond the Colonial period. The American's inability to enjoy the pleasures of life persisted into the Industrial era with its unprecedented accumulation of material wealth. The ethic of moral asceticism (linking morality to self-denial, austerity, and the renunciation of pleasures) was disseminated from nineteenth-century church pulpits in small towns across the land, while advice books preached the supreme virtue of self-control. There was no better indication of residual asceticism than the vitriolic rhetoric of the American clergy directed at the amusements of the Industrial Age. It remained a presence when baseball and other sports began to assume their institutional forms in the closing decades of the century.[214]

Thus did asceticism transcend the monasteries and hermitages of the Middle Ages to exert its influence in the secular world. It evolved from its Reformation era incarnations into a highly moralistic discipline characterized by abhorrence of idleness, a marked need for control, a strong drive toward action, and the pursuit of a diligent, planned, and constant life. Its anti-ritualism and avoidance of the irrational translated into a ferocious hatred of anything that smacked of superstition and led to an attempt to eliminate all forms of magic from the world.[215] The descendants of Puritans emphasized mind over emotion and revealed a profound fear of sensual pleasures and extravagance. Spontaneous activities such as play and dance were especially feared. Work alone was allowed as the only human activity that met the stringent requirements for redemption.

As asceticism evolved within secular Protestant society, it became increasingly rationalized. These rationalist tendencies not only reshaped historical asceticism but endured as an autonomous force in the world. Rationalization surfaced as the distinctive trait in personal lives and in social institutions wherever the Protestant ethic prevailed.

II. Rationalization

> What is required is not brotherly love or faith, hope and
> charity, but self-interested rational labor.
> –Allan Bloom

The element within Protestant asceticism that set it apart from earlier forms was its proclivity toward rationalization. Rationalization refers to the process during which human action became increasingly subject to calculation, measurement, standardization, and control. It is in this sense that the word will be used here (not in its psychological meaning as an explanation to justify actions that disturb the ego). Rationalization as a component of the Protestant ethic derived from two major sources: the rational asceticism within Protestant theology and the secular tendencies inherent in the culture. The Protestant call for mastery over the world led irrevocably to the rationalization of individual and institutional behaviors. It is fair to say that Protestantism has represented the extreme instance among religions of the rational organization of life in the world.[216]

In discussing rationalization within the context of secularization, it is important to distinguish between the sense in which the latter term implies a loss of interest in the supernatural (in providence, guilt, redemption, atonement, etc.) and the clinging to nonrational beliefs and acts but no longer calling them "religious." Protestants retained a strong interest in the supernatural concept of salvation while their beliefs about secular behaviors as a means to this end can be viewed as nonrational. Examples of nonrational beliefs include the exaggerated connection between labor in a calling and salvation, and a blind faith in the power of human will to control the world. In effect, Reformed Protestantism promoted an *irrational* belief in a *rationalized* life.[217]

Protestant rationalism was the doctrine that human reason unaided by divine revelation constituted the sole guide to religious truth. This framework was accompanied by a belief that the world was rationally ordered. As a consequence of these beliefs, no longer was anything held sacred merely because it had been a tradition; instead it had to be justified by resort to reason. This attitude invoked a bizarre reciprocity within Protestant culture: as rationalism broke with tradition, every break involved a need for further rationalization. A kind of ethical universalism prevailed that obligated each individual to bring a high degree of order into his or her life. All things had to be tested anew according to some universal standard. On the personal level, this attitude meant human conduct had to be systematized and justified according to acceptable norms. No act stood on its own merits; its value was judged in terms of its bearing on the entire system of rational conduct. Everyone and everything was treated categorically according to generalized, impersonal standards, as rationalism contained a powerful animus against nepotism and favoritism in its drive to establish a meritocracy.[218]

This exact ordering of secular life required the adoption of formal rules, quantification, and methods of calculable efficiency. Such tendencies were readily apparent in such institutions as the military. Puritan military commanders like Oliver Cromwell proved to be unusually open to innovation. They transformed what had always been a traditionalized profession. The Protestant armies of the early seventeenth century demonstrated a single-minded pursuit of definite goals and clear-cut purpose. They rationalized internal procedures to improve efficiency. As a result, they were more inclined than most of the armies of Europe to adopt standard uniforms and orderly tactics such as marching in step.[219]

The tendencies toward order and efficiency were apparent in a wide range of civil institutions. Innovators like Benjamin Franklin applied these principles to business. For Franklin, efficiency became virtually a moral obligation, a matter of conscience. Failure to be completely efficient weighed like a sense of sin on the Protestant. No one ever became efficient enough, so individuals engaged in an unrelenting effort to improve personal efficiency. In the effort to become more and more efficient, the rational Protestant increasingly sought assistance through technology and the scientific method. Tasks were specialized, rules were codified, and control was centralized. A dominion of technique emerged—what Herbert Marcuse labeled "technical reason." Trained expertise acquired an unprecedented prestige. The Protestant was relentlessly methodical, scientific, and calculating in personal actions and institutional behaviors. This "technical" rationalization promoted organizational efforts, reshaped the structure of modern social institutions and—in the process—paved the way for industrial capitalism.[220]

In 1776, a student of the Presbyterian moral philosopher Francis Hutcheson published a magnificent book, *The Wealth of Nations*. In this work, the author Adam Smith included the first detailed explanation of how the division of labor could increase productivity. Smith's principles were applied expeditiously in the emerging factories of the industrial nations. What Smith contributed to theory, the Quaker industrialist Frederick W. Taylor and his disciples carried out in practice on this side of the Atlantic. Taylor's revolutionary methods of scientific management would bring about the rationalization of the structure and function of the nineteenth-century workplace.[221]

Although industry provided the perfect laboratory for this type of exuberant rationalization, scientific management quickly branched out from the workplace to influence virtually every level of social structure. The rationalization of work was followed by rationalization of the family (transforming it into a vocational unit), the rationalization of politics, and even the rationalization of sport and recreation. In regard to the latter,

Taylor's experiments with scientific management actually began on the tennis courts (where he first applied them), then in the factory.[222]

As rationalization evolved, it increasingly incorporated the values of utilitarianism and materialism. These two forces, which had been incipient tendencies within rational asceticism, came into full bloom under industrial capitalism. The Anglo-American brand of utilitarianism linked usefulness to virtue. The Puritan was expected to engage in behaviors that were eminently practical.[223] As the religious concept of the calling faded from common speech, the shibboleth "usefulness" took its place. Usefulness became a saving grace. Human activity of all types was increasingly constrained by that which was necessary and useful. Utilitarianism was carried to new heights; it became the "tail that wagged the dog." The doctrine even affected churches to the point that ethicist H. Richard Niebuhr chastised institutional religion for having "sold out" to the doctrine of usefulness.[224]

The rational tendencies within Protestant culture also led to "scientification"—that is, the instrumental application of scientific methods to a wide range of practices. Protestantism had always held a hospitable view toward empirical science that extolled the prized value of useful applications. Though the fruits of the empirical methodology could be short-sighted, overly practical, and occasionally disappointing, such science would continue to garner generous support as long as it produced practical results. Thus, Protestants displayed a pronounced tendency to transform virtually every human endeavor into a practical, applied "science," regardless of appropriateness.[225]

Scientific rationalization emphasized what was measurable and quantifiable and, in turn, spawned an exaggerated concern for material things over spiritual values. This "materialism" committed the human mind to quantitative values and methods of reasoning and also to tangible, verifiable evidence. Numbers and numerical data came to occupy a place in the modern vocabulary they hadn't previously enjoyed. Arguably, one can trace the receptive interest in quantitative values directly to the rise of Protestantism. Sir Dudley North observed in the early seventeenth century, "Knowledge in great measure is becoming mechanical."[226] This was an age interested in mathematics and physics, in which the object was to express oneself in terms of number, weight, or measure; to use only arguments of sense; and to consider only such causes as have visible foundations. The era revealed a notable increase in the tendency to keep records and accounts. An interest emerged in quantitative values such as rates of increase. At the same time, historians could discern a shift in production away from items wanted primarily for their beauty and ornamental value to production of common commodities in which quantity and utility became the main concern of producers and consumers.[227]

Tendencies toward materialism developed concurrently with the early stages of a market economy. In the world of industrial capitalism, strict discipline of workers served to further stifle spiritual attitudes in favor of crass materialism. These developments were encouraged by a religion that had become more discipline than faith. Calvinist doctrine originally tied to other-worldly purposes was transmuted into an efficient stimulus for material gain. The new materialist adopted a matter-of-fact temperament that neither recognized any animistic propensities in things nor resorted to preternatural explanations even for the most perplexing phenomena. Materialists showed no predilection for belief in an "unseen hand" to shape the course of events. The materialist gospel was evident in the work of Isaac Newton, who viewed the workings of the world exclusively in terms of mechanistic, dispassionate forces.[228]

Thus, the indelible stamp of rationalization left its mark on a wide range of social institutions and human behaviors. A dynamic tour de force had been unleashed. Rational asceticism spawned scientific management and technical rationalization that, in turn, promoted utilitarian and materialist values. These latter developments led to a form of instrumentalism that would manifest itself on both the personal and organizational levels as goal-directed behavior. The Protestants' quest to find salvation through rational conduct led to the subjugating of means to ends in ways that radically reshaped motives for social action.

III. Goal-Directed Behavior

> Show us not the aim without the way. For ends and means on earth are so
> entangled //That changing one, you change the other too; Each different
> path brings other ends in view.
> —   Frederick Lasalle

The need for a goal constitutes the fundamental relationship between "what we do and what we get." Anthropologists inform us that early humans lived in a natural state where each act related to an immediate goal. Primitive people hunted in order to find food, danced to express their sense of joy, copulated to satisfy the compelling urge to reproduce, and retired to rest their exhausted bodies. However, as human society became more complex, simple acts were divorced from their ultimate consequences by complex chains of means and ends. Human actions came to be connected with remote, even transmundane goals. Advanced civilizations sought an ultimate goal in life to give their actions meaning. For the philosopher Nietzsche, this compelling need to identify meaning expressed the basic fact of the human will. Meaning was not a "given" but was created out of human thought and experience, and humans appropriated abstract concepts like loyalty, honor, prestige, and immortality to imbue their actions with purpose.[229] Philosophers and theologians endeavored to provide the ultimate meaning and goals in life.

Societies define themselves by their ultimate goals and then subordinate social structures to these ideals. Religion often has provided the highest goals and ideals toward which group efforts are directed. Assumptions about the relationship between human actions and ultimate ends have been a part of all major religious and ethical systems: the Buddhist seeks detachment; the Muslim, righteous victory over the forces of Evil; the Roman Catholic, oneness with God; the Protestant, mastery of self and the world.[230] Adherents to these various belief systems occasionally lose sight of goals, but orientation to an ultimate goal continues to provide meaning and purpose in the lives of people in all religions and cultures.

Nowhere in the array of belief systems has single-minded, goal-directed behavior been as salient as among Protestants. More than any other religious system, Protestantism required individuals to justify actions in terms of a higher goal. Protestants set their goals in the context of human progress. Each individual was an instrument of God's will, with an important role in the collective effort to improve the world. The Protestant was compelled to work in the service of impersonal goals. However, the goal of communal salvation didn't free the Protestant from concern about personal salvation. The demands of these two agendas fueled much of the goal-directed action that was characteristic of Protestantism (as discussed previously).

The relentless pursuit of the goal of salvation created a situation wherein no one did anything for its own sake. All action, in effect, was subordinated to this particular goal. Recalling St. Paul's words that, "Nothing is unclean of itself," the Protestant appeared to extrapolate that nothing was valuable in and of itself, short of salvation. Within the Protestant scheme of morality every attainment seemed to be accomplished for the sake of something else.[231] The early twentieth-century British clergyman Frederick Chambers Spurr attempted to explain this orientation to life by noting that it is philosophic nonsense to speak of doing things for their own sake. "Nothing can be done for its own sake, since nothing we do is an absolute thing: it is always related to something else, and [thus] its value depends upon the reality and truth of its relation."[232] For Protestants, the implied subordination of means to ends constituted a fact of life.

Spurr's admonition reflected the traditional Calvinist predilection to assign a neutral status to all natural things. Human action was neither good nor evil per se, but out of its relation to other things. The value of human actions lay in their effect. For example, work was good if it bore fruit (although the laborer was not to dwell upon the fruits of his labor). Play could be either good or evil depending upon its effects upon the individual and the community. If play disrupted the Sabbath, led people to lust, or engrossed them in slothful habits, it was evil. But if play provided rest and recreation so as to allow the individual to return to his or her vocation refreshed with renewed energy, then it was good. Not only work and play, but virtually every human activity was judged by its relation to higher goals.

Psychological tensions were built into this orientation toward goals. The compelling relationship between means and ends could lead individuals to resort to rationalizations (in the ego-protecting sense) and to logical circumlocutions to justify personal actions. A contemporary folktale from the American Northwest illustrates this point. The story tells of a peripatetic philosopher who came upon a pig farmer in his travels. Their chance meeting led to the following dialogue:

Philosopher: "What do you do for a living?"
Farmer: "I raise pigs."
P: "Why do you raise pigs?"
F: "So I can eat."
P: "Why do you eat?"
F: "So I can live."
P: "And why do you live?"
F: "So I can raise pigs."

This tautology encapsulates an aspect of the Protestant mindset. No modern-day yeoman descended from Calvinists could admit to raising pigs, eating—or living, for that matter—without justifying his actions by tying them to an external goal. The farmer's responses recall Spurr's dictum: "No true Protestant is able to do anything for its own sake."

Goal-directed behavior exerted its effect just as strongly upon group behavior as it had upon individuals. Post-Reformation organizations were highly rationalized and goal directed. They could no longer rely upon tradition alone to justify their existence. An organization was granted a charter only if its goals were deemed important, and the programs established to acquire these goals were judged rational and purposeful. Administrators were required to rationally explain the purpose of their programs and to justify them as contributing to the overall goals of the organization and society.[233] Thus, Protestant culture moved toward a system of highly goal-directed individuals functioning within goal-oriented organizations.

As society became increasingly goal-directed, the goals derived from traditional religious values proved unstable. This instability was due in part to the remoteness of religious goals. Transmundane goals lacked the degree of specificity that was required by the worldly and pragmatic Protestants. In this sense, religious goals failed to perform the important psychological function of providing clear directions for action and unambiguous criteria for evaluating success. Consequently, transcendental goals receded and were replaced by more mundane goals. In this process of goal displacement, the means to the original goals became goals in themselves. The new goals were expected to provide a more precise standard against which the Protestant could test the effectiveness of personal actions. But similar problems surfaced with new goals, many of which proved relatively remote and impersonal. The Protestant continued to substitute more concrete (i.e., verifiable) goals through a series of goal displacements.[234]

At the head of this process stood the goal of personal salvation. Under the Calvinist doctrine of predestination, the ability to determine one's progress toward achieving salvation was crucially important. But how did one ensure the proper steps had been taken to attain salvation? The answer wasn't clear; the goal of salvation proved unsatisfactory precisely because its realization was uncertain and postponed to the next life. Thus, salvation became an inaccessible goal, and less remote goals were sought to replace it. Personal success provided a more specific goal, a fixed target against which to test personal achievement.[235] This goal worked as a viable substitute because Calvinist doctrine linked success in one's calling to assurance of salvation. Proof of salvation required visible signs, and measurable success fit this need. Thus, worldly success (which was a more verifiable goal) displaced the goal of salvation. As the late novelist John Fowles noted, in "end-oriented societies" one cannot be content unless he is successful.[236]

Under Protestant capitalism, material success became the new standard of salvation because it appeared to be unambiguous. Everyone played by, or counted by, the same rules in defining success. However, success was soon redefined in more concrete terms as productivity, but so defined, still harbored a degree of moral ambiguity. It became apparent to the capitalist that productivity was meaningless without profit. This problem led to a further displacement: profit displaced the goal of productivity. Financial profit now emerged as the paramount goal, the unmistakable sign of worldly success. Thus, the ultimate goal of the Protestant capitalist was to make money, as its acquisition offered a concrete sense of salvation.[237]

Money-making had displaced the goal of production, which had been the measure of financial success, and worldly success had provided the evidence of salvation. Thus, through a series of goal displacements, the acquisition of money provided the assurance that one was saved. Here was the classic case of remote and ambiguous goals being displaced by ones that could be more easily assessed.[238] Aristotle, in his *Ethics*, had suggested that a life of moneymaking was undertaken out of compulsion. Indeed, the Protestant capitalist was compelled to direct all personal efforts at money-making. Other endeavors acquired meaning only as they contributed to this end.

This series of goal displacements brought about dramatic changes in social institutions under Protestant capitalism. The behavior of capitalist economic institutions was rerouted in the direction of ruthless money-making. The excesses of the robber barons (some of them strict Calvinists) of the late nineteenth century was prelude to the single-minded emphasis on money that displaced productivity as a goal under advanced capitalism. Over the decades, corporations that had originally manufactured steel or refined motor oil shifted the focus of their efforts. They diversified their holdings, manipulated the money market, bought out less powerful corporations, "farmed out" production, and grew into mammoth conglomerates with the singular goal of maximizing profits. This trend was quite evident in the American economy by the last quarter of the twentieth century. Economists lamented that corporations were no longer interested in "making something" but only in making money. The steel mills and factories were supplanted by brokerage houses and holding companies.

Corporate executives spoke less of quality control than of leveraged buyouts. Even traditional nonproprietary institutions such as colleges were influenced by the single-minded emphasis on economic status.

On the level of the individual, goal-directed behavior proved to be an equally perfidious virtue. The Protestant became a victim of his own impersonal ends. Once upon a time, creating a new thing constituted healthy industry. But when nothing was done for its own sake, when work was performed mainly for the ulterior object of making money, the Protestant at his calling was left feeling barren. The Protestant ethic had decreed: sacrifice, work, suffer, and it will all be worth it in the end; but labor became increasingly divorced from any larger set of meanings and values other than the sheer instrumentality of making money. While this instrumental focus aptly conditioned workers to perform the required tasks under early capitalism, ultimately it left them with vague feelings of purposeless despair.[239]

This orientation toward goals also had an effect upon human relations under Protestant capitalism. The impersonal instrumentalism inherent in industrial labor led to a corresponding orientation toward one's fellow beings. Cohorts often were treated as means to ends. "Business is business," it was stated, and friendship shouldn't be allowed to "get in the way." Once in a while one might have to "step on somebody" to get a promotion and "make it to the top." This pervasive goal-directed focus affected a wide range of motivations and social behaviors beyond the workplace. Individuals might marry to advance their social standing, join a church in order to rub shoulders with the right people, or join fraternal organizations to advance their careers. Executives played golf or tennis at the country club less for the exercise than the status and business contacts it provided.[240] Everything was done for the sake of some external goal.

As Tawney wrote in his seminal study *Religion and the Rise of Capitalism,* "Men are to be judged by their reach as well as their grasp, by the ends at which they aim as by the success with which they attain them."[241] Tawney's statement reflects the orientation toward higher goals that has characterized the Protestant ethic. Goal-directed Protestants had to find good reasons to justify personal behaviors. They were always aware of what they were doing and why they were doing it. Individuals were compelled to act for a good purpose, a higher cause. In this moral context, human action came to be judged less by its intrinsic qualities than by the ends that were attained. The goal-directed focus began and ended with the singular focus on personal salvation.

IV. Achieved Status

> Be assured that every man's success is in proportion to his average ability.
> –Henry David Thoreau

The importance of personal achievement is instilled in Protestants at an early age and follows them through life. It begins in the family setting and accompanies the child to school and onto the playground. For adults, achievement is the defining characteristic of both vocation and avocation. Indeed, there is no respite from the need to achieve until the final reckoning at which time one's life achievements are tallied. The moral import of achievement is clearly understood: to achieve implies that one has acquired status among the elect.

Achievement became closely tied to status following the Protestant Reformation. In pre-Reformation Europe status had been treated as a "given." This view of status was based on the Catholic conception of the spiritual equality of humans. The fundamental assumption was that each individual had a salvageable soul and that once that person had been made to "see the light," it was possible for him to receive salvation.[242] Social status was determined by birth or affiliation. One was a noble or a commoner, a cleric or a layperson, etc. This form of identity is what sociologists label "ascribed status."

The basis for determining status changed dramatically following the Reformation. In Protestant society, individuals were judged less by who they were than in terms of what they did: achieved status. The reasons for the revised view of status can be linked directly to the Protestant's distinct view of salvation. Protestant election was reflected in the Calvinist admonition, "Many are called, but few are chosen." Thus, salvation wasn't to be taken for granted, but was the province of a chosen elite. Its acquisition was an elusive prize for which one had to compete with his fellow beings. Strict criteria governed admission to the elect. Achievement became the outward sign, the technical proof, that one belonged a priori (given the doctrine of predestination) to the elect.[243]

The Calvinists drew a distinct line between salvation and damnation. The fear of damnation served as the "engine" that drove individuals to achieve. Failure carried the connotation of sin and damnation, and individuals went to great lengths to avoid this stigma. The singular drive to be successful and not be labeled a failure led to unbridled competition and to invidious comparisons among people. The perception of one's progress toward salvation was conditional upon what others accomplished, or failed to accomplish.[244] This mindset has carried into the modern era. Thus did Oscar Wilde concede that it was not enough that he succeed; his friends must fail. The American writer Gore Vidal confessed, "Each time a friend succeeds, I die a little." When the ranks of the elect are so exclusive, achieving status is perceived as a zero-sum game: someone has to win; someone has to lose.

The need to achieve carries both religious and secular import. Protestants have to prove themselves before God by attaining the signs of salvation while simultaneously proving themselves before their fellow beings by holding their own within the community. The effort to acquire the marks of salvation becomes a constant labor. The individual is obliged to feel discontent with his or her present lot and to be forever striving to improve one's position in society. This lifelong endeavor to achieve status in the community led to a preoccupation with profitable habits.[245]

The fundamental offer of salvation sanctified economic success. In effect, piety was integrated with the profit motive. The Protestant Gospel of Success taught that "God Himself" blessed "His chosen" through the profit of their labors. Sermons carried such titles as "Godliness Is Profitable." Jonathan Edwards wrote in *Charity and Its Fruits* (1738), "If you place your happiness in God, in glorifying Him and in serving Him by doing good, you will promote your wealth and honor here below."[246] God, it was said, "sprinkled holy water on economic success." It became the accepted sign of divine approval, the ticket into the parlor of the elect. A system developed under Protestant capitalism wherein the achievements of entrepreneurs were reinforced by moral and religious sanctions.[247]

Over time, success within the capitalist system worked to erode the Calvinist fear of riches. To strive for wealth by engaging in one's calling was not only permissible but commendable. The achievement of wealth as the result of individual effort symbolized God's reward for industriousness. Money and the things it could buy became valued as symbolic evidence of personal worth. The means, if not the goal, in life was to strive for a higher standard of living. In capitalist societies with relatively high social mobility, and in which one's position on the social scale was tied to occupational achievement, wealth became the universally accepted sign of personal status.[248]

The close tie between economic achievement and salvation hinged upon a crucial modification of the doctrine of election that occurred during the seventeenth century. This revision implied that worldly success wasn't merely a *sign* of salvation but actually a way of *earning* salvation. Although the revised doctrine seemed to contradict the logic of predestination, it carried strong emotional appeal. The implication that salvation could be earned created a *need* to achieve, distinct from actual achievement (as appetite is distinct from eating). Protestantism didn't actually create the need for achievement, but it did provide strong moral reinforcement for it. Generally, in achievement-oriented societies, individuals with a strong need for achievement tend to be oriented toward economic success, and this course became markedly evident under Protestant capitalism.[249]

On the individual level, the ideological justification for economic success strongly reinforced behaviors leading to personal achievement. The moral attributes that accompanied profitable habits can be recognized as the virtues of rational asceticism: industry, sobriety, frugality, pragmatism, optimism, reliability, temperance, simplicity in living, continual striving, and deferred gratification.[250] Generally, an orientation toward achievement has been linked empirically to values in the Protestant ethic.

The antecedents of achievement motivation are evident in the childrearing methods of Protestants. Certain parenting practices produce a type of high-need achiever who then demonstrates a strong need to achieve success—as opposed to merely avoiding failure. This type emerges from a background that emphasizes the goals of competence and autonomy, along with parents who set high expectations for success. The high-need achiever requires and tends to seek out evaluation in social situations. As opportunities present themselves to gain information from evaluations, the achiever becomes competitive as a function of the comparison process. Where a dearth of opportunities exist for high-need achievers to prove their competence, they experience feelings of uneasiness and then seek out new and appropriate experiences in which comparisons can be made. Young people who are high-need achievers require opportunities for positive reinforcement of appropriate behaviors if they are to persist.[251]

The need to achieve appeared particularly strong among the inhabitants of the developing nations in the post-Reformation West. These new nations offered an openness and flexibility that, when tied to the Protestant ethic, resulted in achievement-minded and economically oriented behaviors. It was in these open societies that individuals were most likely to be judged in terms of what they could do rather than who they were. Thus, the inclination to tie status to achievement has been characteristic of Americans. The factors that promoted the need for achievement were enhanced by the nation's class structure. The need proved strongest in the broad middle class where the realization of status through achievement was a viable goal. This need translated into planning for the future, a drive toward active accomplishments, and valuing practical results. Individual achievement occurred within a framework of group competition that created a distinct sense of responsibilities. The values and behaviors of the middle class facilitated the attainment of material success, which became the identifying mark of the American class structure.[252]

Weber recognized that societies were organized not merely in terms of social classes but also in terms of status groups. Status groups were differentiated from one another in terms of social honor or prestige—as well as on economic grounds. Status was recognized with an array of symbols: titles, degrees, insignia, medals, honorary decorations, and trophies.[253] One effect of status groups was to foster exclusivity and elitism (independent of class consciousness). That such elitism could be accommodated in a social democracy is a testament to the residual strength of social status as a symbol of election. Elements of social exclusiveness and separatism had been present in the early Protestant sects in America. Even at the outset, the voyage of the *Mayflower* to the New World was an act of Separatists. John Winthrop represented the views of most New Englanders when he stated, "In all times some must be rich, some poor; some high and eminent in power and dignity; others mean and in subjection."[254] Those who didn't accept the goal of high aspiration were assigned subordinate status.

The workings of an open, competitive market economy reinforced—and were reinforced by—this elitism by providing for a visible number of failures that allowed for comparison.[255] The elect weren't shy about placing labels on the society's failures. The nineteenth-century Congregational minister Henry Ward Beecher opined, "No man in this land suffers from poverty unless it be more than his fault—unless it be his *sin*."[256] Moreover, the prevailing belief was that the stigma of failure was somehow contagious, and that the lost souls should be segregated from the elect so that they didn't infect them. Thus, individuals who failed economically were expelled from the circle of the elect and denied social intercourse with the successful members of the community.[257]

Elitism and exclusivity were evident in Protestant religious institutions.

The Puritans were so strict in their admission of members to their churches that over half of the people in some parishes were excluded. They required a careful testing of all who desired entrance into the communion of saints. Qualification into the church depended upon perceptions of the individual's behavior. The gatekeepers monitored their members' standing in the eyes of the community prior to admitting them to religious ceremonies in order to preserve the purity of the congregation. The church fathers claimed the right to exclude even their kinfolk and neighbors in order to maintain a clear distinction between the godly and the sinful.[258]

These exclusive practices seemed to deny the evangelical function of the Protestant church. Critics asked how a church could be an instrument of conversion if it consisted only of those who had already been converted. The response was that the church wasn't there to convert souls but to serve those already converted. In this sense, Protestants formed not churches, but sects—as churches are institutions into which one is born, while sect membership implies an "earned certificate" of moral qualification.[259] As Weber noted, "Sects operated from a voluntaristic principle, but only the qualified could apply for admission."[260] Local churches tended to be discriminatory, the numbers of members restricted; hence, they tended to remain small.

Elitist practices carried over from religious institutions to secular ones. Various forms of boycotting prospective members were practiced by fraternal lodges, social clubs, and college Greek organizations as part of the status ritual. In the everyday world, the elitist valuation of status created a judgmental climate in which an exalted group of the elect would form and then relegate others to an inferior status. It seemed altogether natural and inevitable to Protestants that some had to be assigned inferior status. They believed that the good must be contrasted with the bad, and the borders of goodness were marked out exactly so that none "outside the borders were allowed to cross, for they had no business there."[261] In the late nineteenth century, the political philosophy of Social Darwinism served to reinforce status norms in America. The churches, the schools, the military, and the political order all practiced their own forms of exclusivity.

One of the key assumptions of the Protestant ethic was that achieved success was due neither to luck nor to the environment but to individual qualities. Thus, persons failing to achieve were charged with a character defect. In Santayana's *The Last Puritan*, the Catholic Mario was criticized by his Protestant peers for his character defects: "[While] at Harvard he hadn't done, in any way, what was expected of him. He hadn't distinguished himself in any sport; he hadn't been asked to join any well-known club."[262] Such examples of social failure performed a signal service to the successful members of a Protestant society. They removed the pangs of conscience associated with membership in elitist organizations. The elect harbored no sense of guilt about the unfortunate of the world whose lot might be attributed to idleness, failure of effort, or lack of diligence. In functionalist terms, people were classified in order to demarcate the symbolic boundaries between the society of insiders and the deviant outsiders.[263]

In summary, the emphasis upon achieved status in Protestant culture created a social climate characterized by achievement motivation and social activism and lubricated by elitism and exclusivity. The achievement of status was reinforced by religious doctrine and by the requisites of the free-market economy. Achievement became the primary way to acquire status in the community. Over time, achievement came to be interpreted more and more as economic success. Under Protestant capitalism, one achieved status by making money through constant effort applied in one's vocation. Thus, the need for achieved status strongly reinforced individualism and the work ethic.

V. Individualism

> ONE'S-SELF I sing, a simple separate person.
> –Walt Whitman

The modern concept of the individual took form in the aftermath of the Protestant Reformation. Prior to that time, personal identity was tied to membership in a segment of the established social order: one was a serf, a burgher, a cleric, a member of an artisans' guild. The medieval social structure had both theological and practical significance. As long as people followed the rules of conduct laid down for their class or order, they got along in the world and their salvation was assured. Protestantism didn't immediately alter this communal scheme. A notable corporate spirit was evident in early Protestant communities. John Calvin's Geneva imposed an authoritarian regimentation upon its citizens that has been characterized as "iron collectivism." But as post-Reformation culture evolved, the individualistic tendencies inherent in Protestantism gradually prevailed.[264]

Ultimately, Protestant society became not an aggregate of groups, as was medieval society, but of individuals. Daniel Bell commented on the dramatic social change that took place following the Protestant Reformation: "The fundamental assumption of modernity, the thread that has run through Western civilization since the sixteenth century, is that the social unit of society is not the group, the guild, the tribe, or the city, but the person. The Western ideal was the autonomous man who, in becoming self-determining, would achieve freedom."[265] The roots for this change could be found in religious doctrine. Both Luther and Calvin sought to extinguish the importance of social orders and the heavy hand of the institutional Church and its priests. They eliminated all intermediaries between God and humans, and in the process, they virtually invented the autonomous individual responsible for his or her own spiritual state. No Protestant sect was more individualistic than the Calvinists. The doctrine of predestination implied a highly personal experience with the deity. One's destiny hung on a private transaction between "Self and Maker."[266] As salvation became personalized, a strict sense of individual responsibility developed. The individual conscience became the source of judgment that scrutinized every act, and self-judgment could be as severe a master as any external judge.

Individualism reached its zenith among the English Calvinists. Just as the British Isles stood apart geographically from continental Europe, so did the Puritans pursue their own separate ideology by eschewing the communal elements of Protestantism that had survived on the continent. The Puritan exemplified moral self-sufficiency. It was a quality that nerved the individual will but undermined social solidarity. Quarrels and schisms proved common where the Puritans prevailed.[267]

Protestantism witnessed a continuing dialectic between the centripetal inertia of the social compact and the centrifugal force of individualism. The individualistic impulses of the Puritans were ameliorated by their persecution in England and by their common struggle for survival in the New England wilderness. Other forces worked to pull them together. For Puritans, the good life could be embraced only in the relations of two or more like-minded individuals. Within the community of the elect, members were so linked together as to have their spiritual fortunes in common. The Puritan enforced his personal creed upon his neighbors while being subjected to their constant scrutiny. Notwithstanding these communal forces, the Puritan remained a soldier whose battles were fought out within the self before they were waged in the community. The highly personal approach to righteous living constituted a sort of "moral autarchy." Individualism was to become a defining characteristic of mature

Puritanism.[268]

Individualism was built into the structure of churches and religious practice. Within its congregational configuration, the Puritan church was essentially a group of individuals searching separately for the godly way of life. The central role of the individual was apparent in the religious forms: confession, eulogy, and exhortation. The highly personalized conversion experience was represented as an annihilation of the self that preceded a rebirth of self. The chief concern for the Puritan was the welfare of his own soul. All discipline was ultimately self-discipline. Likewise, self-approval was conditional upon pursuit of personal goals. Over time, this individualized brand of religion would influence a wide range of Protestant denominations, from the mainstream Baptists and Methodists to the radical Society of Friends and the Unitarians. Methodism came to emphasize the "methodical" personal life at the expense of church tradition. While the Baptists were separating into dozens of sects based upon differing interpretations of scripture, autonomy for Unitarians meant that individuals held differing beliefs within the same congregation.[269]

Protestants derived not only their religion but the simple pleasures of life from successful self-projection. The secular focus of Protestantism bolstered the sense of individual autonomy, especially for the educated elite. As alluded to above, the Protestant lived more easily outside the Church. When elements of the worldly order came into conflict with religious values, these conflicts played out largely on the level of the individual. Secularization led to an increase in individual choice and individual self-expression.[270]

The emphasis upon self was expressed in the language. "Self" compounds were abundant in Protestant sermons and religious tracts: self-affection, self-confidence, self-control, self-discipline, self-sufficiency, self-trial, self-examination, and self-discipline, among others. Not only the language but the content of literature—both religious and secular—centered on the individual. The popular Bible stories for Protestants dramatized the trials of individuals—for instance, Job, Jonah, Samson, and Daniel in the lion's den. The archetypical success story in the secular literature chronicled the morally worthy individual's rising "from rags to riches" through personal effort. The Horatio Alger stories became America's archetypical narrative.[271]

Protestantism's redefinition of personal identity engendered dramatic psychological effects (both positive and negative) upon the individual. At its best, the emphasis on individualism brought about the development of an independent, self-sufficient personality. But as McNeill noted, such a highly personal view of salvation led to an unprecedented sense of inner loneliness.[272] The Protestant often felt naked in a reformed world, haunted by a sense of ambivalence and unfulfilled narcissism. Individuals were discouraged from associating too closely with others who were perceived as potentially dangerous to their salvation. Regardless of their outward conduct, one's neighbors were suspected of being "unsaved" and to be avoided when possible. In this climate, neighborly love often was reduced to little more than an attitude of service and sacrifice without any feelings of mutuality in relationships.[273]

In a more positive light, the tensions created by individualism motivated an active life. This activism was enhanced by the strong need for achievement and a healthy element of egoism. Achievement needs were fulfilled largely through vocation, and this goal provided Protestants with the incentive to shape the economic world. The expanding market economy that emerged in the nineteenth century "annihilated organic forms of existence and replaced them with atomistic ones."[274] Protestant capitalism brought about a setting of individual competition. Its tenets were routinely invoked as a means of allocating scarce rewards. The nexus of individualism, scarcity, and competition served to legitimate the reorganization of society under Protestant capitalism.[275]

This social restructuring was consistent with a Protestant tradition that held that prosperity and economic progress came through individual enterprise and individual initiative. The emerging class of entrepreneurs felt ethically authorized to act individually. The archetypical entrepreneur was a "loner" whose interpersonal relations remained contractual in nature.[276] Tawney noted that the Protestant businessman would ascribe his achievements to his own unaided efforts as if unconscious of the social order without whose continuous support and vigilant protection he would have been "as a lamb bleating in the desert."[277] Yet, the Protestant continued to interpret social well-being as a reward for the sum total of individual qualities and personal merits.

The Protestant capitalist couldn't become totally preoccupied with personal effort but was obliged to seek active involvement with others for the sake of doing business. Yet in doing so, the individual actor never sought the type of organic involvement that had characterized medieval trade guilds, for example. Economic and social life for Protestants continued to reflect laissez-faire individualism. Everyone was personally responsible for his own well-being. The individual might work for a company but his ultimate sense of loyalty was to himself, and he would promptly hire out to a competitor if the remuneration proved personally advantageous.

The free-market economy encouraged workers to compete as individuals for jobs, promotions, and better wages—all which translated into individual rewards. In the process, individualism defined not only economic life but social life. Social identity became less and less group bound. This brave new world placed its emphasis on individual initiative, individual choice, individual responsibility, individual achievement, and individual rights. The Protestant looked toward his neighbor only to compare accomplishments and material possessions that had become extensions of the self.

VI. The Work Ethic

> Now I wake me up to work. I pray the Lord I may not shirk. If I should die
> before the night I pray the Lord my work's all right. Amen.
> –Jack London

Imagine a society in which work becomes the fundamental goal in life, the activity through which individuals define themselves and give meaning to their existence. In this social climate, the absence of meaningful work would lead to an existential crisis. Eugene Zamiatin described such a society in his dystopic novel *We,* in which three citizens of the modern state were exempted for a whole month from any work:

> The unhappy three spent their whole time wandering around their usual place of work and gazing within with hungry eyes. They would...busy themselves for hours repeating the motions which they had been used to making during certain hours of the day.... They would saw and plane in the air; with unseen sledge hammers they would bang upon unseen stakes. Finally on the tenth day, they could bear it no longer, they took one another by the hand, entered the river and...waded deeper and deeper until the water ended their sufferings forever.[278]

Not everyone in the real world has shared this compulsion to work. Throughout much of history, work has been perceived as something to be endured at best, if not avoided altogether. The advantages of wealth or position included the opportunity to avoid physical work. Whenever possible, manual labor was delegated to servants, serfs, slaves, and criminals.

In order to appreciate the implications of the Protestant work ethic, it is helpful to review briefly the meanings and contexts of work in the pre-Reformation world. Preliterate societies made a distinction between profane work and sacred work. The latter related to communal obligations tied to myths and traditions. Without the rituals of sacred work, work would have lost all meaning. Profane work was purposeful work, but traditional societies didn't separate it sharply from nonwork in terms of time, effort, or attitude. Purposeful work, like sacred work, was carried out within an interpersonal texture and filled with customs, rites, and religious observances. These cultural elements provided relief from the strain of purpose and efficiency. Moreover, traditional work like farming and artisanship included a great deal of variety and creativeness that alleviated the boredom of routine. Since most traditional work was tied to the land, it was difficult to compartmentalize it. Generally, such work wasn't time intensive, and it held less import in the public mind than it does in contemporary industrial societies. Indeed, it is fair to say that much of traditional labor didn't represent work in the modern sense.[279]

The pace of work is influenced significantly by culture and environment. Anthropologists have a fairly accurate picture of the work rhythms of ancient hunter-gatherer societies. Typically, one or two days of hunting—each lasting about six to eight hours—was followed by a day or two of rest. Women usually did the gathering about every two or three days. Thus, the general pattern was to alternate days of work with days of rest. Contemporary tribal hunters average about twenty hours a week in their major occupation of hunting for food. The traditional pace of work varies with the grazing patterns of wild animals and the seasonal ripening of various roots and berries. Historically, seasonal patterns of work persisted following the agricultural revolution with the cycles of planting and harvesting.[280]

The advances of civilization brought significant changes in attitudes toward work, both positive and negative. To the ancient Greeks, work signified the revenge of the gods; their word for "work" (ponos) had the same root as the Latin word for "sorrow." The Greeks viewed manual labor as having few redeeming qualities and held that it had a brutalizing effect on the mind. The happy citizen was the one who could avoid labor, and whenever possible, the Greeks delegated most manual labor to slaves and foreigners. Menial tasks were despised, and even free artisans and craftsmen were looked down upon. The only physical work that was grudgingly accepted as worthy of a Greek citizen was agriculture, because it provided an independent livelihood. In contrast, the ancient Hebrews viewed work as a form of expiation through which humans atoned for the sins of their ancestors (see the biblical book of Genesis). Early Christianity seemed to recommend work not because it had any intrinsic value but because it was uncomfortable and humiliating—an appropriate scourge for pride of the flesh.[281]

In the Middle Ages, the monasteries imposed physical labor as a form of religious discipline, but the idea enjoyed little popularity outside this setting. The tempo of life in medieval Europe was leisurely, the pace of secular labor relaxed. Labor may have extended from dawn to dusk, but was intermittent. Work was halted for breakfast, lunch, and dinner, as well as the customary afternoon nap. Labor tied to the land was moderated by seasonal variations, reaching its peak at harvest time. It is estimated that peasant families put in about 150 days a year on their land. Such labor was free of haste and exactitude and characterized by lack of concern for productivity. The pace and intensity of urban labor was not much different. Steady employment is a modern invention. The medieval trade guilds were exceptional in instilling pride in craftsmanship, and this ethic led to more positive connotations of work.[282]

Following the Protestant Reformation, the significance and context of work changed dramatically. Meaningful work now was to be carried out not in the cloisters but in the counting houses. As the locus of work shifted to the secular world, work became a virtual sacrament. Martin Luther's idea of a personal calling signified serving God in one's vocation. The Calvinists amplified the principle of a calling, defining work as a moral duty for everyone.[283] The Puritan minister Samuel Hieron branded work the "testimony of one's religion."[284] Work for Protestants became a self-affirming activity. This mindset is captured in lines from a poem by Rudyard Kipling: "And no one shall work for money, And no one shall work for fame; But each for the joy of working."[285] Work, in and of itself, took on values of dignity and worth. The type of work made little difference, as a spiritual equality existed among callings. The godly individual got up early in the morning and dutifully took care of necessary business, whatever it might be.

The Protestant work ethic was less a single conviction than an evolving complex of ideas and attitudes about work. Three of the most salient state that: (1) one should work in a gainful occupation for personal satisfaction and as a sign of virtue, (2) work in one's calling carries its own intrinsic reward, and (3) work is a form of ascetic discipline.[286] Indeed, work for Protestants was infused with a strong dose of moral asceticism. It was touted as the very foundation of morality, providing a prophylactic against the dual sins of sloth and sensuality. Called by God to "labor in the vineyard," the individual had within the self a principle of order. Diligent work kept the tradesman from frequenting taverns by pinning him to the shop. Those reprobates who wouldn't work were dealt with harshly. In 1649 the English Parliament passed an act that established the power to apprehend vagrants and, when caught, offered them a choice between work and whipping. English law set to compulsory labor all poor persons, including children. Various schemes for workhouses were advanced. Captain John Smith stated the rule of the Jamestown Colony quite succinctly: "He that will not work, shall not eat."[287]

Work as a calling implied a form of labor more regular and assiduous than the world had every seen, short of servitude. The Protestant conception of work stood in stark contrast to the Catholic concept of "good works" as compensation for particular sins. Protestant doctrine demanded not "works" but work, not a few meritorious acts but a lifetime of unceasing labor in the service of God.[288] Protestants set out to save the world by building a utopia through assiduous labor. The fate of one's soul and the fate of society were inextricably tied to the efforts put into one's vocation. God rewarded hard work.

The work ethic had to adjust to a series of cultural and economic developments. In England, a steadily rising interest in the scientific management and rational organization of work took hold in the second half of the seventeenth century. At the same time, the emphasis on an active work life created a climate conducive to industrial labor under capitalism.[289] However, the actual nature of industrial labor stifled much of the personal satisfaction one was supposed to experience from work. Industrialism changed the fundamental nature of work. In the relentless quest for efficiency and productivity, work was shorn of ritual, customs, and traditions. Moreover, the pace and intensity of industrial labor contrasted sharply with traditional forms of work. Artisanship and handicraft were replaced by repetitive movements of machine work isolated from social interaction, as the worker was increasingly bound to the machine. No longer were there alternating patterns of work and leisure; work now filled the hours of the day and the days of the week. Furthermore, industrial labor was not seasonal; it lasted the entire year.

Nevertheless, the work ethic endured amidst the changing climate of industrialization, rationalization, and secularization. The ethic governed the Victorian Era. One of the Era's early prophets was the Scottish Calvinist Thomas Carlyle, labeled the "conscience of the nineteenth century." His popular writings were a testament to the sustaining influence of religious beliefs in the industrial era. Carlyle envisioned a utopia of work. His *Past and Present* (1843) offered an unrestrained paean to work: "Work is a blessing." "All work is noble and sacred; work *alone* is noble." "The only human unhappiness is not being able to work." "Work provides well-being." "Work gives hope, a life-purpose." "Work is life." "From the heart of the worker rises a 'God-given Force,' the sacred celestial Life-essence." "All true Work is Religion." The encomiums poured from his pen. For Carlyle, even the meanest sorts of labor brought harmony to one's soul. He waxed on about happy laborers energetically heaving and struggling with shoulders at the wheel, their hearts pulsing, every muscle swelling.[290]

Carlyle's writings had a broad influence in the United States. The American industrialist Frederick Taylor echoed these sentiments regarding work: "I look upon it as the greatest blessing we have."[291] Equal enthusiasm poured forth from America's clergy, politicians, and writers. The gospel of work spewed from church pulpits while children's storybooks, editorial pages of newspapers, and the stump rhetoric of office seekers praised work in all its forms. The ethic survived the marginalizing of organized religion and the hedonism of the profligate 1920s. It persisted in spite of widespread unemployment during the global breakdown of the world economy in the 1930s.[292] In the midst of the Great Depression, the British clergyman Frederick Spurr wrote: "The coronation of all life is achieved through work...it is a boon be-stowed upon our humanity. It is a blessing for the *Individual*. It is good for his *body*...Good for his *mind*...Good for his *heart*. We should therefore find in it a real joy and pride. Work is a blessing for Society."[293] For Carlyle and Spurr—as for the citizens of Zamiatin's fictional modern state—work provided the central purpose and meaning of life. Work remained a duty for Protestants even when it had ceased to be a material responsibility or necessity. Max Weber's biographer Reinhard

Bendix commented that "duty in one's calling still prowls about in our lives like the ghost of dead religious beliefs."[294]

The work ethic was as evident in the literature of Protestant culture as in its religious tracts. In his novel *The Magic Mountain*, set in post-World War I Germany, the author Thomas Mann, a native of Lutheran Lübeck, describes the novel's protagonist Hans Castorp, the scion of a long line of Reformed Protestants: "Work was for him...the most estimable attribute of life; when you came down to it, there was nothing else that was estimable. It was the principle by which one stood or fell, the Absolute of the time; it was, so to speak, its own justification. His regard for it was thus religious in its character, and so far as he knew, unquestioning."[295]

This ingenuous faith in work was to be sorely tested by the consumer culture that emerged following World War II, in America and then in Europe, but the work ethic survived in a form. Amidst the artifacts of a materialist society, among the ranks of dispirited factory and office workers, the ethic would retain its traditional meanings within the professions while it was finding new meaning in the institutions of organized sport and physical recreation. The descendants of Lutherans and Calvinists would regain the sense of a calling and rediscover the atavistic rituals of homo faber—if not in corporate "games," then in the serious games that were pursued in the athletic arena.

VII. The Time Ethic

> "Oh dear! Oh dear! I shall be too late," [exclaimed] the Rabbit [who]
> actually took a watch out of its waistcoat-pocket, and looked at it,
> and then hurried on.
> —Lewis Carroll, *Alice's Adventures in Wonderland*

Time, like work, has taken on radically different meanings across cultures. The Native American Hopi reputedly had no word for time. In contrast, the concept of time was pivotal to the ancient Hebrews' view of reality.[296] Time continued to hold a central position in Judeo-Christian theology. Significantly, the central message in the New Testament was presented in the context of the impending end of time. Life on earth was to the Christian a journey in time prefatory to the second coming. Paul admonished in Ephesians 5:15–16, "See then that ye walke circumspectly, not as fools, but as [the] wise...redeeming the time."

Protestantism has been an eminently time-conscious religion. In

Protestant theology, time was instilled with the qualities of a moral force that governed how individuals should relate to the secular world. In an effort to control use of time, Protestant culture multiplied its nuances. By the Industrial era, the Western world had been divided into time zones and the days into hours, minutes, and seconds. The sundial and church bells were supplanted by clocks and watches. Ultimately, scientists would measure the dimensions of time from the infinitesimal nanosecond to the incomprehensible light year. However, time in Protestant culture isn't simply a function of the speed of electric circuits or of planetary motion. Time also has psychological and religious implications. Following the Reformation, a Protestant time ethic emerged that included three moral imperatives: (1) time is dear, (2) time must be filled with productive activity, and (3) orientation should be to the future.

As to the first imperative, it is pertinent to note that there are cultures with time surplus and cultures with time famine. Protestant culture suffers from time famine for reasons that relate directly to Lutheran and Calvinist doctrines. Time is dear; stretched between the moment of one's appearance on earth to one's death was the finite opportunity to improve oneself. Thus, Protestants experienced time as an arena in which individuals worked out their personal salvation. Everything done *in* time and *with* time came under God's scrutiny.[297] This outlook leads to the second moral imperative regarding use of time.

The Protestant was compelled to use time to advantage. One's calling was carried out within a definite time frame; every hour and minute had to be accounted for and not wasted. Time had to be used carefully, prudently, profitably, and devoutly. The righteous individual was methodical and time-conscious, passing not a minute in unprofitable activities. Every moment spent in idleness, leisure, excessive sleep, or the enjoyment of luxury was a waste of time.[298] Time was infinitely valuable; every hour lost detracted from the glory of God. Calvin possessed an absolute horror of wasting time; it was an attitude that infiltrated other Protestant sects. The Methodist minister John Wesley advised his followers to "sav[e] all the time you can for the best purposes, buying every fleeting moment out of sin and Satan, out of the hand of sloth."[299] Sloth ranked high among the Seven Deadly Sins for Protestants. Sermons abounded with references to the despicable examples set by reprobates who had testified to their damnation caused by losing time in wasteful pursuits.[300]

Time-consciousness carried into the modern era where it continued to pervade Protestant culture. One of the characters in *The Magic Mountain* offers the following lecture:

We Europeans, we cannot [wait]. We have as little time as our great and finely articulated continent has space, we must be as economical of the one as of the other.... Just as...space becomes[s] more and more precious so, in the same measure, does time. *Carpe diem*! That was the song of a dweller in a great city. Time is a gift of God, given to man that he might use it...to serve the advancement of humanity.[301]

The lecturer's linking of the dearness of time to limited space was belied by the experiences of the frontier nations. It isn't cramped continents that account for the feeling of time scarcity. *"Carpe diem"* also was writer Walt Whitman's cry to the settlers of the vast North American continent. The feeling that time is dear has more to do with the shared Protestant heritage of Germans and Americans than with geography.

The moral imperative to fill time productively held sway in secular Protestant culture. Benjamin Franklin advised his neighbors, "Employ thy Time well...and since thou art not sure of a Minute, throw not away an Hour."[302] Franklin's contemporaries appeared quite consumed with the obligation to use time productively and to monitor and record their uses of time. This singular focus on time "well used" heightened time-consciousness. To paraphrase a biblical admonition, "Whatever the right hand finds to do, the left hand records with a timepiece." Like Lewis Carroll's white rabbit, Protestants hustled through life with one eye on the clock.

The moral imperative to fill time productively is inherently connected to the work ethic (as alluded to above). Time-consciousness and time application were influenced by the changing nature of work. An English tradition has it that the medieval King Alfred established the three-eighths division of the day into work, rest, and leisure. The division of the year into model work weeks and standard workdays also appeared early on in the English-speaking Protestant nations. The five-day work week was one in which Monday through Friday were characterized by work, meals, and sleep—with meals and sleep also framed as duties. Friday evening and Saturday were appropriate for recreation as permitted within religious and social constraints. Sunday wasn't only a day of worship but a day of rest to make up for the fatigue of the previous week's work and to get ready for work during the week ahead. In most of these instances, time was defined in its relation to work.[303]

The relationship between time and work is apparent in Linder's model of how time is utilized within modern society. Linder lists five categories of time use: (1) working time in specialized production, (2) time for personal maintenance (sleep, hygiene, etc.), (3) consumption time, (4) cultural time (devoted to mind and spirit), and (5) free time (idleness).[304] The further down Linder's list one finds each use of time, the more divorced it is from work and the more problematic it becomes for Protestants.

A characteristic problem with use of time occurs during holidays. Protestant holidays have been influenced both by the work ethic and the time ethic. It is not surprising that the number of holidays from work has been greater in non-Protestant culture. Protestants have placed themselves on a tight schedule to prosperity by way of their labor and have gradually eliminated numerous medieval holidays from the annual calendar. By the nineteenth century, British and American agricultural laborers were working six-day weeks with only Good Friday and Christmas as time off.[305] Where holidays have remained, these "off-days" changed in meaning and practices. The leisurely *holy* days of Catholic culture were replaced by activity-filled *holidays* for Protestants. The American holiday provides the classic instance of the nonleisurely day off. For the Americans, time must be used productively whether at work or at leisure. Leisure time, just like work time, is subject to scheduling and other rational manipulation.[306]

The Protestant time ethic has impinged most heavily on the middle and upper-middle classes. Generally, the better educated people are, the more they feel a shortage of time. Only the lowest social classes have been able to resist the compulsive time-consciousness that has impinged upon Protestant culture. It has been asserted that the poor accepted a life of poverty in part because it provided them with a certain freedom. In effect, they rejected the ethic of the working class that would rob them of time. The working class, in contrast, felt compelled to march to the cadence of the clock's pendulum.[307]

To the extent that the Protestant ethic encouraged industrial capitalism, time-consciousness was solidified. Capitalist labor lacked traditional labor's resistance to the clock. (It is easy to forget that people living in the past didn't divide up time in such a way as to know the exact hour and minute of the day.) The primary way of regarding time in industrial culture was in terms of clock time. "Clock consciousness" impelled the industrial worker to get up, work, eat, sleep, and even recreate by the clock.[308] Historians believe that the first public clocks (bells, initially) appeared in the textile centers of Europe to signal workers when to arrive, when to take meal breaks, and when to close out the workday. In effect, the employers owned a worker's time for part of the day. The day itself was increasingly split into kinds of time—a time to work and personal time, which in theory could be used for leisure. Workers no longer experienced time as a milieu in which they lived, but as an objective force in which they were confined.[309]

Mindfulness of clock time was facilitated by advancement of technology. The large-scale production of brass clocks, beginning about the 1830s, was succeeded by common employment of pocket watches a generation later. Exact time was available within the moment needed to pull a chain from a watch pocket and open the case. This progression was followed by sweep-hand wrist watches that gave accurate time at a glance, and then digital watches with the month, day, hour, minute, and second displayed on the face. All this refinement of time measurement increased the habit of being "on time." Humans fell increasingly under a constant (if unconscious) strain to get somewhere or do something at some definite point in the near future.[310]

Time-consciousness was intensified by the faster pace of life. In the modern world, time became a scarcer commodity as increasing claims were made upon it. Work time was filled with pressures to increase productivity and make money; consumption time was influenced by the availability and requirements of more consumer goods. Consumption actually decreased free time due to the shopping, servicing, and maintenance dictated by consumer goods. The trade-off was accepted: preoccupation with making money and the things it could buy in exchange for the loss of free time. Substituting money for time meant those with the highest incomes often had the least time to enjoy their material possessions. This exchange was indicative of a people more comfortable with money and material possessions than with unfilled time. In many ways time itself had become a form of currency—something to spend rather than to pass.[311]

The use of "free" time has remained problematic. Those who feel impelled by the Protestant time ethic ultimately reach the point where no time is free of normative constraints. What passes for free time actually suffers most from constraints, because the commitments during free time are voluntary and thus carry an increased burden of individual responsibility.[312]

Time-conscious individuals have little trouble deciding how to use their daytime Monday through Friday, but how to occupy themselves on Sunday afternoons can present a real dilemma. Free-time avoidance is a commonly felt impulse in the context of a strong work ethic and time ethic.

For many individuals, the job and its attendant responsibilities impinge upon free time. Health professionals remain on call; business managers have to check in with the office by phone during evenings and weekends; salespeople go on holiday accompanied by their pagers. Ken Dryden, who played professional hockey for several years, expresses a sense of time constraint that must be shared by many athletes and performers. He describes the degree to which his private life is framed by his occupation. On "practice days," he notes, it is "before practice," "practice," or "after practice," and on "game days," "before the team meal," or "after the meal." Today is a "practice day," as yesterday was; tomorrow and the next day are "game days." Today, we are "at home," tomorrow we'll be "on the road."[313] He elaborates:

> [O]ur time is fragmented and turned upside-down. Awake half the night, asleep half the morning, with three hours until practice, then three hours until dinner, nighttime no different from daytime, weekends from week days. At home, in the rhythm of the road, on the road, needing to go home. Then home again, and wives, children, friends, lawyers, agents, eating, drinking sleeping…and we're on the road again.[314]

The third element in the Protestant time ethic governs orientation to time. As an illustration, consider that there are three ways to consciously walk across an area: one can walk across and think about where one has come from and what was left behind; one can walk focused on the present, on the immediate experience of putting one foot in front of the other; or one can walk toward a destination, thinking about what is to be expected upon arrival. The Protestant journeys through physical areas, and through life, pre-eminently in the latter frame of mind.

Calvin, in his *Institutes*, admonished his followers "to habituate ourselves to a contempt for the present life."[315] He was implying that the focus must be on the future. Orientation to the future is exemplified in John Bunyan's *Pilgrim's Progress* (the book most likely to be on the shelf next to the King James Bible in nineteenth-century America). The pilgrim metaphor implies being "on the road" to somewhere or something important. This mindset is reinforced by other values in Protestant culture. McClelland noted that individuals with a high need for achievement characteristically are oriented to the future.[316] Likewise, goal-directed behavior has led to deferred gratification. Work provides activity to mindlessly fill the present, while as Novak observed, worry about the future constitutes an additional form of "work" for Protestants.[317]

Individuals influenced by the Protestant ethic are future oriented to a degree quite incomprehensible to a Catholic or Buddhist. George Beard relates the story of a late nineteenth-century American tourist who, upon going to an Italian boot maker to have some slight repair performed, was met with the craftsman's refusal to do the work. On being asked why he wouldn't make the repair, the boot maker replied that he had enough money to last him the day and didn't care to work any more. The American inquired, "But what about tomorrow?" "Who ever saw tomorrow?" was the Italian's response.[318] The answer, of course, is that the American Protestant—instilled with the time ethic—saw tomorrow with a clarity that was unfathomable to the continental Catholic.

Lord Keynes wrote of the "purposive man" who is always trying to secure immortality for his acts by pushing his interest in them forward into time. Future orientation intermeshes with rational asceticism so that preoccupation with long-range goals effectively blocks out any pleasures of the moment.[319] In pursuing an active mastery over the world, the Protestant has been impelled to work in service of remote ends. This imperative blocks not only pleasure but immediate interests as well. Human activity, unsatisfying in the present, can serve only as a means to some source of future satisfaction.

The Protestant is engaged in a lifelong struggle with the moral constraints of the time ethic. This struggle has been evident from the Reformation through much of the twentieth century. George Goodwin, in his early seventeenth-century poem *Auto-Machia*, wrote, "The *Victories* I howrely lose and win; The *dayly Duel*, the continual Strife, The *Warr* that ends not, till I end my life." Americans continue to struggle with the constraints of time.[320] In the early 1990s an athletic shoe company advertised its product in the television market with the terse slogan: "Life's short. Play hard." The message succinctly states the liturgy of time-conscious Protestants. With their gaze focused firmly on the future, those who live by the time ethic seem unmoved by the implication of Keynes's famous retort to the long-term investor: "In the *long term*, sir, we all are dead!" As Goodwin reminds us, only in death does the Protestant gain release from the tyranny of time.

5

Protestantism and the American Ethos

The Protestant Establishment

> It seems to me that I can see the entire destiny of America
> contained in the first Puritan who came ashore.
> —Alexis de Tocqueville

In an important sense, the Protestant Reformation established the preconditions of British Colonial America. The values carried to the nation's shores by early immigrants were essentially Calvinist and set the tone for the nation's early intellectual and cultural history. Most New England settlements were distinctly Puritan, while the Southern colonies were populated by Anglicans at a time when their theology was noticeably Calvinist.[321] This religious milieu shaped the politics and social mores of the developing nation as it spread westward beyond the Rocky Mountains and south to the Gulf shore and Rio Grande. Pulitzer Prize-winning poet Phyllis McGinley would refer to this legacy as the "Calvinistic and Puritan traditions of which we are all spiritual heirs."[322]

The Calvinist foundation germinated a set of values and ideas that coalesced in the Protestant ethic. This ethic would govern the nation's mindset and shape the American dream. Weber saw Benjamin Franklin as a paragon of this ethic. Franklin's brand of secular Protestantism encompassed a cluster of concepts that would make America prosperous: thrift, utility, inventiveness, the profit motive, and the accumulation of wealth. The historical Franklin is framed as a paragon of virtues, somewhat larger than life. (In truth, he didn't always live by his own maxims dispensed in *Poor Richard's Almanac*.) Franklin symbolizes the American myth that champions both spiritual and material freedom and promotes self-assertion—even while confusing it with social assertion. In this sense, the American ethos accomplished the primary function of all national myths: to reconcile antithetical ideas and cultural contradictions.[323]

Calvinist ideology influenced not only personal behavior but political institutions and their relationship with religious life. This religious ethic, in tandem with Enlightenment principles, exerted a seminal influence upon the founders as they constructed their unique version of a free society. The founding documents of the United States were written largely by people from Protestant backgrounds who had escaped from European state-imposed religion. Their experience with European monarchs coupled with a Calvinist distrust of human nature prompted them to institutionalize the system of checks and balances within the federal government. The framers constructed a federal constitution that provided for the strict separation of church and state, while supporting religious tolerance. No religious establishment by law would be allowed to exist, and individual conscience was free from restraint. Offices of government were open to all, regardless of religion, and no tithes were levied to support a church.[324]

Despite constitutional safeguards separating church and state, the Puritan social agenda generated close ties between religion and society. The development of public education and the nature of political parties reflected the nation's religious roots. In the private sector, sectarian (mostly Protestant) colleges sprang up like dandelions in towns and villages across the continent. Through the end of the eighteenth century, more college graduates went into the ministry than any other profession. An early survey of the clergy found 247 Presbyterian and Reformed ministers in the colonies in 1776. Reformed Protestant denominations essentially controlled institutional religion in the new nation. Other religions would make their presence felt, but Protestants, especially the Calvinist sects, would dominate American social, religious, and political life.[325]

As with the leaders of government and religion, Protestants prevailed among the common people. During George Washington's first term of office, Protestants constituted nearly four-fifths of the American population. Protestantism remained a cultural force despite the influx of hundreds of thousands of Catholic immigrants—many of whom would assimilate mainstream Protestant values. De Tocqueville commented on the similarities between American Catholics and Protestants.[326] Catholics were but one of many religious groups to move into the mainstream. Reform Judaism, as it developed in the late nineteenth century, also took on much of the character of upper-middle-class Protestantism.[327] The assimilation of Catholics and Jews into American institutions was most evident by the onset of the Industrial Age. Members of these two minority religions attained prominence in business and the professions.

The blossoming institution of organized sport reflected religious and ethnic assimilation. Oscar Bielaski (1847–1911), a Polish Catholic, became one of the first professional baseball players at a time when the teams were overwhelmingly Protestant in makeup. The New York Celtics, the professional barnstorming basketball team of the 1920s, evolved from an Irish settlement house team. Jewish boxers like featherweight champ Abe Attell were common by the turn of the twentieth century. America was unique in the way that religious affiliation became less significant than a general acceptance of Protestant values. Assimilation was just as evident in popular culture as in the nation's political institutions, if not more so.[328]

While Protestant culture often acted as an assimilative force across religions, it harbored contentious social forces within itself and experienced repeated doctrinal schisms. Early on, an Armenian component pitted its more egalitarian view of "election" against the strict Calvinist interpretation. This schism reflected the uneasy tension between elitism and egalitarianism that would always be present in American religion and politics. In accord with prevailing democratic principles, the more egalitarian churches embraced the hope of extending religious conversion to all. The campaign to convert led to a rash of religious revivals that flourished during the first two-thirds of the nineteenth century. The enthusiasm for revivals waned as Protestant sects shifted their strategy to that of forming churches and federating members. As the efforts to extend grace became institutionalized, diverse organizations emerged as extensions of the proselytizing churches. Americans felt an irresistible impulse to extend salvation through organized activities.[329]

This spirit fueled a steady stream of social movements: the Great Awakening, the Temperance Movement, the Social Gospel, and other campaigns carrying well into the twentieth century. The above-mentioned efforts reflected the growing interest of churches in social and moral reform. The more progressive Protestant churches founded agencies to care for the poor and to educate the ignorant. Most of the activities within the reform movement were Protestant-sponsored and unabashedly promoted the "Protestant way of life." Reformers directed their efforts particularly at Irish-Catholic immigrants, revealing elements of nativism and anti-Catholicism. Moralists reacted to the perception of urban corruption and vice that was going on around them and sought to restore order in a fragmented and uncertain world in which Protestant values seemed to be eroding.[330]

The Age of Reform persevered from the 1890s through the 1920s. In this era, Progressivism made its mark on American politics. The Progressives had inherited the moral traditions of the rural evangelists but recruited many liberal clergymen who bolstered the prestige of the movement. The Progressive mind was preeminently a Protestant mind, as reflected in its rhetoric. The key terms in the Progressives' vocabulary were "character, conscience, soul, morals, service, duty," and their counterparts, "shame, disgrace, sin and selfishness." This spirit of reform would remain a strong influence in the nation's politics into the modern era.[331]

The Protestant establishment represented America's power brokers. By the Industrial Age, positions in business, government, and education were held in disproportion by Protestants. Politicians elected to all levels of government were overwhelmingly Protestants (allowing for exceptions like the Irish wards in New York City). Every president and vice president of the United States through the mid-twentieth century belonged to one of the Protestant sects. Most of the early innovators in American industry were Protestant reformers. Frederick Taylor was typical in his campaign to rationalize labor when the work force increasingly was drawn from non-Protestant immigrants. And what was generally true in business and politics was true for the sports establishment. During the early decades of organized sport, Protestant patricians held the vast majority of positions of power and influence on teams and in league offices and continued to do so for decades—despite the presence of Catholics and Jews among the ranks of athletes.[332]

By the post-World War I era, traditional small-town Protestantism no longer dominated cultural symbols, even as outward respect for religion remained strong among the American people. By the 1920s, social convention had replaced religious commitment to a large extent. Membership in churches was as much a status symbol and social ritual as a religious practice. However, the core values of Protestantism continued to thrive beyond the walls of the churches.[333] The American journalist H. L. Mencken observed on the threshold of the roaring twenties that Calvinism was dying a much harder death than expected, that in many respects America was still a "nation of Puritans."[334] Throughout the remainder of the century, this culturally diverse nation showed itself to be distinctly Calvinist in its values, attitudes, and institutions—from the family to the workplace to the country club. As Morone remarks in his history of American moralism, "The Puritan trope lives on."[335]

Protestantism took on varying forms at different times and in different places throughout history, but nowhere did it exert a stronger influence than on the North American continent. The United States became the quintessential Protestant nation. Americans fully embraced the values of inner-worldly asceticism, activism, anti-ritualism, and rationalism. As a people, they were distinguished by their focus on the community, on leadership, and especially on individual salvation. The forms of American Protestantism were as unique as its substance. A pattern of organized religion emerged that differed from both the medieval and Reformation religions of Europe. Where no established state religion reigned, the American laissez-faire approach allowed for change and diversity as the nation's people became increasingly diverse. Though each religious denomination was distinct, a common set of secular Protestant values endured within the broad culture.[336]

The Secularization of Protestant Values

> If we are to find Grace it is to be found in the world and not overhead.
> —Amos Niven Wilder

America's Puritan colonies may have been theocracies in a technical sense, but New Englanders actually were rather stingy in extending authority to the clergy. Historians point out that Puritans referred to their places of worship not as churches but as meeting houses. Indeed, New England Puritanism was less of a creed than a way of life. What held Puritans together was their common approach to living in the world. The Puritan experience led to a set of secularized values and ideals that were reaffirmed in a wide range of social institutions. America's social agencies, clubs, and civic organizations have been, to a large extent, secularized imitations of the prototype Puritan sect. Benjamin Franklin's utilitarian brand of religion would prove more palatable to the common people than Jonathan Edwards's intellectualized Protestantism, with which Americans flirted briefly during the Great Awakening. Over time, American religion shed its contemplative and esoteric character to become worldly, pragmatic, and anti-intellectual.[337]

The challenge for American religion wasn't merely to adjust to the changing context but to manipulate it. Religion could remain a cultural force only by redefining its role in society. During the last three decades of the nineteenth century, the role of the clergy as moral and intellectual leaders diminished as the churches lost control over the working classes. But as

American religion ceded its traditional functions, it retained its core functions of regulating the commitment of individuals to a common ethic. Generally, people didn't separate their religious beliefs from their secular world views. In their daily lives they employed religion to rationalize their behaviors. One still hears Americans say things like, "That's the way we've always done things," or "It's the Christian thing to do."[338]

This process of constantly redefining doctrine and adjusting practices reveals an American paradox. Religion endured despite America's becoming a progressively secularized society. Indeed, Americans have always prided themselves on their religiosity. Comparative studies across nations have shown that a relatively high percentage of Americans attend religious services. Where no official state religion existed, the intense religious feeling of the people endured. This sentiment has been manifest at a variety of public functions that include quasi-religious ceremonies revealing the legacy of secular Protestantism. At the same time, many of the functions fulfilled by American churches have been secular rather than religious in the traditional sense.[339]

As secular Protestant values became institutionalized, they formed the focus of what Talcott Parsons referred to as the "definition of the situation" for the conduct of individuals in their secular roles in society.[340] America was to become not a Calvinist theocracy but a secularized Protestant society with a broadly accepted religious ethic. The American sociologist Will Herberg noted that what has been labeled the American way of life "is, at bottom, a spiritual structure, a structure of ideas and ideals, of aspiration and values, of beliefs and standards." This "way of life" points Americans to the right, the good, and the true.[341]

The Protestant Middle Class

> There can be no doubt that the middle rank...is the chief source of all that
> has exalted and refined human nature.
> —James Mill

The United States developed into the major middle-class civilization of modern times. An inclusive middle class incorporated much of the working classes, farmers, small-town merchants, and artisans, and expanded to encompass white-collar workers including technicians, engineers, production managers, and other professionals. In America, the terms "Protestant" and "middle class" would become inextricably joined (while the nation's religious minorities readily assimilated middle-class values). The middle class fully embraced the Protestant ethic and exemplified the spirit of capitalism. The bourgeois virtues of industry, sobriety, frugality, reliability, temperance, and simplicity of living ensured the nation's success. The entrepreneurs of this class were the catalysts for the burgeoning market economy that arose in the nineteenth century.[342]

Middle-class attitudes and behavior carried beyond the economic sector to encompass the nation's social and cultural institutions, not the least of which was the American family. Middle-class values influenced the fundamental nature of parents' relationships with their children. This class redefined the concept of youth as a time for preparation. Middle-class parents were willing to sacrifice the labor of their children in favor of prolonging their education. To a large extent, American schools reproduced the middle-class ideology. Their curricula emphasized career-oriented values such as individual achievement, rational calculation, forward planning, and deferment of immediate gratification for attaining long-term goals. Even the free time of middle-class children has been devoted to activities that would prepare them for successful social adjustment: structured lessons in music, dance, or participation in organized youth sports. Thus, a distinct conception of desirable behavior was imposed upon middle-class youth. Their parents gave high priority to values that reflected the internal dynamics of the personality. Young people were judged on a stage largely dominated by middle-class adults employing middle-class standards consistent with the Protestant ethic. Parents of this class were far more controlling and effective in training their children for success than were the lower classes.[343]

Lower-class values appeared antithetical to the Protestant ethic. They deprecated ambition, and encouraged immediate gratification, collective rather than individual enterprise, and communal rather than private property. Working-class parents had lower aspirations for their children and preferred conformity over achievement. Despite these distinctions, children of the America's lower classes have demonstrated a relatively high need for achievement. The laboring classes were encouraged to work hard by the promise of upward mobility. For immigrants coming to America, social mobility seemed to be a natural extension of their physical mobility, and this belief was passed on to their children. Upward mobility was especially characteristic of "third-generation" Americans who seemed always to be moving on and moving up. In times of economic growth and change that have characterized most of American history, disadvantaged minorities moved into positions of leadership in business and the professions like teaching that were open to upwardly mobile religious and ethnic minorities.[344]

Although the nation contained distinct social classes, the fluidity of movement between them created the perception of classlessness. America's social fences have had to be repaired constantly. Moreover, there has been little class conflict. As long as the distinction between social classes remained transient, the members of each stratum accepted as their ideal the lifestyle of the next higher group.[345] Veblen may have exaggerated the extent to which the wealthy leisure classes set the standards for emulation and underestimated the influence of the middle class, but he understood well the idea that class emulation had replaced class conflict in America. The dynamics of a free-market economy extended to the working classes who imitated the upper-middle class.[346]

The nation's upper class diverged from the archetypical leisure class. Abstention from labor had been the conventional evidence of high social standing in Europe, but the American upper class was little influenced by European models of gentility. Outside of the South, the country revealed scant evidence of a hereditary, propertied class. Members of the New England upper class were wont to admonish the plantation aristocracy of Old Virginia for their idleness and decadent recreations. Unlike their Southern neighbors, the Yankee aristocracy was typically nouveau riche, and having recently ascended from the middle class, they found it natural to live by the work ethic and to deprecate purposeless leisure.[347]

The American upper class, despite its wealth, could not entirely give up the idea of a worthy vocation. Status and prestige were tied to achievement rather than to social origin. Thus, the Protestant ethic retained a residual influence even among the wealthiest Americans. It was characteristic of this class that even their sports—polo, golf, and sailing—lost their spirit of amateurism early on and began to reflect middle-class values of competitiveness and achievement.[348] Ultimately, Veblen's thesis about the leisure class was "stood on its head." While the middle class admired the lifestyle of a leisure class (at least, its materialism), the American upper class tended to embrace middle-class values in their work and play.

Many members of the American middle class had arisen from the working classes and emulated the material success of the upper class, but they looked with disdain upon leisure class and lower-class morals and mores. The opposite ends of the social spectrum were viewed—regardless of the reality—as less appreciative of the work ethic and more inclined to eschew the ascetic temperament for a life of pleasure or idleness. The middle class remained the class with which most Americans chose to identify. Mainstream sentiment reflected Tawney's characterization of "the middle rank" as the true and best citizens.[349]

The Legacy of Moral and Rational Asceticism

> God meant human society to be organized always, and on the whole, in the
> interest of the industrious, prudent, self-denying, ingenious, shrewd and
> honest people; and will on no account permit it to be controlled by
> the lazy, stupid, and shiftless.
> —E. L. Godkin, journalist

The Colonial American had been injected with a strong dose of moralism that manifested itself as pragmatic righteousness. It was a force that permeated both religious sects and the nation's secular institutions, and it has endured. "The moral cacophony of colonial Puritanism filters into every nook and cranny of our common lives," observed Morone.[350] However, as the nation evolved, the legacy of asceticism became less moralistic and more rational in character. The tandem of moralism and rationalism was exemplified in America's political and business leaders who espoused the values of rational labor, service, discipline, and restraint. Industrialists John D. Rockefeller, Sr., Henry Ford, and Frederick W. Taylor ("the father of scientific management") were personifications of Protestant asceticism. These archetypes of industrial capitalism attested to the positive energy this ethic engendered.

The national brand of asceticism may have created positive energy, but it also suppressed the enjoyment of life. Sigmund Freud could be thinking of Americans when he noted that Protestant capitalism leads to an effective stifling of the libido. It was true that the ascetic American found it difficult to admit pleasure or to trust activities that brought pleasure. Emotion was held as somehow sinful or shameful; most certainly showing it was. Americans loved the idea of "coolness." Denial of pleasure served as a sort of moral test. Immediate gratification was deferred with the goal of reaping substantial rewards in some receding point in time. Americans continued to practice self-denial even when they became affluent. The generation that went through the Great Depression of the 1930s persisted in hoarding resources even in the post-World War II era of prosperity. They found it easier to acquire luxuries than to enjoy them. A feeling of moral rectitude was evident in the denial of the comforts and pleasures of modern life. On the other hand, anything causing discomfort was viewed as morally redeeming, beneficial to the formation of character of the sufferer for having endured it.[351]

The descendants of Puritans harbored the ascetic's mistrust of human appetite. Foregoing Aristotle's advice as to moderation in all things, they instead framed the moral issue of appetite as a struggle between the polarities of indulgence and abstinence. There is no better illustration than the nation's struggle with the consumption of alcohol. The American moralist refused to admit to the possibility that most individuals could drink responsibly. The issue of alcohol consumption was framed as a choice between falling into inevitable drunkenness or practicing abstention. The belief in the necessity of prohibition led to a series of moral campaigns beginning with the American Temperance Society, which was established in 1826. The Women's Christian Temperance Union took up the cause against the evils of alcohol after the Civil War. The campaign against selling alcohol expanded into the political arena. The National Anti-Saloon League, founded in 1895, was a political lobbying group that presaged the forming of a national Prohibition Party and culminating in national Prohibition in the 1920s.[352]

The "religious" crusade against drinking didn't cease following the repeal of Prohibition. Alcoholics Anonymous, formed in 1935 as a support group for recovering alcoholics, discounted the possibility of moderate drinking in favor of total abstention. The group's meetings featured public confession, repentance, testifying, and obeisance to a higher power, much in the style of a revival meeting. The extolling of abstention from alcohol carried over to campaigns against other recreational drugs. One national campaign against drug abuse adopted the slogan "Just Say No" as a panacea. This slogan encapsulates the ascetic's remedy to the excesses of appetite. Eventually, the Puritanical view of drug use would roil American sports.[353]

The American commitment to self-denial carried into areas of diet and exercise. The characteristic nutrition-related problems of the contemporary era are gluttony (manifested in obesity) at one pole and willful starvation (i.e., anorexia nervosa) at the other. Reduction diets became a national obsession, particularly among young women. Likewise, the remedy for sedentary living habits has been sought in strenuous exercise programs.

Health-conscious Americans competed in grueling marathons and triathlons. For the ascetic, both society's problems and their solutions were framed in extremes.

The moral overtones of rational asceticism were evident throughout the nation's transformation into a modern society. During the 1920s and 1930s, church and business leaders had assessed the daily habits of the common people in distinctly moralist terms. Not until the post-World War II era would social and economic changes mitigate the influence of traditional values. Mass consumerism brought forth other ethics. Americans would struggle to bridge the gap between the moral imperatives of Protestant asceticism and an emerging consumer culture. Philip Rieff suggested that asceticism had been eclipsed by what he labeled the "therapeutic" ethic, implying that Americans no longer judged behavior on the basis of strict morality. However, others identified elements of asceticism in the anti-materialistic communes of the radical 1960s and in social welfare agencies working at the grass-roots level during these politically turbulent times. While attempts to adapt rational ascetic values to new lifestyles often were strained, the efforts were in themselves a testament to the continuing influence of this ethic.[354]

The late twentieth century witnessed an anti-pornography campaign, a "three strikes and you're out" policy toward criminals, and a "war on drugs" that emphasizes harsh punishment over drug treatment. All of these social movements reveal elements of moral asceticism. One can cite national figures like consumer advocate Ralph Nader and the late Muslim radical Malcolm X who have been widely admired for their ascetic lifestyles. Despite rampant materialism and the hedonistic elements of popular culture, Americans continue to admire austere individuals as they join reform campaigns that embody elements of moral and rational asceticism.

Rugged Individualism

[The American is] a lonely racer in a high speed air-conditioned automobile.
He is going faster, he will "get there" sooner, but he will not feel much on
the way, except, perhaps, his isolation.
–Lewis Austin

The American's deepest image of himself or herself is that of a loner. Of all the national icons, that of the lonesome cowboy riding across the Western range may be the most powerful. The myths of individualism have persisted despite the realities of the nation's social experience. The first European settlers came to America in groups and, once here, formed tightly knit communities. For the most part, their descendants carried out the westward expansion in groups—on wagon trains and river boats. Yet, the pioneering spirit became a symbol for individual effort, and this image has endured.

American literature and film are replete with images of loners: mountain men, frontier sheriffs and their modern counterparts—jet pilots, secret agents, and private detectives. The contemporary protagonist in popular drama is often the isolated urbanite "bucking the system." Even within the crowded megalopolises, Americans have emphasized "going it alone." Americans continue to believe that everyone acts individually out of self-interest and ends up happy, that the independent approach to life assures not only survival but salvation.[355]

Crucial historical circumstances fostered individualism in the forming of the new nation that became the United States. Notably, the continent was populated by groups of European emigrants who had little in common beyond their need to survive and a shared geography. Immigrants had come from disparate places and arrived at different periods; thus, they often lacked common traditions or a common history. The Protestant ethic did not create the physical and social conditions that promoted individualism, but it did sanction them. The ethic taught that a genuinely moral life could be lived only by a community of individuals, each focused on self-improvement. This view was summed up in Benjamin Franklin's dictum: "God helps those who help themselves."

Calvinism, early on, had contained a strong sense of communalism (evident in Calvin's Geneva), but the individualistic tendencies in this religious sect eventually prevailed. Plymouth colony's governor William Bradford offered a justification of the abandonment of the initial communal economy on the ground of unequal distribution of talents and incentives. By the third generation of New Englanders, individual initiative had replaced the feelings of mutuality that had dominated the tightly knit first and second-generation Puritans. Individual welfare began to take precedence over that of community welfare. The grandchildren of the founders strayed from the communal ties that bound their parents, and succeeding generations demonstrated more and more self-reliance and self-expression.[356]

This emphasis upon individual responsibility and personal salvation influenced the formation of American government in the eighteenth century.

Protestantism was sympathetic to an Enlightenment political philosophy that recognized the role of the individual. Thomas Jefferson became the symbol of Republican individualism, the political philosopher who championed sensitivity to individual rights, individual responsibility, and self-reliance. The political philosophy and ethic of individualism would take hold in America to a greater degree than in any other post-Reformation society.[357]

Individualism remained relatively unfettered in America until confronted with the late nineteenth-century corporate ethic. In the wake of bureaucratization, the individualist values inherent in the Protestant ethic retained meaning as symbols of social striving, but individualism no longer functioned in its classic economic and sociological forms. By the end of the first quarter of the twentieth century, the rugged individualism of the previous era had become an anachronism in the corporate world. These changes would affect virtually every segment of the social hierarchy. The individualism of the middle classes was being eroded by large-scale business. Workers now were little more than highly regimented "individuals within groups" required to operate in a framework of *group* competition and *collective* responsibility. As the self-sufficient worker and independent entrepreneur declined, the long-held ideals of self-sufficiency slowly gave way to the reality of teamwork more suited to industry in a bureaucratic economy.[358]

During the Great Depression, the idea of uncompromising individualism became insupportable, as the best efforts of individuals availed them to little or nothing. A new kind of public responsibility was born that culminated in the Roosevelt administration's New Deal. Not surprisingly, the strong valuation of individualism within the Protestant ethic strained against the rapidly changing economic and social realities. While the remedies were collective, the end product was fulfillment of the individual life. The morality of self-interest prevailed. The average American continued to think in terms of individuality and self-reliance.[359]

Gunnar Myrdal observed that at mid-twentieth century, the strength of the American ideal of individualism was still felt to an extraordinary degree in spite of the changes in social conditions brought about by corporate capitalism.[360] The American psychiatrist Willard Gaylin commented on the ideology of late twentieth-century Americans: "We see everything in terms of personal autonomy—in terms not only of my rights under law, but also in terms of pleasure, in terms of privilege. I think we have trained a whole generation of people to think in terms of an isolated 'I'."[361] Of course, the phenomenon of undeterred individualism preceded Dr. Gaylin's generation; it had been evident throughout much of the American experience.

The continuing strength of individualism could be observed in late twentieth-century political philosophy that emphasized personal rights and responsibilities. Despite the recognition of compelling state interests, the ethos of the political/legal system reflected the individualistic philosophy of the nation's founders. The Reagan revolution of the 1980s equated the quality of life with freedom of individual choice. Every citizen would be free to improve the quality of his or her own life. This idea was the traditional politics of self-improvement. Once free from the structural constraints of the bureaucracy, moral responsibility could be reconceptualized on the individual level. Public issues such as the breakdown of family structure or the failure of health care have been redefined as matters of individual concern and responsibility. The American government has resisted implementing national health insurance after virtually every other Western democracy has done so. In the matter of mental health, psychotherapy (a European invention) experienced its greatest popularity in the United States because its primary appeal is on the level of the individual. For Americans, emotional problems—like physical health problems—are thought to be personal ones, individually caused and individually corrected.

As America moved to a consumer culture, the accumulation of material goods functioned as a symbol of individual success. Each family strived for its own piece of property with a stand-alone dwelling and their own means of transportation in the garage. The affluent built their own tennis courts and swimming pools. Status remained tied to the number of personal possessions individuals acquired. Everyone was supposed to make his or her own way in the world through individual effort, for which he or she would be rewarded. Amidst a social bureaucracy made up of larger and larger organizations, within densely populated urban settings individualism would endure as an ideology reflective of the Protestant ethic.

A Nation of Volunteers

> The American Puritan...was not content with the rescue of his own soul; he felt an irresistible impulse to hand salvation on, to disperse and multiply it...to make it free and compulsory. All that was needed was organization. –
> —H. L. Mencken

One is confronted with an anomaly in explaining the American character: how to interpret a nation of individualists with a compelling need to form voluntary associations. David Riesman highlighted this incongruity with his oxymoron "the lonely crowd." [362] The fact is that American individualism has always been played out in and through groups. As the tightly knit New England colonies of the seventeenth century dispersed, the impulse to organize voluntarily arose to replace the lost sense of community. The penchant for organizing has deep roots in Calvinism. The post-Reformation churches were early examples of voluntary associations. John Calvin was an "organization man," a reformer who relied upon organizations, and he imparted upon his followers his organizational initiative and stamina. Indeed, a Calvinist's piety was matched by his activism and sense of involvement. The impulse to improve oneself and to improve society translated into the active formation of associations to implement goals. The propensity to organize satisfied the Calvinist's felt obligation to "do good." The descendants of the Puritans found themselves engrossed in the agendas of voluntary organizations.[363]

However, the sense of communalism wasn't completely regained in voluntary organizations that turned out to be little more than loose aggregates of members banded together to meet limited goals. In truth, the formal and informal organizations in Protestant societies have remained relatively impersonal in contrast with the guilds, cliques, and kinship groupings of the pre-Reformation era.[364] However, these loosely bound organizations seemed to strike the right balance for the individualistic Americans. While touting personal virtues and zealously guarding their individual rights, they initiated a surfeit of voluntary ventures bent to every imaginable purpose. From early on, this flurry of organizing and joining was apparent to foreign visitors. De Tocqueville commented during his visit to the United States that Americans of all ages, all conditions, and all dispositions were forever forming associations—religious, economic, and civic.[365]

The compelling impulse to organize carried into the modern era. It is estimated that 80 percent of contemporary Americans belong to some type of organized membership group. A perusal of the telephone directory of any large city provides convincing evidence of the large number of volunteer organizations that prevail. Private citizens associate not only to save souls and cure social ills but also to bring together persons with similar interests or idiosyncrasies. America can be viewed as a "kind of Rotarian nation, a people primed to sign up for any communal effort." This energy can be directed at positive ends such as bowling leagues and fraternal organizations, or negative ones such as street gangs and right-wing militias.[366]

As America's churches became "institutionalized," they initiated structured activities and formed affiliated groups for a variety of purposes. In doing so, the churches set the pattern for interdenominational lay organizations. Established religion played on the feelings of Americans that organizations had to be established to safeguard morality. These newly formed groups of volunteers were drawn into all sorts of social causes. Interdenominational organizations became so numerous in the late nineteenth century that there appeared to be one for almost every social cause: temperance, playgrounds, and Sabbath-keeping, among others. The Victorian Era was a particularly fertile period for such organizational activity among both men and women. Married and single women began to assume active roles in organized fundraising efforts, charity drives, and social work.[367] Commenting on the voluntary associations of the era, Calvin Colton concluded, "so numerous, so great, so active and influential" are their numbers that they "lead the public mind and govern the country."[368] Community spirit and civic "boosterism" became the secular equivalents of the evangelical impulse that operated within religious settings. Margaret Mead and Max Weber remarked on the extemporaneous associations that are such a prominent feature of American life.[369] Fraternal organizations, service clubs, and honor societies pursue their own versions of Protestant activism and Christian stewardship.

Much of the American initiative to form organizations has focused on young people. Beginning late in the nineteenth century, churches, community organizations, and schools became particularly concerned with the problems of youth. The Sunday-school movement, the Young Men's Christian Association, and the Boy Scouts (and their counterparts for young women) began organizing the leisure time of school children, while Protestant churches directed their adolescents into associations for self-improvement and recreation.[370]

Notably, organizational proclivities have been applied to recreation. Sports programs in the US have largely relied upon the willingness of individuals to volunteer their time and energy. Unlike the modern socialist democracies with state-supported programs, America's sports have been organized largely through volunteer efforts. Golf is a classic example of a game that required a permanent organization on the local level to bring about the conditions necessary for its pursuit. The requisite organization was the "country" club (primarily as a venue for golf). By the 1930s, over 1,200 clubs had been formed on the model of business corporations.[371] Similar organizations like the Amateur Athletic Union were formed around dozens of other participant sports, from track and field to water polo. The Turners, German-American gymnastic clubs with political overtones, flourished in America's inner cities as country clubs emerged in the suburbs.

Thus, as a modifier to the marked individualism that arose out of the national experience, Americans developed a strong penchant for forming and joining organizations among whose purposes were the betterment of the individual and the community. These organizations did not stifle individualism. There was no dissolution of "self" in the collective. Instead, voluntary organizations functioned as "secular congregations" that reaffirmed the individual's place in the community. This accord has been part and parcel of the continuing dialectic between individuality and communalism that has played out in American society.

The American Dream: Achieving Success

> There is only one complete unblushing America[n]: Protestant...college
> educat[ed], fully employed, of good complexion...and a recent
> record in sports.
> –Erving Goffman

Americans demand above all else fair opportunity and a free scope for individual effort. While equal opportunity provides a sense of self-respect, achieved status is what motivates individuals to strive for improvement. Together, these conditions have created an "aristocracy of merit." The values of equality and individual achievement haven't always constituted a harmonious tandem, however. Democratic ideals often proved antagonistic to the elitist elements inherent in American Protestantism. Though individual Americans may have been created equal in the eyes of the law, they proved to be less than equal in practice. The New England Calvinists took note of these discrepancies.[372]

The Puritans framed status as a reflection of the inequality of innate endowment. They rationalized inequality by referring to the angelic orders or to Plato's metaphor of gold, silver, and base metals. The Calvinist Joseph Hall proclaimed, "Equality hath no place, either in earth or in hell."[373] To the Puritans, opportunity was the only thing that had to be equal. While they acknowledged that even the lowborn might rise above others through achievement, ambition to succeed was certainly not equally distributed. Sentiments about equality could be viewed as actually inhibiting achievement. Thus, a greater value was placed upon achievement. The dialectic that played out between inequitable achievement and equality of opportunity was to remain pivotal in shaping the American psyche and the nation's institutions.[374]

The goals "to get ahead" or "to make good" had to incorporate visible signs of success. Evidence of achievement typically was couched in terms of material gain. John Cotton had declared that just as the strongest are most able to do battle, so are the virtuous most apt to attain riches. To the mature Puritan mind, riches became less an object of suspicion than evidence of God's blessing. Poverty, on the other hand, provided an example of the "wages of sloth." The poor were viewed not as victims of circumstance but of their own idle, irregular courses; misfortune wasn't to be pitied but condemned. The Puritans' summation was that God prospered the good individual and withdrew from the evil one. Material success was taken as an immediate outward and visible sign that one so lived as to find favor in the sight of God. It was a judgment that survived the transition from the New England theocracies to a more secular world. Ralph Waldo Emerson was fond of the term "inner resources" in explaining success. Whether the motivation was internal or external, the need to rise in status through one's individual efforts constituted a moral imperative.[375]

The emphasis upon individual achievement appeared as an enduring theme in American myth and literature. An entire genre was created around the rise to success. Narratives of individuals rising from "rags to riches" dated from Cotton Mather's time and would include Ben Franklin's record of his own rise to prosperity. The idea of success through achievement was prominent in the nation's popular literature. Examples include Horatio Alger's stories of young men climbing to the top of the ladder of success through perseverance and good fortune. During the peak of his popularity in the early twentieth century, Alger had a reported readership of some fifty million. The size of his audience attested to the force that the idea of achieved success exerted upon the American imagination. The so-called "success tracts" written for middle-class consumption continued to be a popular well into the twentieth century when sport autobiographies and biographies offered a new type of success story.[376]

Americans tended to dwell on obstacles to success and the specific means to overcome them rather than on specific goals. Life became a marathon to reach goals that were not fixed but constantly receding. Feelings of achieved success proved elusive. An American could never be fully content with his or her personal achievements; life was a constant tugging and scheming to get ahead, "a great scramble in which all are troubled and none are satisfied," as Nichols put it.[377] One could never be successful enough, for the attainment of success proved to be a boundless aspiration. One triumph must lead to another, on and on *ad infinitum.* The drive to achieve success became virtually a "life sentence."[378]

Thus, the act of achieving success became more important than the substance of achievement. It mattered less *what* one accomplished than that one succeeded in his or her efforts. Success in acquiring a large fleet of automobiles, or in racing them, was just as legitimate as success in manufacturing them. The ethic of achieved success ultimately became self-serving and self-justifying. Americans didn't reflect on why they obsessively pursued success, nor did they integrate the pleasures and duties of their lives amidst their single-minded pursuit of it. In the singular effort to achieve, a large part of life's satisfactions were relinquished in the quest for self-justification. The question of why someone should relentlessly pursue success in a milieu of often distorted values was generally ignored. Achievement of success came to be an end in its own right.[379]

In a system where it was imperative to achieve social status, vocation became the principal criterion. The wealthy businessman was the archrepresentative of success in America. But as the nation became increasingly prosperous, financial success led to increases in leisure and consumption. Both developments became problematic for the achievement ethic. One had to reconcile these changes with the work ethic and the residual asceticism in American Protestantism. Bruce Barton's bestselling guides to personal success reflected the transition from the traditional production-centered system to the new consumer-oriented one. His famous book, *The Man Nobody Knows* (1925), depicted Jesus Christ as a successful salesman, publicist, and role model for the modern businessman. Barton's writings illustrate an attempt to breach the gap between the demands of the traditional ethic of hard work, self-denial, and savings and the emerging consumer demands of spending and using up goods.[380]

Thus, the achievement ethic survived the transition to a consumer culture, but over the course of the twentieth century, the pattern for achieving success was redefined. Americans were concerned not only with how to achieve through work but with how to consume the fruits of their achievement. Status became an article to be purchased; consumption emerged as a recognizable sign of achievement.[381] What Veblen defined as "conspicuous consumption" was a practice of displaying wealth as the visible sign of success, and thus of status. The onlooker had no way of telling how a neighbor's wealth had been acquired (this was the mystique surrounding Scott Fitzgerald's title character in *The Great Gatsby*). A degree of moral ambiguity accompanied the new system of achieving status. Affluence was thrust upon Americans by circumstances that hardly existed for the Puritans. Despite all the rationalizations, the prosperity accompanying achievement of success remained a problem. The main danger for the descendants of Puritans was in the temptation to indulge in sensuous living and to be distracted from one's calling.[382]

This relentless quest for achieved status created a climate of unrestrained competitiveness. Competition manifested itself in almost every facet of social and cultural life: politics, business, education, even recreation. Success always seemed sweeter when attained through competitive effort. What constituted success was that one had outdistanced others who sought the same goal. The American counted personal successes by the number of competitors passed on the road. Despite the fact that industrial capitalism developed the potential to eliminate scarcity, to do so would have been antithetical to achieved status in a climate of residual asceticism. Thus, artificial scarcities were "built into the system" to insure individual competition as a means of allocating scarce rewards.[383]

Competitiveness

> [America is] a perpetual football match, a brave struggle
> with no further purpose.
> –George Santayana

Legend has it that an emperor of ancient China was invited by one of his courtiers to attend a horse race. The ruler politely declined, commenting that he was quite aware one horse could run faster than another. How strange this attitude must seem to the American whose very life resembles a virtual steeple-chase of competitors scrambling for the prize. Indeed, Americans have demonstrated an unbridled propensity to compete in everything from horse races to beauty contests to sales quotas, and hold an abiding interest in who prevails in these contests. From its very beginnings, the nation was held together by pitting group against group, state against state, region against region.[384] The contemporary writer Tom Wolfe characterized the Great American Land Rush: "People used to get to the starting line and run into Kansas. If you could get to a plot of ground and stand on it, it was yours."[385] The Land Rush is a relic of the past, but Americans still compete for territory through sales franchises and on football fields.

Unlike the British, who seemed to take competition for granted and assumed it would exist even if one didn't set up an ideology for it, Americans were of the paradoxical opinion that competition is natural only if it is constantly recreated by artificial condition and reinforced by ideology. This competitiveness had ideological roots in Protestantism, and as the nineteenth-century clergyman Lyman Beecher noted, it dominated American religion along with the other national institutions. Where no state religion existed and religious association was purely voluntary, individual denominations vied with each other in an open marketplace for influence and membership. Thus, the penchant for competition would define the nation's institutions, religious and secular.[386]

The love of competition had an equally profound effect upon individual behavior. The roots for this can be found in Calvinism's agonic view of life as a constant struggle in which few rise to the status of the elect. American Protestants are fond of quoting Paul in his first Letter to the Corinthians (9:24-27): "I run straight to the finish line…. I am like a boxer, who doesn't waste his punches. I harden my body with blows and bring it under complete control, to keep from being rejected myself after having called others into the contest."[387] Moral life was represented as a battle, a conquest, an overcoming. The progeny of this legacy appeared to be engaged in a perpetual trial, haunted by the ever-present question, "Can I?" It was as though competition were the only mode of existence understood. Life was framed as a zero-sum game in which someone always has to win, someone to lose. In its extreme form, competition encouraged ruthlessness and selfishness.[388] To the extent that the competitors could free themselves from scruple, sympathy, honesty, and regard for life, they were assured of furthering their chances of success; to the degree that their human qualities included a sense of equitableness and an indiscriminate sympathy for others, they placed themselves at a disadvantage—or so it seemed to Veblen.[389] This is not to say there were not positive outcomes of competition, as any defender of the economic free market will avow.

Competitiveness was ingrained in the American child's psyche within the family setting, in the schools, and on the playgrounds. Sociologists note that in the absence of laws of primogeniture, sibling position promoted intense competition within American families. Parents regularly bragged about which child could walk or talk at the earliest age. The term "sibling rivalry" was coined to explain this phenomenon. Frederick W. Taylor's mother instituted a system of child training that remorselessly pitted her children against one another in spelling bees and other competitions. Taylor's upbringing may have been a bit extreme but not uncharacteristic.[390] American parents have routinely directed their children into competitive activities against siblings, neighbors, and schoolmates. The child who couldn't compete successfully was put to open shame by parents, teachers, and coaches.

American schools were structured around competition. The spelling bee became a national institution. The curriculum and methodology reflected a view of human nature in which intellectual gifts were unevenly distributed. Teachers graded "on the curve," and children had to compete for high grades and honors. Scholastic competition meant some students passed and some failed. At Phillips Exeter Academy, an elite preparatory school in the East, half of the class was "dropped" annually during the 1870s.[391] (Similarly, I recall my freshman year at a Big Ten university when the professor in a large lecture room pronounced, "A third of you won't be here next year!") American youth soon learned that teachers' approval could be won only by out-competing their peers. Competition was rationalized as good training for success beyond the family and school, especially in the business world.

Indeed, business provided the classic model for competition. It became a sort of game in which the "contestants" relied upon self-assertion and exploitation to get ahead. Every impulse in the business person encouraged him or her to exploit society and the natural world for all one could get. American business adopted an adversary model both in relations with competitors in a free market and in the negotiations between labor and management. Businesses attempted to undercut their competitors even if it meant fixing prices and creating artificial barriers to fair competition. Labor-management negotiations were conducted in an atmosphere of contentious confrontation. Contract agreements were effected through offensive tactics calculated to force the adversary to make concessions, and defensive tactics calculated to prevent the adversary from gaining concessions. Notably, labor relations in professional sport would reflect this strategy.[392]

The competitiveness that characterized America's large corporations was imitated by the small-town business community where competition was always vibrant, and occasionally underhanded. Here too existed the mutual maneuvering to "get the best of the other guy." Business entrepreneurs demonstrated a ruthless suppression of opponents and exerted their dominance over subordinates. Some would even resort to force, blackmail, and bribes when necessary. The perception was that a formally blameless evasion of the rules could be beneficial. The competitor who was able to "beat the game" was met with admiration. Gamesmanship appeared to be profitable. The only limits on breaking the formal rules of competition occurred when tact or collusion seemed more expedient to maintain or augment one's collective hold on a corner of trade. In such a system the number of failures were numerous, but dropouts were replaced by others eager to join in the contest. The openly competitive business climate reinforced the Calvinists' harsh view of the world. Those who had succeeded were persuaded that they enjoyed the blessings of God, while the failures in society were pronounced as deserving their fate for lack of character.[393]

When viewed objectively, this ruthless competitiveness wasn't entirely rational. Like so much of the Calvinist legacy, it operated on the psychological level. Psychoanalyst Karen Horney recognized the neurotic elements in unrestrained competitiveness. Foremost among these was the constant need to measure oneself against others, even in situations that didn't call for it. This propensity was accompanied by a sense of discontent. *What* one was doing became less valued than the success or prestige gained from it. There was a felt need not only to compare oneself with others but to be superlative.[394] The inherent hostility in this mindset often went unappreciated among Americans. Individuals driven by a strong need to achieve showed few qualms about taking unreasonable risks or hurting others. Such behavior could always be excused somehow by one's own successes. Exaggerated competitiveness proved ultimately self-destructive. The narrowly conceived scenario of relentless competition rendered the descendants of Puritans "cold and dumb in spirit," to recall Van Wyck Brooks's characterization.[395]

Unrestrained competition in the economic sector prevailed until late in the nineteenth century when the openly competitive forms of immature capitalism were replaced by what resembled an oligopoly. Once large business corporations began to dominate the scene, the profit incentive no longer operated in the same way. Yet, the changing external reality of corporate America did little to dampen the spirit of competition. Americans still believed in economic competition even when it was muted by tariffs, monopolies, cartels, and anti-trust laws.[396]

As competition was being modified in the arena of production, it moved into the new arena of consumption. Americans refocused their efforts on what has been called "keeping up with the Joneses." The nation was becoming wealthy, and the affluent members of this society remembered well the moral admonition, "By their fruits ye will know them." Protestantism, as no other religion before, put its stamp of moral approval on individual accumulation of private property. The nation's unlimited frontier and burgeoning market economy provided ample opportunity for the acquisitive impulse to be satisfied. What emerged from the unique combination of competitiveness and opportunity was an unprecedented struggle for possession of the spoils that lay before Americans, and no one followed any rules of "equitable grab." The competitive spirit shifted much of its energy to acquisition.[397]

The enduring emphasis upon competition in the face of dramatic social changes illustrates Weber's contention that ideas can be just as influential as economic forces. Despite the shift of a capitalist economy away from the unbridled and ruthless competition that characterized the era of the Robber Barons, competitiveness continued to be viewed as the mode of behavior through which individuals were assured of success. Americans chose to ignore the persuasive empirical evidence that indicated cooperation was responsible for much of the progress of modern societies. They would continue to insist on the efficacy of competition. It remained an item of faith that each individual through his or her own efforts was responsible for personal success or failure in life.

The distinct form of Protestantism outlined in this chapter—with its emphasis on moral asceticism, rationalism, individualism, achieved status, and competitiveness—also spawned a strong work ethic. This ethic also became problematic amidst the nation's rapid industrialization and the emergence of corporate culture. The following chapter chronicles the evolution of the work ethic and its displacement into the world of sport.

6

The Evolution of the American Work Ethic

The American Gospel of Work

> That the American, by temperament, worked to excess, was true;
> work and whiskey were his stimulants.
> –Henry Adams

In spring 1932, the aging camera manufacturer George Eastman composed a suicide note that read, "My work is done. Why wait?"—and took his own life. His act expressed a prevailing sentiment: that life without work has no purpose. For Americans like Eastman, work was the reason for living, the path to salvation in a secular world. Eastman's life personified the work ethic. Following his early employment at an insurance company and a bank, he founded his own company to make cameras and film for popular photography. He went on to build Eastman Kodak into one of the largest companies in the photographic industry. Eastman lived by the principle that spending capital for reasons other than reinvestment or philanthropy was a cardinal sin. The camera manufacturer gave away more than half of his immense fortune of $75 million to charity before ending his life.[398]

Americans believe honest work carries the import of a moral duty. The roots of the work ethic reach back to Lutheran and Calvinist concepts of the calling that imbued work with religious significance. The obligation to labor diligently in one's calling had been particularly strong among the Puritans who carried the gospel of work to the new world. There it fueled the taming of a continent and the building of a new nation. The ethic would endure through the nation's history. Michael Walzer noted that the Puritan "emphasis upon methodical endeavor and self-control, was an admirable preparation for systematic work in shops, offices, and factories." He elaborates:

> It trained men for the minute-to-minute attentiveness required in a modern economic system; it taught them to forego their afternoon naps—as they had but recently foregone their saint's day holidays—

and to devote spare hours to bookkeeping and moral introspection. It somehow made the deprivation and repression inevitable in sustained labor bearable and even desirable.[399]

What the actual work was seemed less important than the fact that one was working at something and that this labor reaped rewards. The concept of work as a calling applied not only to gainful activity pursued in the marketplace but to vocations as varied as those of clergyman, soldier, physician, and bureaucrat. The work ethic readily accommodated new professions and occupational mobility in an open society. Though no one was to remain idle, individuals no longer were obligated to spend an entire lifetime at a single job.[400] And, it didn't matter whether one's vocation was white collar or blue collar.

Only among a small minority of New England aristocrats who had inherited their wealth, and the leisure class in the South, did the concepts of manual labor and trade carry a stigma. But these classes were exceptions to the rule in American society where a working middle class set the standards. Moreover, in a frontier nation the land itself served as a continuous reminder of the relationships between work, survival, and spiritual rewards.[401] The American gospel of work incorporated geography, economics, and religion. The national experience continued to reinforce faith in the moral worth and efficacy of hard work. As the work ethic evolved over the course of American history, it incorporated the following components: (1) faith in work as a creative act, (2) the belief that work must be useful, (3) fear of idleness, and (4) work as the path to personal salvation and success in the secular world.

The gospel of work was not held together by any logical consistency, but carried various and incongruous meanings. Work could constitute an ascetic exercise and simultaneously provide the means to material success.[402] The resiliency of the work ethic became clear as the nature of work evolved. The socially useful work of the Puritans in building a New Jerusalem gave way to the regimented industrial labor of the nineteenth century. As the obsessional energy of the work ethic was transplanted into the workshops and factories, the elasticity of the ethic was strained. But it endured as a moral and social force through the Industrial era and beyond.

Americans continued to exhibit an unswerving faith in work as a creative act inextricably connected with the American dream. Hard work, self-control, and dogged persistence constituted the formula for accomplishment. Work not only brought success but made up the very core of moral life. Honest work was expected to develop personal qualities and to shape individual identity. The model of active, conscientious labor was epitomized in the biographies of national heroes like Abraham Lincoln, the rail splitter, and the visibly energetic Theodore Roosevelt. American folklore celebrated archetypical laborers like Paul Bunyan, Casey Jones, and John Henry. Following their examples, thousands of unsung American workers cleared the forests, poled the keel boats, and laid railroad tracks to help build a burgeoning industrial economy.[403]

The work ethic was both utilitarian and pragmatic. Americans had a distaste for futile effort; work had to be purposeful and effective. The importance of useful work had been touted by the popular epigramist Benjamin Franklin. The practical wisdom of *Poor Richard's Almanac* (1732–1757) shaped the American's image as a self-reliant laborer, whether pioneer, farmer, or mechanic. The resourceful worker applied his or her skills and muscle power to nature's abundance, fashioning new tools and machines, imagining innovative products, and carrying out new construction. It seemed as if Americans were always busy making something.[404]

De Tocqueville remarked upon his visit that Americans centered their lives around work, to the detriment of leisure.[405] Indeed, work appeared to be a national obsession. The average manual laborer of the early nineteenth century worked from dawn to dusk. Economists speculate that this period witnessed what may have been the longest and most arduous work schedules in the history of humankind. (The steel industry didn't relinquish the twelve-hour day or the seven-day week until 1923.)[406] This regimen seemed not only acceptable but desirable to the Protestant capitalists. Political wisdom and religious opinion shared the conviction that long working hours promoted the welfare and moral fiber of the laboring classes. Only the beleaguered workers questioned the value of the long hours, but their arguments for a shorter workday reached an unsympathetic audience. Complaints about unreasonable work hours were viewed as a threat to the nation's destiny. When labor unions urged a reduction of the work day from twelve to ten hours, they wisely avoided claims for more free time but argued for time to use for self-improvement, a Protestant virtue.[407]

One of the more durable myths of industrial capitalism was that it reduced human toil. Yet, when unions succeeded in negotiating shorter work hours, the reduction was accomplished by squeezing periods of relaxation and amusement out of work—in effect, trading long hours of casual work for more concentrated labor. Thus, a decrease in the nominal work hours was not a true sign of the diminution of work. As the hours were reduced, the pace of work increased to compensate for the reduction. Labor leaders advisedly turned their attention away from the goal of shorter working hours and toward better working conditions and benefits for workers. Unions took into account the fact that paying workers by the hour was becoming the norm. Thus, fewer hours meant less pay, except when unions succeeded in bargaining for higher wage rates.[408] The nation's factory workers labored intensively and enjoyed little leisure in the Industrial era.

Public speakers in the nineteenth century addressed the importance of work and the peril of idleness. Tributes to the work ethic pervaded sermons and political oratory. One prominent lecturer of the period proclaimed, "The sweat drops on the brow of honest toil are more precious than the jewels of a ducal coronet," and admonished, "We tolerate no drones in our hive."[409] Work was extolled as a panacea for a wide range of social ills beyond the workplace. To remedy psychic disorders, asylum superintendents adopted the precepts of "occupational therapy," with the effect that the insane were rarely left idle. Similar tendencies were manifest in the institutions for the sane. The manual labor movement gained wide popularity in the schools and colleges of the early nineteenth century. The proponents argued that teaching job skills provided a more practical education than purely academic learning. In the burgeoning cities, child labor was defended as a remedy for juvenile delinquency.[410]

The popular fiction of the Industrial Age extolled the work ethic, as did biography. Success through hard work was a central theme in the widely read books of Frank Merriwell. One of Merriwell's characters boasted, "Work is the greatest sport in the world, for it is a game at which one plays to win the prize of life."[411] Elbert Hubbard became the literary champion of the dignity of work by penning his famous essay "A Message to Garcia" (1899), which celebrated unquestioned obedience in getting the job done. Even the clothing styles of Americans demonstrated the high regard for work. Long trousers, traditionally the garb of common laborers, were adopted by both middle and upper-class men, and eventually by women. This trend reached its zenith in the post-World War II era with the adoption of a style caricatured as "proletarian chic." Blue jeans, originally work clothes, were donned by the social elite as a fashion statement.[412]

The work ethic was just as compelling for the professions as among the working class. America's professionals routinely reported seventy-hour work weeks. Driven by motives beyond the obligation to serve their clients, medical doctors and lawyers revealed a passionate drive to advance their practices and accumulate more and more income.[413] The normative behavior of the professional and business classes provides a fundamental insight into the work ethic: the getting of a living is not a necessity incidental to some higher and more disinterested end, but the prime and central end itself.[414] The professional man or woman continued to labor unceasingly at "getting a living" even after the living had been got! Thus did work become less the path to salvation than its own salvation.

Hungarian Count Vay de Vaya, on his visit to the United States in 1908, observed that wealthy Americans eschewed the European idea that people of independent means should work gratuitously or, at least, preserve the appearance of doing so. The traditional model of the liberal professional who placed an emphasis on responsibility, personal service, and creativity eroded into an unrelenting effort directed at economic success. America's professions lacked a sense of *noblesse oblige*; instead, they were pursued in a manner that was both strenuous and time consuming.[415] The term "professional" acquired the popular meaning of "work for pay" at the expense of more high-minded connotations.

No Americans held a stronger belief in the moral worth of work than those who made their living through business. The American business person—having attained gains sufficient to meet individual needs, guarantee his or her security, and gratify personal tastes—did not cease from labor but continued to go to the office diligently until carried to the graveyard.[416] This lifelong ritual was not merely an act of ascetic discipline. A typical sentiment came from the president of an American grocery company, as reported in a popular journal of the 1920s. The grocer declared, "I get more joy out of selling than of anything else."[417] The typical American business executive obtained satisfaction from work rather than leisure.

Business executives continued to exemplify the gospel of work into the post-World War II era. Austin, in his comparative study of American and Japanese executives, described the American as "an unwilling Puritan, staggering under the weight of an ethic his parents and his teachers imprinted on his soul."[418] Theobald characterized the American executives he studied as "workaholics" (a term coined in the 1960s).[419] By the 1980s, the typical business executive's work hours actually had increased from a decade earlier. High-level managers avoided taking regular vacations or utilized time off to catch up on their work. Those on pensions found ways to remain busy in work-related activities during their retirement.[420] One of the more influential of this group was banker David Rockefeller, Sr., grandson of oil tycoon John D. Rockefeller. His words exemplify a conviction in the Protestant work ethic: "To me, honest labor is a means through which we earn our way in the world. My own work and that of my family have contributed valuably to our sense of achievement and self-esteem. Work is one way of justifying our existence to our Creator, by enhancing the magnificent legacy of nature and turning it to the service of our fellow man."[421] For Rockefeller, work still held the import of a calling: the idea of self-justification through work and the strong sense of stewardship.

The strength of the work ethic carried beyond the board rooms of private corporations into the public sector. David Riesman concluded from his research in the post-World War II era that civil servants were working as hard or harder than they ever had.[422] Civil service no longer implied a soft, cushioned position in the political spoils system, as it might have in the previous century when Nathaniel Hawthorne held a civil service sinecure as a way of supporting himself as a writer. The implication is that Hawthorne's duties weren't too demanding. However, the civil servants of the following century were expected to perform, as is evident in the experience of a more recent writer. William Faulkner was fired by the US Postal Service for failure to do his job. He then harnessed himself to his writing desk where he exemplified Henry Adams's characterization of the American: work and whiskey were his stimulants.

The force of the work ethic remained equally strong among those who labored in factories of the mid-twentieth century. Riesman found that blue-collar workers had little enthusiasm for an extra day off. Many of them commented that they would use an additional day to take another job. In fact, the level of multiple job holding by workers remained steady despite increasing affluence.[423] Workers reported they would go on working even if there was no financial need. A survey conducted in the Midwest found that nearly one-fifth of factory workers held a full-time second job, and another 40 percent worked at a part-time job. Regardless of their motivation, American workers clearly preferred extra work to more free time.[424]

Feelings about work seemed to be unrelated to the number of workdays or work hours put in. A field experiment in the 1970s found that changing to a four-day, forty-hour work week had little effect on job satisfaction. Absenteeism in industrial plants was explained less by malingering than by workers holding a second job or running their own businesses on the side. It seemed as though workers toiled beyond reason, as if to avoid the vacuum of free time. Such behavior isn't unexpected in a society that disdained educating the working classes in the cultivation of leisure.[425] Riesman concluded that the Protestant work ethic was a pivotal factor responsible for Americans clinging to the job, while fear of leisure acts as a contributing factor.[426]

The amount of time Americans spend on the job has been increasing according to a report by the International Labor Organization. The UN agency reported in 2001 that American workers were putting in almost a full week more in total hours than in 1990. Americans work longer hours than workers in most other developed nations, and the US is exceptional in increasing the number of working hours. Salaried professionals often work sixty or more hours a week, while low-wage workers hold down two or three jobs. The American obligation to work is reflected in the average annual vacation—two to three weeks—when compared to Europe, where workers enjoy four to six weeks off. Very few American employers have been that generous, nor have labor unions pressed management for vacations comparable to those of Europeans. In addition, Americans resist forced retirement for reasons only partially based on economic concerns. Mandatory retirement at age sixty-five, a policy stemming from the New Deal era, is no longer enforceable in most jobs due to current federal legislation, and many Americans opt to work beyond traditional retirement age.[427] A further testament to the continuing strength of the work ethic is the national goal of full employment rather than optional nonemployment, with the opportunity for more leisure time.

Historically, women also were impacted by the imperatives of the work ethic. The full-time housewife and mother had always worked long hours. Even with the appearance of domestic labor-saving devices and smaller families, housework didn't get much easier. Norms for cleanliness increased, while the standards of mothering became more rigorous. Arguably, preparing meals became more complicated with the new kitchen technology and the disappearance of the family garden. Surveys indicate that twentieth-century housewives worked at least fifty hours a week, and this figure held fairly constant over time. Moreover, women had been entering the workforce in large numbers since the 1920s, and this trend meant juggling housekeeping with a job. In the post-World War II era, about a quarter of housewives with children held paying jobs, and this number would increase to two-thirds of married women by 1990.[428]

Significantly, the women's liberation movement focused on job access and equal pay. The prevailing symbol of the liberated woman was the holder of a job previously held by a man. Thus, liberation translated as better opportunities to work for a living. As important as this goal is, little effort was made to extend the concept of liberation into the realm of leisure culture. (Even the advances in women's access to sport had little relevance to leisurely recreation.) These changes affected the pattern of American family life. By the 1980s the two-income family became the norm. At the same time, greater numbers of adolescents were entering the work force, juggling part-time jobs with school. It was not unusual for all family members to be working and for the head of the household to be holding a second part-time job.[429]

Just as the gospel of work carried across gender and class, it made few religious distinctions. The work ethic impinged upon Catholics as strongly as Protestants.[430] Conclusions drawn from empirical data are bolstered by anecdotal evidence. Sociologist Albert Reiss, Jr. wrote about a Catholic surgeon whose daily routine included going to mass every morning, then to the hospital, and on to his private practice. In addition to these obligations, he belonged to almost every imaginable community organization, and he and his wife entertained three or four nights a week. Here was an individual who worked hard at his job, worked hard at his religion, worked hard at his social life, and worked diligently at his public commitment to the community.[431] Similar accounts can be found describing American Jews, Muslims, or Buddhists. Whether descended from the Puritans or from more recent immigrants, Americans of various religious persuasions readily assimilated the work ethic.

For those Americans cut off from the opportunity to work for a living, a stigma has been attached to their predicament. But even among the chronically unemployed, the imperative to work is palpable. This is because all Americans are defined largely by their relationship to work. As Herbert Marcuse observed, the public consciousness routinely has evaluated individuals in terms of what and how much they produced rather than who they were.[432] Psychiatrists have identified failure in work as a primary source of anxiety for contemporary American men.[433] And women are becoming more like men in this regard.

More than a century ago, Henry Adams had characterized Americans as working to excess, working beyond need, and often working beyond reason.

At the same time, work provided meaning and a purpose in life. Work filled time, conveyed a sense of salvation, and served as the guarantor of morality. As long as meaningful work existed, the experiment called America seemed to work. However, as the America of Benjamin Franklin gave way to that of the Industrial Age and then the post-Industrial Age, the traditional work ethic was put to a demanding test.

The Changing Nature of Work and Frustration of the Work Ethic

> John Henry told his captain, "A man ain't nothing but a man, But before I'll
> let that steam drill beat me down I'll die with my hammer in my hand, Lord,
> Lord, I'll die with my hammer in my hand."
> —John Henry, ca. 1873

Tradition held that prosperity and progress came through hard work, that individual enterprise provided a moral reward based on personal merit. Traditional values die hard. The question loomed, "What will happen to the American work ethic when the fundamental nature of work has changed?" Factory work—with its imposition of regularity, requisite attentiveness, and demand for unthinking obedience—was losing its validity as a medium for self-fulfillment and a productive life. Instead, industrial labor was generating feelings of powerlessness, isolation, and self-estrangement.[434]

As industrial capitalism muted the transcendental overtones of work, it left American workers with a lingering sense of betrayal. Work was no longer a blessing that alleviated human suffering but merely a diversion from suffering. What was once a calling had become a job. The broad middle-class who held strongly to the Protestant work ethic still required productive activity to which they felt called, that was self-justifying, and that would provide them with feelings of accomplishment. When work failed to meet these needs, it created a sense of ennui. This feeling was palpable in the Industrial Age but carried into the era when the majority of workers no longer worked on assembly lines.[435] A human dilemma emerged for those who believed in the work ethic as they attempted to adjust to the jobs offered by the factories, the corporate offices, and the public bureaucracy. Workers found little meaning in tasks assigned to them or in their impersonal work roles. In a fundamental sense, workers became alienated from their work.

Factories alienated workers in at least four ways. First, workers were alienated from the products they produced. Unlike craft laborers, industrial workers found their labor so fragmented, the product so standardized, their individual contribution so minimal, that any sense of personal involvement and pride was completely destroyed. Second, workers were alienated by and from the machine. The worker and the machine did not form a cooperative tandem in production, as did the crafts laborer using tools controlled by his own hands. The industrial worker became an instrument controlled by the machine rather than the controller of it—a mere "appendage of the machine," to borrow Marx's phrase. Third, workers were alienated from their colleagues. The work situation no longer was a family partnership of parent and child, of siblings, or the mutual compact of master and apprentice. Under industrialism, the worker became a commodity in a competitive labor market. The competition was not that of independent craft workers striving to produce superior products for a larger share of the market, but that of unskilled laborers competing for subsistence wages. Finally, workers were alienated from themselves. Labor was divorced from other facets of life to an unprecedented degree. What was once an organic form of existence was now an atomistic one. Industrial capitalism separated work from the worker's physical, cultural, and psychological existence, and ultimately from spiritual life. At the same time, wage labor became the central life activity, the organizing principle of daily existence. There was not a great deal of difference between the slavery of wages and bond slavery.[436]

Industrial capitalism continued to diminish worker autonomy as the economic sector moved inexorably toward bureaucratization. Bureaucracy meant elaborate hierarchies of authority and normative controls. Bureaucratic work environments imposed impersonal surroundings, external constraints, and formal contractual obligations. Thus, by its very nature, the bureaucracy seemed inimical to a personal work ethic. The coercive and cooperative functions inherent to mass labor were at loggerheads with the individualized, entrepreneurial forms of activity that derived from the Protestant ethic and thrived under pre-industrial capitalism.[437] Herbert Spencer stated the point succinctly: "[The] deadening influence of bureaucratic officialdom lessens individual initiative."[438]

Clearly, by the late nineteenth-century the evidence suggested that working-class Americans had developed a sense of mistrust toward large employers. They found it difficult to accept the emerging role that monopolistic corporate bureaucracies came to play in the nation's social and economic progress. The profit incentive no longer operated the same way it once had; competition was being inhibited by price agreements and oligopolies. Bureaucratization and the institutionalization of power made individual striving seem irrelevant. Thus came the end of an era; rugged individualism succumbed to the corporate ethic. By the World War I era, the corporate ethic would be fully realized.[439]

The subjectivity of modern work was just as evident in corporate offices as in the factories. By the close of the 1920s, one quarter of American men were working in white-collar jobs, joined by large numbers of women who held clerical positions.[440] These numbers would increase dramatically during the following decades. Men and women who worked in offices were confronted with the disconcerting realization that these jobs didn't necessarily imply meaningful work either. Not much had changed two generations later when a newspaper article reported that many secretaries in the public sector spent their hours on the job reading for lack of anything better to do. It chronicled a typical workday for one secretary at a federal government office in the Midwest:

8:00 A.M. Came to work. Read newspaper and book for two hours.
10:00   Typed envelope address.
10:12   Photocopied report.
10:26   Mailed two letters.
10:48   Placed phone call for boss.
11:22   Typed revised job description.
11:30   Went to lunch.
Noon   Returned from lunch; transferred phone call. Read.
2:15 P.M. Typed voucher.
2:25   Passed out mail to four people.
2:50   Passed out more mail, and then read.
4:30   Went home.[441]

The above ledger reveals office "work" that constitutes little more than an occasional shuffling of paper. Nor did office workers make anything with their hands, unless typing an occasional letter could be viewed as such. A day at the office often consisted of filling time, appearing busy for appearance's sake. Like the industrial worker, the office worker was not free to engage in meaningful work of his or her own choosing.

The frustration of the work ethic was evident in the emerging surveys of workers' attitudes and job satisfaction. These studies provide telling insights into the relationship between workers and the changing nature of the workplace. Social scientists have identified the structural factors that promote job satisfaction as autonomy, freedom to make decisions and take on responsibilities, permissive leadership, and a voice in decision-making. When workers in one survey were asked directly what made their work satisfying, they responded: creating something, using skills, working wholeheartedly in the absence of rate-fixing, having responsibility and using initiative, and working with people who know their job. Feelings of productivity related to job satisfaction. Workers who were pitted against their environment reported a sense of accomplishment and pride. Job dissatisfaction, on the other hand, correlated with doing repetitive work, making only a small part of something, doing useless tasks, feeling a sense of insecurity, frustration, or a lack of purpose, and being too closely supervised.[442]

The above dimensions of worker satisfaction and dissatisfaction provide a basis for assessing the strains placed on the work ethic as the nature of work changed under corporate capitalism. One implication seems clear: as management procedures imposed greater and greater control over the lives of workers, they squelched any remaining sense of individual responsibility. This transformation of the locus of control was lethal to the work ethic. Satisfying work had always meant having a chance to accomplish things and to contribute as an individual. Given these prerequisites, it is not surprising that the nature of work in modern factories and offices proved less than satisfying.[443]

In the late twentieth century, psychologists began to assess adverse effects of the dull routine of modern work. One study set up a low-scope task, similar to many industrial jobs, that was highly repetitive, low in autonomy, low in task identity, and low in feedback about performance. The Protestant ethic (measured by a standard scale) failed to correlate with either performance or satisfaction in this type of work.[444] The key factor was that labor had become depersonalized. Workers felt disengaged from routine forms of work that were merely the means to impersonal ends. In a broader sense, workers had lost control over their destiny, the means of acquiring a sense of personal worth through pursuit of a meaningful vocation.[445]

The nation had changed substantially since the era when work had been concerned with wrestling sustenance from the earth and providing shelter for one's family. Despite the changes, the work ethic could retain its ideological significance and meaning as long as human labor was tied to providing the necessities for a good life and transmitting a sense of personal accomplishment. However, workers would no longer experience a sense of personal salvation in and through work done mainly to meet production goals or simply to make money. When human labor became a series of fragmented tasks required for producing the meaningless appurtenances of a consumer culture, the traditional work ethic was tested to its limits.[446] Changes in American society were quite evident in the World War II era. They included a rising standard of living, better wages, and a transformation in the relationships between labor, wages, and consumption. Even so, the post-war decades witnessed lower standards of work proficiency. Social scientists began to refer to a "post-industrial" society in which the work ethic and the achievement motive had waned as general cultural influences.[447]

Caught in the throes of dramatic change, the work ethic became more idealized and less dependent on actual work. The ethic now operated on a symbolic level for many Americans. Work remained functional for those in high-status occupations who were at the reins of control, but among many nonprofessionals work became little more than a ritual. Work failed to provide any rewards beyond material ones. It was no longer a central life interest. The job was chosen as the most satisfying part of life by only a small minority of factory workers. All the while, workers retained the expectation that work should have moral content. When such contradictions occur between normative systems and social systems, one adaptive response is for the individual to withdraw. In this instance, workers withdrew emotionally and spiritually from their labor.[448]

Compensatory behaviors began to emerge to fill the emotional vacuum of work. Given routine jobs that lacked any need for creativity or opportunity for meaningful interaction with others, some workers engaged in escapist behaviors. Factory employees who manipulated the same bolts or rivets day in and day out confessed to daydreaming on the job. Others engaged in pranks and "playing around." A study by Lloyd Street found that play in some form occurred every day in a metal trades plant. Such diversions served as a release for the workers from the negative and frustrating content of their workday.[449] However, play and escapist behaviors in the workplace didn't address the basic need for meaningful labor. It was becoming evident that a more functional form of compensation must be found outside the traditional workplace. The crisis of work under industrial capitalism cried out for a surrogate, an activity in which the traditional work ethic could still find meaning. The following section examines the extent to which sport and physical recreation would fill this role.

Displacement of the Work Ethic to Sport

> In America, few can be induced to work for money as hard as some will
> voluntarily work at recreational activities like mountain
> climbing or playing football.
> –Goodwin Watson

Organized sport arose in the shadows of the factories. Many of America's early athletes and the fans who followed them came from the mill towns and steel towns of the East and Midwest. Industrialism facilitated the rise of sports. It created the technical capacity to promote and market sport to a mass audience. The railroads provided transportation for professional and college teams to compete on the road and carried fans to contests. Mass-production techniques were applied to the manufacture of sporting equipment and the construction of stadiums. Later, the invention of public lighting made night contests possible. In addition, industrialization led to greater discretionary income for workers to spend on spectator sports and on commercial recreation. As a result, sport would become an important part of the lives of many working Americans.[450]

At the same time, sport represented a reaction to industrialized life. The burden of regulated work in factories and offices created a need for an "escape valve," and sports provided such a release. Organized sport provided relief from the constraining environment of the workplace and bureaucratic controls. Both participant and spectator sports offered a palliative to the mechanization, standardization, and specialization that dominated workers' lives.[451] Historian Arnold Toynbee viewed sport as a conscious attempt to counterbalance the "soul-destroying specialization" of industrial capitalism. Lewis Mumford proposed that sport reinstituted the glorification of chance that was erased in the mechanical routine of industry. It became apparent to many observers that sport could provide a form of compensation for what was lacking in the corporate work experience.[452]

Through the natural motions of sport, the stifled artisan was able to rediscover activities in which he could compete against himself, manipulate innate forces, and actively execute the craftsman-like skills inherent to traditional work. It was as if the work ethic had discovered a new outlet.

Thorstein Veblen had predicted that when American society developed into "a civilized industrial organization," the instinct of workmanship (his term for the work ethic) might have to work itself out in activities such as golf and yachting.[453] Recent history seems to corroborate Veblen. To a great extent the work ethic has shifted from the factories and offices to the stadiums and playing fields. "Men seek in play the difficulties and demands—both intellectual and physical—which they no longer find in work," in the words of social critic Christopher Lasch.[454]

The following discussion of the displacement of the work ethic to sport addresses both the meanings and forms of work and nonwork. It explores the specific conditions under which compensation for work and the spillover of work into nonwork occur. As previously noted, much of the change in the nature of industrial work was precipitated by the impetus for greater productivity. The focus on production goals had several effects, one of which was a sharper distinction of work from all that was not work. This compartmentalization of work was problematic for workers. Jobs, then and now, don't exist in a social vacuum, and workers don't view their jobs as independent of nonwork dimensions of their lives. Workers are affected by what happens both on and off the job. These circumstances led to a form of displacement. While the work ethic continued to define the moral context of work, the focus of its meaning shifted to nonwork activities.[455]

According to John Carroll, the displacement of the work ethic from the job setting unfolded in four stages. In the initial stage, the Protestant worked at a calling that provided a sense of salvation. In the second stage, work was pursued for its own sake in a vocation that was still harnessed to salvational hopes. In the third, utilitarian work was engaged in solely as a means to material ends. Finally, as the meaning of work further deteriorated, the worker attempted to compensate through nonwork activities. These four stages did not unfold in lockstep progression. However, the fourth stage was evident within several contexts by the second half of the nineteenth century.[456]

As noted above, when work was transformed by the new technology and tied to production goals, industrial workers felt a disruption in the traditional relation of their work to their bodies. These impositions deprived workers of a sense of artistic accomplishment and physical satisfaction. In contrast, sport offered somatic experiences and a sense of control and personal achievement that were missing in industrial labor. It was as if sport sought to restore to the body some of the functions of which the machine had deprived it. Workers rediscovered in sport the demands and challenges, both aesthetic and physical, that they no longer found in work. Sport not only compensated for the "demuscularization" of work, but it also provided the participants with a sense of connection with the goals of their physical efforts, and sport re-established the lost relationship with fellow workers.[457]

The deprivation of somatic experiences in industrial labor was accompanied by a loss of work motivation. Motivation on the job was displaced by emotional involvement in meaningful sporting activities through which workers could achieve personal goals and share in team victories. Sports teams recreated the ambiance of a personal vocation within a small-scale, closely knit moral community. The team, like the traditional work gang, was directed by a manager/coach with devoted followers. Recall that America's small towns were working communities in which the close relationship between individual effort and group success was the norm. Sport, in this sense, reflected the handicraft stage of production; the experience of the athlete was more akin to that of the artisan than the assembly-line worker. Thus, the social structure of sport duplicated, in several respects, the setting in which the Protestant work ethic had originally flourished.[458]

In a sense, the sports clubs effectively recreated the historical relationship between the individual and community, as avocation supplemented vocation in American life. Workers seeking a communal experience began to utilize their limited leisure hours to form leagues and tournaments with games scheduled in the early morning hours or after work. They organized bowling and baseball teams or accompanied friends and family to the ballparks to watch the local team play. The sense of satisfaction and meaning heretofore connected with work activities increasingly were sought in leisure pursuits.[459]

The displacement of the work ethic was a classic illustration of what happens when one social institution fails to meet the functional requirements of the system: another compensates by assuming this function. The nature of industrial labor had failed to support the strongly held ethic that equated personal effort with the products and satisfaction of work. Sport provided a counterweight to the existential impoverishment of work. The rise of organized sports occurred at the very time work was being transformed from handicraft techniques to those of the factory assembly line. Workers, whose jobs were becoming increasingly depersonalized, discovered significant and meaningful activity in the emerging forms of sport, and these activities tended to be quite unlike standardized work in the factories and offices.[460]

However, in a society where the work ethic was so highly valued, it was inevitable that the behaviors and mindsets acquired in performing work would infiltrate nonwork contexts. Sport began by serving as compensation for work only to absorb the ambiance of work. Forms and meanings of work spilled over into sport. The psychological and social lifestyles of work reappeared in sporting activities. What was supposed to be leisurely recreational activity was inexorably transformed into a productive enterprise. Organized sport began to incorporate performance standards within the same technocratic frame of reference as work. The outcome of sports contests took on increasing importance as they acquired connotations of productivity and achievement. The culture of sport increasingly emphasized recorded performances by participants and focused narrowly on winning.[461]

By the turn of the century, sport had become as much a product of industrialization as its corrective. Sport no longer constituted a reaction to the mechanized division of labor and standardization of life; instead, it began to take on the very qualities of the assembly line.[462] Examples of the spillover of industrial forms into sport could be seen in American football as it evolved from a spontaneous, rugby-like game into a highly structured and synchronized contest. Reuel Denney commented on football's "industrial folk ways": the atomistic patterns, the recurrent starting and stopping of field action around the timed snapping of the ball, the trend toward a formalized division of labor, and the increasing synchronization of men in motion.[463] (See chapter 9 for a discussion of the forms and meanings of work spilling over into sport.)

Lewis Mumford observed that workers sought compensation in physical recreation only to serve the clock there as well.[464] Even as the work week shortened, workers spent the periods of nonwork during evenings and weekends in a frame of mind that related to the work context. Thus, the extent to which sport could be therapeutic for meaningless work was compromised by spillover of work traits into recreational time and space. In effect, industry took back the gift of leisure technology had bestowed. Sport was reconceptualized within the context of work. Americans had always found it difficult to utilize leisure as a cultural medium free from work values. Inherent tendencies within the Protestant ethic facilitated the displacement of the work ethic to sport. Sport had emerged as a form of redemption from meaningless work, but soon came to look like a vocation rather than an avocation. This transformation was built on a strong tradition that encouraged productive use of leisure. In truth, the displacement of the work ethic to sport owed much to residual Puritan values.[465]

Organized sport in its early forms had captured the ambiance of pre-industrial handicraft labor. To this extent, it served as compensation for the stilted work environment of the factories and offices. However, the escape from the mechanical routine of industry through sport proved ephemeral. Sport had become as much an artifact of industrial labor as the antidote.[466] Moreover, the work ethic appeared to be more functional within the context of sport than in the workplace. This lesson was not lost on the labor managers.

The Corporate Sponsorship of Sport

> [It] was discovered that play added to the worker's efficiency...
> and was, therefore, of economic value.
> –Robert L. Duffus, journalist

Industrial-era employers recognized what had been palpable to workers on the assembly lines—that recreational activities provided compensation for the dull routine of industrial labor. Management took note that workers were participating increasingly in recreational sports during their off-work hours. In response, a growing number of companies began to organize their own employee programs. The business motive for supervised recreation was buttressed by a longstanding class prejudice. The American establishment harbored a deep mistrust of working-class leisure, which they viewed as time wasted or used for immoral purposes. The managerial class was easily convinced that workers wouldn't know how to use their free time without guidance. (The Puritans never did trust their neighbors to employ leisure productively and were more than eager to offer advice on how to fill it.) Nineteenth-century moralists expressed particular concern regarding commercialized recreation—the dance halls, saloons, pool rooms, and amusement parks that appealed to the working classes. It was feared that these crude diversions were instilling values antithetical to the Protestant work ethic. To counter these uses of leisure, employers sponsored sports and recreation programs with the idea of imparting on workers a set of behaviors consistent with the corporate ethic and supportive of American middle-class values.[467]

In truth, the corporate endeavor to uplift workers through recreational sports had as much to do with promoting increased productivity as with rectifying misuse of leisure. It was becoming apparent that productivity in the factories was not reaching the levels predicted by the proponents of scientific management. Astute labor managers began to question the blind adherence to the principles of Taylorism with its rigid protocol for worker performance. The more progressive employers introduced work breaks for relaxation and recuperation. The next step was to conceptualize work and recreation as different expressions of production, and to promote sport programs as a strategy to improve workers' efficiency. The motives behind these innovations were to manipulate labor power and to extract the maximum value from it. Managers exploited sport to integrate the work force into the company, overcome worker fatigue, and sublimate employees' natural drives into productive efforts. The overriding purpose of employee sports programs was tied to production.[468]

Employers sought to transfer the spirit of competitive sport to the workplace. They promoted the idea of "work as sport." Images and metaphors drawn from the sporting experience were appropriated to reinforce the mental paradigms workers carried in their heads that motivated them to perform work tasks.[469] Slogans like "team spirit" were utilized to enhance the work process. The concept of loyalty transferred to the shop floor was designed to reinforce attitudes and behaviors appropriate for highly synchronized work. Management realized that team sports, in particular, emphasized mutual interdependence and loyalty, and these traits promoted compliance by the workers and the internalization of company goals and values. Competition between work units and efficiency contests were instituted to further motivate workers to perform.[470]

The spillover of values between work and sport was bidirectional. Companies hired specialists to determine appropriate types of employee recreation and then applied standards and measures of success to these programs. Corporate recreation directors were hired to design employee sports programs that reflected the characteristics of the workplace. When they succeeded, such attributes as specialization, calculation, planning, efficiency, self-discipline, and subordination to experts could be detected in the sporting activities on the corporate playing fields.[471] Here was another instance of the reciprocal relationship between work and sport: the spirit of sport was insinuated into the workplace while the characteristics of work infiltrated sport.

The intuition that company-sponsored recreation would increase efficiency in the workplace proved to be accurate. Research confirmed the benefits of employee sports programs. Industry analysts reported decreased absenteeism, less labor turnover, and increased productivity. They concluded that company-sponsored sports served as a creative release for the individual from the negative content of the workday and preserved workers' capacity to perform. Organized recreation apparently reinforced the naturalness of discipline and achievement-oriented feelings of workers.[472] A study conducted in the mid-1980s determined that if stressed-out employees were given an opportunity for recreation, their stress levels returned to their optimum state and their performance improved. Another study of shipyard workers found that jobs were made more pleasurable and acceptable by adding doses of recreation. Further studies on worker efficiency in the United States and Europe confirmed the positive effects of participation in recreation on workers' performance. Thus, American employers became thoroughly convinced that sponsorship of physical recreation enabled workers to adapt themselves to their jobs better, eased tension in the workplace, and improved labor relations.[473]

It is instructive to look at the historical development of corporate sport. In the last half of the nineteenth century, company managers initiated programs to provide sports and recreation for employees. In doing so, companies built upon a longstanding practice among American workers who—much like college students—had informally organized their own sports and recreation. The first baseball clubs, dating from the 1850s, tended to be organized around a single occupation: fireman, shipbuilders, schoolteachers, etc. Fire companies sponsored not only baseball teams but also running competitions and ladder-raising contests. A decade later, a few factories had begun to organize workers into sports teams. National Cash Register (now NCR Corporation) was one of the first employers to endorse recreation programs for workers, convinced they would contribute to reducing production costs and increase the profits of the company. Other corporations followed their lead. Several companies sponsored baseball clubs, eventually leading to the development of commercial leagues. This trend was quite evident in the Midwest and South. Company teams were formed in Chicago and Rockford, Illinois, in the 1860s. By the World War I era, companies of all types were promoting baseball teams for their employees. Nearly every industry had a league: textiles, coal and iron, meat packing. Large crowds would come out on weekends to watch the factory games. There were teams and leagues for both men and women employees.[474]

As corporations continued to sponsor sports teams for the above-mentioned reasons, they began to appreciate the public relations benefits of company teams. While early teams had been made up of current employees, the more aggressive companies recruited expert ball players by offering them paying jobs. Albert Spalding's career as a professional baseball player began as a well-paid member of a company team. Spalding's experience was an early example of what was to become a common practice among American companies as spectator sports increased in popularity. In the 1920s, the Chicago Labor Sports Union reported that 5,000 spectators (mostly company employees) attended one interdepartmental athletic contest. Company managers increased their efforts to employ outstanding athletes to play on company teams as public interest in the teams increased. Corporate teams were evident in the American South from the turn of the century, when the textile mills began sponsoring baseball teams. From the mill team, players like "Shoeless" Joe Jackson went on to play in the major leagues. By the 1930s, club and company baseball teams had formed in San Francisco They were grouped into leagues that scheduled three or four games in a row in city parks on Saturdays and Sundays year round. Joe DiMaggio and his brothers were prominent among the local athletes who played in these leagues. The corporate teams were often referred to as "semi-professional," acknowledging the high quality of their players and level of competition.[475]

Companies in the Pittsburgh area were sponsoring football teams in the 1920s. By the mid-1930s there were semi-pro and factory clubs competing over much of the country. Art Rooney, the future owner of the NFL Pittsburgh Steelers, organized several teams in the Midwest. A. E. Stanley, a starchmaker in Decatur, Illinois, was one of several corporations to sponsor semiprofessional football and baseball teams in that area. Stanley offered George Halas the position of company athletic director, but Halas declined the offer in order to organize the American Professional Football Association, which later became the National Football League. Industrial firms not only sponsored semipro teams, but some of them financed professional teams. In 1911, Indian Packing Company of Green Bay, Wisconsin, gave money to Earl "Curly" Lambeau to form a football team. The team, subsequently known as the Packers, was considered a business project and was allowed to use the company's athletic field.[476]

Industry's keen interest in sponsoring sports teams continued through the twentieth century. The large breweries demonstrated a keen interest in sponsoring professional sports teams, while a larger number of companies continued to field teams in the semipro leagues. In the period following World War II, local and regional industrial sports leagues flourished.[477] Notable semipro basketball teams of the era included the Phillips Oilers, sponsored by the Phillips oil company of Bartlesville, Oklahoma, and the one sponsored by National Homes Corporation of Lafayette, Indiana. Phillips and National were typical in hiring former college and high-school players to work at rather perfunctory jobs for good salaries (much like A. G. Spalding's experience a century earlier) and to play on company teams that competed in interregional leagues. As the teams traveled around the country, they promoted their companies' names and products.[478]

Thus, corporate sports evolved from recreational programs whose purpose was to promote worthy use of leisure and instill employees with work values to the promotion of highly publicized semipro teams competing as a public relations arm of their companies. Many of the star players for the company teams were athletes first and workers second. In effect, they were paid by their employers to play sports. The original goals of corporate sports may be seen as a classic extension of the values inherent in the Protestant work ethic. However, the spirit of capitalism emerged as a predominant influence on corporate-sponsored sports. The recent trend has been away from company-sponsored teams made up of highly skilled athletes. Television dampened the semi-pro teams' spectator draw. Today, progressive companies continue to sponsor employee recreation and fitness programs in an attempt to instill loyalty, improve job satisfaction, and enhance workers' health. Concurrently, the larger corporations promote their services and products through advertising connected to televised professional sports.

Part II

The Spirit of Sport

7

The Protestant Ethic and the Institutionalization of American Sport

The Institutionalization of Sport

> Games are much less carefree than puritanic thought implied. They are
> tightly bound to the cultural situation of the players.
> –Brian Sutton-Smith

Ask a sociologist what the term "institutionalization" means, and you'll get a response along the line of, "It is the point at which human activities become sufficiently regular, reveal well-established systems that incorporate a set of norms and values, and acquire traditions, rationalized myths, and guidelines for their continuation." To the layperson and sports fan, this scholarly argot describes the process by which pickup games and playground ball are transformed into organized teams, leagues, and tournaments. It means the replacement of choosing sides on the spot ("You're on my team") with first-round draft choices and bonus babies. No more playing ball in knickers and tennis shoes, but suited up in team uniforms with numbers on the back, purchased by a commercial sponsor. Institutionalization means that games like "one o'cat" and stickball are transformed into the national pastime.

Virtually all American sports—baseball, football, basketball, golf, and tennis, for example—have been institutionalized. They contain norms (fair play), values (winning), traditions (bowl games), and myths (Abner Doubleday invented baseball). Over time, institutionalized sports acquire universalized and accepted practices, codified rules and regulations, sanctions, an agreed means of arbitration within contests, a regular pattern of events, and a visible concern for the perpetuation of their own existence. They also interrelate with other social institutions in mutually reinforcing ways. Organized sport and American political institutions have had a long relationship: the national anthem is sung before ballgames and the national flag appears at sports stadiums; presidents throw out the first ball at the opening of baseball season and invite champion teams to the White House for "photo ops."[479]

Organization is a byproduct of institutionalization. Modern societies, in general, have demonstrated a tendency to create large and complex organizations that routinely evolve into bureaucracies with impersonal, hierarchical authority, specialized venues, and division of labor. Sports are no exception. They utilize both bureaucratic and nonbureaucratic structures including sponsoring bodies, governing associations, and permanent teams that promote formally organized activities. Under Protestant capitalism, sports also have acquired the trappings of commercialism and professionalism, including paying spectators, paid performers, promoters, public advertisement of events, and journalistic reports of outcomes.[480]

As American sports acquired the trappings of modern bureaucracy, they became increasingly distinguishable from pre-Modern sports. Adelman offers a comparative model of the two patterns:

Pre-Modern Sport	_Modern Sport_
Organization	
nonexistent or informal, sporadic	formal, institutionally differentiated on various levels
Rules	
simple, unwritten, unvarying, based on local custom, tradition	formal, standardized, written, rational, pragmatic, legitimized
Competition	
local	national, superimposed
Role Differentiation	
low among participants, loose distinctions between players and spectators	high, specialists, strict distinctions between players and spectators
Public Information	
limited, local	reported regularly, important, records sanctioned
Statistics and Records	
nonexistent	kept, published regularly, given importance, sanctioned[481]

Turning from social theory to social history, one of the more striking developments in American society has been the alacrity and the degree to which sport and physical recreation were organized and institutionalized. The early play of Americans revealed little formality. Players simply got together and organized a game on the spot. Informal games of town ball (a precursor to baseball) were played by children and adults in the parks and on city streets. On college campuses, sports contests were initiated by students without adult supervision. Throughout much of the nineteenth century, the nation's games and recreational pastimes were casually and locally organized. However, in the second half of the century a network of sport-specific, voluntary governing bodies emerged. This development was stimulated by regional and national competitions with the accompanying need for agreed-on rules and an effective organizing capacity. American sport began to reflect the rational ascetic impulse within Protestantism to legitimize human activity through organization and control.[482]

Americans inherited their sporting tradition and the proclivity to institutionalize sport from the British, who began forming sports clubs and leagues during the eighteenth century. Regularly scheduled cricket matches and prize fights were evident in England as early as the 1730s. The famous Marylebone Cricket Club was founded in 1787. Other sports clubs were formed around soccer, rowing, rugby, tennis, and track and field. Americans tended to follow the British model. Organized turf sports and baseball were early examples. The New York Trotting Club was established in 1824–1835. The Knickerbocker Base Ball Club organized in 1845, and by the end of the next decade, the latter club had adopted uniform rules and was competing against a dozen other baseball clubs in the East. These local sporting endeavors became widespread and invariably led to the establishment of regional and national governing bodies. The National Trotting Association formed in 1870 to promote harness racing. The National (baseball) League was established in 1876. In addition to professional associations, Americans created an elaborate infrastructure of voluntary organizations and national governing bodies for sports: tennis's USLTA (1881), the multi-sport AAU (1888), golf's USGA (1894), and the forerunner of the current NCAA in 1905, to name a few.[483]

The early promoters of organized sport typically were members of the Protestant establishment. One representative was Robert Bonner, a staunch Scotch Presbyterian, who exerted a great impact upon the organization of harness racing in America. Most trotting-horse owners, including Bonner, were members of the Protestant upper-middle class. While these men of property were promoting adult recreation, Luther H. Gulick, the son of a Protestant missionary, was a prominent organizer of youth sport and recreation. In the 1880s, Gulick became part of a national movement to organize children's play that culminated in the formation of the Playground Association in 1907. His efforts were characteristic of the Progressive era campaign to formalize and regulate leisure activities.[484]

The impetus for organizing youth sport and games gained momentum during the early twentieth century. In the period from 1900 to 1917, a concerted effort was made by reformers to convert free play into highly regulated and ordered recreation with well-established goals. What is now known as Pop Warner football was organized for boys ages seven to fifteen in Philadelphia in 1929 as a remedy for youth vandalism in the city. Ten years later, Carl Stotz founded Little League baseball for boys. Little League eventually incorporated and became a multimillion-dollar organization with large cash reserves, real estate holdings, its own insurance company, summer camps, and other income-producing activities. The founding of these early leagues opened the way for other youth sport organizations. The twentieth century witnessed a plethora of basketball leagues, hockey leagues, and similar organizations in virtually every sport that could be modified for children from preschool age to high-school level. American youth sports typically were organized by age groups. In baseball, age-based leagues included Little League, American Legion, Pony League, and the eponymous Connie Mack, Sandy Koufax, and Mickey Mantle leagues. These local organizations, along with the efforts of the YMCA, brought organized sports to millions of children and adolescents.[485]

The community-based programs were accompanied by organized sports in the public schools beginning in the 1890s and flourishing by the 1920s. In 1903, General George Wingate and Luther Gulick established a sports program for boys in New York City schools. Seven years later, the program boasted 150,000 participants. By 1910, seventeen other cities had formed athletic leagues modeled after the one in New York City. Public senior and junior high schools would offer an increasing number of sports for students on both the intramural and interscholastic levels during the course of the century. A parallel effort was underway in private schools. Groton, the prestigious college preparatory academy founded on the British model in 1884 by the Episcopalian priest Endicott Peabody, set the pattern for Northeast boarding schools by emphasizing the character-building qualities of sport.[486]

Organizations at the state and national levels were formed to oversee school sports. By the mid-1920s, school athletic associations existed in all the states. These groups merged into the National Federation of State High

School [Athletic] Associations, whose primary concerns were regulation and control. The number of public high schools grew rapidly in the second quarter of the century. By this time, the games of adolescents had evolved into a system of highly organized, highly competitive programs both within and outside the schools, featuring full-time coaches, scheduled seasons, and state and regional tournaments.[487]

Organized sports on college campuses had provided the model for school sports. Early on, "intramural" sports had been organized rather informally by college students. Fraternities and class organizations had made efforts to initiate and regulate student sports, but problems with rowdiness, injuries, gambling, and other unsavory influences prompted college authorities to take charge of them. The organizational emphasis in college sports quickly shifted from campus competition to the intercollegiate model. Colleges appointed directors of athletics to take control over the programs. These administrators pursued an agenda to standardize rules, procedures for recruitment, eligibility, and finances. Athletic conferences formed in the 1890s around football competition. The early efforts were at the state level, such as the Indiana Intercollegiate Athletic Association, made up of both public and private colleges. The first interstate conference was the Western Conference—now popularly known as The Big Ten— organized by Purdue University President James Smart in 1895. Smart's efforts were motivated by the need to regulate college scheduling practices. The precursor to the National Collegiate Athletic Association was formed a decade later out of a growing concern over the lack of control over undesirable influences and practices.[488]

By the mid-twentieth century, most large American colleges had established departments for the promotion and regulation of sports. College athletic staffs' responsibilities reflected a sophisticated division of labor including business affairs, ticket management, publicity, and recruiting of athletes. The larger colleges offered dozens of sports for men (less for women) and employed several coaches for major sports like football. Some colleges' athletic budgets ran in the millions of dollars by the post-World War II era. The athletic physical plants included an impressive collection of buildings and fields that rivaled the academic structures on campuses.[489]

Even more impressive was the institutionalization of professional sports in the United States (see chapter 12). Baseball made its initial attempt to organize into leagues beginning in the 1870s. It set a precedent for other sports like basketball and football. The American Professional Football

Association was established in 1919. A National Hockey League had formed two years earlier. Professional basketball leagues were evident by the 1930s. Through the course of the century, individual sports like bowling, and the formerly amateur sports of golf and tennis, organized into professional associations.[490]

In addition, participatory sports and fitness activities formed their own local, regional, and national associations. National organizations would be established for virtually every recreational pursuit imaginable, from Frisbee throwing (World Flying Disc Association) to yachting (United States Yacht Racing Union). These organizations promoted competition, set rules, and communicated with members through newsletters and various publications. The National Jogging Association claimed over 25,000 members, while a dozen magazines devoted to running were being published by the late 1970s. Americans have acted on the assumption that one should not simply participate in a sport casually and recreationally but should form organizations to promote and regulate it.[491] Sociologist George Sage speculated that American sports were organized less as outlets for human expression and self-fulfillment than as the result of a bureaucratic ethic.[492] Whatever the motivations, regulatory and promotional organizations would dominate American sport.

Several theories have been proposed to explain why American sport became so highly organized. Certainly the closing of the frontier and the rise of cities played a key role. The industrial cities with an accumulation of people and capital were a necessary precondition for mass sport. Richard Gruneau noted that no general theory adequately explains why modern sports have flourished concurrently with industrialization.[493] Neither the frontier thesis nor an urban thesis entirely explains the rise of organized sport. Other nations experienced frontier cultures followed by rapid urban growth and industrialization, and yet failed to organize and institutionalize sport on the scale of the Americans. While a large urban population was necessary for spectator sports, the congregation of people in cities didn't preordain thousands of them crowding into stadiums and gymnasiums to watch games. The accumulation of wealth was a prerequisite to spectator sports and the large facilities that housed them, but there was nothing inherent in the nature of this largess that suggested its investment in sport.[494]

The explanation for this phenomenon lies elsewhere. The thesis of this book is that the institutionalization of American sport is attributable in large part to the influence of the Protestant ethic. Dominant tendencies within secular Protestant culture worked to transform what initially were informal and spontaneous activities into highly organized ones. The rationalization of America's social institutions led to sport acquiring its own bureaucratic structure. Sport became institutionalized as it absorbed the values of rational asceticism, goal-directed behavior, competitiveness, the work ethic, and individual achievement. Sport as a cultural institution fully integrated with the other major institutions in American society: the family, schools, business and industry, the churches and quasi-religious organizations. Sport also was integrated into the American class structure. Protestant middle-class values prevailed, and it was this class that exerted the major influence upon the nation's sports.

Sport as a Middle-Class Institution

> The higher an American's social-class position, the likelier he is to be a sports "doer" than a sports "viewer."
> –Harold M. Hodges, Jr.

The upper and lower tiers of America's class structure provided the initial impetus for sport. At a time when gentlemen amateurs were racing yachts and horses and the lower classes indulged in cruder forms of recreation, those in the middle ranks were constrained by lingering Puritan admonitions against disporting and idleness. The members of the middle class were equally disdainful of polo matches and pocket billiards. In due course, however, it was the middle class that would set the tone for both spectator sports and participant sports.[495]

Upper-class sports emerged in hunting clubs, country clubs, and urban social clubs. Early on, baseball organized through private clubs like the exclusive New York Knickerbocker Club. Urban sports clubs were succeeded by exclusive country clubs that began appearing in the East in the 1880s and 1890s. These clubs featured outdoor sports like polo and yachting, along with clubhouse accommodations for billiards. These were pastimes the working classes had neither the time nor money to pursue. Golf became popular in the US around the turn of the century and soon became the archetypical country club sport. Clubs actually doubled in number during the era of the Great Depression. Golf remained an upper-class sport until the pre-World War II era when it began to draw players like Ben Hogan from the working middle class. In a similar pattern, country club sports were an established element in private preparatory schools and colleges in the Eastern states before appearing in the extracurriculum of public schools and colleges.[496]

Sport had distinct forms and meanings within the various social classes. Upper-class sports were pursued leisurely, and the interaction among the participants was casual. The class norm was to play fair, to be gracious in victory, and to neither cheat nor question the decision of an official. The upper-class sportsman or woman considered it gauche to "work too hard" at winning. The rich were comfortable with sport that showed no apparent utility other than assuring social status. Apart from its functions as a status ritual, the primary purpose of sport for gentlemen and ladies (who could take for granted their social position) was its capability to fill an excess of spare time and to promote socializing. As Veblen noted, the sports of the leisure class were more of a diversion and a *display* of status than a way to *gain* status.[497]

What upper-class sport drew from the Protestant ethic was elitism. The privileged of American society were wary of democratic pretensions to their status and their version of gentility. Characteristically, the patrician social clubs sponsored exclusive sporting events that were closed to the public. For example, the national ladies' tennis championship held at the Philadelphia Country Club (established in 1890) allowed no one to enter competition without an invitation, and only those of assured social position were invited. Moreover, the clubs required substantial subscription fees, and the typical sports like polo required large outlays of money for equipment and the maintenance of necessary facilities. These provisions served as a barrier against incursions from the lower classes.[498]

The tenor of upper-class sports contrasted sharply with the highly competitive and rowdy sports of the lower classes. Wrestling, boxing, and the other working-class sports were pursued with a reckless intensity and a loose interpretation of the rules that encouraged winning at all costs. Gambling and heavy drinking regularly accompanied these affairs, and they occasionally culminated in a general free-for-all. Middle-class sporting behavior carried its own distinctions. The bourgeoisie, when they played at all, were more inclined to participate in the emerging professional sports for financial gain. Eventually, the industrial economy produced an economic surplus sufficient to support large-scale involvement in sport by the masses. At that point, sports experienced a degree of democratization. Baseball in the early years had been taken up by Eastern gentlemen who played the game in private clubs, but soon it was drawing players across classes.[499]

American football developed as a relatively classless sport. A review of players' surnames on the "All America" football team rosters in the 1890s suggests that what once had been an Anglo-Saxon (and thus, a Protestant) monopoly was experiencing inroads from Irish and other ethnic groups. Throughout the twentieth century, a significant number of football players would be drawn from working-class coal and steel towns of Ohio and Pennsylvania. These class inroads occurred despite the fact that the nation's rather exclusive colleges played a pivotal role in the development of football. In a similar manner, other popular team sports that got their start in private clubs and on college campuses would open up to the middle and working classes.[500]

Throughout much of American history, the urban working classes satisfied their sporting impulses largely as spectators. Among spectator sports, boxing matches were quite popular with the newly arrived immigrant groups, as well as the emerging class of resident ethnics, notably the Irish and people of color. Entrepreneurs like Albert Spalding recognized the popular market for baseball. The promoters of spectator sports realized that in order to lure more customers, it was necessary to get the working classes to identify with the game. They consciously promoted local teams made up of factory workers. Sports owners fielded teams with names like "Steelers," "Packers," and "Trolley Dodgers" that appealed to working-class fans. While the workers provided spectators for professional sports like baseball, they also indulged in commercial recreation like bowling and pocket billiards. The relatively good wages and living conditions in America provided unique opportunities for sport involvement among the working classes. However, they were spectators more often than participants.[501]

While sports spectators came largely from the working classes, the middle class cultivated their own recreational sports. Cycling became popular with this class in the Victorian Era as did competitive swimming. Golf and tennis emerged later as upper-middle-class sports. Class-distinct sporting behaviors would remain salient throughout much of the twentieth century.[502] A 1983 survey of leisure activities showed that although class differences had diminished, business-class families reported somewhat greater participation in athletic sports. The working classes preferred outdoor recreation such as fishing, hunting, and camping,[503] while middle-class families showed a preference for "conceptual" rather than purely physical recreation.[504] Thus, while most sports were now open to everyone, distinct upper-class sports (polo), upper-middle-class sports (swimming), and working-class sports (bowling) were identifiable. American sport would continue to reflect class distinctions in what remained a relatively open society.[505]

However, it was the American middle class ultimately whose mark would be stamped indelibly upon the institution of sport. The Protestant ethic shaped middle-class values, and these values were reproduced in the arenas of competition. The codified rules, norms, and goals for sporting behavior reflected middle-class ideology: "Set yourself a goal. Prepare yourself conscientiously for your task. Recognize the coach's authority. Be a brave loser." Sport facilitated success through individual achievement within the framework of group competition. Unlike upper-class and working-class recreation, middle-class sport blurred the distinction between work and leisure.[506]

The American middle class also placed their distinct stamp upon youth sport (see chapter 10). Studies indicate that middle-class fathers participate more in sport with their children than do working-class fathers. The parents in attendance at children's games typically are of the middle classes. Involvement in children's sport provides the middle-class family with a sense of cohesion. At the same time, sport has functioned as a medium for socialization of children into middle-class values of achievement and success. Parents of this class view organized youth sport as an opportunity for their children to display physical skills that demonstrate their abilities. In contrast, the working-class family has regarded youth sport more as a form of social control.[507]

At the same time, sport became an important institution for facilitating social mobility within a class system that was far more open than in Europe. Americans patterned their sports after the English, whose sports revealed less separation between classes than on the continent. (In the English sport of boxing, one could observe aristocrats competing in the ring against members of the lower classes.) In America, social status was even more fluid than in England. The New England Puritans—despite their accommodation of elitism and exclusivity—supported the principle of open access to all social positions. The Protestant ethic implied that society should operate as a meritocracy and that status should be a function of achievement, not birth. Anyone could rise to the elect through hard work and talent. This prospect for rise in social status included athletes.[508]

Moreover, a less rigid tradition of amateurism was in place in the United States than in Europe. Most American sports eventually were open to those who demonstrated the necessary skills, regardless of their social class. Countless athletes from the working classes, and from ethnic and religious minorities, exploited sport as a way to achieve social status—at first, the Jews and Irish, and later African Americans and Latinos. Early on, boxing and then football provided visible channels for social mobility. Those who were pulled into the sports stadiums as spectators were instilled with the belief that they too had an opportunity to become successful athletes.[509] Former professional football player Alex Karras, the son of a Greek immigrant, commented that athletes coming from the lower classes felt they were "looked down upon" and needed to prove to the world they had value. They acquired a sense of value on the athletic fields.[510] Sportswriter John Tunis described sport as "the modern way up the ladder," the goal to acceptance and complete Americanization.[511] The possibility of gaining fame and fortune was often more illusion than reality, but the belief in social mobility via sport remained a part of the American myth. It was an item of faith that anyone, regardless of money or social connections, could rise to the top through achievement in sport.

Thus, the nation's sports in their various incarnations encompassed athletes and fans across the socioeconomic spectrum, but it was the Protestant middle class that defined the character of American sport. This class pursued sport with intensity as if it were a vocation rather than an avocation, and it imbued sport with high purpose and great expectations. The middle class promoted the idea that an individual could develop character on the athletic field, and this discipline would serve the athlete well in life. Given the moral pretensions of middle-class sport, it is not surprising that sport was adopted by mainstream institutional religion as a remedy for vice, as well as a school for success.

Sport and Institutional Religion

> Out of that new will to power came many enterprises…with the "institutional" church at their head. Piety was cunningly disguised as basketball, billiards, and squash.
> –H. L. Mencken

When the Reverend Henry C. Wright was observed swimming in the Connecticut River in the 1870s, the elders of his church relieved him of his ministerial duties. Such activity was thought unbefitting a man of the cloth. But the times and mores were changing. Two decades after the New

England clergyman's fateful plunge, the writer Finley Peter Dunne counted eighteen ministers in attendance at a baseball game in Chicago. Organized religion was making its peace with sport. The more progressive Protestant churches had reconciled traditional religious beliefs with the emerging recreational uses of leisure.[512]

The truth is that organized religion was losing its effective control over vast areas of social and cultural life once constrained by its watchful eye. Religion's monopoly on the definition of reality was giving way to modernist ideals. The church's authority receded in the wake of rapid urbanization and secularization. By the last half of the nineteenth century, the Protestant church no longer wielded the influence over popular culture it had previously enjoyed.[513] A growing awareness emerged among the more astute clergy that the churches were fighting a losing battle against change. At the same time, institutional religion was too deeply involved in social issues to isolate itself from the secular world. The beleaguered churches adopted a revisionist attitude toward sport and recreation expressed by the American colloquialism, "If you can't lick 'em, join 'em."

A growing number of ministers found it acceptable to voice public support for wholesome physical recreation. The liberal Unitarian minister Thomas Wentworth Higginson wrote an early article titled "Saints and Their Bodies" for the *Atlantic Monthly* in which he extolled the idea that physical fitness and morality go hand in hand. A like-minded article in the *Unitarian Review* of 1889 went a step further in commenting, "A man who does not exercise properly is not a moral man." Another prominent minister of the era proclaimed that good wholesome recreation was first cousin to religion and that the refreshing of the body went a long way toward giving the soul a chance. In the theological schools, a new generation of ministers was instructed that their mission included ministering to the body as well as to the soul. The Social Gospel encouraged these developments. A book entitled *The Minister and the Boy,* published in 1912, contained a chapter on "The Ethical Value of Organized Play." By the early twentieth century, Protestantism had begun to openly embrace the positive values of sport and recreation.[514]

American religious leaders had recognized the facts of life, such as they were. Theology had become rather exotic with little appeal to the common people. The more popular religions had downplayed their emphasis on doctrine to focus on human needs for ritual, communion, regeneration, and renewal. Sport and recreation seemed to meet many of the needs formal religion was having difficulty addressing. Church leaders were not blind to the potential of recreational sport nor reluctant to exploit it for religious purposes. Faced with an autonomous leisure subculture, the churches adopted a strategy of replication. They had no other choice if they were going to compete successfully with secular organizations for bodies and souls.[515]

Organized religion had a strong incentive for initiating programs to compete with unsavory commercial recreation. The clergy sought to counteract the growing popularity of pool halls and bowling alleys with their own offerings that promised to be more uplifting. Toward this end, Protestant churches began a campaign to build gymnasiums and organize athletic leagues. They installed billiard tables in fellowship halls as an alternative to the commercial pool halls. Ministers would invite their Sunday-school classes to the parsonage one night a week to play pool, after which they engaged in a thirty-minute Bible study class. In small towns across America, as churches established societies for the betterment of young people, many of these efforts featured sports and recreational activities. A tremendous growth in such programs occurred around the end of the nineteenth century and carried into the next century. Episcopal bishop William T. Manning dedicated a sports bay in the Cathedral of St. John the Divine in New York City in 1929. Church recreation had arrived.[516]

The reconciliation of sport and religion was realized not only in the churches but also through quasi-religious organizations like the Young Men's Christian Association. The YMCA, another British import closely tied to Protestantism, had sponsored recreational games and sports as part of its mission. It did much to alleviate residual Puritan reservations about youth sport. In the inner city, the YMCA served as a sanctuary devoted to protecting young men against moral decay. (The organization had narrowed its focus by the 1880s to working with boys opposed to girls, and to adolescents rather than adult males.) Typically, the early YMCA gyms were housed in separate buildings from the clubs and libraries. Consequently, many young men took part in the recreational activities without showing any interest in the other programs. The religious agenda continued to lag behind athletics until the arrival of Luther H. Gulick from Springfield College in 1887. Gulick began integrating sports and religion around the concept of body building. Quoting scripture and taking advantage of the new doctrines of experimental psychology, Gulick argued for a union of body, mind, and spirit symbolized by the inverted triangle that became the logo of the

YMCA. Sports were touted as a necessary element in the education of the whole man and as a means of redemption. Thus did Gulick "Christianize" sports within this distinctly Protestant institution.[517]

One happenstance that aided the rapid development of YMCA sports was the invention of basketball at Springfield College, a school where the emphasis on Christian athleticism had gained an effective footing. James Naismith, the architect of the sport, had been a student of Gulick. Naismith conceived of basketball as a laboratory for the development of moral attributes in its players, assuming a competent Christian coach. The YMCA continued to promote basketball in the growing cities of industrial America, and the sport of basketball reciprocated by promoting the YMCA. The local Y gym became the facility used by church basketball leagues well into the following century, as most churches were without their own gyms.[518] The Christian mission of sport was embraced by the YMCA's long-time general secretary John R. Mott (1895–1920). Mott praised the contribution of physical training to the "Kingdom of God in the world" in his Nobel Peace Prize speech. The religious mission of the organization carried through the World War II era; however, the modern YMCA has shifted its emphasis to personal fitness and family recreation.[519]

The traditional religious prejudice against sport continued to wane during the course of the twentieth century. The progressive clergy endorsed sport as a positive good and an effective tool to promote religious goals. Given the American history of assimilation, it was not surprising that Roman Catholics forged their own alliances with sport. Catholic schools and colleges, along with Catholic Youth Organizations (beginning in the 1930s), developed strong sports programs. But it was mainstream Protestants who had established the strongest ties to sport. Historically, their churches were more likely to sponsor sport ministries, their colleges and seminaries to field varsity sports teams. Baptist, Methodist, and Presbyterian churches, in particular, were known to sponsor athletics programs and build and equip gymnasiums. No one surpassed the efforts of the Southern Baptists in the size and scope of their sports programs. Their endeavors were complemented by the Methodist campaign to erect playgrounds. In 1920, the General Conference of the Methodist Episcopal Church approved a plan for Methodist churches to employ a recreational director wherever conditions warranted. By the end of that decade, few religious restrictions on church recreation remained, excepting Sabbath prohibitions.[520]

Physical recreation was incorporated within the context of the religious mission. Sports were viewed as serving the church through four roles: community outreach, fellowship, Christian education, and fundraising. Large Protestant churches hired full-time recreation directors, established sports leagues with dozens of teams, and invested large sums in sports equipment and facilities. As these efforts continued to supplement traditional worship and service, many church leaders attempted to weld a stronger link by sponsoring sports events under religious auspices and by bringing athletes into their churches as missionaries to spread the word and recruit new members.[521]

Sports programs in mainstream churches did have their detractors. An assortment of critics expressed discomfort with the uses made of sport by institutional religion. One editor of a religious publication referred to the expanding phenomenon of church recreation as the "basketballization of American religion."[522] Indeed, American religion was co-opting a wide range of sports for its purposes. Even martial arts, with historical ties to Buddhism, were exploited as an instrument for proselytizing, what some pundits labeled "Karate for Christ." Other observers referred to the exploitation of sport by fundamental Protestantism as "Sportianity," or more derisively as "Jocks for Jesus." Traditionalists felt that in many cases the tail was wagging the dog.[523]

At the same time, evangelical Protestantism was infiltrating American sport at several levels. Christian athletes could be observed in locker rooms poring over passages of the Bible or convening religious services with like-minded teammates. Coaches who presented themselves as "born-again Christians," like Joe Gibbs of the NFL Washington Redskins and Dan Reeves of the Denver Broncos, promoted pre-game chapel services for their players beginning in the 1980s. Organizations like Pro Basketball Fellowship and Hockey Ministries International sponsored regular religious services for athletes. Estimates in the late 1980s were that about a fourth of professional athletes in the four major team sports participated in sport-related religious services. Some of these athletes engaged in religious testifying in much the same way as teammates endorsed commercial products. No one in American society had a better platform to deliver the message of Evangelical Christianity than the successful athlete.[524]

The Fellowship of Christian Athletes, founded in 1954, is the oldest and largest of the evangelical religious organizations for athletes, with over 20,000 members by the late 1960s, an annual budget in the millions of dollars, and its own magazine, *Christian Athlete*. Similar organizations included Campus Crusade for Christ, which begat Pro Athletes Outreach, Sports Ambassadors, and Athletes in Action (AIA). AIA came into being as a missionary arm of Campus Crusade and sponsored sports teams beginning in the 1970s. The colleges became a focal point for sports evangelism. Oral Roberts University, a fundamentalist Christian college, was founded in 1965 with sports as an integral part of its Christian witness (followed shortly by the founding of the National Christian Collegiate Athletic Association). Notably, almost all the leaders in the Christian athletic movement of the late twentieth century were Protestant fundamentalists. The thrust of the movement came from the "Bible Belt" in the American South but soon spread nationally.[525]

The modern evangelical movement can be understood as an artifact of American Protestantism, with both secular and sectarian dimensions. The relationship between religion and sport has reflected the nation's pragmatic and populist brand of religion. Over time, the common people eschewed the esoteric theology of Cotton Mather and Jonathan Edwards in favor of the popular religion of the Reverend Dwight Moody (1837–1899), an early champion of athletic Christianity. His successors included the former Olympic decathlete the Reverend Bob Richards; Reverend Billy Graham, golfing partner of presidents and sports writers; and Reverend Jerry Falwell, founder of Liberty University, an avid football fan who boasted his school would be the "Protestant Notre Dame." The major objective of evangelical Protestantism has been to spread the gospel and convert young adults through sport. In effect, organized sport has been appropriated for the promotion of an evangelical religious agenda. As such, its significance is peripheral to the general discussion of the Protestant ethic and the American sport ethos.[526]

Contemporary Americans have come to accept a minister who enters the river for a swim as well as for a baptism, whose *vade mecum* might be a basketball instead of a Bible. The general public has learned to accommodate clergy on the golf courses as well as at the altar. Churches continue to build gymnasiums adjacent to their sanctuaries; Sunday-school classes still combine Bible lessons and pocket billiards. In one way or another, American religion has made its peace with sport. In order to fully appreciate how this accord came about, it is necessary to take a brief look at the historical movement labeled "Muscular Christianity."

Muscular Christianity

> A man's body is given to him to be trained and brought into subjection, and
> then used for the protection of the weak, the advancement of all righteous
> causes and subduing of the earth which God has given to the
> children of men.
> –Thomas Hughes

Institutional religion's acceptance of sport was built, in large part, upon a belief in the necessity of action as the basis of character. For America's Protestants, physical activity has always been perceived as a corollary of moral activity. This conviction was evident in Colonial New England and stood at the basis of the muscular Christianity movement that emerged in the last half of the nineteenth century. The promoters of muscular Christianity espoused the view that physical and moral behavior were linked, that the body was an extension of moral power, and that the will displayed physical courage. The movement's emphasis upon the positive relationship between sound health and sound morals was consonant with the tenets of inner-worldly asceticism within the Protestant ethic.[527]

Muscular Christianity, like much of American sport, was an immigrant from Great Britain. The British version had combined the exemplar of the medieval Christian knight with the more physical forms of post-Reformation religious discipline as a counterforce to spiritual asceticism. In the words of British author Charles Kingsley, "There had always seemed...something impious in the neglect of personal health, strength, and beauty." Muscular Christianity offered a vigorous and manly form of asceticism that promoted the virtues of developing "a broad chest, a tireless stride, and a strong body."[528]

The model of muscular Christianity was promulgated in the popular literature of Victorian England, most notably in the works of Kingsley and his friend Thomas Hughes. In Kingsley's novel *Two Years Ago*, he vigorously endorsed an athletic brand of Christianity. Kingsley wrote, "Games teach boys virtues which no books can give them." He boasted, "I could not do half the little good I do here, if it were not for that strength...I gained in snipe shooting and hunting, and rowing, and jack-fishing." Hughes's novel *Tom Brown's Schooldays* about a young English boy at rugby school extolled the idea that masculine character was learned on the athletic fields. In the sequel, *Tom Brown at Oxford*, the protagonist advises, "Love God and walk one thousand miles in one thousand hours." Kingsley, for his part, had once walked from Cambridge to London (forty miles) in a day.[529]

However, mere strength or physical activity in themselves weren't worthy of respect. Hughes distinguished between the muscular Christian and the mere "muscle man," commenting that the only common point between the two types was "that both hold it to be a good thing to have strong and well-exercised bodies, ready to be put at the shortest notice to any work which bodies are capable and to do it well." He continues: "Here all likeness ends, for the muscle man seems to have no belief whatever as to the purposes for which his body has been given him, except some lazy idea that it is to go up and down in the world with him, belaboring men and captivating women for his benefit or pleasure."[530] The muscular Christian, in contrast, displayed a sense of duty and employed his strength for the betterment of self and society. The characteristics of muscular Christianity were manliness, morality, health, and patriotism. The idea was advanced that athletic sports like cricket and soccer contributed significantly to the development of moral character.[531] Hughes's and Kingsley's writings were instrumental in promoting these character-building team sports in British public schools.

Given the goal-directed and moralistic focus, it is not surprising that muscular Christianity was transplanted successfully on American soil. Following the American Civil War, the evangelical minister Dwight Moody (routinely flanked by the British cricketers C. T. and J. E. K. Studd) promoted this brand of athletic Christianity from the pulpit, while physical educators like Luther Gulick, Amos Alonzo Stagg, and James Naismith organized programs along these principles at YMCAs and in schools and colleges. Muscular Christianity had particular appeal to a generation who embraced social Darwinism, an ideology that (mis)applied the idea of "survival of the fittest" to human society. Those individuals who survived and prospered were seen not only as biologically fit but also morally fit.[532]

No one spoke more ardently for the "gospel of the body" than Gulick, who began his affiliation with the YMCA in 1886. He believed the health and disposition of the muscles determined one's moral predispositions, that the right type of play had a greater influence over the character of a person than any other activity, and that morals rose no higher than they did in play. Implicit in this view was the contention that some forms of play were more uplifting than others. Simply stated, the intent of these reformers was to safeguard morality by forbidding games classified as evil and by encouraging the playing of games recognized as good.[533] One YMCA worker of the era observed that the association had "wrested the gymnasium from the hands of prizefighters and professional athletes and put it into the hands of Christian gymnasts...."[534]

Gulick's transformation of the YMCA was consonant with the spirit of the times. The noted psychologist G. Stanley Hall supported the idea that the character of young people could be better achieved through physical conditioning than by intellectual training. Hall believed morality could be stamped on the nerve cells and fibers through repeated physical drill until right conduct became habitual. Washington Gladden, a prominent Congregationalist minister, added his voice to the prevailing conviction that physical recreation could shape character. Testimonials of great men like William Gladstone and Abraham Lincoln were appropriated to extol the merits of physical exercise by the adherents of muscular Christianity.[535]

As the American version of muscular Christianity evolved over the decades, it revealed less and less of the British legacy and became increasingly evangelical—essentially a campaign for bringing young men to Christ. Characteristic of this trend was the popular preacher Billy Sunday, who had spent nine years (1883–1891) playing major league baseball, mostly in Chicago. In spring 1891, he converted to evangelical Christianity and, in his words, gave up drinking, swearing, gambling, going to theaters, and playing ball on the Sabbath. After retiring from baseball, Sunday moved into work at the YMCA in Chicago. In his sermons, he contrasted what he saw as the immoral features of professional sports with the positive elements of muscular Christianity.[536]

But in truth, muscular Christianity would never supplant secular sport. As the 1933 Hoover Commission on Social Trends noted in its report, while many of the amusements once vigorously banned were by then accepted by the church, there was no evidence the church exercised control over recreation in any way compatible to the censorship it once exerted. Religion had even lost the battle over banning Sunday amusements. With Billy Sunday's death in 1935, "the vestiges of nineteenth-century muscular Christianity were put to rest." A major cultural shift would take place. In response, evangelical Protestants moved from justifying sport by appeals to religion to promoting religion by appeals to sport. The use of sport to promote religion was the focus of the movement as it was reformulated in the mid 1960s. By the decade of the 1980s, a growing number of evangelical Protestant churches and affiliated groups were employing sports celebrities and church-run programs to proselytize for converts. [537]

Institutional religion has staked out its own territory within the world of sport, but plays an increasingly marginal role in what has become a dominant cultural phenomenon in American popular culture. The spirit of contemporary sport owes more to the cultural forces of professionalism and consumer capitalism than to evangelical Protestantism. At the same time, one can still identify the transplanted virtues of secular Protestantism in the American sport ethic. At the heart of this ethic are the persistent forces of moral and rational asceticism.

8

The American Sport Ethic: I

Introduction

> The spirit, the will to win and the will to excel—these are the things that
> endure and these are the qualities that are so much more important than…the
> events that occasion them.
> –Vince Lombardi

As the Protestant ethic imparted a distinct character upon American culture, a derivative sport ethic emerged to shape the nation's games and athletic contests. This ethic pervaded sporting venues from Little League to the Super Bowl. It has inspired city recreation leagues, school athletic tournaments, and community 10K runs. Its influence is even more pronounced within the intercollegiate, national Olympic, and professional sports establishments. The values inherent in this ethic determine the moral compass of American sport, while the spirit of sport charges athletes and their mentors with a compelling need to achieve. This tandem of purpose and action has carried rationalized competitiveness to an unsurpassed level.

Public sport in America constitutes a sort of Protestant morality play, a staged struggle among ostensibly equal antagonists who confront each other under contrived circumstances in order to bestow precise and incontestable merit upon the victors. It is a scenario in which luck and chance are discounted in favor of skill, strategy, and effort—for these are the qualities that allow the competitors to attribute their victory to personal merit. In leagues and tournament play, there can be only one deserving winner though the losers may be many. The losers are equally deserving of their fate, for they have failed to do what was morally necessary to achieve victory. In this sense, they have committed a kind of sin for which their failure is proof.

The sports contest provides a test acted out in an arena where the outcome is visibly apparent to everyone in attendance. In providing a setting for this ritual of achieved success, spectator sport extends the connotations beyond the level of the participants to the larger community. A collective feeling of moral justification encompasses the audience following a victory.

When a team wins a championship, an entire city or state vicariously celebrates their elevation to the realm of the elect. In this sense, winning at sport reaffirms and extends the Calvinist conceit that the worthy are rewarded. An illustration from contemporary New England exemplifies this ethos. *Boston Globe* writer Nathan Cobb coined the term "Red Sox Nation" to characterize the long-suffering fans of the city's professional baseball team. The team's eighty-six-year hiatus from winning the World Series was framed in the context of the "Curse of the Bambino" (a reference to a former team owner's selling Babe Ruth to the archrival New York Yankees in 1919). Local journalists attributed the self-perpetuating fatalism surrounding the Red Sox to the legacy of the Puritans who settled Boston and instilled in the region's inhabitants a deep-seated determinism. It was in this historical context that Boston's victory in the 2004 World Series became more than winning a national championship; it represented a sign of moral redemption.[538]

The American sport ethic generates both centrifugal and centripetal energy. The core values are distilled in the athletic coach. This revered figure personifies the seriousness with which Americans undertake physical games and contests. Much like a film producer, the coach presents the sporting event to the public for its consumption—and more significantly, its edification. The message is cogent. Coaches emphasize hard work, sacrifice, and discipline to achieve mastery of self and events on the field of competition and beyond. The coach's role in American society has been institutionalized in community leagues, schools, and colleges. Professional coaches are the high priests of sport. The aphorisms and admonitions of acclaimed mentors like Vince Lombardi grace the walls of locker rooms, ignite pre-game pep talks, and echo from the rafters of banquet halls. These maxims resonate in church pulpits and political forums. Athletic coaches are the heralds of the American sport ethic.

Scholars have sought out the values that prevail in American sport. Sociologist Harry Edwards conceptualized an American sports creed that incorporates character development, discipline, individual achievement through competition, physical fitness, mental fitness, religiosity, nationalism, high aspirations, unbridled competitiveness, and an emphasis upon winning. Empirical studies have confirmed that outstanding athletes share a set of traits that imply a common ethic. Among these are the need for achievement, realistic goals, high organization, order, respect for authority, psychological endurance, and self-control.[539]

The concept of an American sport ethic is based on the supposition that sport incorporates values and behaviors characteristic of the larger society. There seems little doubt that this occurs. Anyone equally familiar with the values inherent in the nation's sports and in the Protestant ethic cannot fail to notice the overlap and link between them. Both systems of values enforce and maintain a strict code of behavior reinforced by accepted rituals; both project a lucid belief system that is adopted and internalized by participants; both exert a cohesive social control function; and both present a system of meaning.[540] Consistent with perspective, I have extrapolated from the Protestant ethic, as conceptualized in chapter 4, a related set of constructs that represent an American sport ethic. The seven major elements are: (1) moral asceticism, (2) rationalization, (3) goal-directed behavior, (4) the work ethic, (5) individualism, (6) competitiveness, and (7) achieved status.

Components of the sport ethic such as rationalization and individualism have direct corollaries in the Protestant ethic. Other values like competitiveness are derivative. The Protestant time ethic has no direct corollary on the above list but clearly shapes attitudes and behaviors within the world of sport. Its particular influence is evident in the pace of games and contests, their internal time constraints, and the consciousness of coaches and athletes.

The present chapter and the next offer an examination of the components of the American sport ethic. We begin with moral asceticism followed by a discussion of the rationalization of sport.

Moral Asceticism

> Athletics supplies a splendid motive against all errors and
> vices that weaken or corrupt the body.
> –G. Stanley Hall

Mike "King" Kelly of the Chicago White Stockings once inquired of his manager Al Spalding, "What are you running here, a Sunday school or a baseball club?" The ballplayer's rhetorical question expressed his objection to the intrusive discipline imposed upon the team. Kelly, an outstanding player in the decade of the 1880s, was an equally outstanding carouser and imbiber off the field, and generally considered to be a bad influence on his teammates. At one point, Spalding hired Billy Pinkerton's detectives to monitor the extracurricular activities of the Chicago team. The ballplayers were "tailed" up and down Clark Street and around the Tenderloin district's saloons by Pinkerton's men. Kelly's teammate Billy Sunday—destined to become a celebrated preacher—was given a "clean bill of health," but the "King" was repeatedly reprimanded for his off-field conduct to the point that his reign was put in jeopardy.[541]

The Chicago manager's zeal for enforcing team rules was characteristic of the moral tone that pervaded the Victorian Era. The enterprising Spalding would publish a popular baseball guide that promoted "playing for the side," by which he meant athletes were to avoid indulging in the standard vices. Borrowing a theme from the Women's Christian Temperance Union, Spalding required every member of his team to sign a pledge of total abstinence for the duration of the baseball season, with stiff fines imposed on those who broke the pledge. This was at a time when the sport attracted a rather unrefined cast of characters. Spalding's code met with opposition not only among players but with several of his fellow managers.[542]

A battle over alcohol had embroiled the owners of professional baseball clubs from early on. Cincinnati's team had been struggling financially in the late 1870s, so the owners (aligned with a brewery) decided to sell beer on the club grounds as a way to increase revenue in this city with a large German-American population. The decision was met with disapproval in the National League offices, and when the club refused to cease selling beer, it was dropped by the league in 1880. Throughout that decade, the owners, in keeping with the morals of the day, forbade Sunday games as well as liquor in ballparks. They touted baseball as a gentleman's game. Then the rival American Association appeared on the scene, and baseball would never be the same. The upstart association challenged the senior league's hold on the national pastime by cutting admission in half, playing games on Sundays, and selling liquor in its ballparks. It was quickly dubbed the "Beer and Whisky League." Here was a classic confrontation between Calvinist moralism and consumer capitalism. The business interests of the brewers gained the upper hand until 1920, when the Volstead act took effect. The next dozen years were "dry." While Prohibition (ending in 1933) imposed official abstinence on the ballparks, it hardly drove alcohol out of baseball. Fans simply brought their own flasks of moonshine to the stadiums and waited for repeal.[543]

Despite the return of alcohol to ballparks, America's moral crusaders persisted in their efforts to manage sport "like a Sunday School" down to the playground level. The nation's youth were instilled with a sportsman's code that instructed the morally upright athlete to refrain from smoking, drinking, gambling, ungentlemanly conduct, and for the most part, contact with the opposite sex. This ethic was reflected in children's books dating from the 1880s in which the sports heroes were always self-disciplined, responsible, hardworking boys who were by implication the most moral among their peers. The training rules for young athletes encompassed a wide variety of behavioral constraints applying both on and off the fields of play. This moralistic climate carried through to the contemporary era. Today's youth sports programs still promulgate codes of conduct. Examples are evident in high-school handbooks.[544]

Concerns about the personal behavior of athletes have not been limited to amateur sport. This moral legacy survives in the professional ranks. Contemporary coaches and managers routinely establish rules for personal conduct, enforcing curfews and policing behaviors of the adult athletes who play for them. When Chuck Knox coached the NFL Seattle Seahawks in the 1980s, he would require his players (many of them married) to check into a hotel by eight o'clock the night before a game, home and away. The coaching staff scheduled team meetings leading up to a meal together before enforced bedtime at eleven. The players' rooms were monitored by an assistant coach or trainer along with a security officer.[545] Knox's tactics were not unusual. Bed checks for ballplayers were a standard practice at NFL training camps dating from the 1920s.[546]

Athletes, however, have continued to pursue their own agenda. Echoing King Kelly's experience, Mickey Mantle and his teammates on the 1950s-era New York Yankees found themselves tailed by private detectives at the behest of a ball club concerned about their players' "painting the town." However, a mixed message about personal behavior emanated from management. The surveillance of carousing ballplayers occurred at a time when Ballantine Beer was one on the team's major sponsors. The Yankees, like most teams, were inclined to enforce the rules with run-of-the mill ballplayers but had a tendency to "look the other way" when one of their stars misbehaved. Such was their response to Mantle showing up at games "hung over" after a night out on the town.[547] This charade can be interpreted as a replay of the Puritan penchant to set high standards and expect most individuals to miss the mark.

The ascetic discipline foisted upon American athletes was derivative of, and yet distinct from, the athletic asceticism of the ancient Greeks.[548] The Roman poet Juvenal's phrase, "Mens sana in corpore sano"—translated as "A sound mind in a sound body"—was a guiding principle of Victorian athleticism, although it would be more consistent with Protestant moralism to restate the dictum as, "A sound *will* in a sound body." The essence of this ethic was to promote a methodical manipulation of the body as a way to obtain subjugation to the will. The ascetic ethic not only set the standards for personal behavior but demarcated the import of athleticism. The pursuit of a perfected body became the badge of a righteous soul. A distorted version of this legacy can be observed among participants in the contemporary sport of bodybuilding. Bodybuilders do not enjoy their bodies so much as exploit them to obtain a kind of perfection. In this sense, bodybuilding constitutes an ascetic discipline but with a marked element of narcissism. The mirror becomes as indispensable as the barbells.[549]

Historically, sports programs that promulgated moral discipline and self-control complemented the traditional agents of discipline like the family and church. The overriding objective was control: control of the body, control of the will, and control of the strength of the personality. American athletes were encouraged to practice physical training to get their physical desires in check. Training for sport was a way to discipline the inner-self, to develop self-command, to resist influences that impaired the will and the power to act.[550] Participants were expected to demonstrate self-control during competition as well as in their private lives. Athletes or coaches who lost control could be cited for what was labeled "unsportsmanlike conduct." Although a strict standard of controlled behavior might seem foreign to the nature of competitive sport with all the passion it engenders, the display of passion or the lack of restraint remained a sign of moral weakness.

Indeed, virtually every facet of organized sport suggests control. The athlete's sense of self-discipline has been reinforced by various external controls. Coaches routinely direct athletes to restrain their emotions, not to swear, curse, or brawl. More broadly, foolish or idle talk is to be avoided during competition—notwithstanding "trash talk," whose intent is to cause one's opponent to lose control. Practice sessions are strictly monitored, with athletes admonished to stay on task and quit "playing around." American coaches actively manage contests from the sidelines by directing strategy, calling plays, reproving players, and interacting with officials. In the 1960s, NFL linemen were still calling blocking schemes and informing the coaches what worked. Team captains made the decisions and directed the flow of the game. By the early 1970s, play-calling had shifted to the coaches.[551] Another manifestation of control was the curtailing of on-field and post-game celebrations by athletes during the season. The momentary elation following success is quickly eclipsed by a "back-to-work, prepare-for-the next-game" focus. Football conferences have restricted end-zone celebrations by players following a touchdown. Penalties can be meted out for "excessive celebration."

The athletic coach is expected to set an example of control, to be a paragon of self-discipline. John Wooden, long-time basketball coach at UCLA, was a classic illustration of this persona. Today the standard still applies even if the practice is left wanting. When contests get out of control, much of the blame is placed on coaches. The American coach is expected to keep his emotions in check and is subject to censure when he fails to do so. Baseball umpires eject managers from the game when they lose their composure (notwithstanding contrived tantrums). The volatile college basketball coach Bobby Knight was widely criticized for repeated episodes during which he lost his temper. Coach Knight violated the moral standard that holds self-control as the foundation of character even while expecting his players to adhere strictly to it.[552]

The emphasis on control within athletic asceticism is buttressed by the meanings given to pain and pleasure. The Puritans distrusted physical pleasure and held under suspicion any forms of sport and recreation that provided a means for enjoyment, spontaneous expression of undisciplined impulses, or awakened human instincts. Henry Atkinson, in his early twentieth-century religious tract, admonished that "[if] we can take our recreations soberly and without getting any pleasure out of them, they are good; but amusements prompted by any other motive bear ill fruit."[553] As for pain, the Puritans believed its endurance denoted a test of moral fiber. The idea developed that competing in sports should hurt somewhat—or at least be uncomfortable.[554] The athletic subculture is one in which playing with pain and injury is the norm, something to be admired. Indeed, managers, coaches, trainers, and peers coerce athletes to compete despite painful injuries. Often, coercion is not necessary. Pain becomes part of an athlete's identity. Someone once asked cyclist Lance Armstrong what pleasure he took in riding for so long. His response: "Pleasure?... I don't understand the question. I didn't do it for pleasure. I did it for pain." He characterized competitive cycling as "a contest in purposeless suffering."[555]

Competing against the elements as in cycling, mountain climbing, cross-country skiing—or against a superior adversary—constitutes an endeavor that, in its extreme incarnations, compares with the discipline of suffering practiced by early religious ascetics. Football games are scheduled in settings like Green Bay, Wisconsin, or Buffalo, New York, in the middle of winter under conditions of subzero cold or during snow storms. The archetypical event was the 1967 NFL championship game, dubbed the "Ice Bowl," where the temperature at game time was -13° Fahrenheit with a wind chill factor estimated at -48°. When a referee attempted to blow his whistle to start play, it froze to his lips. Dallas Cowboys quarterback Don Meredith came down with pneumonia after the game and had to be hospitalized. No one seriously considered canceling the contest because of the weather; playing football under arctic conditions builds moral fiber.[556]

Likewise, athletic contests are scheduled where temperatures on the fields and courts reach triple digits. Rudyard Kipling's line stating, "Only mad dogs and Englishmen go out in the midday sun," was a commentary on British soldiers' laboring in the tropical sun of India, often bareheaded. This verse could be applied just as fittingly to "mad-dog" Americans' competing in tennis, marathons, or football in extreme heat. Football players routinely suffer heat exhaustion during grueling two-hour practice sessions in the August sun. Until recently, coaches were known to deny their athletes water, assuming they were making them tough. Only after a number of deaths from heat stroke was this regimen curtailed. However, team practices in extreme temperatures and resulting fatalities persist. Minnesota Viking offensive tackle Korey Stringer died in 2001 from heat stroke during a practice session when the heat index approached 110°.[557]

The obligation to endure extreme conditions is tied to the practice of physical denial that lies at the core of asceticism. Adherence to a puritanical code of self-denial becomes part of the athlete's identity. Wrestlers, boxers, and jockeys have been known to starve themselves prior to competition in order to make their weight class. Pool players deprive themselves of sleep in the midst of tournaments that run for days on end.[558] Competitive running has an obvious appeal to the ascetic athlete. A study at the University of Arizona concluded that serious runners display symptoms similar to those suffering from the eating disorder anorexia nervosa. Runners control their diets as rigidly as they adhere to an exercise regimen. The more dedicated among them are known to persist at their activity through the ordeal of sore muscles, stress fractures, and protests from neglected families.[559] Journalist Charles Krauthammer commented on what he labeled "the self-inflicted ordeal" of sport, noting that for the more competitive runners, a marathon has become the choice of weekend recreation.[560] Marathoners have been known to run up to 200 miles a week in training. A club in New York staged a six-day run, while a California city held its annual Multi-Day Classic Run, during which a fifty-two-year-old man ran 213 miles and a thirty-nine-year-old woman ran 141 miles.

Even drug use among athletes can be tied to asceticism. Most of the drugs utilized by athletes cannot be attributed to hedonistic impulses. Abuse of recreational drugs has been secondary to use of performance-enhancing drugs or palliatives: anabolic steroids, amphetamines, and painkillers. Reliance upon these chemicals can be explained as a reaction to the demands that athletes strive to perform amidst pain and injuries, and in spite of deteriorating bodies. The practice of using drugs to enhance performance has been labeled "positive deviance"; in other words, the athlete deviates from the societal norms governing the use of drugs to achieve optimal performance within the subculture of sport.[561]

At the same time, dedicated athletes deny themselves sex, alcohol, tobacco, food, sleep, physical comforts, and other pleasures. NFL linebacker Bill Romanowski recalls his mindset as a football player at Boston College: "Nothing—and I mean nothing—was going to stop me. There wasn't a party that was going to keep me from being the best I could be. Not even a girlfriend.... [I]f my teammates would head out for pizza and beer, I'd have pizza and milk. When they headed to parties after the game, I stayed behind to take care of my body...."[562] Romanowski's performance ethic illustrates that Calvinist asceticism infiltrates sport at Catholic (notably Jesuit) institutions as well.

The puritanical fear of carnality remains strong in American sport. Coaches have been resolute in discouraging sexual activity among their athletes. Linebacker Dave Meggyesy recalls that the St. Louis Cardinals coaching staff purposely kept players from going home to their wives the night before home games, having bought into the belief that sexual intercourse would sap the players' energy and keep them from playing well.[563] Romanowski recounts that during team meetings before an NFL game, San Francisco Forty-Niner coach Bill Walsh would turn to assistant coach Tommy Hart and inquire, "Green light or red light?" Green meant that players could have sex during the days before the game, red that they could not.[564] The myth about sex and physical performance has been deeply ingrained in the psyches of athletes both married and single. A few rogues like New York Jets quarterback Joe Namath did not put much of a dent in this perception. Significantly, athletes like Namath who admit to sexual promiscuity tend to frame sex encounters as an achievement; they are, in effect, "sexual athletes." Dave Meggyesy observed of his teammates' accounts of sexual activity, "[T]hey worry a lot about 'staying power' and 'performance.'"[565]

Abstinence provides the more ascetic athlete with a sense of moral rectitude. The belief ensues that denying oneself carnal pleasure will be rewarded with success in the arena, and vice versa. More than a few young sportsmen have obsessed about surrendering to sexual desires and the effect upon performance. Minor league pitcher Pat Jordan recalls a resolution he made during a road trip when he was having problems on the mound. He became convinced the higher powers were punishing him for his indiscretions with a girlfriend. So he decided to abstain from sex. He writes in his memoir, "My celibacy…would be rewarded with a string of gems (no hitters, shutouts, etc.) that would lift me out of the Midwest League and deposit me in the majors."[566]

Conversely, sport has been touted as a remedy for carnal lust. Like a cold shower, physical training is supposed to dampen the sex drive. This idea became widely popular in the late nineteenth century. The American social reformer Jane Addams, who was troubled by the base instincts of some of her inner-city clients, expressed her hope that recreation could "get the best of vice."[567] Likewise, the YMCA's Social Service Committee promulgated the idea that sport was a means of stifling lust. Addams's contemporary, the Reverend John Todd, advocated body exercise as a remedy for the "secret vice" of masturbation. The Victorians were particularly uncomfortable with female sexuality. Dr. Augustus Kingsley Gardner, a pioneer of gynecology and purveyor of sexual guidance literature, argued that sports were valuable in putting a damper on women's sexual activity by sublimating their sex drive. Organized sports would help women to focus on duty rather than gratification.[568]

The theme of moral redemption via sport and recreation runs through American history and literature, from James Fenimore Cooper's depiction of hunting and fishing as "correct conduct" to Ernest Hemingway's fictional characters who pursue outdoor sports as joyless male games. For Hemingway, who was a good athlete in his school days and an avid sportsman throughout his life, sport was an activity to be carried out with moral correctness.[569] The preoccupation with morality is evident in Bernard Malamud's classic baseball novel *The Natural*, whose plot explores the issues of bribery and sexual indiscretion. The book's fictional reporter, Max Mercy, is the prototype of the modern investigative reporter who snoops into celebrity athletes' lives for evidence of moral turpitude.[570] Indeed, the sports sections of today's newspapers are as much a record of athletes' private peccadilloes as a chronicle of their feats in the public arena.

The moral reprobates share the sports scene with evangelists and crusaders. American moralism embraces the notion that participating in sports can be justified if it changes the world for the better. Writer and critic Walter Kerr remarked on the element of "do-goodism" evident in the nation's sports and recreation. He commented that the typical American can't go bowling or play golf without the comforting feeling that he is contributing to some charity or community improvement.[571] Americans have increasingly tied sporting events and physical exercise to charitable causes. Typical of these efforts was the Walk for Mankind. Beginning in the 1970s, this event staged a multi-mile "walkathon" in several cities as a fundraising arm of Project Concern International, a charity that assisted needy children. Several sports, each with its own pet charity, have built on this model. Numerous charity golf events are held annually in the United States, raising several billion dollars collectively, according to the National Golf Foundation. Community-based charities in league with the American Cancer Society, United Way, and Special Olympics host tournaments to raise money. The American mindset has been that sport and fitness activities can be justified by appropriating them for a good cause. To walk, swim, or golf for charity provides an imprimatur of moral worth.

Replete with moral overtones and prophylactic pretensions, sport becomes less a channel for recreation than a moral obligation. This mindset is explored in George Santayana's novel *The Last Puritan*. Of the titular Oliver Arden, the author writes, "All his lessons and sports seemed to be taken as duties, and executed unswervingly, as if to get rid of them as quickly and thoroughly as possible." The narrator elaborates, "At Harvard, Oliver's fellow students told him that he might make the crew and that in that case it was his duty to try for it. When the football season was over, Oliver sighed in relief, 'No more football for me this year... No more football ever.' He felt a great peace. One duty at least was finished and done for."[572]

The idea of sport as duty is built into the socialization process of American youth. Sport sociologist Gary Fine concluded that Little League baseball players were taught to relate to their sport as a form of moral commitment. Consistent with the didactic pretensions of moralism, commitment is tied to character development. The organizers of youth sport believe the child who plays by the rules will not, as an adult, cheat in business or cheat in his marriage, and that obedience to the rules of games encourages loyalty to the laws of the state.[573] Thus does organized youth sport appear obligatory for families who wish to rear morally upright children.

Sport must be pursued not only to good purpose and free of vices, but exempt from spontaneous enjoyment and uncontrolled movement that might lead its participants to vice. Sport is allowed to be unpleasant, even painful, but not pleasurable. Worthy sports are characterized by discipline, subjugation of the body, and control of the emotions. The similarities between religious asceticism and athletic asceticism have been evident to American scholars. Ralph Barton Perry compared the lives of modern Olympic athletes to those of Puritan "moral athletes" (his label) like Cotton Mather and Jonathan Edwards. Perry suggested that just as Mather and Edwards sought to strengthen their will with a set of moral "daily dozens," so have modern athletes disciplined themselves through rigorous physical calisthenics.[574]

Arguably, many contemporary observers of the sports scene would find it difficult to discern a general climate of moral asceticism. At first blush, it is the egoism, hedonism, and mercenary inclinations of sports figures that appear most salient. Athletes as a group receive a great deal of notoriety in the popular media for their personal indulgences. But the very fact that famous athletes are held to a higher standard of behavior than other young adults speaks to the abiding moralism in contemporary American society. They are constantly admonished to be good role models. The film hero of American sports fans is Rocky Balboa, not the dilettantes of *Caddyshack*. Real-world sports heroes like Lance Armstrong do not suggest casual sportsmen, let alone playboys, (although, Lance Armstrong has acquired a reputation as something of a playboy in recent years) but men (and women) with a "religious" dedication to their sports.

Thus, American sport continues to provide a sounding board for the traditional values inherent in Protestant asceticism. The moralism that originally argued against casual sport was inverted to promote a brand of disciplined athletics directed toward a higher purpose. In the process, sport evolved into an activity characterized by its seriousness and intensity. The spontaneous enjoyment inherent in the play impulse has been displaced by highly controlled forms of physical training and relentless competition. Contemporary athletes who grace the sports arenas and training camps echo the zeal of the Puritan "moral athlete." In pursuing this ascetic ethic, sport has incorporated a pragmatic, utilitarian brand of rationalism.

The Rationalization of Sport

> The sports hero is a hero of efficiency.
> –Lewis Mumford

In fall 1873, students from Yale and Princeton colleges met to play their first football game in what was to become an enduring rivalry. The players on the two teams had no uniforms and virtually no equipment. The game was played under ad hoc rules agreed upon a month earlier. As it turned out, no one had remembered to bring a football, and the game was delayed an hour and a half until one could be found. This rather casual approach reflected the nature of amateur sport at the time.[575]

America's colleges didn't conduct their athletic contests in such a haphazard manner for long. As sport was institutionalized within mainstream culture, its systematic rationalization became increasingly apparent. In contrast to the initial Yale-Princeton game, intercollegiate contests in the following decades were systematically scheduled a season in advance with written guarantees. Players were outfitted in standard uniforms, technically sophisticated equipment was provided, and impressive facilities were erected for the staging of athletic events. Professional coaches, equipment managers, and trainers were employed by the schools. Rules were codified by governing bodies, ratified by the contestants, and enforced by officials. Virtually every aspect of sport was rationalized, both on and off the field. School sports, like professional sports, incorporated expert management techniques, systematic recruiting and scouting systems, uses of technology to analyze performance, sophisticated playbooks, enforcement of discipline, scientific conditioning and training programs, and divisions of competition culminating in championship tournaments.[576]

Rationalization was to become a significant cultural force in American sport. It engendered a constellation of values and practices that transformed the fundamental nature of athletic competition. Sport became progressively instrumental, utilitarian, pragmatic, and reliant upon scientific methodology. The organizers of sport exploited expertise and technology, incorporated quantification and measurement, and implemented standardization and regimentation. Sports organizations were professionalized and bureaucratized. Field managers and coaches sought ways to control game play and reduce the contingencies of competition. Even the practice of wagering on sports became increasingly rationalized; intricate systems were applied to betting on horses, while professional bookmakers developed sophisticated formulas for determining odds and point spreads. The following discussion explores the ways in which the nation's sports became increasingly rationalized.

By the late nineteenth century, America was witnessing what cultural studies professor William Morgan termed the "ubiquitous rationalization" of social institutions including work, the family, politics, and leisure. The rise of "scientism" bolstered the application of rational methodology and applied technology to a wide range of human activities.[577] Although the neologism "sport science" did not gain currency until the twentieth century, scientific methods were being applied to sport before the turn of the century. One finds examples in the popular literature. In 1884, *St. Nicholas*, a children's magazine, featured a story titled, "How Science Won the Game." It told of how a boy pitcher mastered the curve ball to defeat the opposing batters. In essence, the story was about applying technological knowledge to the art of throwing a baseball.[578]

A boyhood friend of Frederick Taylor commented on how the young prodigy insisted the games he played with his friends be subjected to exact formulas in order to improve efficiency. The playmate described Taylor's behavior thus: "In a game of croquet he would carefully work out the angles of the various strokes, the force of impact, and the advantages, and disadvantages of the understroke, overstroke, and so on, before he started to play."[579] Taylor's childhood preoccupation with rational methodology carried over into his adult recreations. In cross-country walks, he constantly experimented with his legs in an endeavor to discover the step that would cover the greatest distance with the least expenditure of energy. At age forty, Taylor took up golf. Not surprisingly, the sport was no mere pastime but yet another activity in which to carry out his invariable experimenting. He invented a two-hand putter and tinkered with the weight and length of clubs to get the right balance. He developed a driver that was ten inches longer and with a much thinner lower shaft than the normal one. Taylor applied the principles of motion study to his swing and hit upon an effectively deviant style, to which he applied the epithet "watch spring."[580]

This inclination to analyze and improve human performance was equally apparent in an unordained Presbyterian minister who applied his rational bent to solve an assigned problem for a class at Springfield College.

The problem was how to keep the college's football players in shape during the cold New England winters. The student, James Naismith, examined the problem, followed a sequence of logical steps, and developed the game of basketball as the solution. He settled on the placement of a narrow horizontal goal (a peach basket) above the heads of the players to ensure the ball had to be thrown in a soft arc, thus avoiding potential injuries that might be caused by a ball thrown with force. He then proceeded to contrive the other elements of the game, such as the requirement for players to dribble the ball when moving, by applying the same rational criteria.[581]

This attraction to reasoned methodology in tandem with the need to achieve would contribute significantly to the character of American sport. Achievement required rationalized benchmarks against which to measure performance. The industrial model provided criteria and standards that were readily appropriated by sport. By their very nature, athletic feats proved to be well adapted to objective measures as they consisted of highly visible actions that were easily assessed. Sport accommodated additional principles and methods of industrialized labor: specialization, calculation, planning, efficiency, self-discipline, and subordination to experts. Training for sport would evolve into a process that was as rationalized as the production process in the factories. For an achievement-oriented society that prided itself on productive work and disdained futility of effort, it was predictable that the casual play of amateur athletes would give way to the rationalized techniques of the professional manager.[582]

The rationalization of sport led to a new class of experts focused on human movement. The emerging profession of physical educators sought to shape sport to the ends of health and fitness. Typical of this group was Dudley A. Sargent, a nineteenth-century educator who was less interested in winning at sport than improving bodies. To this end, Sargent developed a highly rationalized system of corrective gymnastics. Concurrently, specialists in the new science of anthropometry were carrying out measurements of the structure and functions of the human body. Studies of "animal mechanism" included Eadweard Muybridge's famous photographs of the structure and dynamics of human movement in work and sport in the 1880s. While physical educators encouraged well-rounded exercises for human development, the sports coaches set more expedient goals. They applied the new scientific knowledge to promote physiological economy in the training of athletes. Walter Camp, the influential Yale University football coach (later, at Stanford), was representative of this pragmatic bias in expressing his preference for physical detail over theory.[583]

Similarly, the coach began to play a larger role in American sport. The number and variety of coaches multiplied as the profession became increasingly specialized. Their professional status implied expertise, and the use of scientific knowledge gave these "sports experts" a certain legitimacy. The popular belief spread that a knowledgeable coach provided the difference between victory and defeat through the application of specialized knowledge and rational methodology. The outcome of sports contests was attributed to the coach's efforts as much as to that of the players. Coaches responded to the unrelenting pressure to win by becoming highly expedient. These new rationalists downplayed the random "bounce of the ball" or other indeterminate factors outside the command of human will. The image of the coach in control of well-trained athletes and able to orchestrate game strategies fulfilled the Calvinist expectation that humans in charge determined their fate by right efforts.[584]

Salaried coaches became a fixture not only in professional sports but in colleges by the close of the nineteenth century. Cornell University was one of the first to hire an athletic coach when Charles E. Courtney was retained to coach crew, a sport that became popular in the 1860s. Courtney had studied the sport systematically. He applied scientific methods to teaching his students how to row and rig the shell more efficiently. He instituted a business-like air that promoted strict discipline among his athletes. Courtney exemplified the new breed of coaches in applying rational methodology. Other colleges followed Cornell's lead by hiring their own coaches in a variety of sports. The practice that began in the Eastern colleges spread westward. Amos Alonzo Stagg, hired by the University of Chicago in 1892, was responsible for many of the innovations of modern college coaching. Following suit, the University of Michigan phased out its "graduate" coaching system in 1906, replacing amateur alumni coaches with salaried ones. A few schools hired former professional athletes as coaches. By the early twentieth century, most of the colleges with athletics programs were employing salaried coaches.[585]

These experts were obliged to implement the systematic forms of training viewed as necessary for success in athletic competition. The developing body of coaching knowledge was passed down from teacher to pupil. The more successful coaches and managers transferred their knowledge into print. Earlier, Albert Spalding had pioneered scientific coaching techniques in baseball and published booklets of ready-made instructions for would-be coaches and athletes. Fielding Yost, the coach at University of Michigan, published a book on football in 1905. Other coaches and athletes followed suit. In 1912, major league baseball's Christy Mathewson published his own instructional book, *Pitching in a Pinch* (with the assistance of *New York Herald* writer John N. Wheeler).[586]

The application of rationalized training techniques challenged the traditional concept of natural athletic ability. Coaches and physical trainers were persuaded that athletic performance depended less upon intrinsic talent than what had been assumed. Success in highly skill-oriented sports like golf and tennis was attributed increasingly to training methods and proper techniques. As a consequence, the dazzling feats by naturally endowed athletes lost some of its appeal in favor of predictable, methodical, standardized play. The greater reliance upon training and proper execution was bolstered by the use of statistical analysis, as this developing mathematical science found another practical application.[587] The emerging mindset was testament to the general body of knowledge forming around the applied science of human performance.

Clearly, rational methodology was changing the approach to athletic training. Previously, the athlete was responsible to a great extent for planning and carrying out his or her training program—that is, when any pre-training took place at all. The impression is that surprisingly little training (by today's standards) preceded early athletic competition. Notably, at the first modern Olympic games in 1896, the athlete who won the discus throw had never thrown, or even held, a discus before. He simply picked it up and threw it farther than anyone else! But this laissez-faire approach to preparing for competition was eclipsed by a system of intensive, methodical training. Subsequent discus throwers, like most other athletes, would practice systematically for months prior to competing in championship events.[588]

Both the quantity and quality of training was revolutionized. Early on, training had been directed almost exclusively to practicing the event itself, the so-called "whole method." Rationalization led to the increased use of the "part-whole" method. Applied to an event like discus-throwing, this method incorporated drills on footwork and practicing the release separately, as well as prescribing a weight-training regimen to build strength in the appropriate muscles. Likewise, swimmers would take laps with kickboards, and golfers practiced for hours on their backswings. Scientific data were collected and analyzed to determine what particular methods were most effective.

Coaches were interested in the balance between performance skills and physical fitness that could be attained through the new training. "Conditioning" became a common term in athletic circles by the 1890s, and conditioning programs for athletes were routine by the early twentieth century. Conditioning equipment including weights and mechanical devices became common. Football tackling and blocking dummies had been introduced in the late 1880s, primitive blocking sleds by 1905. Rowing machines appeared soon after. The main virtue of these devices was their potential for reducing the amount of time needed to train athletes and gain optimal efficiency. In professional baseball, the methodical Methodist Wesley Branch Rickey was largely responsible for creating a rational system of training and conditioning for players. While serving as the general manager of the St. Louis Cardinals in the 1930s, he implemented a regime that included calisthenics and skill drills. Later, with the Brooklyn Dodgers he would encourage use of the batting cage and pitching machines. Rickey also was responsible for baseball's first permanent spring training facility.[589]

Peter D. Haughton reputedly was the first coach to apply the principles of the assembly line to the game of football. Beginning his career at Harvard University in 1908, he developed a mechanistic system of training that left almost nothing to chance. Haughton was a drillmaster who required his players to concentrate on selected plays until they executed them perfectly. At a time when chalkboard talks and playbooks were still a novelty, he required his athletes to learn the assignments of every other player on the team.[590] Training and competition were increasingly rationalized and managed. In team sports like American football, the need to coordinate the movements of a number of athletes led to the "scientific management" of competition. Purposeful planning of strategies and execution transformed the type of loose team play that had typified early kicking games into a kind of tactical operation based upon specialized skills and division of labor.[591] Naismith had envisioned basketball as a game to be played, not coached, but this view was soon discarded.

As the influence of coaches increased and sports became more specialized, additional time was devoted to training. College coaches complained of needing more practice time, and training programs expanded to include off-season practice sessions. Serious athletes now trained for several hours a day and, eventually, throughout much of the year to prepare for competition. The greater time put into training had a clear rationale. Training sessions proved more adaptive to rational control than the actual competitive events for which the training was geared (at a time when limited sideline coaching was allowed). Consequently, the time devoted to training continued to expand.[592]

The attention given to pre-contest preparation precipitated the arrival of another expert on the scene, the athletic trainer. The terms "trainer," "training," and "training table" (the latter an innovation by Carlisle College coach Glenn "Pop" Warner) had all appeared in sport argot by the early twentieth century. Increasingly, colleges fielding teams in the major sports put athletic trainers on the payroll. It became the norm for athletes to submit to the requisite taping and other pre-contest prophylactics trainers offered. Trainers also instructed players on how to perform efficiently and to avoid injuries, while they invoked the latest scientific procedures to treating injuries for accelerated recovery. By the late 1920s, the ministrations of athletic trainers were being supplemented by team physicians who could administer drugs and carry out other medical procedures.[593] In the 1950s, sports medicine would develop into a recognized medical specialty with its own association, conferences, and journals.

The success of rationalized coaching did not completely eclipse the belief in natural athletic ability. Despite all the efforts put into the training of athletes, the more astute coaches harbored few illusions about the limits of instruction and drills upon the outcome of contests. They soon realized they couldn't "make a silk purse out of a sow's ear." The solution to this predicament was to apply a similarly rational methodology to the selection of athletes. Coaches proceeded systematically to seek out talented recruits. The recruiting of college athletes dates to the early twentieth century. In 1901, Fielding Yost brought Willie Heston with him to the University of Michigan from the West Coast, an event that did not go unnoticed by other colleges. Within a relatively short period of time, outstanding athletes routinely were foregoing attendance at the local liberal arts college or state university in favor of playing for a distant institution that recruited them through inducements, both legal and illegal.[594]

As the practice of recruiting athletes became widespread in America's colleges, the process was increasingly systematized and rationalized. Time set aside for the "scouting" of outstanding prep-school athletes was built into coaches' schedules. Coaches developed information networks among alumni and cultivated contacts with "feeder" schools that could supply promising athletes. Scouting manuals with criteria and rating systems were developed to aid coaches who sought talented athletes. To make the selection process more reliable, sport psychologists and physiologists developed aptitude tests that would predict success in a particular sport when administered to athletes. Scouts and coaches routinely subjected potential recruits to performance tests before signing them to athletic grants. Football players were timed in the forty-yard dash, and basketball players were measured on their vertical leaping ability. From high-school programs through the professional level, rationalized recruiting efforts became a key element in successful sports programs.[595]

Scientific analysis utilized by professional teams to identify superior ballplayers can be traced to the late 1930s, when Chicago Cubs owner Philip Wrigley hired C. R. Griffin with the Bureau of Institutional Research to measure his ballplayers' physical characteristics and reflexes so he could better assess prospects. For the most part, the players refused to cooperate with Wrigley's experts, and the results were a disappointment. However, the practice would be revived. In the 1960s, Clint Murchison, the owner of the Dallas Cowboys, hired Services Bureau Corporation, a subsidiary of IBM, to devise a computer program that would put player scouting on scientific principles. The experts narrowed football players' characteristics to eight essentials and devised a set of "position-specific" skills, constructed on a nine-point scale. The NFL Rams and 49ers joined with the Cowboys in employing this service for the 1963 season. The corporation rated every player in the 1964 college draft, fed it into their computers, and selected their clients' draft picks for them. By 1966, five other NFL teams had employed their own computer scouting combine.[596]

Economic theory augmented the science of human performance in the endeavor to identify athletic talent. Billy Beane, who took over as general manager of the Oakland Athletics in the late 1990s, appropriated principles borrowed from stock market investors that applied performance statistics to evaluating baseball players with the intent of finding "undervalued players." The theory, which reflects the rational methodology and cost-effective strategies of investment capitalism, is based upon innovative formulas for assessing the effectiveness of batting, pitching, and fielding. Beane had notable success during his tenure at Oakland in getting his ball club into the playoffs by applying these formulas.[597]

Rationalization led inevitably to standardization. Not only were training and coaching techniques standardized, but officials attempted to bring a degree of uniformity to the playing of games. The establishment of eligibility rules for participants was accompanied by efforts to standardize rules for competition, equipment, and team uniforms. Walter Camp was a dominant force behind early efforts to codify rules in collegiate sports at the turn of the twentieth century. He headed several important committees with this goal in mind. These early efforts culminated in unified codes and rules. Rules committees specific to each sport controlled the competition. The National Collegiate Athletic Association, the most prominent body governing intercollegiate sports, published a comprehensive rules manual. State high-school athletic associations developed their own policies and rules to govern sports in secondary schools. The National Federation of State High School [Athletic] Associations was founded in the 1920s as an umbrella organization with the goal of establishing standardized policies across states. Likewise, the Amateur Athletic Union standardized and regulated competition in track and field and other amateur sports.[598]

Manufacturers of sports equipment contributed to standardization in large part for business reasons. A. G. Spalding had promoted the use of standard sporting goods, which he then manufactured through highly rationalized production methods. As Spalding was promoting regulation equipment stamped with his company's trade name, he and other sporting goods manufacturers insinuated themselves into the deliberations of sports rules committees. As a result of these efforts, official equipment was stipulated in the rules for most sports. Subsequently, a small number of manufacturers would supply most of the regulation equipment used.[599] Sports-governing bodies specified official equipment and then required manufacturers to meet their standards. For example, the balls used in various sports are strictly regulated as to composition, design, weight, size, and official markings.

The efforts to rationalize and standardize sport reveal a pervasive need to establish order and control. While Americans inherited much of their sporting tradition from the British, they demonstrated an intolerance for the rather loose rules and regulations that were characteristic of English games like rugby and rounders. American baseball, derived from rounders, began codifying rules quite early in its development. (By 1877, professional baseball had official scoring rules in place, for example, defining what was a "hit.") As the game rose to prominence during the late nineteenth century, it demonstrated a particular affinity for rational control and scientific precision.[600] A British observer commented on baseball's character: "The Americans have a genius for taking a thing, examining its every part, and developing each part to the utmost. This they have done with our game of rounders and from a clumsy primitive pastime, have so tightened its joints, and put such a fine finish on its points that it stands forth as a machine of infinite exactitude."[601]

American football revealed a similar penchant for precision as it emerged out of association football (soccer) and rugby. These British games had been spontaneous and free-flowing, with perfunctory structure, few timeouts, and limited substitutions. Shouted signals and timed movements were atypical. Early on, American football—like the British kicking games—had no definite line of scrimmage and utilized the same players on both offense and defense. However, the American game rapidly evolved toward increased structure and exactitude in play. Walter Camp almost single-handedly crafted the game of modern football. He discarded the rather chaotic rugby scrum in favor of the line of scrimmage, reduced the team to eleven players, and introduced the standard offensive arrangement of seven linemen and four backs.[602]

American football's implementation of a line of scrimmage was followed by the development of "downs" and the calling of play signals. These changes, in turn, facilitated the practice of teams initiating play from a regimented formation in tandem on a signal. Signals, which were at first little more than barks with some signification, evolved toward great subtlety and precision for cueing strategy. Coaches formulated sophisticated game plans and relayed signals from the sidelines during the game. Through the course of the twentieth century, American football evolved into a game characterized by recurrent timeouts, regular huddles for determining strategy, synchronized play, and role specialization facilitated by liberal substitution rules. Athletes no longer played the entire game but assigned positions on offense or defense. Thus, American football evolved into a game where spontaneous play gave way to rational control.[603]

The inclination toward order and precision was accompanied by the relentless quest for increased efficiency. To this end, American coaches routinely implemented innovations in play. In the 1890s, football coaches experimented with momentum plays featuring linemen swinging into motion before the ball was snapped, and with moving wedges of blockers to gain an offensive advantage (although several of these early innovations were subsequently regulated out of existence). Rules were changed to accommodate other inventive strategies. The spiral forward pass that exploited the elongated American football was legalized in 1906. This innovation created a more crafted game. The quest for efficiency led to sophisticated offensive formations that accommodated both the passing game and the running game.[604]

The emphasis on complex formations encouraged the system of specialized playing roles. It was obvious that an individual athlete concentrating on one set of skills could eventually outperform a jack of all trades, and that a team of nonspecialists would have a definite advantage over a team of generalists. Football rapidly evolved toward increasing specialization. Notre Dame coach Knute Rockne began substituting entire teams at one point in the 1920s. The two-platoon system was formally introduced in 1941; two years later, football implemented the free substitution rule. Generally, team-sport athletes were discouraged from playing more than one position. Coaches analyzed each position for precise movement patterns and then trained a player specifically to play that position. Specialized kickers and punters developed skills quite distinct from most other line and backfield players.[605]

Liberal substitution rules facilitated specialization across team sports. As early as 1888, professional baseball altered its substitution rules to give field managers the right to insert a substitute at the end of any inning, even though no player was injured. The following year the number of free substitutes was increased to two, and substitution could take place at any time during the game. Players were being platooned by the 1908 season. The substitution rule also facilitated the use of a specialist known as the relief pitcher—pioneered by the Philadelphia A's manager Connie Mark—a role that would fundamentally change the nature of the game. Baseball, like football, became a game characterized by specialization and the liberal interchange of position players.[606]

During the course of the twentieth century, recreational sports developed similar tendencies toward rationalization. Mountain climbing, which had been a rather leisurely and informal—although rigorous—pursuit, developed into a highly competitive activity incorporating precise calculation and expertise. Serious rock climbers developed a system of ranking mountain climbs by their difficulty. At least three different systems were utilized to rate the difficulty of climbs. The National Climbing Classification System runs from F1 to F15. Meanwhile, climbing gear was scientifically redesigned to improve efficiency. By the second half of the century, climbers were employing refined pitons, carabiners, and cramming devices to climb. Mountain climbing had evolved from a form of adventurous recreation to a highly rationalized form of competition.[607]

As new sports appeared on the American scene, their casual nature inexorably gave way to more rationalized versions of the original. The recreational sport of surfboarding, or "surfing," arrived on the American West Coast in the last half of the twentieth century as an activity that emphasized expressiveness, spontaneity, and harmony with nature. However, the experiential qualities of surfing succumbed to concerted efforts to rationalize and standardize the sport. Within a few years of its beginnings, a national surfing organization formed and exerted its control over the sport. The sponsoring of surfing contests led to the establishment of rating systems to grade performances within divisions of competition. The competition required performance of standardized maneuvers on boards that had been redesigned for greater versatility. A disciplined training regimen became obligatory for serious competitors. A world championship tour was instigated in the 1990s.[608]

Rationalization promoted the quantifying of human performance. Physical games by their very character invite measurement. Athletic performance is easily observed and readily assessed. In few other human endeavors can effort, skill, and results be determined with such precision. Americans relish objective measurement and the resulting data that reflect achievement. Enthusiasm for what can be measured or counted found a ready audience among sports managers, journalists, and spectators. Consequently, sports contests have been subjected to a wholesale application of measurements and statistics. The counting and measuring reflected the rationalist proclivity to judge, rate, and assess success and failure. Numerical rating systems were applied to sports like high diving and gymnastics (lacking inherent units of measurement) based upon contrived criteria and standards.[609] Enthusiasts for measuring sports performance are not averse to totaling discrete elements of performance—or even separate performances—in concocting sophisticated point systems, as evident in combined events like the triathlon, pentathlon, and decathlon.

Sports are subjected to the same exacting and intricate measurements characteristic of science and industry. When sport performances are amenable to being directly measured—as is the case with times, weights, and distances—they are gauged to the centimeter, the gram, or the fraction of a second. Exactitude is limited only by the sophistication of measuring techniques and instruments. The increased accuracy and intricacy in measurement technology have brought about situations in which the winner's performance is not visibly distinguishable from that of other competitors; rankings are based upon exceedingly small differentials detectable only through sophisticated measurements.[610] In sprinting, swimming, and speed skating, the time intervals between the finishers often constitute a few hundredths of a second. And there have been instances when swimmers or runners compete not against competitors in other lanes, but alone against the clock in attempts to set records.

Likewise, sports facilities must be manufactured to precise standards. Swimming pool and running track dimensions are accurate to the centimeter. Standardization has been particularly important for measuring performance in national and international competition. A world's record set in a track and field event on a certain date in California can be measured against another performance years later in Tokyo, as long as external factors like weather conditions are comparable. Indeed, wind speed is measured precisely during championship outdoor running events (allowing officials to disqualify wind-assisted performances). All variables affecting sport performance have to be assessed as accurately as possible in as many ways as possible in order to compare performances. Thus, sports are increasingly subjected to quantification to satisfy the need to determine winners as well as the setting and breaking of records.[611]

The reporting of sports contests by the news media has indulged the American sports fan's preoccupation with performance data. Sports pages of newspapers provide columns of detailed data and statistics for athletic events. The box score was developed less than a decade after the first professional baseball game and remains a standard feature in newspapers.[612] Sports record books have become a genre of popular literature. Recent advances in computer technology have allowed the television sports audience to be routinely briefed on individual and team statistics. For example, baseball commentators might inform viewers that the player in the batter's box batted .290 against left-handed pitchers during the last month, or reference other permutations of arcane performance variables. There are sports fans for whom the passion for data appears to surpass their interest in the actual physical contests. Robert Coover's novel *The Universal Baseball Association, Inc.* is about a man who created an imaginary baseball league and then devoted himself to playing a board game for hours and keeping elaborate statistics on the outcomes.[613] Sports board games have been eclipsed by computer games. Fantasy sports leagues have become a major preoccupation of fans via the Internet.

There are few areas within sport where rational methodology has been applied more diligently than in improving the implements utilized by athletes. Rackets, bats, balls, shoes, and other equipment and gear have been subjected to a wide range of technological advances. As the use of highly sophisticated equipment increases, the very nature of sport is altered. The introduction of fiberglass poles for vaulting in the 1950s, provides a classic case of a revolutionary technological improvement's changing the fundamental nature of an athletic event. The game of tennis has been revolutionized by rackets manufactured out of exotic materials and with shapes reflecting the application of biomechanical principles. Today's players deliver serves recorded at 140 miles per hour. No sport has witnessed a more single-minded application of technology than golf. Graphite golf drivers added fifty meters to tee shots. The composition and surface features of golf balls were redesigned to increase distance of flight. Grooves in golf irons were altered to create backspin on balls. Long-shafted putters allow golfers to employ a pendulum effect that greatly reduced putting errors. By 2004, GPS range finders that measure distance to a target were being sold to amateur golfers.[614] Technology has revolutionized performance across a wide range of sports—automobile racing, target shooting, and archery included.

Similar technological improvements are being built into sports facilities—for example, artificial surfaces for contests traditionally played on turf and domed/roofed stadiums providing controlled climate for formerly outdoor sports. These features reduce the risks of play being adversely affected by imperfections in the playing surface or due to weather conditions. Clearly, they alter the nature of competition. Waveless swimming pools have been scientifically designed to reduce times. New surface materials provide "faster" running tracks. The promoters of ice sports have experimented with the surfaces of rinks to improve the performance of skaters. Groundskeepers have tried various strains of grass for optimum play on golf courses. An equal effort has been put into the design of spectator accommodations at sports arenas, emphasizing comfortable seats, various amenities, and a better view.[615]

The application of rational designs to facilities and equipment improves athletic performance through changes in environmental rather than purely human factors. Critics argue that the actual element of "sport" has lessened as the technical efficiency of implements of performance is improved. The new technology has proved more forgiving by reducing the chance for human error. The skill and judgment of the athlete play a less crucial role.

An amateur baseball player swinging an aluminum bat does not worry about breaking a bat by hitting a pitch off the handle; the deer hunter with a scoped, high-caliber rifle and high-velocity ammunition does not have to consider the direction of the wind; and the golfer swinging a high-tech club has less risk of over-hitting the ball.

Notwithstanding the technical advances in sports equipment and facilities, a great deal of technology is aimed at directly improving the human components of performance. By the late twentieth century, outstanding performances of athletes were less a chance occurrence than the result of an application of sophisticated technology. Contemporary coaches and trainers are accompanied by a coterie of technicians who seek ways to minimize the expenditure of human energy and maximize efficiency. Human movement is dissected into its components; training goals are broken down into parts and phases to be worked on separately or in small sequences. For each technique there is a prescribed and optimally economic (in terms of human effort) sequence of movements. For instance, interval training incorporates repetitive division of temporal, spatial, and quantitative tasks interrupted only by controlled pauses for recovery. Sophisticated training methods are supplemented by rationally crafted game plans. Highly trained athletes are coached to follow these strategies meticulously.[616]

Rationalization led to the applied sciences of biomechanics, exercise physiology, sport psychology, and nutrition. These new fields of study mine scientific knowledge to improve sport performance. Academic journals are published in all of the above sub-disciplines of sport science. Sport psychology journals date from the 1970s. The journal *Sports Engineering* began publication recently. Scholarly tomes are written with titles such as *The Physics of Baseball*. Coaches enroll in university courses in sports science. Athletes themselves become students of their sport; a few have actually earned degrees in biomechanics or kinesiology with the goal of better understanding and improving their personal performance.[617]

Nowhere have scientific methods and technology been utilized to a greater degree than in training athletes on the United States Olympic team. The "cold war" atmosphere surrounding the Olympic games in the post-World War II era led to a ruthlessly instrumental approach to improving athletic performance. The US Olympic Committee established a biomechanics laboratory to evaluate and train top athletes. Scientists and trainers applied engineering principles to the mechanics of the human body and to the body's interaction with sports equipment and facilities. By the

1980s, athletes were being tested with computer software that produced readouts on strength and power of muscles during performances. The data were then analyzed to diagnose muscle imbalances that might hamper performance or cause injury. Technicians and engineers employed high-speed videotapes that were studied frame by frame to pinpoint flaws in techniques. Video imagery was used in conjunction with timing lights to make horizontal speed calculations. In addition, athletes were fitted with heart monitors during workouts to record pulse rates, with the data relayed to a computer for analysis. Technicians experimented with computer programs that could analyze every limb and muscle of the athlete to predict optimal performance patterns. Electrodes were implanted on an athlete's body, and biofeedback devices measured responses during performance.[618]

Computer software packages designed for biomechanical analysis now have the flexibility to be modified to fit an individual athlete's characteristics under any particular set of conditions. Theoretically, a computer readout could be generated to describe how a six-foot-tall pole-vaulter with relatively short legs should vault in a ten-mile-per-hour head wind. Computers have found their way into competition. By the 1990s, hand-held computers were part of the crew's equipment on racing yachts. They were programmed to determine optimal trim for the sails under existing conditions. Computer-enhanced performance was on the horizon in several other sports, including golf (as noted above). These technical innovations recall Theodore Adorno's comment that "sports give man back a part of the functions that the machine has deprived him, but only so that men may be even more remorselessly placed at the service of the machine."[619]

The applications of electronic technology have been accompanied by the increased use of performance-enhancing chemicals. It was portentous that the term "doping" entered the English language a mere six years after the first use of the term "record" to designate an unsurpassed sporting achievement. By the last half of the twentieth century, the use of performance-enhancing drugs by athletes was widespread. In 1954, Dr. John B. Ziegler, a US Olympic team physician, worked with a pharmaceutical firm to develop the original anabolic steroid (an artificially produced derivative of testosterone). Although this chemical eventually was banned, the marriage between drugs and sport had been consummated.[620] Use of steroids, growth hormones, blood-doping techniques, and stimulants were outlawed by sports-governing bodies, but drug use and blood-doping continued as covert practices. In spite of prohibition of amphetamines, Olympic cyclists (who had employed these drugs at least since the 1960 Rome games) have persisted in taking them. Weightlifters covertly take illegal steroids to improve strength. Meanwhile, football players are routinely (and legally) injected with painkillers so they can play while injured. The sense of expediency inherent in intense competitiveness has outweighed most considerations against engaging in risky—and often illegal—practices.[621]

NFL linebacker Bill Romanowski became the poster boy for performance-enhancing chemicals. Sections of his autobiography read like a pharmacopoeia. Over his sixteen-year professional career ending in 2003, Romanowski admitted to using the anti-inflammatories Felden, Naprosyn, Motrin, Supac, and Ephredrin; applying DMSO cream; and taking the amino acid creatine and the hormones cortisol and DHEA. Early in his career he used a variety of uppers including Phentermine, an appetite suppressant with amphetamine-like effects. As a veteran, he relied more on painkillers like Toradol and would have his hip injected with Xylocaine during halftime intermissions. He also was injected with vitamin B12 and took various diet supplements in prodigious amounts. His personal tacklebox, "the size of a welcome mat," was split into two levels containing well over 500 pills, mostly diet supplements. He would swallow assortments of these pills on schedule five times a day. Athletes like Romanowski will try virtually any chemical supplement to gain a competitive advantage.[622]

Athletes are increasingly ingesting nutritional supplements to enhance performance. Nutrition specialists utilize sophisticated computer models to determine optimal amounts of fat, protein, and carbohydrates for athletes' diets. An international center for sports nutrition was founded to offer dietary expertise to athletes and coaches. Amateur wrestlers in some states are required to attend nutrition education classes and to undergo body fat assessment via skinfold measurements prior to matches (to discourage unhealthy dieting). By the late 1980s, the norm was for college and professional athletes' diets to be scientifically designed and supervised by dietitians. A huge commercial market in sports nutrition supplements emerged in the 1980s.[623]

In addition, the behavioral sciences have been exploited progressively to improve athletic performance. Sports psychologists developed psychological profiles that set optimal parameters for different sports. Behavior-modification techniques were applied to performance-enhancement strategies, and hypnosis was used to enhance technique and the proper attitude for performance. Imagery was probably the most important and versatile tool sports psychologists used. When "mental practice" was shown to improve actual performance, athletes were trained to visualize correct movements in their heads before executing a skill. Athletes were taught how to deal with distractions and anxiety that hampered their performance. Archers were instructed to be aware of and to control respiration and heartbeat through biofeedback techniques when it was discovered that shooting was more accurate when the arrow was released between heartbeats.[624]

The early efforts to rationalize sport through the strategies and methods of the industrial workplace culminated in an ever-increasing use of scientific knowledge and technology to enhance athletic performance. Training methods and competitive tactics have relied more and more upon scientifically designed regimens, sophisticated equipment, dietary and pharmaceutical supplements, and the advice of an array of performance experts. As the technological restructuring of sports equipment and facilities was supplemented by the efforts directed at human performance, the very nature of sport was altered. The contemporary athlete seems as much an appendage of technology as master of his or her craft. There is little indication this trend will reverse itself. Given this climate, it is not surprising that the efforts to ensure victory on the fields of play through rational methodology and expediency have carried into the judicial arena.

Sport as Legalism

> The American...is beyond all things else, a judge and policeman; he believes
> firmly that there is a mysterious power in law; he supports and embellishes
> its operation with a fanatical vigilance.
> –H. L. Mencken

Americans are infused with an amalgam of moralism and rationalism. One consequence is the national obsession with exactly measured performance and precise rules, coupled with a finely tuned sense of fairness and justice. Collectively, these inclinations have engendered a rampant legalism. This habit has been evident since the early New England beginnings. The Puritans set high standards for personal conduct; they attempted to regulate and litigate every aspect of life, private and public. Colonial New England has been characterized as "an over-governed society, with every tenth man an official." The outcome of these inclinations was a propensity for litigiousness. As early as 1679, a synod of Puritan ministers concluded that the number of lawsuits had gotten out of hand. One of the characters in Arthur Miller's play *The Crucible*, set during the Salem witch trials, complains he has been in court six times in the past year. His descendants seem to have inherited this malady. The United States boasts more lawyers and harbors more litigation than any other nation.[625]

The penchant for legalism carried over into sport. The first baseball commissioner, Kenesaw Mountain Landis, was a federal judge appointed to stifle corruption following the 1919 Black Sox scandal. Lawyers, including Lawrence O'Brien of the NBA and John Ziegler of the NHL, have served as commissioners in other professional sports. Lawyers were appointed to these positions for good reason. Sport has found itself subject to antitrust laws, labor laws, civil rights legislation, tort law, ADA regulations, and federal broadcasting regulations. Sports leagues and franchises have come to rely on legal advice out of necessity. Moreover, professional athletes retain legal representation as a matter of course. As careers in sport and events on the field of competition acquire more consequences (especially economic ones), the principals increasingly seek redress for alleged injustices through arbitration or adjudication. In response, sports law has become a recognized specialty in the American legal profession.[626]

Americans exhibit a remarkable diligence in policing the rules and regulations governing sports. It is indicative of this national predisposition that half of the major institutions involved in intercollegiate athletics were either sanctioned, censored, or put on probation by the NCAA for rules violations within one ten-year period. In addition, coaches and athletes are routinely subjected to punitive sanctions for violating regulations promulgated by sports-governing bodies. This regulatory predilection is equally evident on the fields of play. The managers of sport have repeatedly augmented the number of officials who supervise competition. Tennis, a sport that involves two to four athletes, currently employs eleven officials at major tournament matches. Game officials are charged with ensuring no competitor breaks the rules, victory is awarded only to the deserving, and no errors are made in determining winners and losers. The predominance of officials reflects the fact that sports are governed by an intricate code of regulations. The overall impression is one of compelling concern for control.

The history of American football provides a typical illustration of the regulatory impulse at work. As the primitive style of play shifted toward more precision, the game took on a legalistic character. Football was increasingly controlled and regulated in an attempt to repress the spontaneous play and legitimate violence typical of English rugby, from which it derived. Penalties that were rather perfunctory in English kicking games were rendered more exact by American footballers. A protracted list of fouls and penalties was propagated in order to restrain the free movement of players. The classic instance was the much used offside rule, the stepping over an invisible but precise line of scrimmage.[627]

Football was not the only sport to multiply the number of regulations and regulators. Early on, baseball assigned only one umpire to call the game. At that time it was considered gauche for gentlemen athletes to question the umpire's decisions. In short course, baseball rules became more numerous and specific, and the umpire's role was enlarged. The current game has reached the point where four umpires are assigned regularly to professional games, six to World Series games. Predictably, play has become more contentious. Modern ballplayers and managers routinely argue with umpires about batted balls judged foul or fair, and calls on the base paths. (MLB implemented the Umpire Information System—over the objection of the umpires' union—which employs a system of cameras in ballparks to determine the accuracy of umpires' "ball" and "strike" calls.) Challenges to the umpire's decisions led to what became an institutionalized ritual in baseball, the "rhubarb."[628] The contentiousness is not unique to baseball. Athletes have been strident in their questioning of officials' decisions, even when there are added penalties for doing so.

Basketball, an American invention, evolved into a game plagued by frequent interruptions to deal with rule violations. By mid-twentieth century, it was not unusual for three or four dozen personal fouls to be called during the course of a game. In addition, technical fouls were assessed for unsportsmanlike behavior by players and coaches, including the berating of officials. The result was a parade of free-throw shooting during which regular play was suspended (until this practice was curtailed by a modified rule giving the fouled team possession of the ball). Despite the numerous rule infractions, the number of court officials was increased to three during the 1988–1989 basketball season. The rationale for the added official was the perception that some fouls were not being detected by only two referees.[629]

Football has employed as many officials as any team sport (currently seven on the field). In the professional game's recent history, an additional official was positioned in the press box above the stadium floor to "second-guess" the field officials by means of reviewing videotapes of the action on the field. Put into operation by the National Football League in 1986, instant-replay officiating was resorted to over 200 times during that season, resulting in numerous reversals of on-field calls. The procedure caused protracted delays. During a televised NFL game between the Los Angeles Raiders and the Detroit Lions in December 1990, play was delayed for eight minutes while replay officials continued to review the videotape of an unusual ruling amidst communication problems between the replay booth and officials on the field. After a few seasons, the practice was discontinued but then reinstituted, and it is currently being considered by other sports. (In August 2008, MLB initiated instant replay to review questionable homeruns.)

In order to participate in a sport, the athlete has had to master a detailed set of rules that cover every aspect of play. A relatively simple game like tennis is governed by some three dozen separate rules that extend to fifteen pages of print. The rule manuals for team sports tend to be thicker. That of the National Football League has grown to more than 120 pages. Regulations that govern play on the field are accompanied by an increasingly sophisticated canon of "extra-contest" regulations covering matters such as eligibility of athletes and number of practice sessions allowed. The National Collegiate Athletic Association publishes a manual of over 400 pages. This guide includes a constitution, by-laws, rules of order, executive regulations, recommended policies, enforcement procedures, administrative provisions, and a case book. It follows that the NCAA employs a director of compliance and a director of legislative services. One anthropologist who studies play commented that in American sport "the rules seemed to be the reason for the game."[630]

Recently, the use of performance-enhancing drugs by athletes has been a major focus of contention and litigation. The United States Anti-Doping Agency began operations in 2000 as a nongovernmental agency responsible for implementation of the Anti-Doping Code in the US. The code was developed by the World Anti-Doping Agency (WADA), a body established by the International Olympic Committee (IOC) in 1999. The USADA governs only Olympic sports; however, national and state athletic associations enforce their own drug regulations for other amateur sports. The major professional team sports (NFL, NHL, NBA, MLB) each have their own regulations and enforcement procedures governing drug use. Athletes are subjected to random drug testing (usually a urine sample). Violators can be suspended from eligibility to compete based on the adjudged seriousness of their transgression. In the 1988 summer Olympics in Seoul, Ben Johnson apparently won the 100-meter event. However, urinalysis tests subsequently revealed Johnson had been using illegal steroids, so he forfeited all his medals from the 1988 games. (It is now known that in addition to Johnson, five Olympic gold-medal winners during the 1980s had been using steroids.) Doping has led to protracted legal battles amidst scientific controversies. Allegations of drug use often rely on "unsupported personal testimonials, abstruse laboratory procedures, legal technicalities...[and] the opaque functioning of remote committees."[631]

Detected rule violations by players or ex post facto rulings by officials (rather than the results of real-time competition) increasingly determine the outcomes of sports contests. In many cases, disputes that originated on the playing fields are carried into the law courts. There are international courts including the Court of Arbitration for Sport, based in Switzerland; however, Americans seem to lead the world in sports-related litigation, and this practice has had a long history. Legal recourse stemming from disputed sports contests is more than a century old. In 1895, a dispute over a referee's call in the Bob Fitzsimmons versus Tom Sharkey prize fight was challenged in the California courts, where the matter acquired a long, drawn-out history.[632]

The nation's courts continue to hear disputes stemming from sports contests. The following examples are illustrative. In 1977, a group of Washington Redskins football fans filed a suit in federal court to overturn a referee's call that had decided a game in favor of a Redskins opponent. A prolonged dispute stemmed from the 1981 Indianapolis 500 auto race. The apparent winner was determined by the track officials to be Mario Andretti after another driver, Bobby Unser—who crossed the finish line first—was disqualified for an apparent rule violation. After a series of reviews by the United States Auto Club (the governing body at the time), the officials' decision was overturned in a court of law some four months after the actual race had ended. In 1990, boxer Michael Olajide filed suit against the New York State Athletic Commission in the State Supreme Court to overturn the boxing commission's ruling upholding the result of a fight that Olajide lost.[633] The final decision regarding the winner of the 1989 America Cup yacht race was determined by an appellate court several months after the event took place. Because of the increase in appeals of outcomes of sporting events, spectators can no longer be certain who the winner is at the end of a contest. Olympic athletes have had their medals revoked years after the event took place.

Sports managers and athletes, buttressed by their attorneys, instigate legal contests that often upstage the contests on the athletic fields. Litigation is pursued increasingly to defend economic interests. Professional athletes and players unions have resorted to lawsuits to challenge contract agreements and to rectify perceived violations of labor laws. Contract disputes between the ballplayers and management became routine by the 1990s. Entire sports seasons have been jeopardized by unresolved contract disputes between players associations and owners. Lawsuits have tested the application of the 1890 Sherman Antitrust Act to sport. (Only baseball franchises remain directly protected by this act.) Related litigation has allowed players "free agency" and sport franchise relocations. There has been a general increase in civil litigation not limited to contract disputes. Fans have sued players, players have sued agents and teams, sports officials' associations have sued leagues, owners have sued leagues, leagues have sued rival leagues, and cities have sued sports franchise owners—and the permutations of possible litigants still have not been exhausted![634]

Amateur sport is not exempt from litigiousness. Lawsuits have been filed by colleges with sports programs to protect their economic interests. In the mid-1990s, the National Collegiate Athletic Association was required to adhere to the general standards of due process for civil suits when placing a college under investigation for NCAA rules violations. State legislators have extended to colleges the right to sue alumni or other parties who compromise the integrity of their athletic programs. These laws, upheld by state and federal courts, have led to further litigation. Neither has high-school sport been immune from civil litigation. The parents of adolescent athletes, contending that participation in interscholastic sports is a prerequisite to a lucrative professional career, have argued that their child's property rights were affected by not being allowed to compete on the school team. In some cases, the courts appear to have redefined participation in school extracurricular activities as a right rather than a privilege. Litigation has carried to the level of children's sports. Little League Baseball, Inc. had to respond to sex-discrimination lawsuits before it opened play to girls.[635] In 2004, Little League in Larchmont, New York, sued to stop a tournament because of a dispute over the interpretation of rules.

One explanation for the propensity to litigate can be found in the element of expediency inherent in rationalism. Expediency implies using every available means to ensure goals are achieved. Contention, arbitration, and litigation are logical consequences. Disputing the rulings or results of a sports contest is a tack employed in the same spirit that applies to game strategies. If one cannot win through skillful performance on the playing field, then manipulation of the rules or intimidation of officials might influence the outcome (a tactic extended to commissioners' offices, mediation tables, and courtrooms). In a highly competitive society, the need to win often overrides the spirit of sportsmanship. Competitors employ whatever rational means are available to achieve victory. The attitude that "winning is everything" translates into, "[I]f you can't win on the tennis court or basketball court, try to prevail in circuit court." Legalism is the inevitable consequence of competitiveness bolstered by moralism and rationalism.

9

The American Sport Ethic: II

Goal-Directed Behavior

> Upon the fields of friendly strife
> Are sown the seeds
> That, upon other fields, on other days,
> Will bear the fruits of victory.
> –Douglas MacArthur

To participate in play is to dwell in the "Kingdom of Ends," as Michael Novak fashioned it. Play is its own end, an activity purposeless outside of itself. To accept this verity is to recognize that the spirit of play is antithetical to goal-directed behavior. A devil's advocate might argue that play also has goals: the player seeks to experience vertigo or to escape reality. But these aren't so much conscious goals as byproducts of play. If the playing of games involves goals at all, they are intrinsic goals—for instance, to avoid being hit with the ball in dodgeball or reaching base in softball. External goals, on the other hand, seem foreign to the very idea of play.[636]

German psychologist William Stern noted that play does not incline toward some systematic objective and, therefore, is not ultimately serious, however seriously the player may pursue it during its course. Stern coined the term "Ernst-spiel" ("serious play") to refer to behavior that, while subjectively serious, lacks objective consequence. Anyone who has watched a small child playing "make-believe" can appreciate the concept of serious play, but also recognizes that the child's fantasies have little significance in the real world. Thus, play harbors internally serious goals but remains externally "nonserious."[637]

However, experience tells us playful activity is not immune to external goals. When elevated to the level of formal games and competitive sport, play often is appropriated for sundry purposes, and its players are drawn into "purposiveness."[638] Mihaly Csikszentmihalyi had such distinctions in mind when he analyzed the activity of mountain climbing. He was able to distinguish between two ideal types of climbers. First are the "mountaineers" who climb for the spiritual and aesthetic dimensions of the experience. These are the intrinsically motivated "players." The second group, labeled "rock climbers," are obsessed with technique and performance and motivated by personal goals of accomplishment. They are more interested in establishing and breaking records and receiving recognition for their feats than in climbing mountains as an end in itself. This group, in effect, is engaging in goal-directed behavior.[639] The American spirit of sport is consonant with the "rock-climber" mindset. The nation's sports and games have been imbued with personal and societal goals.

America's sports and games were rooted in Puritan soil and nurtured in the climate of moral asceticism. When allowed at all, playful activity was appropriated as a means to worthy ends. Recreation was rationalized as physical training and became a corollary to moral training. Such justification was necessary, for if play were allowed to become an end in itself, it could easily escape all control except that generated from within. Tolerance of intrinsic goals such as seeking joy in movement would sever the connection with a higher purpose. Action as a substitute for virtue would become its own end, and sport would be severed from the moral realm. Thus, linking sport to worthy ends kept it within the boundaries of acceptable behavior.[640]

Traditionally, educators and social reformers emphasized the concomitant values of sport. They firmly believed behaviors and attitudes learned on the playing fields would carry over into other areas of life. Notably, these "carry-over" values were expected to prepare individuals to meet the challenges of competition in the world of work.[641] Thus has sport been linked to pragmatic goals. For Americans, sport has to be "good for something." Throughout the nineteenth century, a growing number of liberal clergy and public intellectuals lent their voices to these utilitarian aspirations for sport. The Unitarian minister Thomas Wentworth Higginson (1823–1911) referred to "purposeful, useful sport." Oliver Wendell Holmes, the son of a Calvinist clergyman, noted that the racehorse was little more than a gambling toy while the trotting horse was respectable because it was, after all, a *useful* animal. It followed that human athletes must prove themselves useful in some way.[642] The Protestant message is unambiguous: for sport to be justified, it must lead to positive outcomes or provide experiences that transfer to life success. Given this standard, American athletes have been concerned less with "playing the game" than with extrinsic goals such as physical fitness, acquiring status, or making money.[643]

The military promoted experiences on the athletic fields as a way to prepare soldiers for the battlefield—as implied in the epigraph at the beginning of this chapter. By the 1880s, the US War Department was actively promoting sport as an approach to physical training. Douglas MacArthur was a staunch supporter of athletics at West Point, where he served as superintendent in the post-World War I era. The military academy touted sport as the ideal way to develop leadership skills in its cadets. The nation's schools were encouraged to incorporate military drill into physical education classes. In the field, military officers cited the prophylactic value of sport in preventing indiscipline and immorality among enlisted men. A few enthusiastic commanders made athletics virtually a duty. By the twentieth century, nearly every military post and naval ship was promoting a comprehensive sports program. Regiment champions were crowned in combat sports like boxing and target shooting.[644]

Instrumental goals were equally evident in the framing of women's sport beginning in the late nineteenth century. Only by linking sport to moral ends could Americans accommodate women engaging in recreational activities (see chapter 8). The very idea of a "sportswoman" initially shocked the Victorian sense of propriety; thus, it became essential to rationalize women's sports. Some of the justifications had been employed earlier for men's sport, while others were specific to women. Sports were promoted as beneficial in reducing the too-corpulent curves of women's bodies, ameliorating the female tendency to "nerves," and putting a damper on less desirable (implying sexual) activities while increasing fertility. Apologists claimed sports were helpful in curing "female insanity." Bicycling was vaunted as an activity that rendered women more orderly and rational. This popular recreation was supposed to steer women's focus to duty rather than gratification and unhealthy excitement, while at the same time strengthening the muscles of the uterus to promote efficient childbirth.[645]

The linking of sport to worthy goals was prominent in the rationale for children's activities. Organizations with ambitious social agendas began promoting youth sport in the Progressive era. The Young Men's Christian Association sponsored sport programs as a means to moral ends. The leaders of the YMCA were convinced that boys properly supervised would be less inclined toward youthful vices, and that involvement in wholesome recreational activities ensured youngsters would grow into responsible members of the community.[646] Likewise, the primary objective of New York's Public School Athletic League (PSAL) at the turn of the twentieth century was to promote "useful athletics" among young men (and later young women) attending public schools. After-school activities were organized to work off youngsters' excess energy and deflect them from participation in gangs and other mischief. PSAL officials championed sports' contribution to scholarship, morality, citizenship, health, and school discipline. Intrinsic enjoyment of activities was not mentioned.[647]

American higher education embraced a comparable set of goals for sport, captured in George Santayana's novel *The Last Puritan*. The main character, Oliver Arden, scion of an old Boston family, reflects on his college football experiences: "He remembered all the...reasons which his mother and other high-minded people used to give to justify that game: that it was good for the health, or for young men's morals, or for testing and strengthening character." Oliver internalized the goal-directed predisposition of his elders. He commented that if he were given the opportunity to ride horses, it would not be for idle pleasure or show, but that he might be able to carry on his life's work better and have a greater influence for good in the world.[648]

However, such noble-sounding goals employed to justify sport soon were subordinated to more immediate ones. Athletic coaches showed less interest in sports' potential to mold character and save the world than in developing players who could win athletic contests. By the close of the nineteenth century, American educators began to realize they had an "athletic tiger by the tail," and admonished the ruthlessly pragmatic coaches for stressing the goal of "winning at any cost" while ignoring the character-building goals of sport.[649] Yet, the goal of victory on the athletic fields was consistent with an ethic that equated success with personal worth. Winning carried strong moral overtones. Indeed, no goal in American sport has been more salient than that of winning, often at the expense of the intrinsic values of sport. This single-minded objective attenuated the enjoyment of competing such that it was narrowly confined to celebrating victory.[650] The goal of "playing to win" was supplanted by that of acquiring the symbols of victory. Athletic feats were recognized by an array of ornaments: ribbons, medals, and trophies. These artifacts of victory were supplemented by more practical rewards, including cash prizes. The more mercenary athletes competed for material and financial inducements.[651]

Thus, an ineluctable process of goal displacement reshaped American sport. Intrinsic goals gave way to a progression of incrementally peripheral goals. At the initial stage, the value of playing the game became less important than the moral benefits derived from play; then, winning the game became the paramount goal. The latter objective eclipsed the ethical pretensions of sport. Ultimately, the value of playing to win was subordinated to personal status or financial rewards derived from winning. Rigauer noted that it is implicit in top-level sport to constantly raise the level of achievement, and this demand manifests itself in the establishing of goals that are continuously corrected upward (or downward, depending upon one's viewpoint). This series of goal displacements dramatically affects the way games are played. The goal of outperforming the opponent—an intrinsic element of competition—is sublimated to the single-minded goal of assuring victory. The implications are corrosive to the spirit of sport. The displacement process then subordinates winning to external goals like financial profit.[652] Clearly, the progression of goals tended toward practical concerns at the expense of high-sounding moral pretensions from an earlier time.

The implications of goal displacement are manifest in contemporary sport. One instance is when a team's final league standing inversely determines the order of choice in "drafting" future players or establishes the strength of opponents on the following season's schedule. The long-term interests of a team out of contention are advanced by losing games late in the season in order to improve its prospects for the next season. At this point, coaches might "bench" their best players, or the athletes exert less than maximal effort in competition. In such a case, the natural goals of competitive sport are undermined. Likewise, goal-directed behavior becomes problematic when athletes' personal goals conflict with team goals. Athletes adjust playing strategies to advance their own careers, to qualify for performance-based salary supplements, or to protect themselves from injuries. These goals can be independent of the team's success and corrosive to the spirit of competition. A baseball player is less likely to execute sacrifice bunts or dive headfirst for fly balls in the field if his primary goal is to improve his individual statistics and stay healthy. In extreme cases, athletes have manipulated the point margin of victory in order to win money wagered on the "point spread" of a game. In all the above instances, the intrusion of tangential (and often inappropriate) goals erodes the fundamental authenticity of competition.

Finally, spectator sports are finding it more difficult to avoid intrusions upon their time and structure by peripheral interests with goals extraneous to the competitive event. Of particular concern are interruptions by commercial sponsors and diversions instigated by the electronic media.[653] When sporting events are interrupted repeatedly by advertisements lasting several minutes, the flow of competition is compromised. Television networks, concerned about bored and fickle viewers, routinely divert the focus away from the playing field in an attempt to retain audience interest. Cameras "cut" to interviews, show clips of previous contests or plays ("instant replay"), and switch to commentary in the broadcast booth during live coverage. Diverting attention to these "sideshows" damages the integrity of the main event. Clearly, the goals of tangential parties in the presentation of sport are gaining priority over those of athletes and sports fans.

The above discussion describes sports participation in two antipodal modes: playing and goal-directed behavior. The implication is that one cannot engage in both. American sport tends toward the latter, divulging the goal-oriented bias of the broader culture. While the Protestant ethic induces us to judge sport based on its potential for personal development, the spirit of capitalism equates the value of sport with material reward. In either case, when motives are other than situation-generated, sporting activity invariably becomes goal-directed. The intrusion of external goals has become pervasive in modern sport.[654] This scheme for justifying sport has led us down the "slippery slope" of goal displacements. The progression has been quite evident over the course of the last century. Contemporary Americans participate in sports for health, fitness, glory, money, team, country, and alma mater. Athletes may "win one for the Gipper" but rarely play for themselves. By focusing on such goals, both amateurs and professionals pursue sport as if it were a job.[655]

The Work Ethic

> Sometimes we play so badly that we forget we are playing.
> We think our play is work. It is.
> –David L. Miller

On the surface, work and play appear to be polar opposites. However, it is evident to those who have reflected on the nature of the two concepts that the boundaries are not distinct. Mark Twain observed that "work" and "play" are words used to describe the same thing under differing circumstances. The famous fence-painting episode in *The Adventures of*

Tom Sawyer illustrates his point. Social scientists have arrived at a similar conclusion. They propose that human behavior can be defined in terms of the varying amount of work, play, and "not-play" that are present. The anthropological model perceives work and play as qualities rather than activities. Clearly, characteristics of play can infiltrate work activity and vice versa. American folklore proclaims Benjamin Franklin played with a kite and discovered electricity, while Robert Fulton played with a tea pot and invented the steamboat! Turning to sport, tradition has it that Cy Young "worked" on developing his "slow ball" and forever changed the game of baseball; jockey Tod Sloan "invented" the "forward seat" and revolutionized horseracing.[656]

From a phenomenological perspective, the activities of sport and work share evident similarities. The athlete, like the laborer, manipulates objects with a tool, the tennis player with a racket, the pool player with a cue. The motions of the golfer are not unlike those of the reaper, the motions of the server on the tennis court not dissimilar to those of the lumberjack swinging an ax. Moreover, in sport just as in work, bodily action is often accompanied by mental calculation. Both the worker and the athlete plot strategies; the former diagrams a work project while the latter constructs a game plan. The consequences of action in both cases are observable, whether a stone dropped in place by the mason or a ball placed in the goal by the athlete. Finally, work and sport both offer participants visible evidence of accomplishment upon completion of the task. Mountain climbers looking down from the summit may share feelings of achievement similar to those of a road crew admiring a completed mountain pass.[657]

Cultural meanings are grafted onto basic forms of human activity. Some societies have imbued sport with the qualities and connotations of work. When this occurs, athletes begin to resemble laborers in behaviors and motives. Sporting activities then comprise a medium in which individuals must prove themselves through personal performance and accomplishment. In the process, the playful qualities of sport are diminished. Sport is transformed into a serious, work-like endeavor. Henry David Thoreau observed of nineteenth-century America's games, "There is no play in them." Indeed, Americans have pursued sport to meet the precepts of a strident work ethic. What begins as play often becomes the mirror image of labor.[658]

Despite the ambiguous boundaries between work and play, scholars continue to look for defining characteristics. Convention informs us that work is serious and play is non-serious. In truth, neither work nor play can be defined categorically as either.[659] There are employees who fail to take their jobs seriously, yet will train religiously for marathons and triathlons. If seriousness does not provide a useful distinction between work and play, then what does? Pace might be a crucial element that distinguishes the two forms: work requires a regular, controlled pace and play a more casual one. However, Americans have never revealed a sharp change of pace between their work and play. When observing a yachtsman competing in a regatta, it is difficult to tell from his urgent motions of trimming and tacking whether he is at work or at play. Indeed, many sports emulate the pace of industrial labor. Even the "time-outs" during sports contests appear tightly scheduled and frenetic. In reality, they are intense strategy sessions.

Ultimately, the distinction between work and play may reside in individual motivation. To make this determination, one would have to know why someone is pursuing a particular activity. Someone fishing may be working or playing, depending upon intent. The angler may be planning to eat the fish, to market the fish commercially, or just to fish for the sheer pleasure of the activity. In the latter instance, the catch may be released back into the water. Alternatively, a prize specimen may be carried to a taxidermist to be mounted for display in the den, in which case the point of fishing is to enhance one's reputation as a sportsman. The question remains: does such activity represent labor or leisure?

A fourth criterion to distinguish work from play is based on the freedom versus the compulsion to engage in activity. Play is free by definition, while work implies being compelled by coercion or necessity. The problem with this distinction is that not all work is obligatory. An artisan may work for the love of the craft. One finds millionaires who continue to work long after they have "made a living." It is equally apparent that all play is not free from constraints. Membership on a team or being seeded in a tournament imposes social (or contractual) obligations to play. As for freedom within play, the rules of games impose various constraints. The golfer is restricted as to where, when, and how he may drive the ball down a fairway.[660] Thus, another paradox emerges: sport as a form of play should be free and spontaneous, but in fact, it is subject to certain obligations and restrictions. We can only conclude that the distinctions between work and play remain ambiguous.

Experience with work (e.g., chores) and play both have their beginnings in childhood, when these concepts are not yet independently organized in the child's mind. What children make out to be work or play as they mature depends to a considerable degree upon parents' and society's interpretations. Adults often play with intensity, and they may induce their children to do the same. Adolescence is the period when the transition occurs between the play world of the child and the work world of adults. A teenager confronted with functional ambiguities may find in organized sports a bridge between child's play and the adult world of work.[661] Play-oriented motives of young athletes then come into conflict with the work-like agenda of adults (see chapter 10).

Arnold Beisser, in his psychosocial study of modern sport, comments on the reciprocal development of work and play. He notes that activities that originate as play—like ballgames—have assumed the qualities of serious work while what were once occupations such as boating, hunting, and fishing have become forms of recreation.[662] Thus, sport constitutes a muddle of countertendencies; it can liberate through the spirit of play or bind its participants to a rigid work ethic. While the training regimen of sport is especially work-like, experimentation with form and strategy reveals the qualities of play.[663] Sport appears to be a chameleon-like activity that can change its appearance back and forth from play to work.

Sports psychologist Seppo Iso-Ahola offers three models to explain the relationship between work and recreational sport:

The independent model. Work and recreation are autonomous and have no discernible effect on each other.

The compensation model. People compensate for work experiences by choosing dissimilar recreation, *e.g.,* the clerical worker tied to a computer during the workday goes mountain biking for leisure rather than playing computer games.

The spillover model. People tend to choose recreational activities that are characteristically similar to their jobs, *e.g.,* the forest ranger hunts and fishes during leisure time.[664]

The historical record suggests a progression toward spillover. Arguably, sport and work originally were independent realms of social behavior. Then sport increasingly provided a form of compensation for work, but ultimately work values and behaviors began to spill over into sport. As a result, sport became less independent or compensatory over time.[665] Such spillover may occur for various reasons. Among these are cultural values (e.g., the Protestant work ethic, the spirit of capitalism) supporting work and disparaging leisurely and pleasurable activity. The American experience has corroborated the spillover model (see chapter 6). Sport was acquiring the characteristics of work while it was being touted as preparation for work or justified as a "break" from work. Characteristically, Theodore Roosevelt asserted that sport is preparation "to do work that counts when the time arises, when the occasion calls."[666] The prevailing view was that Americans should work until they were weary and then take recreation so they could work again. But as sport and recreation became more work-like, they offered less in the way of refreshment or compensation. Rodgers noted that workers in the Industrial era frequently used time off to engage in an equally strenuous regimen as members of athletic clubs and YMCAs.[667] The recreation that took place in these settings revealed few compensatory qualities.

America's athletes increasingly emulated disciplined laborers. Winning contests and setting records required maximum output that, in turn, necessitated intensive preparation at a pace and intensity reminiscent of the assembly line. The athlete essentially became a producer of performances and records. Efforts to this end were directed by a trainer or coach (the equivalent of the foreman/supervisor) whose goal was to improve the performance of athletes.[668] The assembly-line methods applied to the game of college football led historian Arnold Toynbee to comment that "Anglo-Saxon football was not a game at all. It was the Industrial System celebrating a triumph over its vanquished antidote, Sport, by masquerading in its guise."[669] Sports heroes were idolized by the public in the same context as heroic laborers. Mark Twain noted that both river boat pilots and athletes were made into heroes not only for their power, authority, and glamour, but also for pride in their jobs and their salaries.[670]

Thus did the work ethic divert sport from the model of amateurism. By the late nineteenth century, coaching had become a paid profession, and talented athletes gained the option of being paid to play sports. There had been early instances of paid athletes in the sports of boxing and horseracing. In 1869 the Cincinnati Red Stockings became the first salaried Major League Baseball team—although some ballplayers had been compensated prior to then. An increasing number of sports careers were made available to athletes who demonstrated the requisite skills. In the first half of the twentieth century, football, basketball, and hockey formed professional leagues with salaried athletes placed under contract. The athlete became a new type of worker who sold his labor power to entertain the general public. Moreover, the work-oriented mentality of paid athletes and coaches gradually infiltrated amateur sports (see chapter 11).[671]

The modern Olympic movement attempted to maintain a spirit of amateurism, and Olympic athletes adhered to this principle for a while. Through the early years of the games and into the 1930s, the typical Olympian participated in his or her sport as an avocation. Medal-winning swimmer and film actor Johnny Weissmuller epitomized the rather carefree spirit of the era. He would begin training for his event about two weeks before a meet. Elizabeth Robinson, who ran for the American team in the 1928 Olympics, normally trained only three days a week. She won her Olympic medal in the fourth track meet in which she had ever competed. Jean Shirley, who won a gold medal in the high jump at the 1932 Olympics, had never participated in a national meet until she qualified for the games. Olympic athletes of that era were amateurs not only in their approach to training, but in the sense that many of them held full-time jobs to support themselves while they trained.[672]

This amateurish approach to training was soon to change. Elements within the American Olympic movement pushed coaches and athletes toward a more disciplined model following the poor showing of the American team in the 1924 Paris games. It was ironic that some of the critics subsequently charged the 1928 Olympic team with being over-coached and over-trained. However, Americans convinced themselves a more work-like approach to training was the key to improving performance.[673] The new emphasis was evident in the escalating training regimen of Olympic swimmers over the following decades. Sixteen-year-old Cathy Ferguson, a gold medal winner at the 1964 games, was swimming 12,000 to 16,000 meters (seven to ten miles) a day. John Nabor, a 1976 gold medal winner, recalled that most trainers by then had established four hours of training a day as the minimum for competitive swimmers.[674]

Sport was becoming a full-time occupation. A comparable devotion to training and regular competition was occurring in American college sports. It is pertinent to note that college athletes ostensibly are full-time students in addition to competing in amateur sports. However, campus athletes, pushed by their coaches, began training longer and more rigorously. Meanwhile, the number of contests in a college sports season increased steadily over the course of the twentieth century. Basketball teams in college conferences played about a dozen games in the early 1900s; by the last decades of the century, the typical college basketball season entailed more than thirty games plus tournaments. By then, college baseball teams were playing sixty-game schedules. College football seasons also lengthened.

Training and practice hours increased accordingly. A study conducted by the NCAA in the late 1980s found that in-season basketball and football athletes averaged thirty hours a week on their sport—more time than they spent in the classroom.[675] (The current NCAA 20/8 rule stipulates that college athletes practice no more than twenty hours a week during the season.) Moreover, rigorous weight-training programs have become mandatory for athletes in several sports, even basketball. I recall student athletes arriving late to my 8:00 A.M. class, exhausted from an early morning workout in the weight room. A distinguishing characteristic of contemporary sport is that training takes up much more time than competing and resembles regimented work more so than what occurs during an actual contest.

The fundamentals for successful athletic performance are calculated, analyzed, dissected, and evaluated just like the work process. Recall the young protégé of Frederick Taylor (chapter 6) who stood over workers with a stopwatch and timed their every movement for efficiency. His successors are the football and track coaches. Scouts and coaches hover over athletes to assess every facet of performance: speed, stamina, power, agility—even mental acuity. To compete successfully in this environment, athletes have had to become increasingly disciplined in their approaches to training. Modern training is suffused with efficiency, self-discipline, and subordination to experts. Training sessions are lengthy, frequent, intense, and tightly scheduled.[676]

Indeed, the argot of sport is replete with the terminology of work: teamwork, workout, speed work, weight work. Coaches punctuate practice sessions with persistent admonitions to "work harder." Athletes have learned to rationalize their sport experience within the context of work.[677] Felipe Lopez, a New York City high-school basketball prospect in the early 1990s, commented, "I work all the time on my game. If Coach…says he wants me to work on my ball handling, then I just work at it, work at it, work at it, until it's right. In basketball, you always are working."[678] The argot of sport reveals its prevailing ethic. Slogans and maxims reflecting the work ethic cover the walls of locker rooms and coaches' offices.[679]

If coaches have been hard on athletes, they are no easier on themselves. America's athletic coaches stand as paragons of the work ethic. Coaching has become one of the most demanding of professions, characterized by long hours and chronic stress. Only those individuals thoroughly imbued with this ethic can coach at the upper levels of competition. Ron Polk, the highly successful baseball coach at Mississippi State University during the 1980s and 1990s (returning briefly in 2002), proudly tagged himself a "workaholic." Coach Polk was quoted as proclaiming that work is the reason the world exists! A typical day for Polk began at 6:30 A.M. and ended around midnight. The MSU coach admitted to an average of forty to fifty phone calls a day (before cell phones) while checking out future prospects, evaluating his recruiting efforts, juggling speaking engagements, and tending to the myriad duties that come with the position. Polk's professed goal was to squeeze the most possible out of his day. He admitted to reading for self improvement even while driving his car, and commented that his pet peeve was watching a person in a restaurant eating breakfast without some sort of work in front of him. This ethic impels the productive use of time, and Coach Polk wastes none. He is representative of a breed of work-oriented individuals who thrive at coaching.[680]

Former University of Maryland track athlete and coach Jim Kehoe offers his version of the work ethic: "[W]inners…are people who work harder. I never ran a race in my life that I didn't run to win. If I didn't win it, I couldn't wait till the next day to get up and start a little earlier and work a little later and put a little more into it. I believe…the people that win are the people that work the hardest and have the greatest commitment and put the most into it."[681] Such sentiments ignore other factors that may determine success in sports. Kehoe seemed to express a faith that hard work alone could overcome any deficiencies in natural ability or the vicissitudes of competition. This conviction is reinforced by athletes' parents. Champion figure-skater Michelle Kwan's father, Danny, proclaimed, "There is nothing called talent." He elaborated, "You have to work hard. There is one simple word: practice, practice, practice."[682] The American spirit of sport is infused with the belief that winning is simply the result of working hard.

The work ethic reinforces the belief that athletes, regardless of talent, who compete successfully are those who accept the imposed discipline and arduous training demanded of them. Professional bowler Carmen Salvino displayed these qualities. At age eighteen, he was bowling three to four hours every weekday while working or attending high school, and all day long on weekends. In a typical two-hour practice session, he would release a sixteen-pound bowling ball some 200 times. He notes that his fingers became deformed from the repetitive trauma. In his memoir, Salvino recounts that bowling entails not only physical, but also mental, labor: analyzing the idiosyncrasies of alleys, determining whether your hook is working, etc. The former champion recalls post-practice headaches that would last three hours, but he stayed with his passion for four decades.[683]

This workaholic mindset can be detected even in athletes who appreciate the playful side of sport. Tennis champion and court hustler Bobby Riggs would offer to play an opponent while wearing a dress and with a chair on his side of the court—and still beat him! But Riggs also was a work fanatic. Hustling on the tennis courts and golf courses was both his occupation and preoccupation. He relates, "I once played fourteen sets of senior singles in one day on a cement court in California." His reward for this effort was a severe case of shin splints, but he persisted in a rigorous regimen through most of his life.[684] Riggs's example brings to mind an observation made by theologian Robert E. Neale that the playboy, despite his title, is not a participant in the world of play. "What is significant is that he cannot *stop* playing; it is disguised work. And he, a drudge."[685] Neale could have substituted the term "hustler" for "playboy."

Turning from biography to American fiction, here too one finds the theme of sport as work. The writings of Ernest Hemingway, a self-proclaimed sportsman, are representative of "work well done" in the context of sport. His best characters are highly competent men "at work," engaged in meticulous rituals of technique. Hemingway's use of "sportsman" is a misnomer, for the author has nothing but disdain for the dilettantes who simply "play games." His heroes show little exuberance or joy while pursuing the male games of hunting and fishing. Santiago, the hero of *The Old Man and the Sea,* typifies this persona. The character's central image is that of the technical expert under difficult circumstances. The type of fishing Santiago pursues requires great skill in its careful manipulations of equipment. He fishes because it is his work, and yet his methods are not those of commercial fishermen but of the skilled artisan. Notably, Joe DiMaggio, master of the craft of hitting a baseball, is the old fisherman's hero. In reading this novel, it is easy to forget that deep-sea fishing is a sport. For Hemingway, sport is a ritual of labor.[686]

The Protestant ethic obliges everyone to engage in work of importance. Individuals establish their status among the elect by the example of the work they accomplish. Work represents worthy use of time, productiveness, success, and ultimately, moral virtue. Work becomes the all-encompassing focus of life. Consequently, Americans have had to recast sport in the guise of work in order to justify it. When professional baseball player Cal Ripken, Jr. surpassed Lou Gehrig's record of 2,130 consecutive games in 1995, his feat was celebrated in the American media as a vindication of the work ethic. No other heroic metaphor could compete with this one compelling interpretation. Ripken was a man who was simply "doing his job," showing up for work every day for thirteen years without missing a day.[687]

Ralph Barton Perry suggested that the American athlete, through his intense efforts to surpass records or defeat opponents, makes work out of what should be play and makes it uncomfortable for those who have neither the time nor the inclination to take games so seriously.[688] Beisser observed, "[M]odern sports are dominated by the spirit of work; arduous practice, long hours of learning signals and plays, sweating, bruising, bone-breaking practice, all in preparation for the big game."[689] A contemporary critic summed it up: "People used to *play* tennis. Now they *work* on their backhand." The motives, meanings, and forms of American sport all reflect the dominance of the work ethic.

Individualism

> The golfer...stands alone.
> He starts and finishes the deed.
> He can blame no one for his failure,
> he can take full credit for his success.
> —Al Barrow

Golf is a sport in which the athlete can genuinely compete against him or herself and the forces of nature (recognizing that tournament ranking of scores is a contrivance). Given the emphasis on individualism in the Protestant ethic, one might expect that sports like golf would typify America at play. Indeed, golf is a popular recreational sport. Estimates are that some thirty million play, and professional golf generates a huge television audience. However, it is not individual sports that garner the most public interest and enthusiasm. Team sports draw the largest numbers of fans and the greatest coverage by the electronic and print media. Notwithstanding the recent popularity of golfer Tiger Woods, most of the nation's sports heroes have been baseball, basketball, and football players. Baseball has been christened "The Great American Pastime." The term "contact sport" brings to mind football rather than boxing. Basketball, not bowling, became the "city game." How does one explain the anomaly of cultural individualism and the reigning status of team sports?

The attraction of team sports can be traced to the particular strain of individualism that evolved in the course of the nation's history. America's individualism reflects the shared influence of Puritanism and democracy. These ideologies shaped individual behaviors and values within the context of social institutions. Traditionally, Americans pursued their individual callings within community settings (as noted in chapter 4). Democratic values promoted a "level playing field" upon which individuals were given equal opportunity to achieve, while the Puritan emphasis on personal salvation promoted competitiveness and personal achievement. Early on, sport remained outside this scheme. The Calvinist stifling of sport and recreation preordained these pastimes to become expressions of individual nonconformity at the expense of communal loyalty. The story of Rip Van Winkle covertly playing at nine-pins is illustrative. But as religious objections waned, leisure activities like bowling were engaged in openly. Today's large churches feature recreational wings and sponsor bowling teams. Ultimately, Calvinism and democracy worked in tandem—if not in constant harmony—to promote institutionalized sport with an individualist ethic. Sports stadiums and ballparks provide venues for athletes to perform in public view. In this arena, athletes are held accountable for personal achievements along with their contribution to the team effort. Thus, American sport has performed the important ritual function of affirming the quest for self-identity and self-worth within the context of the group.[690]

During the Industrial age, sport also provided a venue for the struggle between remnants of pre-Industrial individualism and the ascendant corporate mentality. This was the era when sports entrepreneurs first made their appeal to the urban masses by marketing individual athletes as heroes of achievement. The sports fan identified with the successes of athletes as much as with a winning team. Baseball fans followed the individual careers of Cy Young and Ty Cobb. Focus on heroes provided the working class with an illusion of autonomy to counter the rising conformity within large business corporations for whom they labored.[691]

The corporate model redefined the relationship between the individual and the group. Within the context of corporate capitalism, "rugged individualism" eventually gave way to the concept of individuals as building blocks in the organization. Prominent voices spoke against extreme individualism in both work and play. Walter Camp (1859–1925), the "Father of American Football," argued that sports such as track and tennis were weakened by their private character, that they did not permit the development of *esprit de corps* as could football, baseball, or rowing in a crew. Camp and his fellow coaches touted team sports as the ideal medium for preparing the individual to fit into other teams: industrial, executive, and military.[692] Progressive-era reformers touted team sports for their potential to teach young people the ideals of cooperation and group loyalty. Leaders of the playground movement praised group activities as an antidote to unfettered individualism and idiosyncratic behaviors.[693]

America's social reformers, however, discovered they were fighting an uphill battle to stifle the appeal of individualism by promoting team competition and group play. While progressive voices continued to decry economic individualism, they could not stifle individual initiative on the playing fields. What emerged was an uneasy synthesis that framed the sports team as a blend of individual and group effort. The mixed success of the reform movement reflected the fundamental ambivalence of Americans about surrendering their individualism completely to the will of the group. The idea persisted that the individual athlete could "work" both for oneself and for the goals of the team without conflict.[694] In the final analysis, the efforts of the reformers did not stifle individualism within sport or the broader society.

In reality, most American team sports are an amalgamation of individual effort and teamwork. Sports teams reveal patterns of interdependently functioning units, an interplay of individual efforts directed at a common goal. Teamwork, as it exists in most sports, consists of "tactically determined cooperation," to borrow Bruno Rigauer's phrase.[695] A team's success or failure is contingent upon the sum of individual contributions to the collective effort. Division of labor and role specialization (early features of American team sports) further enhance the importance of individual effort. Sports routinely feature instances of individual competition within team-level competition. The team may lose but the individual may be eminently successful in his or her own efforts.[696] Conversely, the team may win and the individual may fail to perform up to personal standards. It is not uncommon for athletes to set personal performance or career goals independent of team goals.

Individual performances in team sports are given disproportionate attention by the news media and the public. We speak of the game-winning run in baseball, shot in basketball, or goal in hockey. Bobby Thompson's home run deciding the 1951 National League pennant race (telecast nationally) was extolled by baseball aficionados as "the shot heard 'round the world." The media tend to focus on virtuoso performances of one member of a team. What is true for success applies equally to failures. A team's loss is often attributed to the failure of one athlete (e.g., a dropped pass in football or a soccer goalie's failure to block a shot), and a losing season often is blamed on the coach.[697] Fred Merkle, who played for the New York Giants in the World War I era, made a base running error that cost his team the pennant. He was haunted for the remainder of his life by what was tagged "The Merkle Boner."[698] In American sport, individual athletes and coaches routinely are praised or blamed for the team's fate. The American sport ethic holds individual responsibility to be the central issue.

Professional basketball was struggling financially in the late 1970s when two outstanding athletes, Irwin "Magic" Johnson and Larry Byrd, came onto the scene. These young players, both with highly individualized styles, commanded such a following among spectators that they carried professional basketball into an era of prosperity. Michael Jordan extended this legacy into the 1980s and 1990s. Harold "Red" Grange had done the same thing for college and professional football some fifty years earlier. Such instances demonstrate how individual performance can effect a response in the American public. However, individual achievement in the context of team sport is often overshadowed by unabashed individualism.

Teamwork appears to be a remnant of the past in some sports. Long-time basketball fans decry the evolution of the professional game toward rampant individualism. They view NBA star players as prima donnas who value their own achievements and reputations over team success. The midrange game that relied on passing, screens, and moving without the ball has been replaced by the sensational inside-outside game characterized by long three-point shots or spectacular dunks. The rise of egoism is not limited to basketball, and it extends to athletes beyond the game. Self-promotion and self-expression have become the norm among celebrity athletes.

Professional athletes seek to further their own careers. Within contractual limitations, select athletes can sell their services to the highest bidder. Professionals function as independent contractors in a perpetual search for better offers. At the same time, teams and leagues exploit individual athletes to their own advantage. One effect of this arrangement is that athletes are no longer identified with a particular team. Major League infielder Eddie Brinkman was traded four times in five years during the 1970s. He spent most of his career packing and unpacking luggage.[699] In contrast, Ernie Banks was "Mr. Cub," Joe DiMaggio was revered as the Yankee Clipper, and Bart Starr is remembered as a Baltimore Colt. But today's journeyman athletes may play with a half dozen teams over the course of their careers. Sports fans follow their favorite players as they change uniforms over the seasons. At the beginning of the 1993 baseball season, some 260 major league players from the previous year's roster had changed teams. Even college athletes change schools in spite of eligibility rules discouraging the practice. Sports teams no longer function as closely knit groups of athletes with a mutual history and a common future.

Team owners in professional sports have promoted an emphasis upon individual performance by agreeing to "incentive clauses" in players' contracts. Salaries, bonuses, and fringe benefits are tied to individual statistics. A baseball player's salary is more likely to be contingent upon his batting average than the team's record.[700] Consequently, professional athletes have become just as concerned with their personal performance as they are with their team's success. Keith Hernandez, who played first base in the National League in the 1970s and 1980s, was known as an individualist. He once reflected on the current season, concluding that his team (twenty games out of first place) was going nowhere, and then rationalized that it was not really his team anyway because he had no intention of staying. Hernandez concluded that it made sense for him to play for himself and worry about his personal statistics.[701] This self-interest has carried into amateur sports. Outstanding school athletes are as concerned with getting their names in the newspapers and showcasing their skills for scouts as they are with the fortunes of their team.

Individualism is reinforced through the system of honors and acknowledgments promulgated by the sports community. The custom has been to bestow awards upon individual athletes, even in team sports. In 1871 at a professional baseball game in Louisville, Kentucky, the daughter of a local jeweler handed the president of the National Association club a jeweled medal to be awarded at the end of the season to the best player.[702] This system of awards initiated during the formative years of sport set a lasting precedent for recognizing individual athletes. A century after the jeweler's trophy was presented, the National Hockey League was bestowing the following collection of awards for the season: most valuable player, top defenseman, rookie of the year, scoring champion, top defensive forward, goals-against average, coach of the year, humanitarian contribution, and the Bill Masterton trophy. All these awards were presented to individuals; meanwhile, the NHL championship-winning team is awarded the Stanley Cup. It follows that teams typically do not get inducted into sports halls of fame; individual athletes do.

One rarely finds a team picture on the cover of a sports magazine or in a newspaper. The news media's coverage of team sports focuses on individuals and personalities. A promotional advertisement for a 1991 basketball game between the Chicago Bulls and the Los Angeles Lakers was billed by the NBC television network (which telecast the game) as the "Air and Magic Show," exploiting the well-known sobriquets of the star players. The electronic media frequently presents team contests as a duel between star players. The television camera has a unique capability to focus on individual performances in a way that the human eye cannot. However, the camera also has the ability to pull back and take in the larger view. When watching the Boston Marathon on television from the perspective of the airborne camera, it is easy to conceptualize the vibrating mass of humanity on the screen as an organic entity. Yet, the upshot of this mass event will be the recognition of one individual within each class of runners who has logged the fastest time. The marathon provides a cogent symbol of individual achievement in the context of the group.

The Protestant ethic has held each person responsible for his or her salvation in the secular world. The individual cannot rely upon anyone else in the final reckoning of self worth. American sport has reflected the basic value placed on individualism. The emphasis upon personal achievement shapes the meaning of athletic performances in spectator sports as well as participant sports. Whether the venue is a neighborhood sandlot or the World Series, the emphasis on individual performance prevails. Sports fans celebrate the player who hit a homerun or scored the winning touchdown. Memories gloss over the fact that these victories required the efforts of fellow athletes working as a team. Americans choose to focus on individual achievement in sport, as in life.

Achieved Status

> [I]t wasn't winning that B.A. cared about; or football, or God; it was how
> those things combined to make him successful.
> –Peter Gent, *North Dallas Forty*

General H. Norman Schwarzkopf, in explaining the Allied military tactic that ended the Persian Gulf War of 1991, likened the decisive maneuver to a "Hail Mary" pass in football. In making this analogy, the general was saying that achievement in war is like achievement in sport. Thus has sport provided a model for achievement. Conversely, and more to the point, accomplishments in the sports stadium exemplify the American achievement ethic. Sport performs this function well, as athletic achievement is straightforward and observable, and it occurs under ostensibly equitable circumstances. There are few other social institutions, with the possible exceptions of business or politics, where individual achievement ranks so highly. Success on the athletic fields connotes several important meanings, but most prominent among them is achieved status.[703]

For Americans, the medium in which achieved status occurs has proved less important than achievement per se. The Protestant ethic fosters a single-minded pursuit of individual success regardless of the arena. The ethic was originally tied to vocation but soon encompassed avocations where achievement was manifest. Even on the playing fields and in the sports arena, achievement can provide status and promote feelings of self worth. This ethic is not the sole source of individual motivation in sport, but unquestionably it reinforces, heightens, and legitimizes the meaning of athletic performance.[704]

Games of all types from chess to poker offer opportunities for achievement, but those requiring physical skills afford the most observable expression. In modern industrial societies like the United States, games and sports combining athletic skill with sophisticated strategies are dominant. These types of activities offer symbolic representations of the basic principles of Protestant capitalism. Not surprisingly, members of the entrepreneurial class demonstrate high achievement motivation and reveal a strong interest in games like golf and tennis that combine skill and strategy. Sports that relied on physical superiority originally proved less popular among the upper classes. But the achievement ethic filtered down through the broad middle classes in such a way that it now encompasses a wide range of athletic sports.[705]

The need for achieved status has impelled the American compulsion to win and led to an uninhibited competitiveness. The fear of losing, whether in business or sport, reveals the latent Puritan anxiety about being labeled a failure with all its moral implications. Arguably, no institution has been more ruthlessly unforgiving of the failure to achieve than sport—regardless of disparities in the innate abilities of competitors. NFL coach Vince Lombardi would admonish his players, "I'm going to tell you the facts, gentlemen, and the facts are these: 'At Green Bay we…do not have losers. If you're a loser, mister, you're going to get your ass out of here and you're going to get your ass out of here right now'."[706] Lombardi sensed the threat of "moral contamination" in associating with losers. It is a feeling that is endemic among high achievers. The achievement ethic abides no excuse for losing.

The harsh stigma associated with losing may explain why America's athletic coaches have insisted on calling most of the plays during contests. Coaches often are held personally responsible for a defeat. Indeed, the fear of failure has been so strong that football coaches—in the era before overtime periods—were known to play for a "tie" rather than risk the consequences of losing the game. Psychologists note that individuals with a strong need to achieve are characterized by their drive to be successful as opposed to avoidance of failure, but this personal trait is countered by the cultural guilt assigned to failure. Arguably, it is possible to speak of "achieving a tie" against a better team, but it is more difficult to speak convincingly of achievement in a losing effort. For many coaches and athletes, avoiding defeat seems to be as strong a motivation as achieving victory.[707]

The achievement ethic has carried to the level of children's sport (see chapter 10). Social psychologist Jonathan Brower found that youth sport programs were typically run by success-oriented adults who promulgate an uncompromising emphasis upon achievement at the expense of other values.[708] The youth sport ethic has a long history. The nation's juvenile literature has reflected the theme of athletic achievement. In children's baseball stories dating from the 1880s, achievement appeared as a central theme. Burt Standish's "Frank Merriwell" stories enjoyed immense favor among young readers. They sold 50,000 copies a week at the height of their popularity in the 1930s. The school sports heroes of these stories would recite homilies that reflect the importance of winning at sports and in life.

Thus were the nation's youth socialized for sports achievement through their reading as well as their experiences on the playgrounds.[709]

Although the emphasis on achievement pervades American institutions, nowhere is the need to achieve more pervasive and compelling than in sport. This emphasis is noteworthy, for unlike achievement in one's employment or public service, achievement in sport provides no lasting benefit in the sense of goods produced or services rendered, apart from its entertainment value. The question arises, "What is gained from sport achievement?" The payoff may be symbolic. Games, by their very nature, result in the establishment of differences among individual players or teams where originally there was no established inequality. At the end of the contest, the participants are divided into winners and losers. (In league and tournament standings, the discrimination is even more refined: first, second, third…last.) Showing oneself superior in the outcome of a contest confers upon the winner a sense of superiority. In this respect, winners achieve something more than victory; they achieve status. Herein lies the significance of winning at sport.

Americans tend to be awarded status based on what they achieve, not on their lineage (see chapter 4). Traditionally, when the "well born" excluded others based on ascribed status, they defended this practice by suggesting the out-groups were less capable. Class bias was accompanied by various forms of race prejudice and sexism. The male WASP convinced himself women were too weak and that ethnic minorities lacked the character traits to compete successfully. But racial and gender barriers eventually broke down as highly skilled women and members of minority groups excelled in an increasing number of venues, including sport. Achieved status eventually prevailed. The American sport ethic, with its emphasis on achievement, proved a stronger cultural force than ethnic, gender, or class prejudice. The Jackie Robinsons, Jim Thorpes, and Babe Didriksons were conceded the status they earned on the ballfields, running tracks, and golf courses.[710]

Status has been the reward for athletic achievement. Sport is replete with status labels: champion, all-American, all-star, superstar, most valuable player, hall-of-famer. Americans reveal a compelling need to apply superlatives to achievements, their own and that of others. Nowhere is this more evident than in sport. Upon winning the world's heavyweight championship in boxing, Muhammad Ali exclaimed unabashedly, "I am the greatest. I am the greatest." The employment of such acclamations has become routine among American athletes and sports fans. Boasting suggests not only the importance of status but also its ephemeral nature. As historian John Lukacs noted, when someone has to announce publicly, "I'm number one," it means the person is not sure of him or herself.[711] The frequency with which Americans proclaim themselves champions, with arm raised and index finger extended, divulges the national preoccupation with status and its transience.

The fragility of status in sport is due, in part, to its very nature. Games and athletic contests are subject to happenstance; the difference between winning and losing often depends upon the random bounce of a ball. In this chancy setting, an athlete constantly strives to remain on top. Sport presents a series of unending tests, physical and mental. There is always another game, another match, another season. Status can be particularly vulnerable in the public arena where performance is continually evaluated. Newspapers print the ranking of contenders, the statistics of individual and team performances, and updated league and tournament standings. The public tends to judge the athlete on his most recent performance; no one remembers last season's accomplishments for very long. Athletes cannot rest on their laurels.

Athletes' insecurity about status transcends the nature of sport. It is endemic to a value system that equates status with personal justification and one in which a sense of salvation comes to those very few who are truly deserving. Americans continually strive to acquire status and its trappings in order to convince themselves and others they are among the "elect" and to alleviate the haunting feelings of uncertainty about their personal worth. One way to accomplish this task is to affiliate with high-status organizations such as country clubs or sports teams. The team takes on many of the same functions as a sect. Only the "chosen" can become members, and putting on a team uniform constitutes a ritual of election. To be an active player is to participate in a select circle.[712] Pulitzer Prize-winning writer Garry Wills observed that "America's prep schools and Ivy League colleges had made games the crucible of character. Skill at one of several sports—racing crew, fencing, polo, yachting, golf, tennis—were marks of caste."[713]

In forming sports teams, the undeserving are excluded. Those who fail to "make the team" are relegated to the role of spectators, a designation that offers little status and permits only vicarious participation in the elite athletes' accomplishments. American sport serves more as a filter than a facilitator. By doing so, it carries out an important function consistent with the Protestant ethic: separating the chosen from the masses. America's social institutions are designed to mitigate the basic contradiction between the strongly held principle of equality on one hand and the reality of superior talents on the other. Sport, ostensibly a meritocracy, fulfills this function well. Everyone has an opportunity to try out for the team. At the same time, the selection process systematically denies opportunities for participation to a large portion of the aspirants. By its nature, competitive sport favors the highly skilled, who always constitute a small minority.[714] Thus, American sport has corroborated the Calvinist conceit "that many are called but few are chosen."

Exclusive practices were evident in the nation's early athletic clubs. When these clubs formed in the last half of the nineteenth century, many of them were made up of urban businessmen. These men strived to maintain the elite character of their sport by openly excluding common laborers. The upper classes felt they could exhibit their superiority by demonstrating athletic prowess in a context that reproduced and justified existing social inequality. The term "amateur," by definition, harbored a class bias. The very idea of competing regularly in a sport as an avocation implied one realized an income that allowed time from work to train and compete. Thus, amateur sport as a product of class privilege was pursued in a way that excluded most people. The founder of the modern Olympic movement, Pierre de Coubertin, incorporated an elitist conception of amateur standing by disallowing athletes who had been remunerated for competing.[715]

A less class-conscious, yet elitist, form of sport has been adopted by the American educational system. The process of selecting athletes begins in the early grades and is repeated by high schools and colleges. Those who measure up become "jocks"—an American colloquialism that, in its positive connotation, denotes members of a sporting elite. Athletes are treated as local celebrities by their fellow students and often by adults in the community. Positions on school sports teams traditionally have been reserved for a limited number of the highly skilled. Consequently, a fraction of the student body participates in school sports. A survey conducted in the 1980s found that only 21 percent of secondary school students were members of even one varsity team. Would-be student athletes whose skills were judged insufficient for varsity teams might compete in intramural sports, if their school provides such a program. But intramurals have always been a neglected segment of the American extracurriculum, especially for males. Arguably, more emphasis is placed on students attending varsity sport contests than on participating in intramurals.[716] Many schools require attendance at pep rallies that provide occasions for the nonathletes to recognize the status of the varsity athletes.

Elitism in sport has been most evident in American colleges. Members of athletic teams (disproportionately men) have constituted a tiny fraction of the students on campus. At a typical large Eastern university, football players made up 1.5 percent of the student body. As sociologist Paul Hoch pointed out, "The money and resources that might have been put into intramural sports in which everyone could be a 'player,' instead has been put into sports for an elite."[717] Only recently have colleges put significant effort into campus recreation and intramural sports that provide opportunities for all students. However, the main focus remains on men's varsity football and basketball teams. Women's sports have increased in number following Title IX legislation, but continue to receive less financial support than men's sports.

College administrators realized it was not the academic programs but successful athletic teams that accounted for much of a school's prestige. Sports programs were the most visible component of some colleges' public image. A school's prestige was tied to revenue needed to produce winning athletic teams that, in turn, conveyed status. Much of this money was to come from alumni. A recent example was Oklahoma State University alum T. Boone Pickens's donation of $290 million to his alma mater, $165 million of which went to support varsity athletics programs. College administrators have convinced themselves successful sports teams enhance general economic support for the institution—although this connection has been brought into question by some recent studies.[718]

Through the course of the twentieth century, a sophisticated status structure was built around college sports. A major component in this structure were post-season championship games and tournaments. Not long after college teams began playing each other, post-season tournaments were organized in basketball, baseball, track and field, and other sports. These tournaments provided the winning teams with national recognition. In football, the tradition of appearing in post-season "bowl" games carried immense status. The tradition began in 1902 with the Rose Bowl game. Other bowl games were established and now number close to three dozen. All-star games are another form of high-status competition. In 1935, the Shriners, a fraternal organization, established the East-West Shrine Game, a post-season contest featuring the nation's best football players from various colleges. A player and his college acquired national recognition by his appearing in this game. Currently, NCAA sponsors national tournaments in most sports.[719]

Additional status was accorded through national rankings of college teams by the major newspapers and other news media, most notably in basketball and football. In 1936, the Associated Press news service began to poll its sports writers to select the top ten teams of the year. This practice aroused national interest, and in 1950 United Press followed suit. News services and newspapers listed rankings of teams before, during, and after the seasons. Today, the news media list several national rankings by coaches and journalists. It is fair to say that nothing—short of a Nobel Prize laureate on the faculty—can convey more status than a college's football or basketball teams being highly ranked in a major sport. National rankings and post-season tournament championships are among the ultimate status rituals in college sport.[720]

Individual amateur and professional athletes attain a high level of status as members of so-called all-star or all-America teams. As early as 1889, Casper Whitney, a magazine publisher, selected a team of the eleven best college football players and called it the "All-America" team. Walter Camp later selected his own nominees for these teams at the bequest of national magazines. The newspapers began selecting an all-pro football team in 1943 to recognize the best professional players. Other sports like basketball and baseball select athletes for all-America or all-pro teams. Likewise, status is accorded to retired athletes. Beginning with the Baseball Hall of Fame, dedicated in 1939, virtually every sport has founded a hall of fame. Election to membership in halls is considered the ultimate status recognition for athletes. These shrines are housed in impressive edifices and feature memorabilia and pictures of inducted players. They remain popular tourist attractions for sports fans.[721]

Meanwhile, America's cities have vied for professional sport franchises that confer status on the entire community. The sense of community was eroding in the wake of the urban revolution of the late nineteenth century. City leaders sought a mechanism to satisfy the need for collective identity. This was the era when local sports teams began to attract large numbers of fans. A team that represented the city and carried its name could serve as a focal point of community spirit and pride. Urbanites identified with a local team. Large cities have not been unique in garnering status from a winning sports team. In the 1990s, a visitor to Warner, Oklahoma (population 1,400) was confronted by a prominent billboard at the town limits announcing that the local junior college had won the national basketball tournament. Every American traveler has witnessed similar landmarks proclaiming that a city or county high-school team has won a state championship. When local teams win, citywide celebrations follow. Athletes are paraded down the main thoroughfares. This ritual provides a shared sense of status for everyone who identifies with the event. The entire population can collectively declare, "We're number one."

Status rituals in sport are accompanied by status symbols. As noted above, the sports trophy evolved as one of the symbols of achieved status. Originally, trophies had served as warriors' *objects d'art* placed on display along with booty in a conspicuous place. They provided evidence of successful exploits on the battlefield. The finer houses in the sixteenth and seventeenth centuries set aside rooms for displaying such trophies.[722] Over time, trophies of war were eclipsed by trophies of the hunt, which provided similar status to the owner. American writer John Steinbeck commented sardonically on rooms filled with "stuffed and glass eyed heads...for the man so unsure of himself that he has constantly to prove himself and keep the evidence for others to see."[723]

Sports trophies have generally taken the forms of small metal statues, bowls, or cups. Yachting cups date from the mid-nineteenth century. At the end of that century, the Pabst Brewing Company began offering trophies for the winners of various sports contests. During this era, medals were awarded to American youngsters who met the standards of the Athletic Badge Test. The practice of awarding sport trophies proliferated. Today's schools and clubs display trophies in numbers that would dwarf the collections found in seventeenth-century mansions.[724] School buildings feature huge trophy cases in their main foyers to display the awards. Additional status artifacts came into use to motivate and reward participants in sports. Ribbons traditionally have been awarded to the high finishers at track-and-field meets: blue for first place, red for second, etc. American schools award school letters to be sewn on sweaters or jackets of varsity athletes. These visible symbols of prowess reinforce the status of athletes among their peers.

Sports fans, for their part, avidly collect status objects including autographed sports equipment or clothing used by famous athletes. Likewise, the holder of a hard-to-get season ticket or admission to a championship event enjoys a significant degree of status. Tickets for seats on the fifty-yard line of an important football game are valued possessions with major bragging rights attached. The ultimate status symbol among wealthy sports fans is access to a "skybox," the elite accommodations found nestled in the rafters of modern athletic arenas. Though a prized seat in the reserved section of a stadium may cost hundreds of dollars, a skybox leased for the season can run into the tens of thousands. These climate-controlled facilities routinely offer gourmet food and drink, television monitors, and sundry perquisites. Skyboxes are favored by American business corporations to impress clients and reward executives.

The American preoccupation with status has carried over into adult recreation. Weekend athletes engage in sports ostensibly for pleasure or health benefits, but also for the status they provide. A participant-observer study carried out in an urban tennis club revealed the dominant role status plays in recreational sport. Members of this club had developed a knack for selectively excluding individuals from matches based on their abilities. Both temporal and spatial boundaries were erected by the more skilled players. Top players formed elite cliques and avoided the lesser-skilled players. The researcher Donal Muir observed that it was as if a tacitly agreed-upon nonstop tournament were being played in which status was operationally defined by winning matches over others. Apparently, any status these upper-middle-class club members obtained from other facets in their lives was insufficient, for they pursued status on the tennis courts assiduously.[725]

Weekend athletes display status through the purchase of expensive sports equipment and accoutrements. The aficionado purchases a $200 tennis racket, a $5,000 golf cart, or a $10,000 power boat in part because of the status these items provide. High-priced leisure clothing items with prestigious brand names or team names imprinted on them provide the wearer a sense of status. Nowhere are status objects more evident than in fitness sports.[726] We recognize the "magazine-cover" runner in his or her polyester-blend trunks with bright stripes, five-star-rated jogging shoes, brand-name socks, and head band.[727] Such attire and accompanying paraphernalia identify the purchaser with high-status fitness. A general rule is that the more status-relevant the ritual, the more stereotyped the clothing, accoutrements, and bearing of the participants. Much of sporting behavior appears to be keeping up with the "athletic Joneses." Likewise, rock climbers and extreme-sport athletes are obsessed with their gear, not only for the obvious safety considerations but as a mark of distinction that sets them apart from novices.[728] Recreational athletes from the middle and upper classes appear to be purchasing status as much as functionality.

The conspicuous consumption of sports status symbols is accompanied by what newspaper columnist Charles Krauthammer (borrowing from Thorstein Veblen) has labeled "conspicuous exertion." This term refers to athletic performance itself being utilized as a status device. Status display is exemplified by jogging or running in public places where the participant can be easily observed by a less active audience. By the late 1970s, millions of Americans were participating in local sports events. Participants' names are reported in the local newspapers, and the event is covered by local television news cameras. By participating in such events, one does not simply "recreate" but achieves a feat that provides a certain amount of prestige.[729] For the rising middle class, membership in a private health club has become a status symbol. Memberships carry a certain amount of intrinsic status, which means one does not need to actually "work out" regularly or strenuously at the club, but only make an occasional appearance there in the proper attire to maintain status by affiliation.

The upper classes have a long tradition of purchasing status in sports. In the late nineteenth century, wealthy Americans began joining exclusive country clubs to compete in golf and tennis with their peers, while others paid lavish prices for champion trotting horses and fulfilled the need to demonstrate wealth and status by owning a winner.[730] Other sports status symbols available to the affluent have included backyard tennis courts and racing yachts. American millionaires would purchase professional sports teams, which provided more status than their less visible money-making enterprises. Media mogul Ted Turner is exceptional in having first achieved status as a yachtsman prior to his purchasing professional sports teams. It is more characteristic for members of his class to achieve in the business world, rather than in the arena, and then to *purchase* status through team ownership.

Sport has provided Americans with the opportunity to fill a basic need ingrained in the Protestant ethic: status through achievement. However, the nature of sport has been transformed amidst the constant striving for status. The intrinsic elements of sport have been eclipsed by the need to achieve in the public arena. American sport is preoccupied with championships, the breaking of records, and the honors and recognition that go with them. Neither the athlete nor the sports fan appears content with the spoils of victory but must continually replenish this need. Status needs have led to an accommodation of elitism. Status suggests exclusivity, and the sports team functions well as a vehicle for exclusion. All the while, the political ethos has championed equality of opportunity. Where sport functions as a meritocracy, the quest for status has resulted in unrestrained competitiveness.

Competitiveness

> The zeal to be first in everything has always been American,
> to win and to win and to win.
> —Vince Lombardi

Competitiveness is a consequence of rampant individualism and the compelling need to achieve. Psychologists note that individuals who score high in achievement motivation seek out competition, and when successful, they are more likely to persist in competitive behaviors. Sport adapts itself well to the needs of competitive achievers; its forms of competition lend themselves to objective evaluation and facilitate comparisons.[731] No American has personified competitiveness more than Vince Lombardi. The former Green Bay Packers coach would accept no excuses from his athletes for their failure to win. What came to be known as the Lombardian ethic was encapsulated in the famous maxim attributed to him: "Winning isn't everything; it's the only thing." In response to criticism of this statement, Lombardi explained he had meant to imply that "winning is not everything, but *making the effort* to win is." This sentiment expresses the essence of competitiveness.[732]

Before examining competitiveness as a component of the American sport ethic, it is essential to acknowledge the existence of noncompetitive sports and games within the world's cultures. Among preliterate people, games commonly represent a form of ritual in which the ceremonial, social, or experiential features are given more significance than winning or losing. The Native American Zunis, who emphasize wide participation in games, have been known to ostracize habitual winners. In a game played by the Amazon Indians, the player who scored was required to change teams in order to equalize the competition. Competitiveness in games clearly is an artifact of culture. Societies that are achievement-oriented emphasize the competitive elements in games at the expense of other qualities. The competitive ethic has been characteristic of American sport. Nothing within the experience of playing games takes precedence over competing to win. Noncompetitive games, promoted by groups like the New Games Movement in the 1970s, never transcended the limited context of a counterculture movement in the United States.[733]

During the rise of American sport, amateurism vied for primacy with professionalism. Unbounded competitiveness was antithetical to the code that governed amateur sports. Etiquette implied that the amateur athlete did not pursue victory with an exaggerated effort beyond the importance of the occasion. To do so implied a lack of breeding. Overly aggressive behavior or expedient tactics that skirted the rules violated the spirit of the game. Amateurism emphasized sportsmanship and good form on the field of play. This spirit is enshrined in the oft-quoted sentiment penned by journalist Grantland Rice, "When the One Great Scorer comes to write against your name, He marks—not that you won or lost—but how you played the game."[734] In this tradition, athletes put forth their best effort, and when the game was over, the winner was expected to accept victory graciously. However, this "gentlemen's-club" approach to sport, with its class-conscious code of conduct, was short-lived in the main arena of American sport.[735]

Among the working classes where status was not a "given," competitiveness took precedence over sportsmanship. The typical athlete made no excuses about competing ruthlessly to win. Pragmatism trumped idealism. American sport progressively replicated the features of a competitive society where success was tied to unrestrained effort. A version of Social Darwinism surfaced to provide justification for unfettered competition. The Episcopal minister William Graham Sumner declared, "Competition is the law of nature. Nature…grants her rewards to the fittest…without regard to other considerations of any kind."[736] Given this ethos, it is not surprising that Americans embraced a ruthless brand of competition. Walter Camp, the dean of American college football coaches (and Sumner's brother-in-law), was a strident champion of Social Darwinism in the sports arena. The spirit of competition also influenced the budding women's sport movement. Camp's contemporary Dr. Louisa Smith, Director of the gymnasium at Bryn Mawr College, asserted, "Life is one long competition so why not prepare for it in the gymnasium."[737]

Few dissenting voices could be heard during this period. YMCA leader Luther Gulick, who called for a de-emphasis on fierce competition, stood virtually alone against the juggernaut of competitiveness. Indeed, the competitiveness in sports surpassed that found in any other American institution. The competitive spirit filtered down to the public-school programs and playgrounds. At the turn of the twentieth century, Joseph Lee, a promoter of supervised recreation, observed while watching boys engaged in spontaneous play that no one was trying to win, and even worse, no one seemed to care what the score was! The remedy, of course, was to redesign children's recreation to be more competitive. The public schools in New York City organized interschool competition in baseball, football, and track and field. Championship tournaments were held up to the city level. Other cities followed New York's lead. Americans justified competitive youth sports as preparation for survival in a competitive adult world.[738]

It is understood that competitiveness is an inherent element of sports, and much of the satisfaction of playing sports can be attributed to competition. The idea of athletic excellence implies competing against others or against one's own limitations. The athlete's identity is connected with the struggle and its outcome.[739] However, sport does not embody unadulterated competition, as cooperation is required in agreeing to the objectives of the game and the established rules. Sport incorporates physical force but shades off from combat by drawing a line at some point. Sports competition differs from hostile physical conflict by striving to attain a goal rather than inflicting damage on an opponent (boxing excepted). But when athletes compete without restraint, rules are stretched to their limit, and the field of play becomes an arena where aggression takes precedence over fairness and sportsmanship.[740] At this point, sport escalates into open hostility. Fights may break out, as they often do in ice hockey.

At its worst, competitiveness can lead to unbounded and ruthless forms of violence and cheating. Athletes may employ physical intimidation to prevail in contact sports. Former NFL linebacker Bill Romanowski is an exemplar of this tactic. For him, injuring opponents was part of the game.[741] Athletes become highly expedient, resorting to virtually any conceivable tack to ensure victory. Equipment is altered in violation of regulations to provide its user with an unfair advantage. Baseball players have been caught corking their bats, while football players violate the restraints on taping or use of pads. Rules of play are circumvented to expedite winning, adhered to only when to one's advantage, or obeyed when game officials are directly observing the action. The prevailing modus operandi is not to get caught breaking the rules. Officials' decisions are assertively questioned and disputed. Critics of hyper-competitiveness observe that the incentives for winning are so great, it is a wonder fair play maintains any presence at all in the arena.[742]

Competitiveness is not restricted to athletes and coaches but carries over to spectators. Consistent with its etymology, the "fan" can become a fanatic about winning. The engaged spectator does not go to the stadium just to be entertained but for the satisfaction that accompanies victory by a local team or favored athlete. The inordinate identification of sports fans with teams and athletes is a manifestation of the need to share in the experience of winning. It reveals itself in the ecstasy that follows victory in the arena and the angst that accompanies defeat.[743] Stadium managers have found it necessary to cordon off sections of seating to keep opposing fans apart because of competitive feelings. Outside the stadium, more than one bar fight has been precipitated by sports rivalries among patrons. Such occurrences remind one of George Orwell's comment that "sport is war without the shooting."

In short, competitiveness permeates America's sport in its diverse incarnations. It has reshaped recreational activities that originally were not contests. Historically, fishing was a way to put food on the table. It evolved into a popular form of recreation. However, traditional methods of fishing—casting from the banks of a farm pond or wading in hip boots in a mountain stream—have been upstaged by organized contests. Bass fishing is now an institutionalized form of competition. A national organization of bass fishermen sponsors regional fishing tournaments lasting up to three days. These tournaments, which draw hundreds of competitors, culminate in the national Bassmaster championship. Equipment vendors and boat manufacturers sponsor promising fishermen in these tournaments and bankroll prizes of tens of thousands of dollars. The competitors in these events purchase expensive gear and boats equipped with sophisticated technology to enhance their chances of winning.[744] Fishing has become a competitive sport like golf or tennis.

American competitiveness likewise has transformed the martial arts. The traditional emphasis upon spiritual development, self-knowledge, and selflessness intrinsic to Zen culture has been supplanted by intense training for national tournaments. The American interest in karate is in full contact with the goal of competing to win tournaments.[745] Other recreational activities that were originally noncompetitive have been similarly transformed by the national sporting ethic. Frisbee and skateboarding—initially forms of casual recreation—have been organized into competitive events with national tournaments.

Competitiveness has carried beyond the physical bounds and timeframe of the staged sports contest. Over the course of time, coaches and managers began to realize what they did between contests could be as important to ensure victory as what is achieved during the game. Astute coaches realized that acquiring superior athletes was just as important to winning as was coaching, training, and conditioning. Competition for the best available talent became a major part of sport, and sophisticated systems of recruiting were instigated. By the mid-twentieth century, recruiting constituted one of the most competitive aspects of college and professional sports, and it extended down into the high schools. Recruiting athletes has become a contest with its own set of rules. However, the rules are routinely broken by the more aggressive college recruiters. Cheaters are caught and penalized, but the unbridled competition for athletes has continued despite enforcement measures by governing associations.[746]

Athletes must compete beyond the playing field as well. They vie for the opportunity to play sports. Recruits and "free agents" contend for limited positions on teams, and once on the team, they compete for starting positions and for playing time. Successful high-school athletes vie for the limited positions on college squads, and a select number then compete for the even fewer positions on professional teams. In the early 1990s, there were approximately half a million male high-school basketball players in the United States. Of those who went on to college, only 19,000 played on varsity basketball squads. The best college players then competed for the 400 or so positions on teams in the National Basketball Association, with about forty or fifty new players drafted each year.[747]

Competitiveness extends to the business of sports. The early history of professional baseball was one of ruthless competition among rival governing bodies. Team owners competed in and for markets. This competition led to trusts, cartels, and other contrivances to ensure profits among the established franchises in a highly competitive market. New leagues sporadically emerged to challenge the existing structures in a dog-eat-dog economic environment. The players formed leagues to challenge the owners. In 1922, a US Supreme Court decision exempting major league baseball from antitrust legislation legitimated the monopolistic business model. However, the United States has never seriously contemplated a governmental agency to coordinate sports as do the Europeans nations. The nation's sports continue to operate in a competitive, free-market environment.[748]

Competition among rival professional sport franchises peaked after World War II when new leagues in football, basketball, and hockey challenged the established leagues. Teams and leagues competed against each other for customers in several urban markets. This market competition took its toll. During one season in the early 1990s, the eight professional baseball teams at the bottom of the standings lost money while the top eight teams made a profit. In some sports, everyone lost. The National Professional Soccer League folded in 1968, the World Football League and professional track in 1975, the National Lacrosse League in 1976, the American Basketball Association in 1977, the World Hockey Association in 1979, and World Team Tennis in 1979. The decade of the 1970s symbolized "survival of the fittest" in the sports business.[749]

Another dimension of economic competition has emerged. Spectator events on various levels compete in an increasingly crowded market. Professional sport competes against college sport, which competes against prep-school sport for fans and revenue. Television stations and networks compete with each other and with gate attendance for an audience. Overlap in seasons pits sports against each other. On the professional level, baseball now begins in early spring and runs into October. Football begins with exhibition games in late July and runs for over two dozen weeks through February. Basketball and hockey extend from October to June. At one point, St. Louis hosted 122 home games in professional baseball and hockey, with these two sports competing for an audience during the overlap in their seasons.

Beginning in the 1960s, intense competition arose among American cities to host professional sports franchises. Owners of established teams have taken advantage of this competitive market by "playing" cities against each other. Teams owners threaten to move to rival cities that offer them better financial deals. The cities of Oakland and Los Angeles carried out a long-term competition in the 1980s and 1990s to host the NFL Raiders. Cities compete for established teams, and for new teams when leagues increase the number of franchises. Mass-spectator sports operate in a free market where intense competition is the norm.[750]

Americans remark on the analogies between competition in sport and the business world. However, there remains a distinction. The essence of play is that the test should be as important as the contest, the experience as significant as the results. In this sense, competitive play stands apart from the world of work. Notwithstanding, the capitalist business model has carried over into American sport.[751] The result is that competition takes precedence in both realms. Ironically, competition in the business world has been modulated by economic realities and political constraints. Sport may be the singular institution in which free competition reigns. The American writer Ring Lardner satirized suburban sportsmen of the post-World War I era who "bared their teeth" in competition at the golf course or bridge table, with a frantic desire to win at games that reflected their daily lives in the business world. Contemporary sportsmen and women may be drawn to such games to express a competitive spirit that is stifled in the world of work.[752]

The United States developed as an open society with no pre-existing social structure and a high degree of social mobility. Everything on the new continent was "up for grabs." Life became a series of contests for land, wealth, power, and social position. The competitive spirit was rewarded in virtually every facet of life. The Protestant ethic framed life as a test in which individuals vied for limited rewards granted to a righteous minority. A vulgar form of Social Darwinism reinforced the prevailing view of life as a struggle for survival. The competitive ethos carried over into sport, where it found an ideal setting in which to be played out. American sport embraced open competitiveness and defined itself in the process. What started out as casual play and gentlemen's games inevitably became contests where winning was indeed the only thing.

10

Child-Rearing and Youth Sport in Protestant Culture

The Uses of Childhood

> Now we see that youth probably exists for the sake of play.
> –Karl Groos

Mark Twain's character Tom Sawyer exemplifies the child at play. Tom was a free spirit intent on postponing the responsibilities of growing up. In the eyes of his elders he was the consummate enfant terrible, a boy who fought valiantly against the prescribed liturgy of school lessons, prayers and Bible verses, regular meals, chores, and imposed bedtime. When forced to suffer regular attendance at school or church, Tom livened up these dull proceedings with imaginative pranks. Occasionally he succeeded in escaping altogether the fetters of the adult world, whereupon he beat a retreat to his favorite refuges on the Mississippi River banks and in the woods of Eastern Missouri.

Tom revealed no aspirations to be the model boy of his village, the teacher's pet, an Eagle Scout, an altar boy, or the most valuable player on anyone's team. He got into fights, smoked tobacco, "cussed," swiped doughnuts, told fibs, and went swimming on the sly. But mostly, he indulged in the spirited free play that occupies any self-reliant youngster left to his own devices. Tom played pirate, dug for treasure, and captured imaginary prisoners. He crossed the Mississippi on a homemade raft, camped out, and fished with his best friend Huck. The readers of *The Adventures of Tom Sawyer* follow this fictional hero's exploits through a ten-year period into his early adolescence. We do not know what kind of adult Tom turned out to be except in the example of his creator and alter ego.[753]

The turn-of-the-century boyhood of George Herman "Babe" Ruth began much like that of Tom Sawyer. Ruth's childhood included a repertoire of boyish pranks rivaling those of his fictional counterpart. Young George ran loose in the streets of Baltimore, tossing baseballs through windows and rocks at delivery men. He became such a problem that his father, George, Sr., a saloon owner, dispatched him to St. Mary's Industrial School for Boys. There, a caring mentor, Brother Matthias, taught George, Jr. to put a baseball to more productive use. But despite his stint in the Catholic reformatory where he honed his athletic skills, the Babe never entirely reformed. The adult Ruth was simply an overgrown boy. He continued to play baseball, caroused, clowned around, smoked, ate and drank too much, and generally had a good time.[754]

Babe Ruth's upbringing was a portent of things to come. America was changing and so was the nature of childhood. Boys and girls growing up in the Progressive era would prove less able than Tom Sawyer to challenge societal norms. Like the young Babe Ruth, they would be steered increasingly into adult-supervised settings. Organized sports and recreation became one facet of a reform movement that was usurping the free play that had occupied children for generations. The impact of these "reforms" was apparent to the Reverend Thomas Wentworth Higginson in the late nineteenth century. The liberal minister noted the lack of spontaneous play among America's young men compared to what he had observed in England. This radical transformation of children's play would carry through the next century.[755]

Contemporary athletes, writers, and scholars have commented on the effects of the shift to organized youth sport. John Mayasich was captain of the 1960 gold-medal-winning US Olympic hockey team. When retired, Mayasich reflected on his career as a hockey player, asking himself, "When did I really have fun?" He recalled his childhood in Minnesota "playing the sport where you didn't have people in the stands, you didn't have parents there, just competing with neighborhood kids or kids from your hometown and doing your best and saying, boy, I'm having fun and I'll probably have a chance to make the high school football, baseball, or hockey team...."[756] Franklin Foer, in *How Soccer Explains the World*, notes that when his father played sandlot baseball in Washington, DC, in the post-World War II era, he could walk three blocks to a neighborhood ball diamond. A generation later, Franklin's parents had to load him into their Honda and drive forty minutes into Maryland so he could play soccer on an organized team. Edward Devereux studied children's games in the 1970s. His observations echo those of the Reverend Higginson a century earlier. The psychologist concluded that American children engage less in informal play and games than do children in other cultures. The low-organized pick-up games, once common to childhood and adolescence, were being pre-empted by highly organized, formalized games directed by adults. Devereux labeled this phenomenon the "impoverishment of play."[757]

Structured activities progressively infringe upon the leisure time of children. Following a productive school day, youngsters are routed to ball practice, dance lessons, or music lessons. Kenneth Shore, writing for the *Los Angeles Times* syndicate, describes a typical schedule for the modern American child:

> Matthew has barely a minute to spare. He just finished his after-school swimming class and is on his way home to practice the piano. After his lesson he will spend 20 minutes reviewing addition and subtraction flash cards with his father. Tomorrow he has Little League practice, the next day he is off to an origami program, and the day after that he will attend a computer class. Matthew's week is so full that the only way he can keep track of his activities is by referring to the schedule card his mother puts in his lunch box each day.[758]

Todd Marinovich grew up three generations after Babe Ruth. He didn't spend much time playing in the streets or playing pick-up games in the park. Like Matthew and a growing number of children, he submitted to an imposed regimen of well-meaning adults. Todd's life was planned and scheduled in detail by his father, Marv, a former coach and professional athlete, with one goal in mind—to groom Todd to become a football quarterback. At age four, Todd was introduced to the balance beam to improve his agility. By age eight, he was enrolled in organized flag football. At eleven, he was placed under the tutelage of a "vision development specialist" who required Todd to perform various complicated tasks with exactitude, such as solving multiplication problems while simultaneously bouncing a ball.[759]

Todd's teen years were spent with a series of coaches, including an expert in Soviet Bloc physical-training techniques, a movement specialist, and a throwing coach. Rather than rafting on rivers or exploring the woods like Tom Sawyer, Todd spent summers lifting weights and performing calisthenics. Sometimes the young Californian trained for hours a day to prepare for football. All this activity supplemented the time he spent in school, where he was expected to carry a B+ average.[760] True to his father's designs, the adult Todd signed a contract with a professional football team, the Oakland Raiders, and became its starting quarterback.

While young Todd Marinovich was throwing footballs and lifting weights, many of his peers were swimming laps or practicing on the balance beam for long hours. What was happening to boys in sport became more common for girls. World-class rock climber Lynn Hill recalls being promoted to the advanced "all-star" swim team at age seven. Jennifer Capriati was competing in world-class tennis tournaments just shy of her fourteenth birthday. Golfer Michelle Wie "turned pro" at fifteen. Swimmer Cathy Ferguson, an Olympic gold-medal winner at age sixteen, recalls training five to six hours a day beginning at age ten. As Cathy swam laps, other young female athletes were putting in a full day on the ice rinks and in gymnastic schools. Elite gymnasts train between thirty and forty-five hours a week. These girls, many of them preadolescents, rise at 5 or 6 A.M., train until 9 A.M., go to school till 2 P.M., and then return to the gym to practice until late in the evening. Parents have been known to spend tens of thousands of dollars on the training and travel for these child gymnasts, all for a career that typically ends before age twenty.[761] Thus has American sport culture radically redefined childhood over the course of the last century.

This chapter examines the relationship between child-rearing practices and the play lives of children in the context of the Protestant ethic. We begin by exploring pertinent theories of socialization with an emphasis on parenting. Next, we look at the historical influence of Protestant child-rearing doctrine as it shaped parenting and youth culture from the Victorian Era to the present. We then discuss the emerging phenomenon of organized youth sport and the American youth sport ethic.

The Family as Socializing Agent

> If not for sports, I do not think my father ever would have talked to me.
> –Pat Conroy

Every society attempts to provide a type of "buffeted learning" through which its children can absorb the cultural values that are considered important. In the course of this socializing process, children acquire a sensitivity to the obligations of society. They learn to get along with and behave like others. They absorb accepted motives, values, and opinions. They are introduced to rituals, laws, taboos, legends, folktales, standards, and cultural beliefs. If society is successful in stamping these basic traits onto the child, they tend to endure throughout the individual's life. By and large, these attributes are acquired in the context of the family, but they are reinforced within other institutions, including schools, churches, and organized sport and recreation.[762]

The main elements of socialization are: 1) significant others who serve as role models, e.g., parents, teachers, athletic coaches; 2) social situations, e.g., home, school, playground; and 3) the role learners, e.g., children, adolescents. The socialization process is influenced by several related factors such as social class, ethnicity, religion, the gender and age of learners, and even the ordinal position among siblings. Social class appears to be particularly relevant to socialization of children. Families within the broad middle class have become a formidable agency of enculturation, and middle-class norms of child rearing have dominated American society. Parents, especially those of the middle class, appear to play a pivotal role in the socialization of children.[763]

There is little question that parental values derive from the larger culture. This broad influence provides for a uniform set of norms and beliefs that apply across a variety of settings. Such uniformity allows us to speak of a prevailing ethic that is absorbed by a cross-section of Americans who may differ in ethnicity or religious affiliation. Within this general context, the diffusion of cultural values occurs within the family setting. Thus, the family is recognized as an important carrier of culture.[764]

Sociologists hold various opinions on how exactly child socialization occurs. They agree that the child absorbs and retains an implicit set of values through the day-by-day behavior of parents, even when these behaviors conflict with parent's advice and exhortations. Regardless of what the exact mechanisms are for explaining this process, little doubt exists that a transfer of values occurs in family settings. Studies have shown consistently that parental values are transmitted to their offspring and are then internalized by these impressionable learners. From parents' conceptions of what characteristics are desirable in their children, we often can discern their values and objectives in child-rearing.[765]

The longer the exposure to significant others, the greater their impact of socialization upon the child. The family may constitute a lifelong relationship, which explains why it serves as a potent socializing agent. As David Riesman noted, the pressure applied through strict child-rearing prolongs the period in which socialization takes place.[766] Family structures that are evident from infancy may endure through the period of adolescence. Teenagers remain strongly influenced by parents and continue to be concerned with adult approval or disapproval. This process seems particularly true of children groomed by parents to be athletes. Mickey Mantle felt incredible pressure to please his father, Mutt. From the time he was five, he felt he couldn't face his father if he failed on the baseball field. During his early professional career with the New York Yankees, the nineteen-year-old ballplayer was sent down to the minors. Hanging his head in defeat, he was confronted by Mutt, who admonished, "I thought I raised a man. You ain't a man. You're a coward." Both men ended up in tears, with Mickey begging his father to give him one more chance.[767]

Peer influence, though quite formidable during adolescence, is largely supplemental to that of parents who remain the major authority in their children's lives. Mickey Mantle reveled in locker room camaraderie and the fraternal bonding of fellow ballplayers. His cronies on the Yankees were notorious for their after-game drinking and partying. But his father's authority never waned. Parents like Mutt Mantle persist in attempting to socialize their offspring through the teen years because they feel the job has not been completed. Adolescence constitutes a period of training and preparation for adult roles, and this fact obligates parents and society to continue the effort to exert an influence. Moreover, many young men and women remain at home during adolescence, and those who do not often fall under the influence of surrogate parents. Brother Matthias played this role in Babe Ruth's formative years.[768]

Thus, the family stands out as the primary socializing agent of children and adolescents. In the present context, it is important to note the family's role in socializing children into behaviors and roles in organized sport. Sport provides a specific instance of the broad socialization process at work. Generally, children tend to be like their parents. Parents who reward the acquisition of physical skills, who value achievement, and who themselves engage in sports generally will produce children who show similar interests. Children may "catch" the mood of the family toward sport rather than being formally taught. Contemporary boys and girls are more apt to see their fathers at recreation than at their occupations. Whether children are influenced to participate in sport directly by parents' formal teaching or indirectly by them as role models, it is well established that families socialize children into organized sport.[769]

However, before we discuss families and youth sports programs in depth, it is instructive to look at American parents' approach to rearing children within the historical and cultural contexts of secular Protestantism.

The methods of child-rearing that derived from the Reformation and carried into Colonial Puritan society placed a distinct stamp on the parent-child relationship. Vestiges of this influence can be detected in the more traditional approaches to parenting that have carried into the modern era. This legacy reaches from the city streets of Baltimore to small-town Oklahoma and the suburbs of California—anyplace where children are groomed to become athletes.

Protestant Child Rearing

For we are changed and become good not by birth but by education. Therefore parents must…correct and sharply reprove their children….
–*A Godly Form of Household Government* (1621)

America's child-rearing practices were cast in Reformed Protestantism with its severe conception of the nature of childhood. The doctrine of original sin was carried forward into the post-Reformation world. Calvinists viewed children as innately depraved vessels, creatures whose desires had to be repressed in the interest of personal salvation and the good of the social order. This view was articulated by John Calvin in the *Institutes*: "Infants themselves, as they bring their condemnation into the world with them, are rendered obnoxious to punishment by their own sinfulness, not by the sinfulness of another. For though they have not yet produced the fruits of their iniquity, yet they have the seed of it within them." The child remained in need of strict discipline even after baptism, for the tendency to sin remained.[770]

Consonant with this doctrine, child-rearing became a matter of "civilizing" children by placing them under stern and authoritarian control. The methods of parenting from birth onward were strictly prescribed by the Protestant establishment. The family's role was to form the child into the proper habits of mind. For this process to occur, it was essential that the child submit to parental authority early in life, and that it be firmly maintained throughout the years of growth. Child-rearing practices reflected the fundamental changes in the family that followed the Reformation. The family acquired a new dignity as it assumed its role as the center of moral life. Thus ensconced, it shared influence with the church and the larger religious community. Essentially, the family served as a "little church and a little commonwealth" reinforcing society's norms within its walls. Children became the primary focus of parents. Parenthood was elevated to the level of a calling in the child-centered family. Parents' duties regarding their progeny took precedence over their affection and feelings toward their children.[771]

The amplified importance accorded to the family developed within an increasingly patriarchal culture. In Protestant families, the father was virtual sovereign in his own house. Sanctions enforced by the father were strict and pervasive. He functioned as schoolmaster, minister, and judge. The father's guidance provided the foundation for the dissemination of religious values. He took on the responsibility to instruct and guide children at daily family worship. He led the family prayers and read the Bible aloud. By this model, the family became a formidable institution for the enculturation of children, the social unit in which the Protestant faith and mission were expressed and reaffirmed.[772]

The role assigned to the head of the family followed the example of the Protestant pastor who, unlike the celibate priest, provided his parishioners with an exemplar—as the pastor often was a married man with his own family. The visibility of the cleric was extended to his wife and children, and the parsonage served as a model for parochial family life. The moral record of the pastor's children was regarded as a kind of certification of the effectiveness or a mark of the ineffectiveness of the minister-father. Children brought up in Protestant parsonages were expected not only to be well behaved but conspicuous for their achievement. All families were assigned the dual charge of safeguarding morality and educating their children.

The Puritans placed a particularly strong emphasis upon the family as an instrument of moral education. Hardly a sermon failed to include exhortations and specific instructions to parents concerning obligations to their children. Puritans were convinced children needed all the marshaled efforts of church, school, and family to keep them from the "sins of Adam."[773] Well into the nineteenth century, tracts on child-rearing continued to reflect the conviction that an infant's nature was corrupt, willful, and selfish, and that this predisposition must be suppressed by strict obedience training. However, a more progressive view was emerging that held the child to be possessed by a divine spark of innocence and an impulse for moral perfection. The moderates of the era viewed the child as a bundle of contrapuntal tendencies that, depending upon the form of nurturing the child received, could result in either good or evil.[774]

Traditional morality continued to influence child-rearing through the

Victorian Era. The child's upbringing was expected to be ruled and regular as a necessary deterrent to depravity. Frederick Taylor's biographer noted of the Victorian family that "an important maternal task was to combat sexual 'sin' in young children. [E]ven the slightest hint of sensuality in a child might goad the mother into a harshness aimed at complete suppression."[775] Repression of carnal impulses in children and the need for their strict control had a dampening effect upon natural play behavior. Playing with a baby was suspect if construed as carrying erotic overtones. Victorian mothers viewed play, at best, as a less objectionable alternative to thumb-sucking and masturbation.[776]

Protestant parents were held directly responsible by the church for their children's behavior, especially that of older children. Cases tried before a Presbyterian church session in the early nineteenth century included charges of "[a]llowing one's children to attend places of 'vain amusement.'"[777] Any signs of sin, particularly rebellion or obstinacy, were to be severely punished. The concerns about defiant children reflected the general fear of disorder. Protestants believed the outward lives of children bore witness to the discipline and self-denial that marked the true believer. Children of "saints" demonstrated by their behavior that they too were saved. The community placed a high level of responsibility upon parents not only for their own sins but for those of their children.[778] Thus, the obligations of child-rearing carried beyond the bounds of the family to the larger community of the elect, who held a compelling interest in the status of children and relentlessly scrutinized them. Every act of the child had a moral and religious significance. A single lapse in behavior might be interpreted as a permanent setback. Any child's apostasy was viewed as a mortal blow to the entire society.[779]

This intense concern for the righteousness of children carried into the modern era. Robert Levine noted that educated families have inherited from their Protestant ancestry much of the ideology of self-control and self-reliance, although shorn of its religious axioms. He elaborates by saying that "child rearing practically from birth onwards is prescribed by religious leaders and designed to foster qualities such as self-control and self-reliance which provides the individual with the means for his own salvation."[780] The obligations of child-rearing have created a contemporary archetype that Levine labels the "Protestant parent." This representation of parenting retains considerable authority as a standard and ideal for rearing children.

The model of Protestant parenting, infused with rationalism and moralism, would serve as prologue to the emerging scientific precepts of child development. The psychology of child-rearing that gained popularity in the late Victorian Era appeared distinctly prescriptive and moralistic. Americans would embrace Sigmund Freud's concept of the "uncivilized infant" as if reaffirming the doctrine of original sin. The new scientific model for parenting placed emphasis on controlling the individual child's environment. The fashionable prescriptions for child-rearing covered everything from feeding and sleeping arrangements to toilet training and play patterns—all seemingly scientifically calculated and infused with moral overtones.[781]

The late nineteenth and early twentieth century represented a crucial period in social history. The rise of science reflected the secularization of culture. It was also an era that witnessed urbanization, radical changes in the American family, the abolition of child labor, and the revolutionary consequences of universal schooling. Together, these developments were instrumental in shaping the culture of childhood and adolescence.

The Changing American Family and the Emergence of Youth Culture

> Among democratic nations each generation is a new people.
> —Alexis de Tocqueville

The American family changed in significant ways in the midst of rampant industrialization and urbanization. The nuclear family of parents and children was increasingly segregated from the broad kinship group of grandparents, aunts, uncles, and cousins. As a consequence, the importance of the immediate family was enhanced and individual roles within the family were redefined. Protestant middle-class families decreased in size, allowing parents to devote more attention to individual children. The father's traditional role in child-rearing became more peripheral due to the demands of his job outside the home. American women stepped into the role of the primary socializing agent for both sons and daughters. (The Puritans had intended that mothers share in the disciplining of their children.) Now it was the mother who ministered to the child's needs, thwarted the child's anti-social impulses, and shaped a home environment in which children learned developmental skills and proper values.[782] Hans Dreitzel refers to "the puritanical socialization procedures of the bourgeois family aimed at the development of a character structure." In his view, the main purpose of parenting in this era was building "a psychological foundation of the Protestant ethic" that would prepare young adults to enter the labor market.[783]

Middle-class families had the option of preparing their offspring for the adult world of work only because children were no longer obliged to work during their youth on the farm or in factories. Following the Industrial Revolution, children routinely were put to work by age seven, and apprenticeships were offered to boys as young as ten. This practice was reflected in popular stories of the time. In Jacob Abbott's book *Rollo at Work* (1837), six-year-old Rollo is weaned by his father from the child's world and thrown into the systematic toil of adulthood. The early introduction of children into the workplace often separated them from the home and pre-empted natural play activity. Children spent their days in tightly controlled factories and shops, often for twelve hours at a turn. Some youngsters were virtual residents of factories, where they cooked their meals and also boarded.[784]

However, by mid-century the requirements of advanced industrialization had the effect of displacing young people from the job market and separating them from the workplace. Early child labor laws accelerated this development. In 1842, children under twelve were prohibited from working in Massachusetts, which passed a ten-hour maximum workday law for older children in 1867. A trend toward eliminating child labor gradually picked up steam in the following decades. By the turn of the twentieth century, a major effort was underway to remove children from the factories and to place them in schools. Juvenile literature of the era reflected these changes. In the popular "Frank Merriwell" series (launched in 1896), the author, Gilbert Patten, provided a fresh model for American youth. He did not advise his young readers to go directly into business as Horatio Alger's books had done a generation earlier, but to learn the formula of success upon the school playing fields.[785]

The shift in favor of schooling was consistent with the post-Reformation view of childhood as a period of preparation. The Protestant middle class, in particular, was inclined to forego the benefits of children's labor in favor of extended education. This trend reflected class aspirations but also a lesser dependence upon the wages of children for the economic survival of the family. The schooling of children pre-empted their productive roles in the family economy. One important consequence of this development was that young people became increasingly dependent, economically and psychologically, upon adults in the household for an extended period of time. The revolutionary changes in middle-class family life kept children at home longer under their parents' roof and under their influence.[786]

Schooling became coextensive with childhood, and this trend had a number of broad implications. At first, schooling was a matter of weeks, then lengthened to months, and eventually took up most of the year. Nonattendance was defined as deviant, and compulsory attendance laws became more common. Concurrently, age segregation imposed by the schools wrought the beginnings of an autonomous youth culture with its own norms and customs. Longer schooling meant that young people were spending more time with their peers, a development that offset parental influence. Schools became the repositories of peer-generated values with the effect that parental values became increasingly challenged.[787]

What was occurring was the creation of "adolescence," that nebulous period between childhood and adulthood in which teenagers were to be prepared for their adult roles. In accord with this stratagem, adolescents were subjected to the imposition of behavioral norms reflective of Protestant middle-class values. However, adult norms increasingly clashed with those of youth culture, and adolescence became problematic. Public officials noted with alarm that delinquent youth gangs were forming in the cities. Juvenile crime increased significantly in poor urban wards after the end of the school day. It was difficult to develop a sense of commitment among a class of young people whose labor was no longer needed—what has been termed the "trivializing" of youth. Feelings of ambivalence and uncertainty developed among adults toward the place of adolescents in society.[788]

By the second decade of the new century, an autonomous youth subculture would be well established. Adolescents arranged their social lives separate from the family. They began to spend more time together in their own company. The adolescent subculture set their own fashions, innovated their own social practices, and established distinct mores. As public high schools increased in number, their students imitated the college crowd. Youth culture formed around leisure, and it thrived as leisure time increased. The schools, unlike the shops and factories, did not preoccupy the waking hours of young people. By the following decade, adolescents were enjoying several hours a day of free time.[789]

Emerging patterns of youth behavior stirred the old Puritan fears about vice, idleness, and lack of control. Adults became increasingly concerned about the independent youth culture that was developing outside the home, largely unsupervised. Children and adolescents were found to be "hanging out" on the streets, using their newfound leisure to engage in informal recreation. Adults worried about unescorted girls and boys strolling about public places and frequenting commercialized recreation establishments like billiard parlors and skating rinks. Leisure activities were becoming increasingly commercialized, and the advertising of products and services directed at the youth market began to play a major role in the lives of adolescents.[790]

Misgivings about the emerging leisure culture led adults to channel America's young people into church programs, clubs, sports leagues, and other supervised activities. Similar institutions had been around for nearly a century but were to experience a marked resurgence. A. B. Hollingshead commented on the strategy of segregating young people into structured programs and activities. He noted, "Adults apparently believed that these institutions built a mysterious something variously called 'citizenship, leadership, or character' which kept the boy or girl from being tempted by the pleasures of adult life."[791] Veblen observed that clergymen and other "pillars of society" were forming boys' brigades and "pseudo-military" organizations for adolescents. He commented that the colleges had become essentially "character factories," more concerned with morals than intellectual development.[792] Faculty were assigned to advise student clubs, regulate student meetings, and supervise campus recreation.

Structured activities directed at youth were most apparent among the Protestant middle class. Joseph Kett, in writing a history of American adolescence, observed that no religious sect surpassed Protestants in their "institutional concern" for youth. The apprehensions of traditional religion coincided with an impetus toward social reform among religious progressives.[793] Progressive-era reformers responded to these unsettling changes in youth culture by redirecting children and adolescents away from unsupervised play and commercial amusements into organized sports and recreation programs infused with high purpose.

The Reformers and the Rise of Organized Youth Sport

A playground is not a playground without supervision.
–Edward Ward (1905)

Reform is a consistent theme running through Protestant culture, as characteristic of the Victorians as the Puritans. The American Progressive era, dating roughly from 1880 to 1920, witnessed several campaigns to bring about the betterment of society through social reform. "Child-saving" was a major goal of the reformers. They were well aware of the plight of the urban family, and they recognized that the emerging youth culture constituted a force of change in moral norms. The reformers sought ways to instill and preserve in young people those traditional values reflected in the Protestant ethic. They promoted supervised play and organized sports programs as one means of inculcating this ethic.[794]

The efforts of play organizers were publicly endorsed by clergy, social workers, and educators. Protestant institutions played a key role in the play movement as sponsors of organized youth activities. When Auburn Seminary, a Presbyterian school in New York, opened its athletic fields as a public playground in summer 1907, the school stated its hopes that the children "will learn more than one lesson of character. The playground will contribute to their true education." There was a good deal of public support for these efforts among the middle and upper classes. Americans were reading *Tom Brown's School Days*, a popular English novel that depicted activities on the playing fields as promoting virtues like fair play and a sense of right and wrong. The sports heroes who graced the pages of Victorian literature achieved victory through hard work and moral fiber. Physical recreation was touted as strengthening the morals of youth as it strengthened their young bodies. The prevailing model linked muscular coordination to moral development, as if the latter could be stamped onto the nervous system by repeated drill until it became a habit.[795]

Play organizers armed with reform notions spent a good deal of time and effort persuading city officials of the importance of supervised play. Their strategy was to transplant youth activity from the city streets onto playgrounds, where "instructors" would keep order and direct play. Playground supervisors would identify the types of activities in which children should engage. Youngsters would be taught to play in a way that was healthy, moral, and socially redeeming. Concurrently, public recreation programs were promoted to counter the corrupting influence of commercial recreation. A study conducted in Kansas City concluded that a third of the commercial amusements were bad influences on youth. Candy stores enticed children with slot machines and the "numbers" game, street vendors peddled cigarettes to children, and saloons sold intoxicating beverages with little concern for the age of the purchasers. Such amusements subverted the efforts directed toward more wholesome recreation.[796]

Reformers argued that supervised playgrounds would insulate adolescents from the pervasive city vices and act as a deterrent against juvenile crime. The evidence seemed to support the idea that organized play had an effect on crime rates among the children of the urban poor. The city of Milwaukee reported that upon providing play facilities for newsboys, the number of children sent to reformatories fell from seventy to three in just three years. A social center was opened in St. Paul, and within a year juvenile delinquency was reduced by 50 percent. A similar study in Chicago showed a decrease of 28 percent in the number of children arrested within a half mile of a playground. A Chicago judge calculated that juvenile crime increased as the distance from the playgrounds increased. In Passaic, New Jersey, the juvenile court was discontinued for lack of business after the opening of a recreation hall.[797]

There were other motives behind play reform. Following the implementation of child labor laws, concern arose about the maintenance of the work ethic among young people. Play organizers intentionally designed youth sports and games to integrate youngsters into "work rhythms" and to think and feel in a "regulated manner." Reformers believed that playgrounds were perfectly suited to train youth to meet the stresses and challenges of industrial society. They envisioned a program of organized and supervised activities that reflected the rhythms of the factories. Indeed, many of the activities on the supervised playgrounds, in schoolyards, social centers, and camps bore a resemblance to work. Notably, craft activities placed children at workstations where they shaped raw materials into useful or decorative objects.[798]

The turn-of-the-century campaign to organize children's sport and recreation represented a significant change in the traditional attitude toward children's play. Before the Civil War, childhood leisure had been filled with spontaneous, unregulated, and unstructured games. These forms of play were tolerated by adults who recognized that they did little to improve the participants. Only in the eyes of the more critical observers was unsupervised play suspected of promoting harmful habits. These reservations led to reform efforts. By the late nineteenth century, organized recreation was being championed as a way to direct youth into appropriate patterns of social behavior. Supervised youth activities gathered steam in the early twentieth century. A concerted effort was undertaken to replace free play with organized games and sports. In 1903, General George Wingate and Luther Gulick established a sport program for boys in the New York City schools. Other cities initiated programs modeled on New York's effort.[799]

Americans were "caught up" in the idea of redemptive youth sport, and the predisposition for creating voluntary organizations was put into gear. Community, regional, and national programs were organized by age group in a wide variety of physical activities. The YMCA offered sports and recreation programs for urban youth. The schools began to sponsor intramural and interscholastic sports. During the twentieth century, more and more boys and girls would play on school sports teams.[800] Early on, most of the organized sports programs were directed at boys. Programs for girls were often limited to intramural sports within the schools, along with a few community programs like those sponsored by the YWCA. A dramatic increase in girls' participation in school sports took hold after Congress passed Title IX of the 1972 Education Amendments. This legislation required schools and colleges that received federal funds to establish some degree of equity between boys' and girls' programs. The movement transcended schools and colleges. By the last decade of the century, organized sports programs for girls were nearly as common as those for boys. Not only did girls enjoy new opportunities to compete with other girls, but they also competed in coeducational sports with boys. Predictably, girls' and women's sports embraced the same values that had been characteristic of boys' programs. Women's sports became highly competitive, rationalized, imbued with the work ethic, and elitist.[801]

As the century progressed, school sports and community-based recreation programs were augmented by instructional camps that offered young athletes an opportunity to improve their skills in sports such as tennis, basketball, baseball, gymnastics, and hockey. These camps, directed by coaches and staffed with adult athletes, usually take place during the summers when school is out. The instruction provided by these camps has become de rigueur for serious young athletes. Most of the camps provide day-long learning and training programs stretching over several days or weeks. The development camp offered by the Amateur Hockey Association of the United States (AHAUS) at Colorado Springs Olympic Training Center is fairly typical. AHAUS offers three camps for different skill levels: midget, midget elite, and junior national. Hundreds of young hockey players attend these camps. Based on their performances in camp, twenty players are then selected to represent the United States in international competition.[802]

Together, a variety of organizations facilitate sports competition for young people, in addition to local public recreation departments and the schools. These include private national agencies (e.g., Little League Baseball); service organizations (e.g., Jaycees); membership organizations (e.g., the YMCA); youth-sport development organizations (e.g., Junior Golf); and commercial organizations (e.g., Ford Motor Company's "Punt, Pass, and Kick" competition).[803]

By the twenty-first century, some two dozen national sport agencies govern programs for children and youth. In the sport of wrestling, the National Kids Council was created by the governing body to deal with issues such as the desirability of national championships, the optimal length of seasons, and rules modification. Most youth sports feature a similar body that makes decisions affecting its young athletes. The National Youth Sports Coaches Association (NYSCA) expresses a collective opinion on the nature of programs and regulations across sports. The combined effect of these local and national efforts is that children's sports are dominated by adult supervisors. The rules are encoded and enforced by adults; the games are scheduled and run by adults; the playing fields and courts are designed, built, regulated, and maintained by adults; the equipment and uniforms are designed, marketed, distributed, and purchased by adults. Adults even buy and sell advertising space on the players' uniforms, as well as on the billboards that adorn the game areas. It is adults who control team membership, keep score and league standings, determine tournament eligibility, and schedule the championship events at the local, regional, and national levels.[804]

The reform efforts of the Progressive era that set out to control the leisure time and activities of children and adolescents culminated in the institutionalization of play and games. In the final reckoning, play has been deemed too important to leave to youth. Play must be supervised and controlled. Achievement-oriented parents with high expectations for their children enroll them in sport programs directed by other adults, with diverse motives. Parents and community activists organize the leagues, coach the teams, and schedule the championship tournaments. These sports and recreation programs reach more and more children at a younger and younger age.

Parents, along with social reformers, have continued to take a strong interest in the development of children and in directing their activities. American parents have felt an intimate attachment to, and responsibility for, the successes and failures of their children, as if their own salvation is tied to what children accomplish. The focus on Protestant morality translated into growing concerns about achievement. When applied to child-rearing, this concern translated into early mastery training. The earlier a child developed and the more he or she achieved, the more likely parents were to feel they had met their responsibilities.

Promoting Precocity: The Prototype for Modern Parenting

O wonderful son, that can so astonish a mother!
–*Hamlet*, 3.2.343-44

Modern child-rearing practices are the culmination of a post-Reformation mindset that stood in distinct contrast to the laissez-faire approach to childhood that had prevailed in the Western world. Throughout much of history, children beyond infancy were simply "left alone" when not appropriated for their labor. They were neither the object of any particular concern nor thought to be in need of special protection. In the worst instances, children were thrown into the adult world without preparation, unshielded from vices and exploitation. The children of medieval Europe could be found in taverns and other unsavory places where they joined in the vulgar amusements of their seniors. Boys and girls often were abused and routinely neglected, with few advocates to protect them. (Many children did not survive the first decade of life.) In contrast, Protestantism conceived of childhood as a separate and shielded period that allowed for the child's preparation for adult life. The entire community concerned itself with the protection and nurture of children.[805]

While Protestants sheltered their offspring from inappropriate adult experiences, they placed new demands on children to meet adult expectations. Parents were held responsible for the comportment and progress of their children, a standard that led to training for early independence. This model of child-rearing carried into the Industrial Age. Studies show that Protestant parents, in particular, consistently promote self-reliance in young children. American children are encouraged at an early age to test themselves by engaging in exercises of mastery. It is a child-rearing practice consonant with the ethic of achieved success.[806]

The demand for mastery and self-reliance reflects the emphasis on progressive maturation of the child, a concept that came into focus following the Protestant Reformation. Behavioral standards for young children garnered little interest before this time. Traditionally, the age of seven had been established as the threshold for presenting the child with responsibilities. In medieval Europe, seven had been advocated in moral and pedagogic literature as the appropriate age for starting school or work.[807] This convention implied that the early years of childhood were relatively free of demands—and in traditional societies this was the norm. The selection of age seven probably derived from Judeo-Christian numerology that accorded significance to the number and its multiples. This scheme explains the age of majority being set at twenty-one.[808]

The concept of progressive maturation carried into the modern era when scientific arguments were used to bolster this approach to child development. The rational predisposition in Protestant culture encouraged use of scientific research to support the view that children were capable of learning at an early age. (Findings by Jean Piaget and others that suggested limitations to premature learning were conveniently ignored.) The practice of placing early demands upon children is one of the hallmarks of Protestant parenting. It has become a salient feature of child-rearing in modern America, where parents tend to push infants and toddlers toward early achievement. The encouragement of precocity includes infants being prodded to walk before they have mastered crawling and rushed into toilet training despite immature bowels and bladders. Parents brag about how early their progenies pronounce words. Cassius Clay, Sr. liked to point out that the first words uttered by Cassius, Jr. (i.e., Muhammad Ali) were "gee gee," a sign that his son was destined to win the Golden Gloves tournament.[809]

American children are steered into structured environments at an early age, including preschool, where they are set at cognitive learning tasks. Six-year-olds enter the first grade of elementary school in spite of mounting evidence suggesting that boys, in particular, are not ready for the demands of disciplined learning at this age. The curriculum in early grades has been accelerated; kindergartners are expected to master what first-graders were taught a generation ago. This trend toward accelerated learning in schools carries over to youth sports. Pee Wee League football players and Little

Leaguers are expected to master sophisticated drills and introduced to complex game strategies by demanding coaches.[810]

Parents place performance expectations on their children particularly when in competition with others. These expectations are manifest in sibling rivalry and among peers in the classrooms and on the playgrounds. Child psychologists comment on the inclination of American parents to forge young children into overachieving students and athletes. David Elkind writes of the "hurried child," forced to grow up too fast, pushed during the early years toward multiple achievements that severely tax adaptive capacities. Many children, like Todd Marinovich and Mickey Mantle, struggled to achieve at a level that would meet their parents' expectations.[811]

The noted pediatrician Benjamin Spock—whose book on child-rearing, first published in 1946, was a bestseller through several editions—commented on the American phenomenon of producing what he labeled "super kids." Dr. Spock, a former Olympic gold-medal winner, described the unreasonable achievement expectations of American parents who "hear that some children can be taught to read at the age of two and...immediately become panicky, worrying that their children are going to be left behind because they're going to schools where they don't expect them to read until kindergarten." Spock's point is that parents are unwilling to "let children be children." However, criticism by a few child-development professionals has been pitted against a strong achievement ethic that continues to encourage early mastery.[812]

The parents of high-achieving children bask in the glory of their accomplishments and accept much of the credit. When children do not achieve to expectations, adults feel themselves to be failures, not only as parents but as members of the community. Such pangs of failure shape the fundamental nature of the parent/child relationship. Jonathan Brower studied the behavior of adults involved with Little League baseball. He comments, "In a sense, little league is a game of errors, and the manner in which children's errors are handled by parents and coaches can prove to be an important input in the development of their sense of self-worth and identity."[813] Riesman was convinced that parents pass on to their children the legacy of their own unfulfilled striving to live up to society's ideals. Adults appropriate children as an extension of their own ego needs as they seek reassurance of their own sense of self-worth. Parents relive personal successes or compensate for their own perceived failures in their children's achievements. Parental standards can prove so unattainable that a constant tension permeates the child's psyche. Mickey Mantle struggled to please his father, Mutt. He wet the bed until he was sixteen years old. His wife Merlyn would observe that "the early pressure on Mickey to play ball...caused real emotional problems for him." Such children can never be certain whether they have lived up to their parents' expectations.[814]

In a society that values achieved status, the child's upward mobility represents for parents an opportunity to recoup the status that they themselves may have desired or been denied. Consequently, parents push their children to achieve in order to share vicariously in their success. This phenomenon seems quite evident in children's sports, where parents feel the need to promote their sons and daughters as athletes.[815] The father who failed in his efforts to play professional ball sets this goal for his child and reinforces the appropriate behaviors toward this goal. More broadly, a connection may exist between parents' vocational dissatisfaction and interest in their child's success in sports. Elkind suggests that the achievements of child athletes serve to alleviate parents' frustrations in the workplace. John Piersall, an often unemployed house painter, was intent upon his son Jim becoming a major league ballplayer. The demanding and often angry father drove his son relentlessly toward this goal, refusing to let him play other sports with his friends. Jim eventually signed with the Boston Red Sox, but continued to suffer from emotional problems that began in his childhood.[816]

Adults often fail to recognize their motives for pushing children into achievement-oriented activities, but instead resort to rationalizations. Despite the pretensions by parents that they steer their children into sport because of the potential for moral and social development, their rabid rooting from the sidelines, their observable delight at winning and disappointment at losing, and the bragging on their children's accomplishments suggest motives other than a concern for the child's development.[817] Observers of youth sport recognize that many parents have extravagant expectations for their children. These parents make a strong commitment to the child's athletic career, and in return for this commitment, they expect a payoff, which is for the child to succeed. Winning is so important to these parents that they emphasize it at the expense of most other values inherent to sport. When the child returns home from a game, the American parent's initial question to the child is, "Did you win?"—not "Did you have fun?"

The more involved parents manipulate youth sports programs and coaches to maximize the likelihood of their own child's success. When

Dennis Rodman tried out for the high-school football team (prior to his phenomenal growth spurt), he was "cut" because he was too small. His mother, Shirley, demanded a meeting with the coach to argue her son's case, but to no avail. The assertive, protective mother declared, "I interfered in my children's lives quite a bit." Anyone who has worked with adults involved in community sports organizations is impressed by the maneuvering that accompanies use of facilities, practice times, team rosters, game schedules—all the variables that influence competitive success. The object of all this manipulation is to garner social status, especially among fellow adults who patronize children's sports. In this way, youth sport functions as a medium to provide parents and surrogate parents (e.g., coaches) with vicariously achieved status.[818]

The promotion of precocity in children reflects the high need for achievement that has carried through the history of Protestant culture. Although the achievement ethic has been strongest among Protestant middle class, American Catholics also have readily assimilated it. Parents with high achievement aspirations, regardless of religious affiliation or ethnicity, provide their children early achievement training and, subsequently, produce children with a high need for achievement. This need carries over into the child's adulthood, resulting in a new generation of achievement-oriented parents.[819] Achievement is demanded beyond the family setting, notably in the schools. Parents are concerned with how their children fare in school, but are less interested in what is learned than in how the child has measured up to other children. Parents expect the schools and community to provide standards by which to measure their children's comparative achievements. The hierarchical system of letter grades adopted by American schools is a reflection of this expectation.[820]

The essential point is that children are conditioned to seek parental acceptance through achievement. As Margaret Mead observed, American parents' love is conditional upon the child's accomplishments. In reinforcing achievement, the parent employs praise and criticism, along with other overt indicators of approval or disapproval.[821] Regardless of the type of feedback, the child "gets the message" at an early age. Psychiatrist Stephen Ward proposed that the successful athlete's drive stems from infancy when the mother greeted every new physical achievement with obvious expressions of love and approval.[822] As childhood achievement is tied to relations with parents, the child must constantly face parents' expectations. Children's anxiety about their achievement is acquired primarily in interpersonal situations. In a study of male gymnasts (ages seven to eighteen), the most frequently reported worries of the young men were "what will my parents say?" and "letting them down." When Roberts and Sutton-Smith observed children's sport in the early 1960s, they found that American boys were given higher achievement training than girls. This gender gap no longer held a generation later. The social revolution in gender equity has meant that both boys and girls are pressed by parents to achieve from an early age in the arena of competitive sports.[823]

The pattern of children's involvement in sport is a specific instance of general tendencies within American parenting. Game forms are directly related to specific child-training variables. Sociologists point out that a strong impetus toward self-mastery relates to the prevalence of games of physical skill. American games are equally high in strategy, and this type of game has been linked specifically to obedience training.[824] Based upon existing models, one would expect that a pattern of child-rearing consonant with the Protestant ethic should lead to an emphasis upon children's games that feature physical skill, prowess, and strategy. These types of games are what we observe in youth sport culture.

Parents' involvement in children's activities and the particular emphasis on early achievement lends support for organized youth sport programs. At the close of the twentieth century, some twenty-six million American children between ages six and seventeen (half of all children) were participating in organized sports.[825] As youth sport evolved as a cultural phenomenon, it established a distinct ethic reflecting traditional Protestant values, among which achieved status was prominent.

The American Youth Sport Ethic

> It's not a question of what the child does to the ball, it's
> what the ball does to the child.
> –Edward C. Devereux

Childhood was framed within Protestant tradition as a separate period of preparation, a doctrine supported later by developmental psychology. Given this perspective, it follows that leisure activities for children should take into account their maturation level. Parents, educators, and community leaders might then encourage age-appropriate developmental play and low-organized games that would prove personally satisfying, while promoting psychological and social development of children. Instead, the American emphasis has been on organized youth sport programs. As George Sage observed, these tightly controlled activities have nothing to do with playfulness, fun, joy, or satisfaction. Sports programs for children have been appropriated for the purpose of inculcating work habits, achievement, and competitiveness.[826] In the final reckoning, that facet of Protestant child-rearing aimed at protecting children from the premature demands of an adult world was trumped by the didactic moralism of Victorian reformers who advocated youth sports based on the adult model. The prevailing tenor of these early programs played a major role in transforming American childhood.

The typical youth sports programs sponsored by local communities and schools are highly rationalized, structured activities instilled with seriousness and high purpose. Coaches and parents set formidable goals for the young athletes who participate. The atmosphere during contests and practice sessions is intense and disciplined. Youth sport provides an effective setting in which to socialize youngsters. There is little doubt that the neophyte stepping onto the practice field will be indoctrinated in the approved norms and behaviors. Organized sport serves as a field laboratory, a model through which children readily incorporate prescribed values. For the most part, these programs reflect the traditional values consonant with the Protestant ethic.[827]

Sociologist George Mead explained the mechanisms of socialization through sport. He observed that children in a game situation are continually taking on the attitude of those about them, especially the people who control them and upon whom they depend. The "morale of the game" takes hold of the child more effectively than the larger morale of the broad community. The game expresses a social situation in which the child can engage completely and acquire a sense of self. The perception of "self as athlete" develops over time in interaction with coaches and peers, and is reinforced by family members. This acquired definition of "self" becomes real in its consequences. The young gymnast who is identified as a "hard worker" or the football player labeled "aggressive and tough" learns to see her/himself in these terms.[828] NFL defensive end Tim Green recalls that at age eight, whenever people called out his name, the next words out of their mouths were, "the football player." That's what he was in their minds. He elaborates: "There are pictures of you in your uniform, one in your mom's wallet, one on your dad's desk...your grandmother has one on her refrigerator. It seems inconceivable to you that you could be anything but the person portrayed in that picture....."[829]

Green's experience demonstrates the extent to which organized sport defines the child's relationship to his or her family. Youth sports become an extension of family life. Parents schedule family events around children's practice sessions and ballgames. A family in Connecticut has a son who plays baseball and soccer and a daughter who swims and plays soccer. The family "shuttles from playing field to playing field" toting sports drinks, high energy snacks, and changes of clothing. In upscale communities where children opt to play "premier" soccer, it is not unusual for games to be scheduled outside the home state. Parents feel obliged to travel to these events. Some youth soccer clubs play as many as sixty games a year. Two or three practices plus one or two games a week are not uncommon. Organized youth sports can dominate the summer season, as family vacation plans are curtailed by insistent coaches who expect the child's attendance at team practices and games to take priority. An inside joke circulates among social scientists, describing the primitive family unit as consisting of father, mother, child, and anthropologist. Sport sociologists refer to the "primary family of sport" as made up of the father, mother, child, and coach. The youth sport coach supplements the parent's authority and influences the family's life. [830]

Parents meld with the larger community through children's sports. At games and meets, they are ensconced on the sidelines along with friends, neighbors, and relatives watching their children compete. Spectators at Pee Wee football games cheer for six- and seven-year olds outfitted in full uniforms and cleats. The young players go through pre-game warm-up drills and calisthenics just like their high-school counterparts. They play under the supervision of uniformed officials. Coaches call plays from the sidelines. Six-year-old cheerleaders perform routines in front of the crowd. A public address system announces each play. Young athletes in some elite soccer clubs compete in million-dollar facilities with fences, lighting, and irrigated or synthetic turf fields. Results of the matches are published in local newspapers. [831] The message is unambiguous: children's sports are to be taken seriously.

Juvenile athletes respond to all the attention directed at them. They internalize values about the importance of structured activity. Children are persuaded that they should spend their time in worthwhile self-improvement. They accede to their parents' preference that they participate on organized teams rather than in neighborhood "pick-up" games. Geoffrey

Watson observed that boys playing Little League baseball reported they valued the game most because it was an activity that organized their summer days.[832] Structure is evident in both games and practice sessions, where activities tend to be tightly controlled and rule-bound. Tardiness and absences are not tolerated, and offenders are disciplined. Coaches show little flexibility in task assignments or in the way they expect tasks to be carried out. Young athletes wait to be told what to do. Most decisions are made by adults, and the participants are expected to respond obediently. Spontaneous behavior, even idle conversation, is discouraged and reprimanded when it interferes with the scheduled activities.[833]

Young athletes rarely rebel openly against this structured format of sport but often become bored or distracted. Boredom leads to peripheral episodes of free play, as sociologist Gary Fine observed. Distinct elements of play appear spontaneously among young athletes during games e.g., throwing dirt, playing with water balloons, chasing one another, playing soccer with a rock in the dugout, tossing hats in the air on a windy day. Fine noted that when this side involvement becomes an incursion on the primary activity, the adults in charge sense the threat and squelch the peripheral play.[834] Youth coaches routinely admonish their charges, "Stop playing around!" or "Cut the horseplay!"

Young athletes are dissuaded not only from "playing around" but from playing more than one sport. Jackie Robinson was a four-sport letter winner at UCLA in the late 1930s. Such accomplishments have become something of an anachronism. Athletes increasingly are molded into specialists at an early age. Coaches and/or parents steer youngsters into a single sport. Mickey Mantle recalls his childhood on the baseball fields of Oklahoma, commenting, "[T]hat's all I did [play baseball].... I had no other enjoyment."[835] Today's young athletes are run through a battery of physical tests to determine their aptitudes, channeled into the most promising sport, and expected to focus on becoming highly skilled and competitive in their specialty.[836] Coaches admonish young athletes for participating in casual sports with friends during free time. Once, the author overheard a fellow coach berating one of his athletes, "You're a basketball player. I don't want to see you playing touch football again." Thus do parents and coaches treat youth sports as if it were a calling, a chosen vocation to which adolescents must devote all their time and energy.

Authoritarianism is pervasive within the rigid structure of youth sport. The moral authority of parents is transferred to the athletic coach, who is ceded broad control over the youngsters' social and technical skills. The coach is a highly respected and revered figure in the community, a person accorded not only a superior knowledge of sport but also the moral development of youth. The coach acts as the embodiment of integrity and authority, someone to be trusted and obeyed implicitly. In this respect, the coach is more of a guru than a teacher, one whose influence carries over into athletes' lives off the field. Training rules extend to social activities, diets, and bedtime. Given the coach's moral authority, noncompliance with training rules invariably results in retribution.[837]

Most of the coaches and other volunteers who direct children's sports have not been schooled in child development. Rarely do these adults work from principles of maturation and readiness for learning in designing or directing physical activities for children. The typical youth sport coach is a former high-school or college athlete, often a frustrated one. Coaches tend to implement a scaled-down version of their own experiences in sport. The high-school and college programs that serve as models for these coaches have themselves imitated professional sport. All too often the adult model has carried down to the level of youth sports. Former NFL running-back Larry Csonka had occasion to observe a group of young boys led by a volunteer coach during a football practice session. What he describes is representative of many youngsters' experience in sports:

> [T]he coach blows his whistle and starts screaming. "All right, men, get into formation for drill Number One!" So two kids, maybe nine or ten years old, line up on opposite sides of the 50-yard line, and the rest of the team splits up and falls into line behind them. Then the coach yells, "Reddie," and comes down hard on the whistle. The kids start going at it, head to head, one on one...then one of the kids catches another one with an elbow in the nose. The kid's nose starts to bleed, and he falls down. The coach goes over to him and starts screaming, "Get up, get up. Show us you're a man and not a quitter." The kid gets up, and the tears are rolling down his cheeks, mixing with the blood, and he goes to the end of the line and waits for his next turn.[838]

Not all football coaches employ this type of head-to-head drill, but the above scenario reflects what parents might expect when they turn their children over to volunteer coaches. Whatever specific methods are employed, such techniques are an effective device through which children can be taught to withstand pain and discomfort, to work hard and strive to be the best. To borrow Sage's description, youth sports reveal "authoritarian and hierarchical organization, endorsement of the performance principle, meritocracy, overemphasis on winning, an assault on records and increasing use of child athletes as public entertainers."[839]

High levels of performance are expected of children, and these expectations are felt acutely by young athletes. The prevailing model for children's sport often stifles worthy outcomes such as sportsmanship or a sense of fair play. Youngsters learn to adopt the practices of adult athletes in order to accommodate demanding parents and coaches. One study found that over a third of young hockey players had learned to use "illegal hits" by watching professional hockey. These young athletes ascertained how to take chances and deceive by imitating veteran hockey players. Such behaviors are hardly ever discouraged by youth sport coaches. The emphasis on winning creates unbounded competitiveness among athletes. The credo that "winning is the only thing" has carried down to the level of children's sports. In order to win, young athletes not only play hard but compete with serious injuries, lie about their age and eligibility (parents of athletes have been known to falsify birth certificates), conspire to violate rules about playing time, and purposely attempt to intimidate and injure opponents.[840]

In their study of youth sports participation, Ewing and Seefeldt found that winning was actually a poor personal motivator for most junior and senior high-school athletes. But at the same time, a significant number of them reported that they played to win in competitive sports because of outside pressure. Almost half of the athletes drew their motivations from approval of adults or from trophies awarded by adults. These adolescents understood that the requisite for adult approval and rewards was winning. At a certain stage of development, children engage in activities not because they offer intrinsic satisfaction, but because they are recognized to have instrumental value or offer extrinsic rewards.[841] This transformation may occur quite early in a child's development. Channel swimmer Sally Friedman recalls winning her first trophy when she was four years old. She describes the event: "The race was half the length of the pool, from the rope across the middle to the wall at the shallow end. Each child [wearing a required inner tube] was held by a parent, who pushed as hard as he or she could, to give their own the best start." Friedman relates that her mother shared her early swimming feats with friends and strangers alike.[842]

The above characterizations reflect what constitutes the American sport ethic (see chapters 8 and 9). Notably, youth sport coaches employ the language and structures of the adult workplace in training and motivating young athletes.[843] Drills are referred to as "workouts." The long hours put into sport are a further testament to the work ethic. Competitive swimmers, many of whom are quite young, train for two or three hours a day, six days a week. Child gymnasts, with their hopes set on an Olympic tryout, train six hours a day in preparation. This regimen requires a unique single-mindedness and total mental concentration with no distractions.[844] Ingham and Hardy suggest that "sport for young athletes has become a form of 'anticipatory productive labor.' Youth sport strives to prepare young athletes to take for granted the norms of specialization and rationalization of the adult work place."[845] A few athletes may get "turned off" by the overemphasis on arduous training or find the experience too time-consuming, and quit. But a significant number continue to endure the regimen in order to please adults.

To a great extent, youth sport is about achieved status. From his study of Little League baseball, Watson concluded that one of the primary functions of this activity for the family was to socialize boys into the values of success and achievement.[846] Sport provides a visible arena (even more than the academic one) for children and adolescents to display achievement behaviors. The crowd of spectators at sporting events provides a sort of "report card" on the child's performance. Parents hear and see the crowd's reaction, signifying that their child is accepted as an achiever. Youth sports experiences reinforce the social skills of children that are expected to carry over to the broader achievement-oriented culture.[847]

The emphasis on achieved status in youth sports is attended by elitism. Sports replicate the elitism of an achievement-oriented society. Unlike free-play settings in which children "choose sides" and casually enter and leave the activity, organized sport employs "gatekeepers" who require an acceptable standard of performance for admission. Typically adults, not peers, determine who is good enough to play on the team. Through this process, youth sports create their own rituals of "election." Premier soccer leagues for children feature highly selective tryouts for positions on teams. Once players are selected, they can be required to sign one-year, binding contracts. Their parents may have to agree to financial-service contracts obligating them to pay annual dues, even if their child drops off the team. Some clubs charge as much as $2,000 for annual dues. Add to this cost another $300 for three jerseys, two pairs of shorts, three pairs of socks, a travel bag, and training suit. Hence, economic elitism augments elitism based on talent.[848]

American children are taught early on that sports are primarily for those who are highly skilled. Terrance Orlick found that three-fourths of the eight- and nine-year-olds he interviewed didn't "go out for a team" because they felt they weren't "good enough."[849] These were youngsters who enjoyed playing the sport but felt their skills did not measure up to the standards. Young athletes who successfully pass the standards of admission must submit to further grading and ranking. Just as there are teams and leagues for the highly skilled athletes, there are others for the marginally skilled, labeled "farm" leagues or B teams. But even the "A"-team athletes are subjected to status grading as starters or reserves—more pejoratively, "bench warmers."

Membership on an elite team translates to significant social status for American youth in the adult community and among their peers. In schools, athletes enjoy more status than do outstanding academic achievers. Varsity athletes are conferred visible status symbols like letter jackets, which they display at school. Tim Green recounts the favorable treatment accorded him and his high-school teammates. The other kids gazed at them starry eyed, and adults fawned over them simply because they were talented athletes.[850] Athletes often wear team jerseys outside the game setting to draw attention to themselves. Inscribed trophies are displayed prominently in school foyers. Star athletes' pictures appear along with a chronicle of their achievements in the local newspapers. High-school games often are televised. Youth sports, like adult sports, provide a visible platform for status display.[851]

In conclusion, we recall that children's activities can assume many forms and meanings within the framework of general culture. In some societies, play and games are not paid much attention. However, Americans have taken an active interest in the sports activities of their children. The meanings attributed to youth sports are a reflection of mainstream cultural values. Historically, the Puritan biases against play have given way to the institutionalization of organized sport and recreation whose purpose has been to inculcate traditional values and social skills. The revision in attitude toward play came about only as children were gradually freed from the consuming labor of factories and farms. As school replaced work, youngsters enjoyed newfound leisure. Adults viewed adolescent leisure and the autonomous subculture that formed around it as a threat to establishment values. They sought ways to reassert their influence by steering young people into worthwhile activities that would acculturate them and prepare them for morally productive lives. Organized sport and recreation have provided a medium for carrying out this agenda. The spirit of youth sport, like that of adult sport, has reaffirmed the values inherent in the Protestant ethic.

11

The Co-opting of Amateur Sport

The Ephemeral Spirit of Amateurism

> The thrill of real sport [is] playing, not for championships, for titles, for cash,
> for publicity, for medals, for applause, but simply for the love of playing.
> –John Tunis

The modern spirit of amateurism emerged in Victorian England's elite universities and private athletic clubs as an artifact of the class system. The amateur athlete was equated with the gentleman sportsman who participated out of love for the game. The distinction of amateur was tied to the requirement that one not receive remuneration for competing. Thus, the amateur athlete was defined as "one who participates and always has participated in sport as an avocation without material gain of any kind." If athletes did not comply with this rule, they lost their amateur status. The standard implied that competitors were either independently wealthy or held occupations sufficient to ensure their livelihood. The average laborer had no conception of "sport for its own sake." Not surprisingly, amateur sport was nowhere the rule in Great Britain. Association football (i.e., soccer), with wide appeal among the masses, had acquired many of the features of professionalism by the end of the nineteenth century.[852]

The British system had a profound influence on early sport in the United States. By the mid-nineteenth century, boating, racing, and cricket were widely popular, and organized club sports began to appear. America's early baseball clubs organized on the amateur model. A club made up its own rules and procedures and chose its members, invariably from a particular social class or occupation. One club would consist of clerks, a second of mechanics, and another of wealthy gentlemen. However, the United States contained a much more fluid class system than England. Steadily, the American clubs began to recruit talented ballplayers from other venues rather than rely on "appropriate members" to win games for them.[853] Competitiveness trumped social and occupational identity. Increasingly, recruits were judged on the basis of their performance rather than their social status.

Cultural and economic forces within Protestant capitalism worked to further erode amateurism within America's sporting institutions. Economic necessity was one crucial factor. Sports clubs had to generate funds to meet expenses, including the high cost of maintaining athletic facilities. Early on, they implemented the practice of renting their facilities to other teams, including professional clubs, to cover costs. In the process, many of the amateur clubs were transformed from exclusive clubs to open clubs and, finally, to "gate-taking" clubs. Sports clubs that presented themselves as "amateur" adopted whatever tactics were necessary to pay the bills. These developments led to what sociologists label the "monetization" of sport.[854] Once amateur sport relied on financial resources to subsist, it was a small step to commercialism and professionalism.

A significant number of athletes had been accepting money "under the table" during the rise of sport. By the late nineteenth century, "amateur" teams outside the college system were regularly paying players (often collegians) several hundred dollars to play under assumed names on Sundays.[855] Some athletes accepted remuneration out of necessity in order to meet daily living expenses, while others took the money for less justifiable reasons. The practice flourished even though it was proscribed by regulatory associations like the Amateur Athletic Union (AAU)—and later the National Collegiate Athletic Association (NCAA), and the United States Olympic Committee (USOC). Athletes caught taking money were penalized sporadically to set an example. The great track and football athlete Jim Thorpe would have his Olympic medals revoked for accepting small amounts of money to cover personal expenses during a summer baseball tour. But such incidents of selective enforcement did not eliminate the practice.[856]

In truth, only a segment of early American sport had been free of the influence of money prizes, cash payments, and wages. Commercial factors were present at mid-nineteenth century when boat races were drawing large, paying crowds. Rowing crews raced for prizes in the thousands of dollars, and spectators routinely made wagers on the outcome of races. Meanwhile, local promoters of footraces were offering purses of up to $1,000, and "prize-fighting" had become a staple. During the course of the century, it became common to charge admission to popular sporting events, and the staging of these contests often depended on the performance of paid athletes. Indeed, the distinction between amateurism and professionalism didn't even exist until the early 1870s. By then, baseball was a thriving professional sport. Sporting events that attracted the working classes, notably baseball and boxing, were early to professionalize; the so-called "country-club" sports remained more resistant.[857]

American lawn tennis dates from the 1880s; the professional circuit formed in the 1920s. Amateur tennis was compromised by elements of professionalism as early as the 1930s, when Bobby Riggs competed on the circuit. Riggs notes that as one of the top-ranked amateur players, he never had a problem supporting himself and his family. He was paid $500 cash, provided full accommodations, hotel, meals, and transportation to compete in one tournament. For at least two years, Riggs was on the personal payroll of tennis aficionado Edmund C. Lynch of the Wall Street brokerage firm Merrill Lynch, Pierce, Fenner & Beane. He received a check for $200 every week from Lynch until the latter's untimely death. Riggs also had a financial arrangement with L. B. Icely of Wilson Sporting Goods, who paid him to work for their advertising company. The "job" provided Riggs with ample time off to play tennis. Riggs notes that the USLTA was aware of sub rosa payments to top amateur players and would occasionally investigate these arrangements. When Riggs told the members of the rules committee the truth about his arrangement, they advised him to keep the relationship quiet and they would not press charges of professionalism against him. Riggs officially turned professional in the 1940s and became a world-ranked player.[858] Amateur and professional tennis would remain officially separate until 1968, when commercial pressures led to abandonment of the pro/amateur distinction. This rule change inaugurated the open era where all players could compete in the sponsored tournaments.

The duplicity within the sport of tennis was indicative of the climate that compromised amateur sport, but the ideal of amateurism persisted. It was promoted largely by three organizations (mentioned previously): the USOC, NCAA, and AAU. These groups attempted to maintain firm and fair standards of amateurism, although the definitions of amateur status would change dramatically over the course of the twentieth century. The Amateur Athletic Union, founded in 1888, exerted a strong influence over track and field, and governed the budding sport of amateur basketball. The AAU was one of the more formidable forces in amateur sport (and the Olympic movement), but had limited influence over sports like football and baseball. The fact is, most Americans accepted professional sport as long as its athletes did not intermingle with amateurs. But the lines of separation were routinely breached.[859] Several sports that presented themselves as amateur were amateur in name only. Much of baseball outside the major league system was accurately labeled "semi-professional."

Ultimately, the ideal of the uncompensated athlete succumbed to cultural biases and to economic reality. By the late twentieth century, "amateur" athletes were openly compensated in ways previously limited to professionals. The Olympic games gradually opened up to professional athletes. America's Olympic athletes found themselves competing against paid athletes from foreign countries. Track and field had once been exemplars of amateurism, but by the 1970s the sport had given way to the forces of professionalization. A winner of the 1987 Los Angeles Marathon was awarded an expensive European car, a camera set, and $15,000 in cash.[860] Top runners were making large sums of money in the 1990s. Golf remained one of the few American sports that preserved a strict distinction between amateurs and professionals.

Moreover, the emphasis on winning necessitated intense and prolonged training, which further compromised the idea of casual amateurism. As time devoted to training increased, it became more difficult to prepare for high-level competition and hold a job simultaneously. Athletes looked for funds to support themselves while training and competing. Financial compensation found its way into the sanctuary of amateur sport. The middle- and working-class athletes felt a particular need for financial support to make up for lost work time due to increased demands of training and competition, as well as for their travel expenses. These realities of life were pitted against the traditional spirit of amateurism. The new breed of amateur athletes were inclined to exploit emerging technologies, the rules, their own strengths, and their opponents' weaknesses. As the more pragmatic approach to competition became obligatory, the label "amateur" took on pejorative connotations. The expression, "He/she played like an amateur," implied a lack of skill, effort, or seriousness.[861]

The following section examines how the forces of commercialism and professionalism played out in three specific areas of amateur sport: college and school sports, the American Olympic movement, and recreational sports. Amateurism was already becoming problematic when intercollegiate athletics took form in the last half of the nineteenth century. The American Olympic movement would struggle to maintain the amateur ideal through the course of the twentieth century. Recreational sports experienced a similar transformation as they abandoned their casual character and became increasingly commercialized.

Amateur Sport, Professionalized and Commercialized

College and School Sports

> Boosters and alumni now act as shareholders... [T]hey seek a return on their
> increased emotional and financial investments in the Program.
> –Selena Roberts, *New York Times*

In 1913, at Princeton University in New Jersey, a life-size bronze statue was erected of a handsome undergraduate in a football uniform with an academic gown slung over his shoulder and a pile of books in one arm. The statue, which students referred to as the "Christian Student" or the "Christian Athlete," intended to set forth a model of what the Princeton undergraduate should be.[862] The icon provides an apt metaphor for American colleges where academics—represented by the books and gown—are peripheral to the student in sports attire. The religious appellation accorded the statue is equally revealing, given that America's colleges began as private institutions affiliated with various religious denominations. However, by the end of the twentieth century, football arguably was the true campus religion in private and public institutions.

Over time, American higher education developed into a diverse system of both public and private, sectarian and secular colleges, and these institutions shed the ecclesiastical model of governance and adopted a business model. A movement emerged among educators to make schools more practical and efficient. The form of scientific management that was transforming American industry was embraced by the National Council of Education and other educational agencies. Industrial metaphors became increasingly popular with school administrators in the post-World War I era. Ellwood Cubberly wrote in his widely used textbook *Public School Administration,* "Our schools are, in a sense, factories in which the raw products (children) are to be shaped and fashioned into products to meet the various demands of life." He went on to state, "[I]t is the business of the schools to build its pupils to the specifications laid down. This demands good tools...continuous measurement of production [and] the elimination of waste in production." His vision reflected Americans' abiding faith in the wisdom of business corporations and their methods. The business model would shape America's colleges and their sports programs.[863]

An explanation of why colleges chose the business model relates to the evolving nature of higher education within a climate of free-market capitalism. American colleges developed in a setting distinct from Europe. European nations established centralized systems of education with a planned number of colleges and universities supported by federal funding. The US Constitution, in contrast, had delegated the responsibility of education to the individual states. Consequently, public funding of colleges was slow to develop and of secondary importance. In this climate of limited federal funding, dual systems of private and state colleges competed for revenue as well as for students. Many early colleges were founded with a surfeit of optimism and a dearth of resources. As the number of American colleges grew rapidly in the nineteenth century, many schools found themselves existing in an environment that reflected the doctrine of Social Darwinism. The "less-fit" colleges went out of business, while survivors were caught in a continuous struggle for adequate resources. The stark reality of this situation was apparent to college presidents who soon were spending the majority of their time in fundraising. Despite their tax-exempt status, colleges—both public and private—realized they had little choice but to secure adequate supplemental revenue through whatever means.[864]

Americans had applied the rules of the market economy to what were essentially nonprofit, eleemosynary institutions, and colleges responded by adopting business strategies. Businessmen began to replace ministers on college boards, and they evaluated college programs based not on their contributions to enlightened morality, but on the criteria of productivity and the contributions individual programs made to revenue generation. Cost-benefit analysis was applied to curriculum and the extra-curriculum. Alumni played an important role in the finances of colleges, and a disproportionate number of business leaders appeared on the rosters of alumni associations. The business bias was reflected in the diverse moneymaking enterprises within higher education. Agricultural colleges operated profitable dairies; research universities and technical colleges applied for patents on scientific processes and inventions. Most colleges invested in the stock and bond markets to enhance their endowments. Colleges also invested in real estate. In 1962, an alumnus of Rice University in Texas willed his alma mater ownership of Yankee Stadium (which New York City later reclaimed via eminent domain for a fee of $2.5 million).[865]

Historically, organized sport appeared on the college campuses at the same time that the business model was replacing the ecclesiastical one. Early on, the attitude of America's colleges toward their students had reflected the paternalistic and moral climate characteristic of a religious cloister. The college fathers showed as much concern for the students' souls as their minds and bodies. They had little interest in providing students with opportunities for physical recreation. The students themselves initiated campus sports in the mid-nineteenth century. The initial sports activities were organized loosely on the British "Oxbridge" model. These intramural activities developed haphazardly under student control. The undergraduates' ability to manage such activities often proved lacking. As campus sports became more competitive, they were plagued with player injuries and the presence of "undesirables," including gamblers. Student control endured until the 1880s amidst increased misgivings about the climate surrounding these campus activities. College presidents moved to place student sports under their direct control.[866]

The takeover of campus sports by college administrators led to an intercollegiate model supplanting the intramural one. For some time, the two forms of sport existed side by side. The first intercollegiate event reputedly took place in 1852 between the rowing clubs representing Harvard and Yale colleges. The fact that the rowing match was staged as a public event a good distance off campus was an indication of the direction college sport was tending. The partisan enthusiasm of college alumni created an incentive for the promotion of such interschool contests on a regular basis. In response, colleges began to hire professional coaches to prepare their teams for a regular schedule of contests. In 1892, Amos Alonzo Stagg at the University of Chicago became the first college coach to be given faculty status. It was less a gesture attributable to Stagg's academic credentials than an indication that the athletic coach had become a recognized figure on college campuses. The fact that Stagg coached football is significant, for it was football that transformed college athletics into commercialized and professionalized mass entertainment.[867]

Sports in American higher education were evolving into a public spectacle distinct from the European model. Colleges on this side of the Atlantic established discrete athletic departments, staffing them with administrators and professional coaches, and erecting huge sports stadiums to accommodate spectators. In contrast, Great Britain and Germany sponsored school athletics through a council of sports clubs. European school sports functioned without an autonomous administrative structure, and the programs relied on volunteer coaches. Cricket, soccer, and rugby teams charged no admission fee to contests, and athletes competed without financial grants. The Americans, on the other hand, had opted for "big-time" intercollegiate athletics with public appeal. The person accorded much of the credit for establishing this model was Walter Camp, Director of the football program at Yale from 1888 to 1891 (and later at Stanford University). For four decades, Camp served on rules committees that developed the game of football as it became decidedly commercialized and professionalized.[868]

In effect, America's colleges adopted a form of athletics that openly imitated professional sports while operating behind a thin veneer of amateurism. This facade was transparent, but most college board members and alumni seemed comfortable with a system that allowed college athletics to generate revenue. William Rainey Harper, President of the University of Chicago (1891–1906), recognized early on the value of winning athletics programs as a means for improving institutional prestige and growth. Other presidents followed Harper's lead and began to rely on spectator sports to garner financial support for their institutions. Sports were tied to the American colleges' identity and prestige in a way that had not occurred in British universities. It is difficult to imagine the reputations of Oxford or Cambridge depending upon the success of their rowing crews or their rugby teams. However, American colleges' prominence would be tied to the success of their sports teams—Notre Dame to football, University of Kentucky to basketball, and Arizona State University to baseball, for instance.[869]

The moneymaking potential of popular intercollegiate sports like football was quite apparent as they drew crowds in the thousands. Colleges exploited the appeal by charging admission to athletic contests. At first, gate receipts were simply a way to meet expenses of the team. (Harvard drew $705 in receipts on football in 1875.) But as the crowds grew, the receipts often exceeded the expenses, and colleges became convinced they could make money on athletics. By 1903, Yale had generated $106,000 from its football program, a sum equal to one-eighth of the total income for the university. Schools built indoor gymnasiums with seating for spectators when basketball became popular. With dollar signs in their eyes, athletic directors adopted the marketing strategies of professional sports. It occurred to the promoters at the University of Pittsburgh that spectators wanted to readily identify the players, so in 1915 they introduced numbers on players' uniforms. This innovation spurred another source of income: the sale of game programs that listed players by numbers. Intercollegiate sports continued to grow rapidly during the course of the young century. In the

1920s, college football attendance doubled and ticket revenue tripled. In the 1930s, college basketball came into its own. College sports multiplied and expanded over the decades. Large universities would offer some two dozen sports for men and women following implementation of Title IX in the 1970s. To support this offering, athletic budgets ran in the millions of dollars. By then, revenue was pouring in from gate receipts, concessions, printed programs, broadcast rights, student fees, and sales of a variety of consumer products featuring their teams' mascots and logos. Income from these sources was supplemented by booster clubs, whose members made contributions to their college's program. Fundraising campaigns were directed at alumni who revealed an avid interest in their colleges' sports programs.[870]

In the post-World War II era, athletic departments adopted the corporate model, hiring large professional staffs to bureaucratize their operations. Athletics were separated from the colleges' academic administration. A few colleges actually established private associations to run their intercollegiate programs. (The University of Florida's athletic association operated as an incorporated private entity outside the direct control of the university.) These private associations allowed more latitude to athletic administrators, who might otherwise be constrained by regulations governing budgets and salaries.[871] In the climate of high finance, athletic departments no longer relied upon former coaches to head their operations. They hired directors with degrees in business administration or with comparable business credentials. Notre Dame chose a former banker to be its athletic director in the early 1990s. Other schools followed this example.

One source of revenue would have a revolutionary impact on college athletics. This was television. By the mid 1980s, a regular-season television appearance by a college team might net half a million dollars for the school. A decade later, the National Collegiate Athletic Association (then governing some 800 colleges and universities) was taking in over $125 million for the sale of television rights. The CBS network paid a billion dollars for the rights to televise the NCAA basketball tournament over seven years. Individual colleges whose teams reached the tournament championship round received over $1 million each by the 1990s. Networks' interest in college football provided an economic boon. By the end of that decade, four-fifths of the revenue for college football came from television contracts. Football teams who played in major bowl games received several million dollars in additional revenue for their appearances.[872]

By this era, colleges were operating through what constituted an economic cartel, similar to the professional sports leagues. The NCAA controlled the cartel by determining how member schools obtained athletes, setting the rules of eligibility and competition, investigating rule violations, and beginning in the 1950s, exercising punitive power over rules violators. This governing association provided a system in which each college program functioned, in effect, as a business enterprise in competition with other colleges. The cartel remained unchallenged by individual members until the late 1980s, when a few schools with large athletics programs protested that the NCAA was not returning enough of the profits to them. A 1984 US Supreme Court antitrust ruling allowed colleges to negotiate individually with television networks. Presented with what constituted a free market, sixty-three colleges formed the College Football Association (CFA) and negotiated a $71 million contract with CBS to televise their football games. Following the collapse of CFA in 1996, the NCAA signed a $6 billion television contract for broadcasting rights to its members' football games.[873]

Meanwhile, athletic conferences began negotiating their own multimillion-dollar contracts with television networks. In 1995, the Southeastern Conference (SEC) signed a five-year, $95 million contract with CBS for television rights to its regular season basketball and football games, and a $20 million deal with ABC to televise its championship football game. Some nonconference schools negotiated their own deals. In the early 1990s, Notre Dame University unilaterally signed a multiyear, $38 million contract with NBC to televise its football games. Thus, the NCAA monopoly continued to erode as athletic conferences and individual schools negotiated independent contracts.[874] In the early twenty-first century, athletic conferences were establishing their own television networks.

In actuality, the profits from intercollegiate athletics were not a panacea for colleges' financial problems. As profits grew, so did the formidable expenses of running an intercollegiate athletics program. One athletic director at a midsized university in the 1990s estimated that he had to find an additional million dollars each successive fiscal year simply to stay competitive. Television revenues rose and fell precipitously with the success of teams in the major sports. Recruiting efforts required an augmented investment, transportation and equipment costs were inflated, and successful athletic coaches demanded and received large salaries. Consequently, most college sports programs found that their expenses exceeded their incomes.

Relatively few schools, like Notre Dame, were "running in the black," but most colleges continued to lose money on athletics. Although college football generated the most revenue, two-thirds of the football programs had been operating "in the red" in the 1960s and 1970s. Nearly the same percentage of colleges were losing money on their total athletics programs by the early 1990s. Experts who analyzed athletic budgets claimed that even the most successful college football programs were costing their universities more than they took in (when hidden costs were taken into account). The laws of the free market reigned; several colleges discontinued their football programs because of "red ink." Apologists claimed that successful programs in the major sports of football and basketball stimulated increased financial donations from alumni to the colleges' general fund, and that this amount compensated for the financial losses of the athletic departments. Empirical evidence for this assertion has been less than convincing, however.[875]

Many colleges have looked for additional money from the business community to supplement television revenues. In the 1980s college athletics began soliciting the same types of corporate sponsorships that would lift the Olympic games out of a financial crisis. The trend started when John Hancock Insurance Company offered to put up a million dollars annually to finance the Sun Bowl, one of the three dozen college football "bowl games" held at the end of the regular season. The offer was accepted by the organizers of this event, and the Sun Bowl became the John Hancock Sun Bowl. Most of the other college bowls went on to acquire corporate sponsors, as reflected in their modified names. They included the Mobil Cotton Bowl, the Mazda Gator Bowl, and the Sea World Holiday Bowl. This trend of commercial sponsorship was an instance of history repeating itself, as the first intercollegiate athletic event, the 1852 Harvard-Yale regatta, had been sponsored by the Concord and Montreal Railroad, which offered to deliver fans to the site of the event for the price of a ticket.[876]

Athletic conferences explored additional sources of income, including endorsement contracts with private corporations interested in promoting their products and services. Universities would accept corporate names for their sports facilities in exchange for revenue. For example, the University of Colorado's field house was named the Coors Events Center, after the brewery. The Missouri Valley Conference sold the rights to Pepsi, Inc. to sponsor their basketball tournament, which then became the Diet Pepsi MVC Tournament. Corporations paid a fee for the right to use the conference name and logos. The Southeastern Conference was among the first college conferences to establish a corporate marketing program, and other conferences soon followed. The SEC licensed Host Communications to run their marketing program. Host arranged for nine corporations, including an automobile company, fast-food restaurant chain, and healthcare provider, to promote their products through the SEC. Hardee's Restaurants sold almost a million basketballs branded with "SEC" under a similar agreement. From 1993–1994, the SEC took in over $600 million in sponsorship royalties. However, not all college athletic conferences made a profit. Some lost money, and a few realigned or became defunct.[877]

Athletic directors initiated their own initiatives to obtain commercial sponsors. Fred Miller, the aggressive A.D. at San Diego State University (SDSU) in the 1980s, resolved his budget problems by selling "titleships," along with other promotional opportunities, to corporations for remunerations in the millions of dollars. Game sponsorships were sold to rental car companies and lumber companies for the college's football and basketball programs. A McDonald's fast-food franchise sponsored a basketball tournament hosted by SDSU. In exchange for their money and services, the corporate sponsors were allowed to place advertising in the university's indoor sports arena and football stadium, as well as at other sporting venues. San Diego State's basketball floor displayed a new ring of panels with advertising. Commercial sponsors also obtained advertising space in the university's brochures, game programs, and on their electronic scoreboards. Miller sought to instigate a national consortium of universities to arrange similar corporate sponsorships. At Wichita State University in Kansas, a beer company was allowed to drape a panel over the scorer's table at basketball games in exchange for financial contributions to the school's athletic program. Pennsylvania State University signed a ten-year, $14 million contract with Pepsi that obtained exclusive distribution rights, sole broadcasting advertising in their product category, and signage (i.e., space for advertising signs) in the football stadium. Commercial sponsorship spread to the smaller NCAA colleges where it often served as the lifeblood of the minor sports.[878]

College athletic departments began marketing a wide variety of products displaying the school name and logo. Felt-cloth pennants, the traditional symbol of loyalty to one's alma mater, gave way to a comprehensive line of clothing, knick-knacks, and souvenirs. Colleges sold their logos to manufacturers who then produced and marketed a variety of articles, such as T-shirts, pens, wastebaskets, even toilet seat covers. Such items were sold in campus bookstores and through the mail, and eventually via the Internet. By the 1990s, athletic powerhouses like Notre Dame were making millions of dollars on consumer products featuring the school's athletic logo. Marketing practices became increasingly commercialized. During the 2005–2006 school year, the University of Texas raked in more than $8 million in licensing royalties. Texas is part of a consortium of Division 1-A schools that have an arrangement with Collegiate Licensing Company.[879]

The spirit of capitalism triggered various forms of entrepreneurial behavior on American college campuses. College professors had hired themselves out as consultants, competed for prestigious research grants, and reaped the benefits of patents on inventions. Coaches followed the example of their academic colleagues and quickly surpassed them as entrepreneurs. As early as the 1940s, some private colleges had paid coaches a commission for recruiting athletes. Other colleges handed their coaches large blocks of game tickets to sell for profit. A coach at the University of Nevada, Las Vegas, had his salary supplemented by a percent of the profit his school made on tournament appearances. By the 1980s, a major portion of some coaches' income came from sources other than the salary paid by the institutions. Private foundations supplemented coaches' pay at several schools. Coaches' total salaries escalated.[880] By the first decade of the twenty-first century, numerous college coaches in the major sports were making a million dollars annually.

Entrepreneurial ventures of college coaches increased in kind and number. The more successful coaches offered their services to a variety of commercial enterprises. Some received additional "perks" from sporting-goods manufacturers, particularly athletic shoe companies, for endorsing their products and seeing that their athletes wore them during televised games. Coaches endorsed other products, such as soft drinks, for which they received additional stipends. Coaches had "tie-ins" with local automobile dealers who provided them with new cars in return for the advertising potential. Popular coaches might deliver fifty speeches a year, charging thousands of dollars per appearance. Many head coaches had their own local radio and television shows with lucrative contracts. Other coaches ran private summer sports camps for profit. The late Jim Valvano, who was basketball coach at North Carolina State University in the 1980s, grossed over half a million dollars in one year based on a variety of off-campus enterprises. Valvano was one of a growing number of college coaches who reported large supplemental incomes.[881] College coaching had traded in the teaching model for the entrepreneurial model. Head coaches in major sports spent more and more time in commercial ventures beyond the stadium, while assistant coaches filled in.

Despite the long history of colleges seeking to make a profit on sports, the system declined to remunerate athletes—except for financial aid covering part of their educational expenses beginning in the 1950s. However, beneath the high-sounding façade of amateurism, a system of covert remuneration and perquisites for athletes was operating. As early as the 1880s, some Ivy League athletes were being paid "under the table" by generous alumni. At that time, covert activity included the practice of paying non-students or quasi-students called "ringers" to play on college teams. A piece of folklore at the author's own alma mater, Purdue University, attributed the Boilermaker mascot to the nineteenth-century practice of recruiting hefty laborers from the Monon Railroad Shop across the Wabash River from campus. These boilermakers, posing as students, produced an impressive string of victories on the football field. In addition to such ringers, a large contingent of "tramp" athletes in the nineteenth century managed to play for a number of different colleges during one season. If true, there was little doubt such mercenaries were being paid either by athletic departments or by alumni.[882]

College athletic associations, including the American Intercollegiate Football Association (1876), were formed in an attempt to standardize play. In the early twentieth century, the NCAA made a more lasting effort to define the rules of college sport, but did not always enforce them effectively. "Under-the-table" inducements to college athletes persisted through the century. A notorious violation of the NCAA code involved Mike Rosier, an all-American football player at the University of Nebraska. In 1983, Rosier was awarded the coveted Heisman Trophy, the pre-eminent emblem of honor in college football. Later, Rosier admitted he had violated his amateur status by signing a contract with an agent and receiving money while a student. This case was not unique. A former University of Kentucky basketball player acknowledged that he accepted approximately $100,000 from benefactors while a member of that university's basketball team. Anecdotes continued to surface about college athletes receiving remuneration in violation of NCAA rules. According to Allen Sack, half of the former college football players he surveyed in 1990 admitted they, or their teammates, had taken illegal payments while in college. Moreover, a large percentage of the surveyed athletes saw nothing wrong with this practice. The sports establishment also relaxed standards. The 1986 Nehemiah Rule invoked by the International Association of Athletics Federations (IAAF) allowed an amateur track athlete to participate as a professional in another sport. This is the current policy in the NCAA.[883]

Over time, high-school sports programs began to emulate the colleges in their quest for revenue and publicity. Currently, Nike, Inc. and other sporting goods companies approach high schools and offer their athletic teams equipment in exchange for exposure of their products. In 2006, a Nike spokesman acknowledged that the company sponsored some twenty high schools, whom they paid as much as $20,000. Publicity for high-school programs has reached a new level. Fox Sports Net and ESPN networks televise selected high-school football games, including the growing number of interstate contests. Local communities also garner publicity and revenue for school sports programs. An athletics booster club in a small town in South Carolina raised over $300,000 for a high-tech scoreboard for the high-school football field. A school athletics director in the state commented, "I find myself studying marketing and business plans as much as I do game planning."[884]

Outstanding athletes bargain in a market where colleges bid for high-school talent. Colleges shop for graduating athletes, who in turn shop for colleges. A contractual arrangement (the letter of intent) binds the signee to a particular college. Unscrupulous college recruiters have been known to offer high-school athletes financial incentives in violation of NCAA rules to play for their respective colleges. If colleges do play within the rules, it is partly out of fear of being punished by the enforcement arm of the NCAA when caught. However, this organization faces a daunting task in enforcing the rules. The open market for athletes continues unabated. An illuminating case was that of Felipe Lopez, a six-foot, five-inch eighteen-year-old who attended a New York City high school in the early 1990s. Mr. Lopez accumulated four crates of letters from interested college basketball coaches and recruiters. Corporate marketing executives wanted Felipe to promote products for them, and the naive young athlete was enticed to appear in a Nintendo television commercial, a misstep that almost cost him his athletic eligibility. In addition, Lopez and his high-school teammates received expensive shoes and uniforms donated by friendly sporting goods companies who had their own agenda.[885]

Felipe Lopez's experience is indicative of the degree to which the marketing of amateur athletes had infiltrated American schools. The recruiting system has become highly rationalized and professionalized. Many trade publications like *The Sporting News,* along with websites (including one sponsored by the NFL), report on promising high-school athletes. Several states have organized "combines" that facilitate school athletes auditioning for college scouts. The "off season" has become a thing of the past for perspective college athletes. During summers, high-school stars attend instructional training camps taught by college coaches or former pro athletes. Football players routinely accelerate their high-school coursework to graduate a semester early so they can begin their college career in time for spring football practice.[886]

Once athletes have completed their college eligibility, the most promising ones can bargain with professional teams for bonuses and large salaries to play for them. Signing bonuses for football and basketball players often exceed a million dollars. Professional sport franchises employ hundreds of scouts to comb the college campuses for athletic talent. By the 1980s, almost three-fourths of the players selected in the annual professional baseball teams' draft were college players. Professional football and basketball draft virtually all their rookie athletes from colleges. A federal court ruling allows college athletes the right to bargain with professional recruiters before their four years of college eligibility are completed. An increasing number of outstanding athletes leave their college teams before their senior year in order to play for professional teams. Within the constraints of the amateur code, college and high-school athletes have been able to market their talents in a quasi-professional environment.[887]

In the above ways, the spirit of amateurism has been compromised on America's college and high-school campuses. Schools and their athletic departments have operated in a climate where only the fittest survive. The existence of their sports programs has depended upon economic fortune as much as success on the playing fields, although the two pursuits are inextricably interwoven. College programs increasingly emulate the professional model and solicit the financial support of the commercial sector. Coaches act as entrepreneurs, and amateur athletes operate as independent agents in contractual arrangements with team talent scouts. The spirit of amateurism, long at risk on college campuses, has been replaced by rampant commercialism and professionalism.

American Capitalism and the Olympic Movement

Mammon a pris rang parmi les dieux du stade.[888]
–Philippe Simonnot

The French anglophile Baron Pierre de Coubertin founded the modern Olympics on the model of British school sport, absent the class bias. For de Coubertin, amateurism meant competitors could come from any class or occupation as long as they were not remunerated as a result of pursuing their sport. Competing for money was believed to corrupt sport. Consistent with this view, the Olympic code defined the amateur "as one who participates and always has participated in sport as an avocation without material gain of any kind." The Olympic games would become a testing ground for the ideal of amateur sport. American capitalism would play a pivotal role in the transformation of the Olympic movement over the course of the twentieth century. The following discussion briefly examines the role of Americans in commercializing and professionalizing the modern games.[889]

De Coubertin had been skeptical about whether the idea of amateurism was workable. However, he and the cofounders of the modern Olympics made a valiant effort to preserve the spirit of amateur sport in the face of encroaching financial interests. For the first couple decades, the Olympic games were largely removed from the insatiable appetite for money that had influenced other sports venues. Notably, many athletes had paid their own way to Athens to compete in the first modern Olympic games in 1896. However, by the decade of the 1920s, the amateur code was being seriously tested. Professional rugby players were allowed to compete in the 1924 Paris games in a stadium bedecked in commercial advertisements. Four years later, the soft drink company Coca Cola donated 1,000 cases of soft drink to the American team sailing to the Amsterdam games. The company's motives were not entirely philanthropic. At the 1932 Los Angeles Games, the American bakery supplying the Olympic Village appropriated the Olympic five-ring logo to market its products nationally. These incidents were harbingers of things to come.[890]

Americans were prominent in the early days of the modern Olympic movement. As officials on the International Olympic Committee (IOC), they contributed to fashioning competition in the amateur tradition. Later, Americans would lead the campaign to bring private-sector financing—and the commercialism that came with it—into the Olympics. Avery Brundage was not one of them. When he assumed the presidency of the International

Olympic Committee in 1952, the organization was confronting creeping commercialism and professionalism. Brundage, who had been a member of the American track team at the 1912 Stockholm games, was stalwart in opposing the intrusion of professional athletes into the Olympics. In 1972, he led the effort to disqualify an Austrian skier for appearing in sports-equipment ads. Brundage's successors, however, would find it necessary to court commercial sponsors and relax the restrictions on professionalism. The golden era of amateur sport would succumb to the economic reality of staging the biggest single event in sports: the quadrennial summer games. These progressively huge spectacles would require larger and larger amounts of capital. The Olympic organizers held few illusions about the facts of life as they were. Dick Yarbrough, Communications Director of the Atlanta Committee for the 1996 Games, put it bluntly: "Instead of Olympic rings, everybody sees dollar signs."[891]

Government entities had become reluctant to directly finance the entire cost of hosting the games after the 1976 Olympics left the city of Montreal, Canada, with a billion-dollar debt. At this juncture, the Olympic organizers began exploring alternative sources of funding. The international committee members assessed the rather bleak financial situation and recognized they needed enhanced funding from private (implying commercial) sources. Only with a fresh formula for funding did the organizers believe that future games might avoid devastating financial deficits. The Olympic charter stated that "the Olympic Games are not for profit." However, that principle would be interpreted liberally following the financial disaster in Montreal.[892]

In fact, innovative approaches to funding had preceded the Montreal games. Two nations known for their capitalist economic systems were at the forefront of this initiative: the West Germans and the Americans. At the Munich Olympics in 1972, banks, insurance companies, and local and national industrial firms were included in the planning sessions of the games organization committee. The result was an improved funding base. The Americans turned to private television networks as a source of private funding. The 1960 winter games at Squaw Valley, California, were the first to be sold to US television networks under a new rights-fee statute. The Olympics were televised internationally beginning with the summer games in Rome in 1960. By the 1970s, Olympic promoters were selling rights to televise the games to networks for hundreds of millions of dollars. The networks, in turn, sold advertising time to private corporations who promoted their products during the telecasts. Additional sources of private funding were sought to supplement the sale of telecast rights.[893]

The fundraising mechanisms considered by the West Germans in 1972 were carried to new heights by the Americans twelve years later. The Los Angeles games proved to be the watershed event that would shape the financing of subsequent Olympic events. Under the direction of American businessman Peter Ueberroth, the 1984 summer games would cultivate a wide range of funding. The stage was set when Los Angeles taxpayers refused to fund the Olympic games out of the public coffers. At that point, the future of the games was placed in doubt. American taxpayers sent a message that public funding was unreliable. The Los Angeles Olympics organizing committee's response to the lack of public support was to acquire commercial sponsors. Despite the gloomy prognostications of its detractors (and initial resistance from some IOC members), the committee's strategy proved to be a resounding success. For a "floor" fee of $4 million, companies were allowed to exploit the Olympic logo and the games to promote their products. A bevy of interested sponsors responded to the offer. Coca Cola purchased the rights to become the official soft drink of the Olympics, and Snickers (a product of Mars Candy Corp.) was conferred the designation of "official snack food of the games." Commercial sponsorships contributed to the Los Angeles games, realizing a profit of about $150 million on total revenues of $619 million. This included $95 million from sponsors and licensee royalties, $280 million from radio and television rights, $123 million from ticket sales, and $18 million from the sale of commemorative coins.[894]

The innovative arrangement that allowed product manufacturers to officially trade on the Olympic name and logo in exchange for a royalty fee would continue to be profitable. Various national Olympic committees subsequently yielded to the necessities of commercial funding, as the promotion of national teams became more and more expensive. Prior to the 1992 games, the USOC had projected a four-year budget for the American team of $285 million. However, funding experts estimated that the combined American effort would require over three times this amount for the games in Barcelona. By then, a large portion of the USOC budget was funded by corporate sponsorships. Individual sports committees adopted the same strategy. The American Olympic track team unilaterally signed a contract with an athletic shoe company prior to the 1992 games to provide adequate funds. Commercial sponsorships were becoming one of the major sources of revenue for national Olympic teams in capitalist nations, and the

Americans led the way.[895]

The influence of the commercial sector on the games was reflected in the changing structure of the Olympic organization in its various agencies, boards, and committees. The USOC was one of the first national committees to adapt an organizational model that closely resembled that of business corporations. On the suggestion of the executive director of the Olympic canoe-kayak team, the Amateur Sports Act of 1978 was amended by Congress to allow the USOC to restructure along corporate lines. The USOC board (made up of eleven members, including corporate executives) reorganized under a president, three vice presidents, a secretary, and a treasurer at the head of what had become a sophisticated bureaucracy.[896] The Olympic movement reflected the business sector's growth strategy. The tendency was for the games to get bigger and bigger—more sports, more athletes, more ceremony, and more bureaucracy. The 1996 games in Atlanta included 15,000 athletes and officials from 197 countries plus 15,000 media representatives, in addition to the estimated 100,000 volunteers working the games. The USOC bureaucracy grew in kind. Its growth was a manifestation of expanded international competition, but also of the necessary resources to deal with emerging commercial considerations.[897]

The Olympic spirit was successfully wedded to high finance in what came to be known as the "Billion-Dollar Games." The 1996 Atlanta games had actually projected a budget of $1.7 billion. One-third of the proposed revenues was to come from commercial sponsorships. More than half the remaining revenue was to derive from the sale of television rights. In effect, the modern Olympics have become television games; television not only pays the bills but creates the lasting images of the games. At the same time, spectators who choose to attend the Olympics get a firsthand lesson in price inflation. A ticket to the opening ceremonies of the Atlanta games was set at over $600. Some of the sporting events charged $75 for admission; baseball competition offered the cheapest tickets at just under $25. In short, the modern games had become huge commercial spectacles with enormous budgets, and increasingly thirsty for revenue.[898]

At the same time, Olympic athletes representing Western nations required adequate financial support to compete. (Communist bloc athletes had been fully funded by their governments since the 1950s.) Americans training year-round might incur expenses exceeding $20,000. Olympic sprinters spent $1,000 a year on the shoes they wore out in training. Traditionally, some financial assistance had been made available to

Olympic-bound athletes in the way of bursaries, "scholarships," and per diems to compensate for training costs, loss of income, and living and travel expenses. Beginning in 1989, the USOC implemented direct cash assistance to athletes, utilizing funds from the sale of official Olympic coins to the public. Currently, the USOC awards $25,000 to gold-medal winners, $15,000 to silver-medal winners, and $10,000 to bronze medalists to offset their financial obligations. In effect, the Olympics no longer distinguish between "amateur" and "professional" athletes. The official distinction was deleted from the Olympic charter in 1986. At Seoul's summer games in 1988, athletes who were overtly professional entered events previously open to amateurs only. Professional basketball players from the NBA dominated competition at the 1992 games. America's so-called "Dream Team" almost boycotted the Barcelona medal ceremony due to a clash between the logos of sponsors Nike and Reebok. Commercial interests are evident both inside and outside the stadium. Many Olympic athletes retain their own business agents to negotiate with commercial sponsors who court them to promote products. American business interests have been prominent in the commercialization of the games and the professionalization of Olympic athletes.[899]

Americans have never seriously considered federal funding of sport. Instead, they hold an abiding belief that sports fare best within the private sector of the economy. Arguably, the model used for funding the 1984 Los Angeles games saved the modern Olympics. It also preordained that the IOC would forthwith become a business partner with private corporations that provide the revenue for the increasingly expensive summer and winter games. The ancient Olympics had been a quasi-religious celebration, not without elements of professionalism. The modern games have become, among other things, a premier marketing spectacle. The lesson may be that if this can happen to the Olympics—with its traditional ideal of pure amateurism—no segment of amateur sports is immune from the influence of money.

Recreational Sports

> Matter-of-fact men who go out shooting are apt to carry an excess of arms
> and accoutrements in order to impress upon their own imagination the
> seriousness of their undertaking.
> –Thorstein Veblen

One outcome of the burgeoning American economic system was an increase in leisure and discretionary income among the broad middle class. This development led to wider participation in recreational sports like bicycling, golf, and tennis. Protestant capitalism would stamp its imprimatur on these activities as well. Participant sports were inoculated with a strong dose of moral asceticism and a work ethic that stifled the spirit of play and overemphasized "productive" free time. In the Victorian Era, use of leisure time was expected to be morally uplifting. Industrialist Andrew Carnegie exhorted, "How a man spends his time at work may be taken for granted, but how he spends his hours of recreation is really the key to his progress in all the virtues." A half century later, sociologist David Riesman observed that Americans on vacation needed to feel that they "are gainfully improving themselves in body and mind." Indeed, Americans occupied their free time with activities that often appeared as energetic as their occupations. Weekend athletes played five sets of tennis, ran in marathons, and scaled mountains.[900]

The cultural bias toward active recreation was apparent in the designing of the new national parks system around the turn of the twentieth century. Natural areas were "improved" with facilities to accommodate the types of tourists who engaged in rigorous sightseeing tours, river-rafting, and hiking. These forms of recreation were promoted at the expense of more leisurely pastimes like simple communion with nature. It was as if the concept of "recreation" had been reframed to exclude the contemplative mode. What occurred in the sport of rock climbing was exemplary of the ethic. Rock climbing became popular in the post-World War II era; it evolved into a quite rigorous pastime. Climbers would spend several days scaling sheer rock faces, suspended in makeshift hammocks at night. Champion Lynn Hill recalls her introduction to the sport in Yosemite Valley in the 1970s: "We indulged ourselves in climbing as if it were more than a full-time job. We worked at it five days a week, eight hours a day, and we put in a lot of overtime. The only problem was that the job of climbing was a job without pay."[901] Today, rock climbing is a competitive sport with championship events and corporate sponsors.

Recreational sports were progressively co-opted by commercial interests. Physical recreation was brought into the realm of objects and services that were produced, marketed, and sold to the public. What Gruneau referred to as the "commoditization of sport" arose at a time when popular culture, in general, was being marketed.[902] Competing in triathlons (running, swimming, and cycling) is a case in point. Triathlete Heather Hedrick lists the items she packs into her "transition bag" before traveling to an event: towel, swimsuit, goggles, cap, suntan lotion, wet suit, Vaseline, bike shoes, helmet, socks, sunglasses, running shoes, racing belt, Gatorade, bottled water, energy bars and gels, and a set of dry clothes for after the race.[903] Meanwhile, golfers and tennis players are toting larger and larger bags of gear onto the greens and courts. To be a weekend athlete is to assume the role of consumer.

The American public increasingly has had to buy its way into sport, as is the case with other forms of popular culture. This phenomenon first appeared with the rise of mass spectator sports but soon encompassed participant sports. Recreation has become a market sector for consumer goods and services. Amateur sportsmen and women have been obliged to purchase the equipment, proper attire, and accoutrements, as well as admission to the appropriate facilities, in order to participate in a chosen sport. Golf, one of the most popular recreational sports, remains a relatively expensive activity. Serious golfers spend hundreds of dollars for a set of clubs. Green fees on the weekends can run as high as $35 to $40. Add to these expenses a rental fee for the obligatory golf cart and the cost of a box of balls as the entrance fee for playing a round at a public course. Private golf courses operated by country clubs require annual dues in the thousands of dollars.[904]

In order to promote sport as a commodity, manufacturers of the related products and services invest in massive advertising and marketing campaigns. The athletic footwear industry has aggressively marketed stylized, high-tech athletic shoes. One leading manufacturer, Reebok International, was selling over $900 million of shoes annually by the late 1980s. Such companies created the concept of specialized shoes for specific sports. They have marketed running shoes, walking shoes, golf shoes, basketball shoes, soccer shoes, baseball shoes, football shoes, and cross-training shoes. The advertising plays up "technological" innovations in shoe design in order to create style consciousness and the promise of improved performance. Gimmicks like shoes that could be pumped up were supposed to improve ankle support and stability. Some of these high-tech, stylized shoes sell for well over $100 a pair. One survey found that only about 30 percent of the buyers of athletic footwear actually participated in the sport for which the shoe was intended. The motivation of consumers apparently was acquiring the cachet of owning the shoes rather than actually using them for their stated purpose, as well as the vicarious identification with the sport's athletes.[905]

Sports clothing has also grown into a billion-dollar market. Exotic synthetic fibers with cotton blends in sophisticated weaves were offered to amateur athletes. Sports clothing manufacturers attempted a similar type of marketing strategy as that of the footwear companies—particular clothing for specific sports and fitness activities. For example, a stylized "uniform" of sorts became obligatory for participants in aerobic exercise in the 1990s. Such items as leg warmers were more symbolic than functional (and proved transitory). The idea was to create a feeling of stylistic obligation for the participants. Bike-riders had their own distinct clothing that would readily identify them with their sport. The subtle nuances in sports clothing functioned to distinguish the dilettante from the true aficionado. People wore sports clothing as general leisurewear to establish their identity with sport and fitness.

Sports equipment and accoutrements multiplied rapidly as sport became increasingly commodified. Contemporary hunters are not the only ones who feel obliged to carry and wear an assortment of accoutrements. Early on, the game of baseball required little more than a bat and ball. Currently, one finds ballplayers equipped with a sophisticated array of batter's gloves, fielder's gloves, helmets, shin guards, flip-up sunglasses, tape, braces, resin, and other paraphernalia. Cyclists attach a variety of items to their persons and the frames of their bikes. Sport-related food and drink also have been marketed with the amateur sports participant in mind, featuring high-energy snacks and nutritional supplements. Although the actual benefits of these products remain questionable, they do satisfy the need of sports consumers to purchase something related to their activity as a way of assuring themselves that they are seriously involved and receiving some benefits from it.

The middle-class American home has become a repository for a large collection of sports equipment: a set of barbells in the corner, an exercycle or rowing machine across the room, a closet filled with tennis rackets, golf clubs, Frisbees, hunting paraphernalia, skies, rollerblades, ice skates, and an assortment of balls for everything from bowling to soccer. The garage or carport may be cluttered with water skies, SCUBA gear, croquet sets, a table-tennis table, archery equipment, and fishing gear. Storage space in the family vehicle is filled with items for more immediate recreational use. American automobiles are marketed by exploiting the sports cachet. Sports utility vehicles became popular during the 1990s. Contrary to their advertised image, SUVs are more likely to be stuck in traffic on the freeways than fording streams and climbing rocks in the outback. In fact, much of the purchased sports paraphernalia is infrequently employed at all. Recent surveys indicate that less than half of the people who purchase exercise equipment for their homes actually utilize it on a regular basis.[906] The unused apparatus has been labeled "fitness furniture" as a commentary. Members of the American middle class have fulfilled their role as consumers by purchasing personal sports and fitness equipment.

Many recreational sports require private facilities, access to which has to be purchased. America has had a long history of private golf courses, tennis clubs, swimming clubs, and hunting clubs that require membership fees. These exclusive facilities are complemented by private health clubs and fitness centers that became popular in the last quarter of the twentieth century. Users pay a membership fee and/or annual dues to maintain privileges. Commercial fitness centers and the YMCA have provided a wide variety of exercise equipment and facilities for members. These fitness centers offer aerobic dance classes, indoor tracks, gymnasiums, swimming pools, and exercise rooms. Franchises like Gold's Gym offer not only equipment but personal trainers and instructors for members. Moreover, recreational sports events held in public venues are becoming highly commercialized. The participants in urban 10K races and marathons are subjected to an array of product placements at the venues, including bottled water, energy bars and gels, etc., often packaged in "goodie bags." The routes they run are lined with commercial advertising.[907]

During the last century and a half, Americans abandoned the spirit of amateurism. Informal and casual recreation yielded to the cultural forces of consumer capitalism and professionalism. This transformation resulted in two approaches to participant sport. The enthusiasts engaged in weekend recreation with the intensity of paid athletes, their earnestness reflected in their outfits and accumulated "tools of the trade." Others simply acquired the paraphernalia of physical recreation, replicating the ritual of conspicuous consumption. Purveyors of consumer goods and services cleverly co-opted physical recreation and converted it into a market campaign. The more sedentary Americans took their recreation by watching others perform from a stadium seat or in front of their televisions. Sports fans watched college games and the quadrennial Olympics, but it was professional sports that dominated the culture of fandom.

12

Professional Sport: The Progeny of Capitalism

Sport and the Spirit of American Capitalism

> The character and scale of sports today is the child of monopoly capitalism.
> –Paul Hoch

By the end of the nineteenth century, business had become a game played by rich men who made up the rules as they went along, while the game of baseball was being converted into a thriving business. In the words of French economist Phillipe Simonnot, the impresarios of the Victorian Era were "faisant du jeu une marchandise et de la marchandise un jeu" ("making sport a commodity and commodities a sport").[908] The new Darwinian world was witnessing the evolution of sport, as the casual games of young men and women in small towns had given way to organized teams of paid athletes and amateur athletic clubs in the cities were eclipsed by professional sport franchises. Spectator sports were being transformed into paid entertainment for the working classes, while recreational sports offered a new market for leisure consumption. America's games were crossbred with capitalism; the progeny of this union would portend the future.[909]

A. G. Spalding expressed the prevailing sentiment of the era when he suggested baseball franchise owners "should abandon the vestiges of the amateur tradition of the Knickerbocker Club and recognize themselves as business organizations employing ballplayers, and trying to make a profit."[910] Thus, American sport developed in the context of burgeoning capitalism, and its growth was nourished by diverse capitalist enterprises. As professionalism supplanted amateurism, a business ethic penetrated the fundamental structure of sport from top to bottom. Sport was transformed into a profit-making enterprise fully integrated with the other major sectors of the economy. Banks, industrial firms, and property companies all joined in to finance sport franchises. Sports leagues began to operate more and more like commercial firms competing in a product market. Even the nominally amateur sports clubs that survived began to adopt business strategies.[911]

Historically, the rise of spectator sports in the US coincided with mass production that created the technical capacity to promote and market sports. The viability of sports was dependent upon the reduction of working hours, modern means of transportation, and improved communication technology. American workers with more leisure and discretionary income provided a ready pool of customers for the new product of sport. Extra money in the pockets of workers translated into potential fans to purchase admission to athletic events. The resulting increase in gate revenue largely determined the early growth and success of sport. Even the colleges began charging admission to athletic contests despite their tax-exempt status and pretensions of amateurism. The newspapers (and later the electronic media) provided fans not able to attend sporting events with descriptions of their teams' performance and, in turn, further popularized sports.[912]

The commercial impact of sport was unmistakable by the mid-1920s, when nine to ten million fans annually paid to watch Major League Baseball and championship boxing matches were taking in million-dollar gates. College sports also began drawing large crowds of spectators. Huge stadiums, seating tens of thousands, were erected to accommodate fans who provided the economic base for athletics programs. What had been a largely amateur venture was converted into its own form of consumer capitalism. The commercial market for sports would explode during the course of the twentieth century, with the news and entertainment media playing a major role. Sport would become a multibillion-dollar enterprise, among the dozen largest industries in the nation by the end of the century.[913]

American sport under the influence of Protestant capitalism has been privatized and commercialized to an extent that remains exceptional. Other developed nations treat sport as a government responsibility and set up bureaucracies to fund and administer programs for the general public. Typical of this model is the French sports division of the Ministry of Youth and Sport, which manages and controls funding to the nation's sports federations and associations (including those in schools and universities) and is also responsible for international sport competition. In the republic of Ireland, almost all the fifty-plus sports-governing bodies receive subsidies from the national government either directly or indirectly. The Gaelic Athletic Association has ties to both the Irish government and to the Catholic Church. The former Soviet Union organized a comprehensive sports program as a public function, while at the same time sponsoring a national training program for elite athletes. A significant percentage of the Soviet Union's gross domestic product was invested in public sport facilities. The Eastern European nations in the Soviet Bloc followed this model, as did the Chinese Communists who came to power in 1949. Likewise, when Fidel Castro took control of Cuba in 1959, he implemented a Soviet-style system of state-sponsored sport.[914]

No federal sport bureaucracy of this sort exists in the United States. The very idea of state-run sport appears to contravene the ethic of individualism and the spirit of capitalism. Americans have generally conceptualized sport as a proprietary enterprise and relegated it to the private sector. This is not to say that Americans have not created public sport and recreation programs at the state and local levels. City leagues sponsor softball and tennis tournaments; public colleges provide campus recreation; state parks offer facilities for participant sports like hiking and fishing. The public has had access to such programs and facilities for a nominal fee throughout much of the nation's history, but increasingly, even recreational sports are being privatized (see chapter 11). As noted, spectator sports developed almost exclusively as profit-making enterprises that charged admission. Consistent with this model, publicly owned teams in the major professional sports like baseball, football, and basketball have become a rarity.[915]

Despite the renunciation of a public sports bureaucracy, Americans have not been averse to supporting private sports with public revenue. Local and state governments routinely subsidize sport franchises through public financing of facilities and preferential application of tax codes. In August 2006, New York City broke ground on a new billion-dollar stadium for the New York Yankees, with the amount of public funds for supporting infrastructure estimated at $220 million. The financing of stadiums is a major example of the influence sports entrepreneurs wield over state and local governments and the public. Urban leaders defend financial subsidies of spectator sports as an incentive for stimulating the local economy and improving the tax base. As a case in point, one New York Mets home game creates 850 game-day jobs and generates over $60,000 in local taxes. Notwithstanding the jobs generated for stadium employees, the major beneficiaries of sports stadiums are private businesses—construction companies, local restaurants, hotels, and of course, the sport franchise owners themselves. A championship game or tournament may fill 15,000 hotel rooms in the host city.[916]

As for ideology, sport has responded to all this largess by making an important contribution to the promotion of capitalism by serving as a bulwark for attitudes and beliefs appropriate to the free-market principles. Capitalism is essentially achievement oriented and competitive; sports present a model consistent with this ethic. In the minds of many Americans, winning is to the spirit of sport what profit-making is to the spirit of capitalism—a saving grace and proof of individual worth. Sport historian John Betts identified the commonalities between sport and the capitalist spirit as including initiative, the need to struggle with one's own physical and mental powers, the premium set on team play and cooperation, and the encouragement of the competitive spirit. "Sport in America was organized to emphasize values such as a commitment to production, competitive success, and the achievement of objectively measurable performance goals," to quote sociologist Jay Coakley. The ethos of sport has been fully integrated with the spirit of capitalism.[917]

American sport could have assumed any of several cultural forms. It might have endured as folk games and informal recreation or, through amateur sports clubs, been made up of young working adults. Sports in these settings would emphasize egalitarian values and inclusiveness. The spirit of play might prevail, with a focus on the joy of movement and the celebration of the human form. Instead, the forms and character of American sport were shaped in the image of capitalism. Team sports like football, basketball, baseball, and hockey have adopted the model of private professional or quasi-professional franchises with athletes (laborers) employed by owners (capitalists) to provide a product (entertainment) to be sold to the general public (consumers). Currently, there are well over 100 professional sport franchises in the United Staes. Professional sport remains the most visible and dominant sector of American sport.

Baseball as Prototype

> Look, we play the *Star Spangled Banner* before every game.
> You want us to pay income taxes too?
> –Bill Veeck, team owner

Baseball has been touted as America's pre-eminent game. In truth, baseball has flourished as both a game and a business. By the turn of the twentieth century, the latter designation overshadowed the former. The popular sport had become a money-making enterprise. Baseball was the offshoot of an unrestrained brand of capitalism characteristic of the Industrial era. The early franchises imitated the structure and strategies of emergent business corporations. Accordingly, team owners treated their ballplayers like hired hands, the fans like customers, and their fellow franchise owners like business rivals. Baseball arose as the first truly professional team sport and provided a model for most other spectator sports.[918]

Exactly when and where baseball first appeared in the United States remains obscure. Primitive forms of the game had existed as early as the eighteenth century. Baseball began to accumulate rules and techniques from related games like "Old Cat," town ball, rounders, and cricket. Amateur cricket and baseball clubs were common on the local level by the mid-nineteenth century. The Knickerbocker club had its own diamond in 1845, and by the 1850s several other baseball clubs were competing in the New York area. Baseball spread in popularity, reaching as far south as New Orleans and westward to San Francisco. As baseball expanded geographically, it also reached out demographically to the middle and working classes. The game was played on club grounds, college campuses, and sandlots across America. It became a popular college sport following the contest between Amherst College and Williams College in 1859. The working classes often played the game on company teams; in fact, the Michigan Central Railroad had their own baseball club in 1857. By 1870, over 400 amateur and professional baseball clubs were represented in the National Association of Baseball Players.[919]

Company teams played a pivotal role in the development of the game. Financial connections between local businesses and sports teams were common. Employers would court outstanding ballplayers with offers of money to play on company-sponsored teams. Businesses hired a promising pitcher or hitter, assigned him a job with light duties, and then paid him an inflated salary to play ball. They "wrote off" contributions to these teams as advertising costs. Some of the players were reimbursed out of gate receipts. These early practices punctuated the growing ties between business and baseball that were to characterize the game for the next century. In 1869, the Red Stockings of Cincinnati became the first truly professional team, made up of players whose full-time job was playing ball. Other ball clubs followed this model, and baseball emerged from being a stepchild of business to becoming a business in its own right. In March 1871, the owners of the Red Stockings and eight other clubs met in New York to form the

National Association of Professional Baseball Players. The managers of the professional ball clubs devised what would become the basic unit of organization for team sports, the league. This arrangement offered two advantages: facilitation of a regular schedule of contests and an administrative structure that codified and controlled competition. Baseball leagues would come and go during the following decades, but the basic form endured to provide the model for other team sports. The league as a contrivance to facilitate competition would be supplemented by elimination tournaments and championship playoff rounds. These organizational devices became mainstays of athletic competition.[920]

The close ties between business and baseball solidified as professional leagues emerged. Financial backing for the fledgling leagues came from established businessmen looking to exploit the game commercially. Prominent among the backers were brewers and distillers who hoped to sell their products to the growing crowds of fans. A. G. Spalding and his brother planned to promote their burgeoning sporting goods business by developing close ties with professional baseball. Vendors of the products used by athletes were instrumental in forming the national league. An interlocking network of trade associations, manufacturers, and rules committees would determine the range and style of the game. Professional baseball teams with established financial backing began to operate as businesses competing in an open market. A few of the more successful teams were paying dividends to stockholders by the mid-1880s.[921]

The sport franchises adopted common business practices including the hiring of specialized personnel. The retinue of employees at ballparks soon included ushers, ticket sellers, security guards, groundskeepers, refreshment workers, cushion concessionaires, and even musicians. Baseball also implemented marketing strategies. The ball clubs were sensitive to the advantages of publicity and made special accommodations for newspaper reporters. In addition, some teams like the Red Stockings went on national promotional tours. Clubs charged admission to games to generate revenue. (It took money to convert a field into a ballpark—an enclosed facility with controlled access.) As early as 1858, a game in New York City drew 1,500 spectators at 50 cents apiece. Such charges had become the rule among the major clubs by the 1870s. Ballparks installed private boxes for parties of "ladies and gentlemen" for which they charged a higher admission fee. In 1881, one ball club reported $30,000 in gate receipts.[922]

The success of baseball created a new class of professional athletes who were paid salaries and travel expenses, as a ready supply of talented players emerged from local teams. But the financial cards were stacked in favor of the owners. Most ballplayers earned wages that were scarcely higher than those of skilled artisans. Even with a supply of relatively cheap labor and expanding markets, several teams failed to meet expenses and folded. The quest for financial profit among baseball teams became as competitive as action on the field of play. Leagues expanded into additional cities as the competition for limited profits escalated. A few owners affiliated with the newly formed rival leagues in order to survive and then raided the former league rosters for players. The national league clubs took a rival league to court in the 1880s for "stealing" players under contract.[923]

Given the ruthless competition for skilled players, it is not surprising that the national league clubs sought to control the labor market. The established practice was that players would sign a contract with any team in exchange for their services. To halt this practice, team owners developed an exclusive contractual relationship with their players, and those who broke their contracts were penalized. This agreement included a "reserve" rule that sought to assure clubs complete control over their players and restrict their rights to negotiate with other teams. What resulted was an immediate cut in players' salaries beginning with the 1880 season. But even with the reserve system in place, it took substantial capital to employ a team of talented players. A few owners invested $60,000 to $70,000 annually in facilities and player salaries (with rosters of fifteen players). Realizing the adverse impact high player salaries could have on profits, they added a clause to contracts in 1887 stipulating that no club could pay a player more than $2,000 a year. So much for the free market![924]

Not surprisingly, players unions began to organize. Baseball's paid athletes recognized their relationship with the team owners as an adversarial one between labor and management. They formed the National Brotherhood of Professional Baseball Players in 1885, and within two years this organization represented a large number of national league ballplayers. In response, the owners resolved that anything looking like a labor union would not be allowed to interfere with their businesses. The situation between players and owners was rapidly approaching an impasse when Spalding, then a team owner, took on the role of mediator. A series of hard-fought negotiations occurred between the two parties. The brotherhood attempted to bargain with the club owners on the reserve rule, but no deal was agreed upon. A new contract was worked out that specifically listed the players' rights and responsibilities and those of the clubs employing them. This so-called "Brotherhood Contract" involved no basic changes in the relationship, however. The owners clearly had won the first battle between baseball labor and management. Player unions would not become a significant factor in negotiations until several decades later.[925]

Meanwhile, baseball entrepreneurs waged their own internal battles. The burgeoning sport was plagued with a series of trade wars between competing leagues and teams in the 1880s and 1890s. Owners recognized the adverse effects of unlimited competition among franchises for profits (and, in some cases, for survival) and moved to operationalize league control over teams. Around the turn of the century, club owners in the national league commenced an effort to save the league from unrestrained competition by opting to form a trust. This trust was proposed to include preferred and common stock that would belong to the league as a body. Stockholders would elect club managers, in the process forming a sort of board of regents. Under this scheme, the clubs were to lose their individual corporate identities, while the board licensed players and managers. The trust idea eventually died, but a compromise was worked out that put the league on the road back to financial health. The final compromise was recognition by team owners that, in order to maximize individual profits, they had to maximize joint profits. They found it in their collective interest to restrict selfish business practices and ensure that franchises operated like participants of a joint venture. Thus, professional baseball moved from the free-market model toward that of a corporate (and territorial) monopoly.[926]

By the opening of the twentieth century, with the initiation of the two-league scheme and a dozen new ballparks, the governing structure and arrangements that characterize modern baseball were largely in place. Management had established a favorable contractual relationship with players and had initiated mechanisms to control external competition and rationalize their internal organizations in order to maximize profits. Realizing that a reliable source for talented ballplayers was crucial, major league clubs began to invest further in minor league teams. In the 1890s, an agreement was framed between the national league and the Eastern and Western leagues. Three decades later, a pivotal minor league agreement was forged when the first baseball commissioner was appointed. This arrangement opened the door for Cardinals president and manager Branch Rickey to pioneer a minor league system that became the model for professional baseball. His impressive organization, developed in the 1930s, provided the St. Louis team with outright ownership or controlling interest in thirty-three "farm" clubs with some 600 players. Rickey understood that one requisite for maintaining a monopoly is controlling the sources of supply. By 1936, two-thirds of major league teams had affiliations with minor league clubs. Baseball began to look like a horizontally and vertically integrated business in the matter of personnel.[927]

During the early decades of the twentieth century, only horseracing and boxing approached the success of baseball. But baseball was the premier spectator sport when Babe Ruth began hitting homeruns with regularity, and it would remain so for decades. In the 1920s, there existed no established professional basketball or football leagues, nor tennis or golf tours of any commercial account. The other major team sports eluded the public's attention until the post-World War II era. Only then did professional football began to rival the popularity of the college game, which itself had adopted a quasi-professional model. Professional basketball teams in the first half of the century were mostly of the barnstorming variety. The current NBA, founded in New York City in 1946 as the Basketball Association of America, struggled during its early years as individual franchises came and went.[928]

In the post-war era, the broadcasting of night games would push baseball across the indistinct line demarcating sport into the realm of entertainment, as it now competed head to head with the movies and television programming. In effect, baseball had become another media enterprise that "happened to use ballgames as its currency." Two individuals dramatically shaped the baseball market in the entertainment era. Branch Rickey, who had moved from St. Louis to Brooklyn, broke the longstanding "color barrier" by placing Jackie Robinson on the Dodgers' roster in 1947, thus creating a new fan base among African Americans. The other was Bill Veeck, who schooled his fellow franchise owners on how to take advantage of new tax laws and advocated that sagging franchises move to emerging markets. The latter strategy extended major league baseball to cities across the nation. Veeck would have yet another pivotal influence on the game. The flamboyant promoter introduced marketing techniques and gimmicks that radically changed the experience of attending ballgames. Many of the promotional events that are now taken for granted—giveaways, special events, garish electronic scoreboards—can be traced back to his brainstorms. Veeck's marketing gimmicks irritated the purists and Rickey's action infuriated the bigots, but these two entrepreneurs brought thousands more fans to major league ballparks.[929]

The golden era for the baseball business was the 1980s, owing to increasing television revenue and rising game attendance and bolstered by its favorable tax status. In 1987, over fifty-two million fans attended regular-season major league games. In the process, they spent $500 million on tickets, parking, beer, souvenirs, and food. Another twenty million attended minor league games, while tens of millions listened to games on their radios or watched on television. The results of this commercial success were dramatic. By the end of the twentieth century, the average baseball franchise would be valued at over a quarter of a billion dollars.[930]

Throughout its history, baseball had cultivated business entrepreneurs like A. G. Spalding, Al Reach, Branch Rickey, Bill Veeck, and August Busch. These men understood implicitly that baseball was first a business, and applied business concepts to their operations. Over the course of the twentieth century, professional baseball would incorporate most principles of capitalism, including productivity, division of labor, allocation of resources, franchise, monopoly, depreciation, tax subsidies, operating revenues, direct and indirect costs, maximization of profits, marketing strategy, and eventually, the accommodation of labor unions and collective bargaining. Professional baseball is the oldest and, arguably, the most successful team sport to endure over the decades; however, it no longer occupies the top spot on the professional sports pyramid. Television would be the great leveler.[931]

Sports Incorporated

> God bless our sponsors, without whom we couldn't be here today.
> —Invocation, NASCAR drivers meeting

By the 1980s, professional sport had spawned its own trade magazines, including Street and Smith's *SportsBusiness Journal* and *Sport Marketing Quarterly*. This type of publication offers detailed analysis of the sports business, with articles on advertising, concessions, products, labor relations, marketing firms, insurance, and government action affecting sports. The format openly imitates other business journals in featuring charts, graphs, and calendars for conferences and trade shows. Their subscriber lists reach beyond professional sport managers to include college athletic directors, marketing departments of corporations, executives of sporting-goods companies, and television/media executives. Such publications confirm what had been apparent to many observers for quite some time—that sport has adopted the forms, tactics, and goals of corporate America.[932]

The sports business traces its roots back to the late nineteenth-century era of the Robber Barons whose strategies and tactics it imitated. Through trusts, reserve clauses, manipulation of tax laws, and antitrust exemptions, team owners quickly accommodated the role of autocratic capitalists, commanding privately held franchises largely protected from public scrutiny. Their goal was to secure professional sport as a self-controlled area in which they could freely operate. Today's team owners and league executives operate like modern corporate managers by entering into various arrangements to promote profitable conditions for their franchises. They may espouse laissez-faire capitalism as an ideal, but all the while, professional sport has merged with the interconnected corporate bureaucracy.[933]

Because the nature of ownership is a key aspect of capitalism, the evolving pattern among sport franchises is instructive. Through much of the twentieth century, team ownership was a family enterprise. Baseball and football set the pattern. Chewing-gum industrialist William Wrigley, Jr., son Philip, and grandson William III, successively managed the Chicago Cubs as a family business over several decades. The late Art Rooney, who purchased the NFL Pittsburgh Steelers in the 1930s, turned day-to-day operations over to his son Dan in 1974 but remained as chairmen of the board until his death in 1988. However, by the mid 1980s, only two professional baseball teams, the Boston Red Sox and Los Angeles Dodgers, were owned by individuals/families whose major business was sports. The Bidwell family's continuing ownership of the Cardinals football team since 1932 is the rare exception in the NFL. When William Wrigley III sold the Cubs to the Tribune Company in 1981, it was the beginning of a new era. The Griffith family, who had purchased the Washington Senators in 1912 and still owned the team when it moved to Minneapolis in 1961, sold the Twins to a banker in 1985. Peter O'Malley then sold the Los Angeles Dodgers to media entrepreneur Rupert Murdoch in 1997. This event signaled the demise of family ownership in major league baseball.[934]

The traditional owners whose emotional investment in the team meant as much as their financial investment had become an anachronism. They were gradually being replaced by brewers, bankers, business tycoons, and media moguls. August A. "Gussie" Busch, Jr., the brewing magnate, purchased the St. Louis Cardinals in 1953. Meanwhile, insurance entrepreneur Charles Finley bought the Kansas City Athletics baseball club in 1960, the same year oil baron Lamar Hunt organized the American Football League, which included his team, the Kansas City Chiefs.[935] In the next phase, franchise ownership shifted to small groups of investors or large corporations (like Murdoch's), many of whom had a secondary interest in sport. Outside interests of the emerging group of franchise owners fell within the more adventuresome areas of investment. A 1980s-era survey of 141 professional team owners found that almost half had made their fortunes in the independent sectors of the economy, such as communications, transportation, real estate/land development, and oil production. By the mid-1990s, nearly a third of the owners of the 120 North America-based franchises in the four major sports were in the entertainment sector. At the close of the century, sole investors made up less than 10 percent of sports team owners.[936]

An event that occurred three decades earlier provided the curtain-raiser for the emergent pattern of ownership. When Gene Autry bought the California Angels baseball club in 1961, his action signaled the amalgamation of professional sport franchises and the media/entertainment industry. Autry owned four radio stations, a TV station, a national radio-time sales firm, and a TV production company. In 1996, the former movie star and recording artist then sold controlling interest in the team to the Walt Disney company. The rationale behind these purchases was unambiguous: media communication conglomerates sought to purchase sport franchises as a means of producing content for their delivery systems. Sporting events provided regular, inexpensive programming.[937]

Multi-franchise ownership by media interests became common in the 1970s. Media entrepreneur Jack Kent Cooke owned the Los Angeles Wolves soccer team, the Los Angeles Lakers in the NBA, the LA Kings in the NHL, and a majority share of the Washington Redskins in the NFL while he also owned the Los Angeles Forum, a sports arena. In the indoor-sports realm of basketball and ice hockey, several individuals and corporations controlled both the arenas and the teams who played in them. The Madison Square Garden Corporation owned the garden arena plus the NBA Knickerbockers and the NHL Rangers. Thus, the same corporate entity could own the teams, the arenas they played in, and the cable or commercial television stations and networks that telecast the games. Such are the advantages usually associated with a monopoly.[938]

The 1990s witnessed the culmination of the marriage between

professional sports and the entertainment business. Rupert Murdoch is typical of this new type of owner. His media conglomerate News Corp has majority ownership in Fox Entertainment Group and Fox Broadcasting (with 200 US television affiliates), along with interests in virtually every major sport in some form. News Corp owns several Australian sport franchises and 15 percent of the MLB Colorado Rockies, and it also owns sports arenas. To effectuate vertical integration, News Corp has acquired sport franchises, TV stations, and networks. It is horizontally integrated through its ownership of subsidiaries in cable, publishing, e-commerce, satellite television, and Internet sites. Another player in these two related sectors is Comcast-Spectator, a subsidiary of Comcast Corporation, a leading provider of cable, entertainment, and communications products and services. In 2010 Comcast-Spectator owned the Philadelphia Flyers of the National Hockey League, the Philadelphia Phantoms of the American Hockey League, and the Philadelphia 76ers of the National Basketball Association.[939]

In the wake of corporate incursions, public ownership of sports has gone the way of family ownership. By the first decade of the new century, three major sport franchises were publicly owned and traded on stock exchanges; they were the NBA's Boston Celtics, MLB's Cleveland Indians, and the NHL's Florida Panthers. The Green Bay Packers remained publicly owned, but their stock was not traded on any of the major exchanges. The decline of family and public ownership reflects the more pragmatic and innovative approach to professional sports. The new corporate managers assess their teams primarily in terms of profits that are realized through an array of novel devices, including inflated salaries, stock dividends, tax benefits charged against other income, the sale of franchise rights or facilities, and shares in fees paid to the league when new teams enter. Today's sports capitalists do not manage a team so much as they market a product to optimize returns on an investment. As baseball historian Leonard Koppett observed, by the late 1990s, "[t]he business of *selling* a team was taking precedence over *running* a team."[940]

Because corporate executives and stockholders who own sports teams are more interested in profits than trophies, sport franchises increasingly imitate large American businesses in their structure and functions. One indicator is the size of a team's front office. Early on, professional teams employed rather small staffs. They operated without corporate sales agents, sponsorship directors, media sales "reps," public relations staff, or even a large ticket sales force. As late as 1959, the Chicago Cubs had a front office made up of eleven people and were operating without job titles in most of the above-mentioned areas. In 1961, the Los Angeles Dodgers listed thirteen people in their front office. Today, the Dodgers have nineteen executive officers alone and over a hundred front office employees working in some two dozen divisions.[941]

Bureaucratic management replaced autocratic and paternalistic leadership. Sport franchises have adopted the hierarchical model of management to plan policies and make decisions. They reveal the distinctive mechanisms of corporate organization: role ordering, explicated relationships, lines of authority, and specific business performance goals. The sport bureaucracy is made up of team owners, board members, professional managers, and field coaches operating within league associations under a complex regulatory structure. The functions of these franchises is to recruit employees, meet payroll, maintain facilities, promote their product, and generate revenue. Today's sport franchises make substantial investments and display most of the other characteristics of high-capital finance.[942]

Despite the restructuring of sport franchises in line with corporate norms, the sports industry has remained unique in several ways. Normally in a free-market system, one attempts to outproduce or outperform the competition in a given market. But professional sports teams have had to cultivate opponents within their market; otherwise, they would have no one with whom to do business. In a sense, competition *is* the product of professional sport. Thus, the very nature of sport has required the fostering of internal competition while limiting external competition. To bring about this essential business arrangement, professional sport has sought to operate as a self-regulated monopoly.[943]

Historically, the federal government regulated monopolies in most industries following the Sherman Antitrust Act of 1890, but generally allowed limited monopolistic privileges in sport. Professional baseball, which enjoyed a powerful monopoly, gained antitrust exemption in a 1922 US Supreme Court ruling. However, other professional sports like football and basketball have been denied a general exemption from antitrust laws. (The National Football League was found to be subject to antitrust laws in 1957.) At the same time, the federal courts and US Congress have favored these sports by underwriting many legal mechanisms limiting external competition. The 1961 Sports Broadcast Act granted teams the right to sell programming to television without being limited by antitrust laws. As a consequence, professional sport has remained less burdened by federal regulations than other monopolies such as public utilities.[944]

Because of its unique status, professional sport has developed as a collection of economic cartels.[945] Team sports cartels consist of franchises in a league that agree to operate under a set of rules to limit economic competition. Such cartels are capable of controlling markets in order to maximize profits of members; for example, the annual NFL player draft functions as a collective to circumvent bidding wars for outstanding recruits. Meanwhile, the goal of each team franchise is to earn more profit than the other cartel members. The idea of the sports cartel has rested on several powerful legal and marketing devices within the favorable antitrust climate. These contrivances, by which team owners act in concert to control their athletes/employees, have included the reserve option and waiver clauses in personal service contracts and other agreements that restrict certain types of competition. Thus, the professional sport franchise owner has been able to operate as a "competitive capitalist," buying into an owner-operated cartel that regulates its own industry out of mutual self-interest—an arrangement that has been considered illegal in nearly all other areas of American business.[946]

Forms of economic competition have persisted within the sport cartels against the backdrop of monopoly capitalism. The cartels could have equalized profit among the individual franchises by pooling revenues from various sources and then providing for the league to pay all player salaries and dividing the profits equally. However, most professional leagues have chosen not to do this. Ideologically, this practice would have violated the revered principle of a competitive free market. Notably, intra-league competition was modified within the cartels to include limited forms of profit-sharing and the player draft apparatus, first installed by the National Football League in 1936. The latter practice reduced competition for athletes within a league, but inequities still remained between the markets in different cities. A more momentous response by owners to inequitable revenue-sharing was to seek more profitable markets. The move of the Boston Braves baseball club to Milwaukee in 1953 triggered a flurry of franchise shifts in the following decades, with a total of sixty-eight professional sport franchises having relocated by 1983. This business strategy has become routine.[947]

Other forms of external competition surfaced. The appearance of rival leagues and new franchises within existing leagues in the 1960s and 1970s changed the structure of professional sports by promoting a classic form of open-market competition. League mergers, as in the case of professional football (1969) and professional basketball (1976), worked to curtail this form of competition. League expansion was recognized as a way to discourage new leagues from forming. In 1959, the four major professional team sports included forty-two teams. A decade later, the figure had doubled. Currently, the number of professional football teams has increased from the original ten to thirty-two (all in the US); professional basketball and baseball now have thirty teams each; the National Hockey League (NHL) expanded from six to twelve teams in the 1960s and now has thirty teams (twenty-four located in the US). With league expansion, more team franchises compete for a finite supply of top athletes. Cities, in turn, compete for new franchises and for existing franchises that are shopping for a better market.[948]

As noted above, franchise owners increasingly were inclined to define success less by what occurred on the playing field than by "black ink." Winning, losing, and playing the game seemed less important than counting the money. Professional football became profitable following the NFL's merger with the AFL. Revenue in all the major professional sports increased significantly during the 1970s and 1980s as the franchises grew into huge business enterprises. The value of sport franchises appreciated significantly. During the inflationary period in the 1970s and 1980s, the worth of sport franchises grew far more rapidly than the consumer price index. This trend continued into the 1990s and 2000s. (The Dallas Cowboys franchise was valued at more than $900 million in 2004.) The assets that came with ownership included the players' contracts, the property rights of the franchise—including rights to an exclusive "home" territory—and broadcast agreements. Because of the lucrative advantages of owning a major league sport franchise, entry fees into leagues inflated into the tens of millions of dollars.[949]

Whether most professional sport franchises actually have made a profit is difficult to discern. One can only wonder why the value of the franchises inflated so rapidly if they were not profitable. Business professor Paul Staudohar claimed that several professional teams were losing money or, at best, breaking even during the decade of the 1980s.[950] Gerald Scully estimated from his detailed analysis that three-fourths of the owners of major league baseball clubs either made money or broke even in 1987. The difficulty in determining profits of sport franchises has been that, with rare exception, they are private businesses whose financial books are not open to public scrutiny. Moreover, owners persistently attempt to disguise profits as costs. Entrepreneurs with diverse business interests purchased sports teams to offset profits in their other holdings. Consequently, financial losses of sport franchises were no longer as easy to isolate from other businesses. For example, the losses suffered by the New York Yankee franchise in 1982 were due in part to nonbaseball business activities of the owner George Steinbrenner, including those incurred by a Florida hotel. In the opinion of some analysts (and the players unions), team owners were hiding profits of their clubs for tax purposes and as a collective bargaining strategy.[951]

The tendency to view franchises in terms of assets and liabilities has been encouraged by the tax code as applied to professional sports. Economists point out that professional sports are a low-tax operation. Federal tax laws in the US have created exclusive investment opportunities in sports designed to attract new money. By the late 1950s, tax regulations provided for accelerated depreciation of real assets, which eventually included personnel. Sports were virtually the only businesses allowed to depreciate their human assets. Congress curtailed some of the excessive amortization practices in the 1970s, but the tax climate remains quite favorable for professional sport. Tax laws continue to allow for an annualized depreciation of human property. Professional football teams have been allowed to depreciate 50 percent of the cost of players over five years. Since the average playing life of a football player is around three years, the owners enjoy a highly favorable tax deduction on personnel. Salaries of players also can be depreciated so that a profitable write-off is allowed within the tax structure.[952]

Ownership of professional teams has remained a lucrative tax haven. Tax advantages were exploited especially by those individuals who could "write off" income from other sources. The 1976 tax rules allowed nonmanaging partners in football franchises to offset income from other sources by losses in their sport franchise. This unique tax climate encouraged wealthy individuals and corporations to buy teams, and it explained why the recent buyers of sport franchises tend to own other profitable businesses. Since one of the principal advantages of team ownership were the tax deductions, not operating profits, teams increasingly were purchased by businesses interested in sheltering income. The tax incentives led some franchise owners to claim bankruptcy and then devise ingenious ways of selling the team to make a profit on what, in effect, was a short-term investment. The key was depreciation of the value of players' contracts. Owners would keep teams for five years or so until the tax benefits were exhausted and then sell the team at a profit. Losses derived from owning an "unsuccessful" sport franchise were then written off against other corporate investments. In effect, sport franchises became a tax shelter.[953]

In addition to the above-mentioned tax breaks for sport franchise owners, local communities that hosted professional teams received tax exemptions on bonds sold to finance the construction of sports facilities. These facilities (many of them financed with public funds) were then rented to sport franchise owners at artificially low rates. This arrangement provided an additional advantage for franchises over other businesses, as they enjoyed artificially low overhead costs for the facilities in which they operated. Few private business enterprises enjoy greater support from the public sector than professional sport.[954]

As implied, some of the new franchise owners had a little more than a token interest in team performance. They recognized that sport was unlike other American businesses in the sense that losing (games) could become winning (financially). This peculiar set of circumstances resulted in less money being invested in teams to make them competitive. This practice was evident in the NFL. Competitive play was not necessary to make a profit from football. In baseball, equalization of team playing strength also has been shown to be inconsistent with profit maximization. Keeping teams in the league championship races during the season does support attendance at games, however. This is one rationale for divisions with fewer teams. When major league baseball divided the two leagues into six divisions with playoffs that involved "wildcard" teams, it may have compromised the validity of the divisional championships, but the change was most attractive from an economic standpoint. Increasing the number of playoff and championship games meant greater ticket revenue and more telecast rights to sell.[955]

Traditionally, franchise owners cultivated three primary sources of revenue: gate receipts, media revenue, and income from auxiliary enterprises. Sports promoters long recognized the advantages of cultivating a relationship with the developing communications industry. Print media had played a significant role in the marketing of sport early on. Later, sport would provide a source of audience interest for radio, and then television. Shortly after the first professional sports leagues appeared in the nineteenth century, mass audience-oriented newspapers were reporting on sports events and advertising sport products. The *New York World* under Joseph Pulitzer's ownership organized the first sports department at a daily newspaper in 1883. By the 1890s, most of the major newspapers in large cities had sports editors and staffs. The newspapers had a natural alliance with sport, a reciprocal relationship. Newspapers created a wider population of fans among those who could not attend games but followed teams through the sports page. There was a game almost every day during the season, and each game provided "news" through its score and result. Daily baseball in the spring, summer, and early fall provided a steady source of copy. Local and regional coverage soon expanded to the national level. In the early decades of the twentieth century, United Press (now UPI) and Associated Press began transmitting wire reports of games to the major newspapers.[956]

Sports coverage in the newspapers and magazines would be augmented by the budding electronic media. In the 1920s and 1930s, the rapidly developing regional and national radio networks began to broadcast sports events into homes. The first baseball game aired on the radio in 1921, and by the mid-1930s, most major league teams were broadcasting at least some of their games. In 1935, Commissioner Landis signed a $400,000 deal with the three radio networks for rights to broadcast the World Series. The 1926 boxing match between Jack Dempsey and Gene Tunney in Philadelphia reached some thirty-nine million radio listeners. In this era, spectator sports were experienced by most Americans not at the stadiums, but through radio broadcasts and the sports pages of newspapers. By the 1950s, radio was broadcasting thousands of baseball, football, and basketball games at every level, from high-school games to professional contests. Tens of millions of Americans were listening not only to the games but to the commercial messages of their sponsors.[957]

Television would have an even greater impact on the sports market. The relationship commenced in 1939 when a baseball game was televised over a national network for the first time. By the late 1940s and early 1950s, commercial sponsorship moved into the national broadcasting of sporting events. NBC and the Gillette company began their well-known relationship sponsoring televised fights in 1946. The subsequent telecasting of boxing and other sporting events would prove a huge success. Professional sports initially had mistrusted television; live telecasts were perceived as a threat to on-site attendance. In 1953, the federal courts upheld the right of the National Football League and other professional sport franchises to "black out" television broadcasts in host cities to protect their gate receipts. It soon became apparent that telecasts of sporting events could provide team owners with an additional source of income without incurring any significant loss of gate receipts. In sports like boxing, there was no question that telecasting matches could increase revenues. Television would be regarded as an electronic King Midas that turned everything it touched into gold.[958]

In 1961, Congress passed the Sports Television Act (amended in 1966), which extended antitrust exemption to the broadcasting of all professional team sports. Team owners began negotiating a series of increasingly lucrative contracts with networks to televise selected games. The last two decades of the twentieth century would set the pattern for relations between sport and media. In the late 1980s, the National Basketball Association signed a four-year, $600 million contract with NBC. Soon after, the National Football League negotiated a four-year deal worth over $1.5 billion from Fox network. In 1995, baseball signed a four-year, multi-network contract for $1.5 billion with NBC, Fox, and ESPN for broadcast rights. Baseball and football became the most watched sports on television. TV contracts proved to be equally lucrative for individual teams. By the early 1990s, each NFL franchise was receiving $30 to $40 million annually in television revenues. These large disbursements were offered for good reason: sporting events provided television with audiences in the millions.[959]

By the last decade of the twentieth century, a radical change took place in sports telecasting as a result of the growth of cable television. Cable networks had established a relationship with sport franchises dating from the mid-1980s. The traditional networks were well aware of the encroachment of cable TV into the market and made adjustments. Both network and cable telecasts of sporting events have been supported through advertisements of a wide range of consumer products. The networks, which pay multimillion-dollar fees for the rights to telecast sporting events, expect to recover this revenue and make a profit by selling commercial time to companies wishing to advertise their products or services to the mostly male audience of sports fans. Televised sports tend to attract advertisements for such products as automobiles, snack food, and beer. Companies that advertise products and services hope to recover the fees paid to the networks for commercial time by increased sales. Advertisers were spending close to a billion dollars annually on commercials during sporting events by the end of the 1980s. Technically, the networks are not in the business of selling sports programming to audiences, but rather, selling audiences to advertisers. The rates charged to advertisers are based on several factors, including the number of viewers estimated (through surveys) to be viewing an event. To complete the picture, when the consumer purchases the advertised six-pack of beer or insurance policy, part of the cost of that product pays for the telecast of the sporting event during which it was advertised.[960]

This interlocking pattern of marketing relationships has not been consistently profitable for all parties. For example, when networks began losing money on televised sports, broadcast executives looked for a way to hedge their bet. They combined their financial interests in sports and the media. This form of "structural osmosis" has become more common, as noted. These business interconnections tend to muddle the product, the medium, and the producer. From one view, we see football promoting beer, and from another, we see beer promoting football, baseball promoting ESPN, and ESPN promoting baseball. This reciprocal arrangement may be an unavoidable corollary to the integration of sport and consumer capitalism.[961]

Sports teams being owned outright or in part by broadcasters makes perfect sense from a marketing standpoint. (Notably, media that do not own sport franchises establish close affiliations with them.) The *Chicago Tribune* bought controlling interest in Chicago-based WGN Television, which controlled the rights to telecast the Chicago Cubs baseball games nationally over its commercial cable television channel. In turn, the *Chicago Tribune* was advertised through commercials during the Cubs games in an effort to increase circulation. Innovative entrepreneur Ted Turner purchased a cable television network (WTBS) and two professional sport teams (the Braves baseball and Hawks basketball franchises), all based in Atlanta. Turner would sell his club's broadcast rights to his own television station at a price well below their market worth—in effect, transferring income from the Braves or Hawks to WTBS-TV.[962] The relationship between sports and television took a new turn in 1987 when Championship Auto Racing Team (CART) began putting together its own television programs and buying network time. Television had entered the sport business, and sports were getting into the television business. The National Football League launched the NFL network in 2003. In late 2007, major league baseball was contemplating its own television network, which had become a reality by 2010.

Television changed the fundamental experience of viewing sports. Game times and locations were adjusted to meet the needs of television. TV timeouts from play were taken for the purpose of accommodating advertising, and the length and number of commercial messages increased over time. It became a common practice for game officials to meet with television producers before a televised sporting event to coordinate signals so that television commercials could be facilitated during a game. The upshot of all this was that the duration of televised sports events increased significantly. As a historical comparison, when the speedy Grover Cleveland Alexander pitched for the Philadelphia Phillies in the World War I era, the game might be over in an hour and a half. Now it is not unusual for a televised nine-inning baseball game to endure for three-plus hours. The telecast of a football game often reaches three and a half hours for the sixty minutes of actual playing time, due in large part to commercial breaks. This extension of game time also enhances on-site profits; more beer and hot dogs can be sold over three-plus hours.[963]

Televised sport has proved a particularly effective advertising medium because of the prominence of commercial messages. Major league baseball games provide time for commercials between each half-inning of a game, plus pre- and post-game commercials, totaling more than forty minutes of advertising during a regular nine-inning game. The time between half-innings of major league baseball games has been extended specifically for the purpose of expanding advertising. Each commercial break typically includes four separate thirty-second paid advertisements. Other ways have been found to incorporate advertisements into the game. It is not uncommon to place promotional messages between batters and even between pitches during televised baseball games. In addition, someone from an advertising sponsor or a promotional event might throw out the ceremonial first pitch of the game, or a product's logo might appear on the screen at selected times. Prominent game occurrences, such as a homerun or the appearance of a relief pitcher, are connected to the mention of a sponsor's name. A beer company has sponsored the "seventh-inning stretch" during the Chicago Cubs' televised games. Celebrity entertainers appear in the broadcast booths to promote a recently released film, album, or upcoming stage performance. Currently, sponsors fill about sixteen minutes (26.6%) of air time for each hour of a sports broadcast. A new term was coined to describe the burgeoning phenomenon: "advertising clutter." Not to be limited by the number of contests in a season, media promoters have realized they can market programs that feature sports analysts. These shows have multiplied on commercial and cable channels. Meanwhile, sponsored coaches' shows have become popular on local network affiliates.

The rampant commercialism that has accompanied televised sport is matched by similar forms of commercial promotions occurring on-site during sporting events. These promotional activities have become part of a marketing strategy designed to appeal to a more diversified audience. While the sports traditionalists have shaken their heads in disdain, the disciples of Bill Veeck transformed the sports stadium into a virtual amusement park with electronic scoreboards, public address systems that produced sound effects, clown/mascots, "ball girls," and fan contests—along with the usual array of fast-food concessions and souvenir stands. Other promotional events and stunts concocted to enhance attendance have included skydivers landing on the infield prior to a baseball game. Ballplayers have been enlisted in cow-milking contests, and firework displays routinely follow holiday games. Games incorporate an array of special events with commercial potential such as "hat day" and "pizza night." Similar spectacles and promotions are just as common at football, basketball, and hockey games.

Sports venues are increasingly embellished with advertising. Phil Schaaf's *Sports, Inc.* includes a photograph showing the interior of the Pontiac Silverdome prior to Super Bowl XVI in 1982. What one notices about the stadium is the complete absence of commercial messages—no billboards, no corporate logos on scoreboards. But professional football soon followed the example of baseball; the interiors of ballparks would become a venue for commercial advertisements. Cubs owner Philip Wrigley remained the lone iconoclast, replacing the advertising on the walls of Wrigley Field with ivy vines (and yet, the name of the ballpark was an advertisement for Wrigley chewing gum).[964] The lucrative practice of advertising on outfield walls spread to most sports facilities. Basketball arenas now provide space for "signage" at courtside or on the court itself, particularly in those areas at which television cameras are aimed. A similar occurrence has taken place around and on tennis courts. Likewise, NASCAR tracks are encased in commercial billboards. Ice rinks in the National Hockey League feature advertisements on the surface of the ice. In effect, hockey players skate on a frozen billboard. In some professional arenas, the backs of chairs that athletes sit on carry advertising, while the seat cushions for fans are emblazoned with commercial logos. To attend an athletic event is to be inundated with commercial messages.[965] In addition to on-site advertising, "virtual" signage is projected onto TV screens via computer technology.

The contracts of professional athletes routinely include requirements to attend promotional functions for the franchise, league, or commercial sponsors. For example, NASCAR drivers are required to appear at Home Depot stores. Promotional obligations include signing autographs at shopping malls, attending sponsors' parties the night before a contest, or wearing a cap with a sponsor's name on it. In auto racing, advertising space is sold on practically every visible inch of the racing cars as well on the uniforms of the drivers. Drivers and their cars are covered with the logos of motor oils, tobacco, beer, and a variety of other retail products. The same is true of professional skiers' outfits. Professional boxers have been embellished with temporary tattoos carrying advertising.[966]

As sporting events become more expensive, promoters become more dependent upon commercial revenue. Auto racing ranks among the most expensive of all sports. By the 1990s, it cost between $30 and $40 million annually to finance a first-class racing team involved in international competition. About 95 percent of auto racing revenue comes from sponsors. Modern auto racing would not exist as a sport without commercial advertising. Racing teams do not promise sponsors they will appear in victory lane; what they offer is high exposure before large crowds of spectators and television audiences. The rationale behind the commercial sponsorship of a race car, strictly speaking, is not to win races—although that unpredictable occurrence is financially advantageous—but to purchase a highly visible, moving billboard. (Tobacco companies increased their sponsorship of auto racing following the federal law restricting televised advertising of tobacco products.)[967]

The attraction of commercial corporations to sporting events has extended beyond purchasing space in stadiums and arenas for advertisements. The venues and events themselves increasingly have acquired the appellations of sponsors. The marketing of naming rights for sports venues began in the 1970s. Currently, arenas and stadiums carry the names of banks, breweries, and insurance companies, to name a few sponsors. Tournaments also have acquired commercial sponsors. Early on, Federal Express sponsored golf matches, and Volvo, tennis tournaments. Tobacco companies had sponsored a large number of sports events in an attempt to present their products in a context of health and physical fitness. R. J. Reynolds Tobacco Company (now part of Reynolds American, Inc.) sponsored as many as 2,500 sporting events a year until confronted with increasing objections to and restrictions on tobacco advertising at sporting events. Other sponsors stepped in to fill the void. Today, very few major tournaments or professional sports facilities remain without a commercial sponsor.[968]

Over the course of time, the ethos of consumer capitalism transformed sport from a participatory activity and local spectacle into a form of mass entertainment, an advertising medium, and a venue for marketing consumer goods. In the final stage of this progression, the main sporting event vied with the peripheral promotions and marketing gimmicks for the attention of the audience. Stadiums have become more than shells built around the field of competition. Many contemporary ballparks and arenas are designed to create commercial and entertainment attractions that have little to do with the game itself. They have the effect of distracting the marginal fans' attention and interest. Stadium amenities peripheral to the sporting event include shopping malls and concourses, food courts, beer gardens and bars, video arcades, ATM machines, and even museums and exhibitions. There are stadiums that incorporate playgrounds for children. The Houston Astrodome complex (built in 1965) included four hotels, an "Astroworld" modeled after Disney World, a bowling alley, barbershops, restaurants, and forty-nine concession stands. The Texas Rangers ballpark in Arlington was built adjacent to the Six Flags Over Texas amusement park.[969]

The encroachment of commercialism is most apparent in minor league baseball stadiums. Local teams have struggled to compete with telecast major league games; they receive very little revenue from the electronic media. The franchises have found ways to compensate for the loss of TV revenue. Fans entering the gates of ballparks are exposed to a gallery of concessions that advertise souvenirs, food, and drink. Commercial interests are allowed to set up displays in the foyers of sports stadiums. The walls of entranceways are lined with small billboards advertising local products and services. Within the arena itself, the prevailing view of the field is dominated by an outfield fence covered with billboards, along with the electronic score/message board featuring a running series of commercial advertisements. Game programs sold to customers typically offer four pages of advertising for every page of game-related information. The programs include contest numbers for between-inning giveaways of local products or services. This marketing device allows local merchants' names to be announced over the public address system. Even the team mascot may be embellished with advertising. Special promotional events include giving the first 100 fans to enter the gate an inexpensive product with a commercial sponsor's name on it—for instance, a baseball cap adorned with the logo of a fast-food restaurant. America's two great national pastimes, baseball and shopping, have melded in the stadium. The sports arena has been successfully colonized by marketing interests.[970]

Sports arenas also have been modernized to enhance profits. Beginning in the 1930s, lighting installed at outdoor arenas allowed night games to attract larger crowds. In the 1950s, lighting facilitated prime-time television. (Wrigley Field in Chicago belatedly added lights in late 1988.) Domes built over modern outdoor sports arenas have eliminated loss of income due to inclement weather. Even the design of seating at sports arenas has taken into account maximum profits and the close ties with corporate America. Chicago's new Comiskey Park (now US Cellular Field), which opened in 1991, set the pattern for modern sports facilities with its concourses, improved sightlines, luxury suites, and concession areas. High-priced seating and luxury boxes supplant the availability of the low-priced bleachers. By the 2001–2002 season, the average price for a ticket to an NBA, NFL, or NHL game was more than $40; season tickets routinely exceeded $1,000. In 2001, it cost a family of four $130 to attend a Colorado Rockies baseball game and over $400 for a Denver Broncos football game. The Carolina Panthers introduced the personal seat license (PSL), an added surcharge for the privilege of buying season tickets. Other professional teams followed their lead. Prices of PSLs now run from a thousand dollars upward.[971]

Luxury suites at stadiums feature elaborate accommodations including climate control, sliding windows, catering service, and wet bars. Business corporations lease these suites to entertain clients (and reward executives) and then write them off as business deductions on their taxes. This marketing device carries back to the mid 1970s, when the prestigious Circle Suites at the newly constructed Dallas Cowboys stadium were sold for $50,000 to $100,000 in stadium bonds. As a result of the focus on upscale seating, less than half of all major league baseball ticket sales currently are for private, single-game tickets. Stadium managers are not limited to drawing revenue from sports contests; stadiums are rented on nongame days for a variety of events from circuses to religious revivals. Site marketing now extends beyond the stadium proper. Professional football fans may be required to purchase "tailgate tickets" to attend pre-game parties in stadium parking lots. Companies like Kingsford Charcoal are emerging as pre-game event sponsors.[972]

The athletic contest itself was repackaged to make it more attractive to fans. During the course of the twentieth century, marketing considerations increasingly influenced the rules, procedures, and forms of play on the fields and courts. In an effort to attract more fans and to earn more money, sports managers altered the structure of the games and the appearances of players and equipment. It is commonly held that fans prefer high-scoring contests. American football altered its rules to encourage a more open game and, thus, more scoring; baseball changed the dimensions of the strike zone, lowered the height of the pitcher's mound, moved the fences closer, and livened the ball to increase run production. Basketball changed the rules governing possession time and personal fouls to speed up the game. Many fans are attracted to aggressive play. NHL officials have been instructed to tolerate a certain level of fighting among players to provide a more exciting game. As the games and playing fields were being altered, new playing surfaces were introduced and player uniforms redesigned to be more attractive. Whenever a sport does not seem able to sustain previous levels of spectator interest, the promoters implement cosmetic changes.[973]

Professional sport has exploited a wide array of consumer markets, especially clothing. Sweatshirts, jogging outfits, caps, and T-shirts with team names and logos are sold through catalog houses. The National Football League licensed the sale of more than 400 items featuring team logos. Products endorsed by the NFL were grossing a billion dollars in sales by the 1990s. Licensed merchandise is one of the fastest-growing sources of income. A National Football League affiliate, "NFL Properties" was founded in 1963 as a marketing, promotion, licensing, and publishing arm. NFL Properties is the exclusive representative of the league and its clubs for licensing logos and symbols and for protecting and enforcing trademark rights. In 1991, NFL Properties contracted to manage former Chicago Bears running-back Walter Payton's auto racing team. The new venture with Payton, named "NFL Team 34" (referring to his retired jersey number), marketed spin-offs including a new line of apparel. Professional basketball capitalized on these commercial opportunities. By the mid-1990s, more than 10 percent of the NBA's profits were coming from consumer products that it marketed.[974]

Sport has adopted the corporate model and gone into the business of providing public entertainment and the marketing of consumer goods. The profit motive has encouraged sport managers to exploit the strategies of the free market while simultaneously attempting to maintain a quasi-monopoly. Professional sport established close ties with the American business community early on. Its more recent relationships with radio and television transformed sport into a major medium for advertising. When sport franchise owners and media executives talk of forming joint ventures, they discuss how they will "administer the product." Increasingly, decisions are being made on the basis of what is good for television. Indeed, spectator sports have begun to look like little more than another consumer product. Koppett observed that by the 1990s sports journalists were writing as much about the "business of sport" as sport itself. It was a sign of the times.[975]

American sport has continued to incorporate the strategies of consumer capitalism (promotion of sport as a product), the methods of investment capitalism (buying and selling teams and athletes), and the structure of monopoly capitalism (forming league cartels that attempt to control competition and wages). Professional sport has been a success by its own standards. Although franchise owners often disguise profits for tax purposes, it appears the great majority of teams in the four major team sports are bringing in substantial revenue for their owners. NASCAR, professional golf, and tennis are also making money. Profit, not winning, has become the "bottom line." The significance attached to making money has not gone unheeded by athletes.

The American Athlete, from Wage Laborer to Entrepreneur

> I have learned three things in life that I try to pass on to my players: The first
> is to make as much money as you can. I forget the other two.
> —Al McGuire, basketball coach

A. G. Spalding's life exemplified the American success story. The boy pitcher from the Illinois prairie parlayed his success on the athletic fields into a career as an internationally known entrepreneur whose name was stamped upon millions of pieces of sports equipment. Spalding's rise began rather modestly as an employee of a Chicago company that paid him double what it paid other clerks to pitch for the company's baseball team. Following his early success on the diamond, Spalding went on to play in the major leagues. While pursuing a baseball career, he employed his notable entrepreneurial skills to form one of the largest US sporting-goods firms, A. G. Spalding & Bros. As the owner of a professional ball club, Spalding was a crucial constituent in organizing the national league and developing the rules of baseball.[976]

Spalding was attuned to the marketing potential of the emerging phenomenon of spectator sport and applied these lessons to baseball. He had been awarded an exclusive contract in 1878 (his final season as a player) to provide baseballs to the budding professional league, which then certified the Spalding baseball as "official." As a businessman, he adopted centralized, oligopolistic practices while exploiting creative advertising and marketing techniques to build a sporting-goods empire. Spalding hired a team of bike-riders to wear his firm's colors in the six-day marathons that were then attracting large crowds. In 1888, he organized a world baseball tour to promote the game and his sporting goods. Both professional baseball and Spalding sporting goods became commercial successes.[977]

Spalding's career foreshadowed the ascent of future generations of athletes from wage-earners to entrepreneurs and businessmen. However, he was exceptional for his time. Early on, professional athletes were simply a new type of worker whose labor power, in the form of their performance on the playing field, was exploited by team owners to attract paying spectators. Baseball would set the tone for professional sport's relationship with its players/employees. As early as 1879, the owners surreptitiously introduced a player reservation rule relegating athletes to the status of virtual serfdom. Athletes could be bought, sold, traded, and released by team owners who dictated contract terms. The teams blacklisted or boycotted players who tried to circumvent the system.[978]

The profit motive determined wages and working conditions for ballplayers. They were subjected to close supervision by coaches and managers and often had to play whether they were sick or injured. Professional baseball offered no guaranteed contracts; if you got hurt, you lost your job, simple as that—and oftentimes the doctor's bills were yours too. This understanding pertained through the early decades of the twentieth century. Joe DiMaggio's teammate Charley Wallgren was cut from the 1933 San Francisco Seals for a persistent case of jock itch. Many athletes, including DiMaggio, played through serious injuries and infections, sacrificing their own well-being in an insecure profession. They signed agreements to deliver services for wages and had to abide by these contracts for fear of being dismissed or sued. Ballplayers had little choice but to submit to unfavorable contract terms in order to finish out their careers and attain a modicum of economic security.[979]

Professional baseball began as an association of players but soon gave way to a partnership of affluent owners. Spalding had broken rank with the players, criticizing them for failing in their attempt to run the "business" of baseball. Indeed, he and the emerging group of sport entrepreneurs proved more adept at business. By the mid-1870s, team owners had turned baseball into a thriving enterprise and were buying and selling players. Athletes were reduced to the position of contract laborers, foreshadowing a century-long struggle between labor and management. The employment plight of baseball players would be repeated in the other early professional sports. Basketball alone would witness player-controlled teams for any length of time. (Not all sports have employed athletes as wage-laborers; for instance, professional golf and tennis players compete for prize money, while top-ranked boxers negotiate fees for fights.)[980]

The owners of the professional teams would retain tight control over athletes without serious challenge to the employer/employee relationship. Baseball players made a few futile attempts in the late nineteenth and early twentieth centuries to organize to protect their self-interests. However, the efforts of the players associations were overshadowed by unilateral actions of a few star players. The talented Ty Cobb became a contract holdout in 1912. Although Cobb's venture was widely noted, he ended up settling for less salary than he demanded, was officially reprimanded, and was fined $50. The lesson from Cobb's experience was that power to negotiate lies in numbers. Babe Ruth would have more success as a contract holdout in the 1920s, but not until the second half of the twentieth century were professional athletes able to gain effective control over their conditions of employment.[981]

Eventually, a few young, highly talented athletes would be able to trade on their potential. In the 1940s, a cadre of baseball scouts vied for the services of top high-school and college players. Incentives to sign with franchises included lucrative bonuses. In 1941, the Detroit Tigers recruited Dick Wakefield out of the University of Michigan, offering him a signing bonus of $52,000. By the early 1950s, baseball was paying out some $4.5 million in player bonuses. Offering bonuses was a crapshoot, as so-called bonus babies often did not "pan out." Despite the risks, the practice persisted in baseball and spread to other sports, fed by intense competition among teams and leagues for players. In 1964, quarterback Joe Namath was offered more than $400,000 to sign with the New York Jets in the NFL rival American Football League. Over the decades, signing bonuses became increasingly lucrative. Today, promising athletes are offered million-dollar bonuses to sign with professional teams. In 2008, sixteen-year-old Dominican outfielder Juan Duran was offered $2 million to sign with the Cincinnati Reds.[982]

However, six- or seven-figure signing bonuses remain the exception. Journeymen athletes have had to wait for other developments to advance their economic standing. Players unions took on a pivotal role in the emerging negotiation wars between labor and management. The Major League Ball Players Association and the National Basketball Players Association formed in 1954. Professional football players organized two years later, and hockey players founded a union in 1957. The principal objective of the unions was to implement collective bargaining. (The National Labor Relations Act of 1935 established a board that set the rules for collective bargaining.) Collective bargaining agreements focused on the length of playing seasons, compensation, job rights such as seniority and discipline, and bargaining rights of unions. The players unions eventually were able to enhance the employment status of their members through bargaining. It is worth noting that when professional basketball players organized in 1954, there were no no health benefits, minimum wage, and no pension plan. In the 1960s, both basketball and baseball players associations bargained successfully for pension plans.[983]

Labor relations and contract agreements began to assume a larger role in professional sport as the balance of power shifted toward the players. The Curt Flood case marked a pivotal point in professional baseball. Following the 1969 season, Flood refused to be traded by the St. Louis Cardinals to Philadelphia. His challenge ended in defeat when the US Supreme Court ruled to uphold the 1922 antitrust exemption, but the centerfielder's actions created a renewed sense of solidarity among ballplayers to challenge the reserve clause and pursue free agency. The main implication of the Flood decision for the players was that they would have to rely on bargaining. The baseball players union achieved a breakthrough in its 1970 agreement with management accepting a grievance arbitration panel with an impartial chairman. In 1973, the players obtained the establishment of binding arbitration for salary and other contract disputes. Arbitration was extended to salary adjustment in 1974. Subsequently, about half of baseball players eligible for arbitration filed for it.[984]

The reserve clause meant that players under contract were the virtual property of the team. They could be put on waivers or traded to another club. The typical short-term (usually annual) contracts offered no job security. A player had little choice but to sign with the team who owned his contract for whatever salary they were willing to pay. This situation prior to free agency constituted what economists label a "monopsony"—only one buyer for workers' services. Eventually, professional athletes were able to negotiate modifications in the reserve clause and attain various degrees of free agency. Free agency for baseball players came through a series of agreements in the 1970s and early 1980s. The key events were the signing of pitcher Jim "Catfish Hunter by the New York Yankees in 1974, and the 1976 court decision upholding an arbitration ruling that Los Angeles Dodgers pitcher Andy Messersmith could become a free agent after playing one year without a contract. Owners were forced to decide whether to meet a player's salary demands or allow him to move to a rival team. This pivotal arbitration ruling turned the buyer's market into a seller's market for talented players. Free agents could, in effect, sign a contract with the highest bidder. A player who had been in the major leagues for six years was eligible to become a free agent and negotiate with any of the twenty-six major league teams in existence at the time. In 1976, the courts ruled that professional football's so-called Rozelle Rule, which was named after the then-current commissioner, and discouraged free agency, to be unequivocally illegal. Subsequently, football, basketball, and hockey players attained various forms of free agency. In the 1980s, multiyear contracts for professional athletes became common.[985]

These initial concessions forced on management would prove to have a direct effect on improving athletes' working conditions and salaries. Baseball players became eligible for binding salary arbitration after their third year of major league service. By 1979, baseball's average player salary was some six times what it had been twelve years earlier. In addition, the ballplayers union would bargain successfully for roughly a third of the lucrative television revenues to enhance their pension fund. By the mid-1970s, television was bringing in over $23 million a year. Baseball players led the way for more aggressive pursuits of self-interest by professional athletes. In the 1990s, athletes in the major team sports employed even more forceful labor tactics to improve their salaries and employment status. By the end of that decade, professional ballplayers were earning the majority of the revenue produced. The NFL was paying out over 60 percent of its revenue to players. Professional baseball players' salaries reached a 50-percent share of the gross receipts by then.[986]

One of the more aggressive tactics used by players unions were job actions. Increasingly, strikes disrupted seasons and caused significant short-term financial losses for all parties. However, athletes gained significant salary increases and benefits from job actions. Baseball had its first strike, lasting eighty-six games, in 1972. It resulted in players gaining an increase in the owners' contribution to their pension fund. The 1981 baseball strike of fifty days led to the cancellation of over 700 games. In the next twenty years, eight work stoppages would occur. The 1994 baseball season was cancelled in early August before completion, and the 1995 season delayed because of a 250-day strike. Professional athletes in other sports also used the strike as a bargaining tactic. Football players first went on strike in 1974, then on a fifty-seven-day strike in 1982, and again in 1987. The traditionally passive National Hockey League players went on a short strike in 1992, the first in the seventy-five-year history of the league. This strike resulted in an agreement that included increases in the playoff fund, new provisions for the entry draft, licensing rights for players, arbitration procedures, an easing of restrictions on free agency, and improvements in the insurance and pension plans. The 1994–1995 hockey season was delayed until January (and shortened to forty-eight games per team) because of a strike. Then the entire 2004–2005 hockey season was cancelled because of the failure of the NHL and the players' association to reach an agreement.[987] Clearly, it was in the interest of both management and the players to avoid such season-long interruptions.

One of the major consequences of arbitration and job actions was their effect on players' salaries. To read the history of professional athletes' remuneration is to gain insight into the monopolistic practices of owners and the evolving economic status of ballplayers. Despite their early exploitation, athletes no longer find themselves in the same predicament as most nonunion workers who have little control over their wages, hours, or working conditions. One difference is that sport constitutes a limited seller's market; in other words, the demand for top talent usually exceeds the supply. As noted, a few top baseball players were selling their services to the highest bidder for rather exorbitant amounts from early on. In 1931, when Babe Ruth garnered $80,000 to play baseball, the president of the United States made only $75,000. Ruth famously quipped that he had a better year than President Hoover. Cases like Ruth's provided team owners the incentive to collude against bidding wars for athletes, as they had done earlier.[988]

The owners maintained effective control over athletes' salaries until the mid-1960s when the salary situation in baseball began to change. At that time, more formal salary negotiations were instigated. Negotiations were carried to a new level with the dramatic action taken by Los Angeles Dodgers pitchers Sandy Koufax and Don Drysdale. The two teammates realized that Dodgers management was playing them against each other in their contract negotiations, and they both held out for higher salaries. They also hired an agent to negotiate for them. Their actions set a precedent. By the 1970s, it became the norm for professional athletes to be represented by agents in salary negotiations. Star athletes found themselves in an enviable position to negotiate their services with management, as they were, in effect, irreplaceable. The run-of-the-mill players also benefited following the 1972 strike because strike-breakers proved an inadequate substitute for established players. A two-tiered system of labor negotiations emerged in professional sport: the "star system." Paul Staudohar described the system as one "in which exceptionally talented people dominate the worker hierarchy. These elite few command a vastly disproportionate influence on their profession and derive substantial incomes from outside sources." On the other tier, the players' unions look out for the marginal players who are more easily replaced.[989]

Arguably, it was the retention of agents as much as players' unions that resulted in the rapid inflation of salaries through the exploitation of individual bargaining power. In the mid-1960s, the average salary of major league baseball players was around $20,000 a year. Baseball salaries increased to an average of $120,000 by 1980 and reached $500,000 by the end of that decade. In 1989, over 100 major league baseball players had signed million-dollar contracts. Baseball salaries soon would average a million dollars a year. The salary phenomenon was not limited to baseball. During the 1980s, the average player salary in the National Football League increased to $300,000, and the National Basketball Association average salary grew from around $175,000 to $750,000. The five-year baseball contract, which retroactively covered the 2002 season, increased minimum player salaries to $300,000. Multimillion-dollar, multiyear contracts for superior athletes became a matter of course. Some top athletes negotiated contracts for tens of millions of dollars. In 2007, pitcher Barry Zito signed a seven-year, $126 million contract with the San Francisco Giants—an average of $18 million a year.[990]

During the course of the twentieth century, professional athletes gained power to negotiate with franchise owners and obtained more control over their professional careers. They improved their salaries almost tenfold since the implementation of free agency. However, all this progress cannot be attributed solely to players' unions and free agency. Television revenue played a major role in the power shift. If owners could no longer buy and sell players "like bushels of corn" or dictate the terms of contracts, this was, in part, because national television networks required that games (i.e., programming) be reliably supplied. In order to meet the terms of their broadcasting contracts, franchise owners were pressured to resolve disputes with labor through bargaining rather than to incite job actions. After all, a great deal of television money was coming in for everyone to share. Television would influence the financial status of athletes in other ways, most notably opening up opportunities for lucrative product endorsements.[991]

As athletes' status improved, they developed a growing interest in and insight into the business prospects of sport. The players on the field learned to exploit the commercial potential of sport. The tendencies that had been there since the Spalding era were to attain new dimensions over the course of time. A few savvy athletes had proved as adept at marketing themselves as were the team owners and sports promoters. As early as the 1870s, Cap Anson and Buck Ewing were featured in beer advertisements. By 1907, Ty Cobb was promoting Coca Cola (and his purchase of their stock eventually made him a millionaire). In the 1920s, Babe Ruth hired an agent, Christy Walsh, to work product endorsements for him. Harold "Red" Grange, who began his professional football career in 1925, also found it advantageous to hire an agent as he toured the country playing in exhibition games.[992]

The examples of these celebrity athletes was not lost on subsequent ballplayers. Sports stars, both active and retired, realized they could trade on their fame to make large sums of money in addition to what they earned in the arena. Athletes in a wide range of sports began to promote commercial products. George Mikan, the first star of the young NBA, signed a contract with Pabst Blue Ribbon brewery to promote its beer in 1950. In the 1960s, sports marketing entered a new era. Golfer Arnold Palmer negotiated a number of lucrative licensing agreements and commercial endorsements that would make him a prototype of the athlete/promoter. Palmer signed as the first client of Mark McCormack, founder of International Management Group, a management agency that handled the business affairs of sports celebrities and would become the world's largest sports management and marketing firm. ProServ, founded by US Davis Cup players Donald Dell and Frank Craighill, entered the market in 1970, eventually representing more than 200 athletes and coaches. It was a new era; independent sports agents now had to compete with international management agencies.[993]

Athletes' commercial exploitation of their celebrity status carried beyond active playing careers. The lyrics of a 1968 song by Paul Simon inquired, "Where have you gone, Joe Dimaggio?" The answer: Joe had gone to autograph shows and on television to promote a popular brand of coffeemaker. By 1989, the retired DiMaggio commanded $40,000 to $50,000 a day for appearing at autograph shows and memorabilia sales. He signed baseball cards, baseballs, and pictures at $150 each, occasionally earning as much as $100,000 for personal appearances. In effect, the retired Yankee "went into the business of being Joe DiMaggio."[994] Few athletes exploited opportunities to trade on their fame more ruthlessly than Pete Rose, who retired in 1986. He was a ubiquitous presence at autograph shows. Rose could scribble more than 600 autographs on various items within an hour. He would appear on the Cable Value Network's Sporting Collections Show and autograph balls for $39, bats for $229, and jerseys for $399. Pete might draw $20,000 from a promoter on such occasions. During the excitement of chasing Cobb's all-time hit record, Rose took advantage of his celebrity by marketing posters, key-chains, limited-edition silver and gold coins, and lithographs. He even sold the bat and ball involved in his record-breaking hit for $129,000. Pete wore a different uniform each inning of the record-setting game and sold them all.[995]

Professional athletes discovered other opportunities for income when using their images as product endorsements became increasingly lucrative. The famous athlete's picture on a box of Wheaties breakfast cereal (beginning with Lou Gehrig in 1934) became an American marketing icon. Athletes promoted an array of products from automobiles to soft drinks. Baseball trading cards (first marketed with tobacco products) had been around since the era of King Kelley and Al Spalding. By the 1970s, professional baseball players contracted collectively with card manufacturers for the use of their images. In 1992, National Hockey League players negotiated as a group for exclusive rights to $16 million in revenue from hockey trading cards with their pictures on them. This was the decade when current and former athletes first appeared on television shopping channels to promote the sale of various memorabilia featuring their autographs or pictures. Not to be outdone by team sport athletes, tennis players and golfers enhanced their tournament earnings with exhibition matches, product endorsements, and public appearances.[996]

No area of product marketing was more lucrative than that of sportswear. Expensive athletic shoes were heavily promoted on television and in the print media beginning in the 1980s. Tennis player Ivan Lendl was paid $2.5 million by Adidas for wearing its clothing and shoes during matches and playing with an Adidas racket. Endorsement opportunities were extended to quite young athletes. Tennis star Venus Williams was approached by racket and shoe companies when she was only eleven years old. Tennis players "rented" spaces on their clothing to advertisers who paid large sums of money for the privilege of displaying their name or logo on these highly visible personalities. Endorsement opportunities were so lucrative for some athletes that commercial remunerations exceeded earnings for their sports performances. Beginning in the 1980s, Michael Jordan made millions from endorsements of various products including athletic shoes and sporting goods. He signed a $2.5 million deal with Nike to promote the brand Air Jordan. In 2003, high-school basketball star LeBron James was drafted by the Cleveland Cavaliers and, before playing his first NBA game, signed a $90 million endorsement contract with Nike to endorse their shoes.[997]

Even the athletes who were not signing autographs or executing lucrative product endorsements enjoyed higher incomes and increased pensions. The result was that a growing number of American athletes were becoming quite wealthy. As this phenomenon grew, more of their time and effort had to be devoted to managing off-field ventures and enterprises. While the players' associations handled business with team owners, agents managed athletes' stock portfolios and real estate investments, and they assisted in tax and estate planning. Some players handed over all their investments to an agent.[998] Baseball player Barry Bonds hired two publicists, a business manager, and a creative director in charge of his licensing. These financial opportunities brought about the final stage in the evolution of the American athlete from wage-laborer to that of investment capitalist.

Arnold Palmer was notable among athletes who took advantage of business investment opportunities. Palmer, who had made a large amount of money in professional golf, made even more in what he referred to as his "commercial career." The popular line of Arnold Palmer products eventually grossed over $100 million annually. In the 1970s, fellow golfer Jack Nicklaus became wealthy by investing in real estate and designing golf courses. An emerging generation of athletes would carry on this tradition. Professional tennis player Chris Evert Lloyd promoted her own line of women's clothing. Retired football player Walter Payton, who owned a chain of twenty-three restaurants, had a promotional contract with NFL Properties (mentioned previously) and made a bid for a new professional football franchise in the 1990s prior to his untimely death. By the late twentieth century, athletes were routinely investing earnings from their sports careers in businesses, real estate, and the stock market. Indeed, some athletes actually incorporated. Tennis's John McEnroe formed John McEnroe, Inc., a multinational corporation with an entertainment division, a personal appearances division, a licensing division, an endorsement division, and a tournament division.[999] By the close of the twentieth century, "Sports, Inc." had coalesced into "Athlete, Inc."

The historical experience of America's professional athletes calls to mind the model presented in *The Theory of the Leisure Class*. The author, Thorstein Veblen, contended that America's social structure was less characterized by economic class conflict than by emulation of the ruling class by the working class.[1000] At the same time, one cannot ignore the classic labor/management struggles that characterized the history of twentieth-century sport. But progressively, well-paid athletes began to emulate Spalding's rise from ballplayer to sports entrepreneur. Today's celebrity athletes have become major players in the American capitalist system. They have recognized that they can trade on their fame to acquire fortunes through product endorsements and become successful business investors. In 2006, a retired Michael Jordan became the second largest shareholder of the Charlotte Bobcats in the Eastern Conference of the NBA. He was the most prominent of several athletes who had moved into sport management.

However, what has been a boon for the most sports superstars has not always been beneficial to mainstream ballplayers or good for sport. The "money game" often overshadows the game taking place on the courts and playing fields. Increasingly, athletes are as caught up in making money as the owners. Professional sport has fully assimilated with capitalism and, in the minds of its critics, become little more than an artifact of American consumer culture. The fundamental question is, will the business ethic prevail, and if so, can sport as we know it survive?

13

Finish Line: Summing up the Ethos of Sport

The certainties of one age are the problems of the next.
–Richard H. Tawney

Viewed through one lens, sport appears to stand apart from the general culture. It sustains a sense of autonomy that separates it from the work-a-day world. Participants cross an existential boundary when they enter the province of play and games. Herein, one finds a social order with its own peculiar forms and meanings. The athlete engages in actions that make sense only within the narrow arena of competition. Sport cultivates its own distinct ethos reflected in maxims like, "It ain't over 'til it's over," and "No pain, no gain." At the same time, we recognize sport is not impervious to influences of the broader culture. The examples are manifest: national flags stand over sports stadiums and victory stands, commercial billboards embellish the periphery of playing fields, pre-game prayers are a susurration within locker rooms and team huddles. The boundaries delineating the domain of sport are, in fact, permeable.

These opening remarks direct our focus to the theme reflected in the book's title: when cultural values infiltrate sport, they alter its very character and spirit. Actions on the field of play no longer constitute their own ends, but become means to other ends. David Miller argues that there is something in the very nature of games that seduces their participants into "purposiveness," in wanting to win something.[1001] Clearly, this tendency reaches beyond the intrinsic goals of games. Sport has been appropriated to serve a wide range of purposes—political, commercial, and religious. Marshall McCluhan has characterized athletic competition as the ultimate conformity. This remark references more than internal orthodoxy, for sport routinely conforms to extrinsic social and cultural agendas.[1002] Significantly, sport has garnered the approval and support of the American political and cultural establishments largely by serving worthy ends, and it has been transformed in the process. The preceding chapters have assayed the influence of the Protestant ethic and the spirit of capitalism on the ethos of sport through recent history.

The interaction between sport and American culture commenced within a Puritan theocracy that harbored a basic distrust of human nature. The Puritans feared human appetite and were uneasy with unrestrained human expression. The body was construed as an object to be subdued in the quest for spiritual enlightenment and personal salvation. In their attempts to purify the world, the Puritans countenanced a narrow range of activities. The strict work ethic left scant time for play or dalliance. Idleness was not countenanced. Although the Puritans would engage in measured recreation, a sense of seriousness pervaded their lives. The patriarchs of Colonial New England seemed particularly uncomfortable with activities that brought pleasure. Pastimes that revealed elements of sensuality were distrusted as temptations to sin. In this climate of moral asceticism, sport was pursued circumspectly and often in defiance of authority. When the authorities proved less than effective in suppressing sport, they resorted to an alternate strategy. The antidote to sport as rebellion was to appropriate sport for high moral purpose. The revisionists justified sport as a way to maintain health and to re-energize oneself in order to work again. Competing in sport was touted as a regimen to build character. With these accommodations, the gates were left open to incorporate sport within secular Protestant culture.

For a period of time following the Colonial era, American sport would enjoy a modicum of freedom that allowed it to develop its own character. While the games of the leisure class imitated the British model of amateurism, the sporting activities of the common people were little inhibited by middle-class conventions. Their games and contests were spontaneous and often raucous. This was an era when children were allowed to engage in folk games and casual recreation with minimal adult interference. However, this ethos proved transitory. The specter of moralism stood in the wings casting a critical eye upon "disporting," especially among those beyond childhood. The reform agenda of the Progressive era was redolent of the Puritan ethic. The Victorians were consumed with standards of decency and morality, with an unquestioning acceptance of orthodoxy and authority. The prevailing inclination was to exert institutional control over human activities to bring them in line with elevated standards. Many of our contemporary institutions are a legacy of the Victorian Era, including public schools, the civil service, and organized recreation. These establishments continue to harbor Victorian values, both puritanical and progressive.

This era also bequeathed us our model of professionalism. While lawyers, educators, and physicians were initiating professional codes of practice, sports managers were developing into a profession. The Victorian concept of professionalism emphasized standards over profits, and this emphasis became the defining characteristic that set professionals apart from other economic actors who were motivated by self-interest. In this regard, the goals of professional associations departed from those of labor organizations that were more concerned with wages and working conditions. However, most professions did not function solely by standards of excellence and altruism. Pecuniary impulses intruded. The sports establishment and the coaching profession reflected the struggle over standards of conduct in conflict with mercenary motives.

Ultimately, sport became both a profession and a business. Spectator sports adopted a corporate model that focused on assets and revenue. Consistent with this model, sport took on the nuances of rational work: long training sessions, division of labor, role specialization, schedules, production quotas, and pay for performance. Activities on the athletic fields increasingly acquired consequences in the real world. In the process, the athlete early on was reduced to little more than an employee who performed assigned tasks. The ethos of the business profession and rationalized labor, like that of moral asceticism before it, stifled many of the natural qualities of sport.

Professionalism, with its impetus toward rationalism, led to the performance principle being applied to sport. Beginning in the Industrial era, an imposed standard of limitless improvement was aided and abetted by the adoption of scientific management and technological innovation. These strategies resulted in unprecedented achievement in the factories—and on the athletic fields. The sport of pole-vaulting was indicative of this phenomenon. The American vaulter Marc Wright won the event in the 1912 Olympic games by clearing four meters (13.1 feet). By the end of the century, vaulters utilizing principles of applied kinesiology and fiberglass poles were clearing six meters (19.7 feet). Across sports, the limits of human performance were extended beyond imagination. Applied science would create athletes who were amalgams of human nature and biotechnology. However, as sport increasingly exploited technique and technology, it became less an activity for escape and expressiveness than one of rigorous routine and goal-directed behavior.

The "technicalizing" of sport shifted the emphasis to superior scientific and economic resources and away from natural athleticism. Competing successfully in most sports would become highly exacting and costly both in time and resources. Sport science developed as a discipline to determine which designs, materials, and other engineering principles could provide the most efficient approach to performance. The expense of preparing athletes became prohibitive to the point of pricing some competitors out of the game. Noted fitness expert Dr. Kenneth Cooper commented that all this technology could well transform sport competition into a "space-age war" between opponents trying to prove their technical superiority. Indeed, today's athletes without significant financial resources and access to scientific expertise have found it more and more difficult to compete in world-class sport.

The American experience harbored another ideology that would dramatically alter the nature of sport. As the reigning spirit of capitalism increasingly influenced popular culture, mass sport would have more and more to do with making money. Nicholas Negroponte, a writer for the *New Yorker*, noted that his son had trouble learning how to add and subtract until the teacher put dollar signs in front of the figures. This story serves as a parable for what has happened to America's athletes. The players of games—along with their managers—have become preoccupied with money. Today's top athletes are reluctant to perform unless someone meets their price. The news media report on professional ballplayers offered $100 million contracts. Meanwhile, amateur athletes appear largely motivated by the promise of reaching the professional ranks where they can demand signing bonuses and large salaries. The financial game has framed the game that is played in the arena of competition.

Thus, sport and commerce have coalesced into a thriving partnership. The money changers have entered the temple of sport. Some professional athletes now receive more remuneration from commercial sponsors than from their playing contracts. Tennis players and golfers have complained that commercial sponsors of tournaments control which athletes can enter competition, with criteria based not only upon their abilities but their commercial relationships with the sponsors. The specific accusation is that tennis and golf professionals who have contracts with a certain agent/promoter are given priority over others. To the extent that these practices exist, skill and achievement have become secondary to commercial considerations.

The advertising of products in conjunction with sporting events has become less a means to finance sport than the rationale for staging the contests. As one cynic put it, "The purpose of televised football is to sell cheap beer." Beginning in the late 1950s, the advertising of beer made possible the televising of professional boxing. But incrementally "the cart replaced the horse." Ballgames and auto races facilitate the marketing not only of alcoholic beverages but a wide range of consumer products. In the process, commercialized spectator sport, with its acute awareness of audience, has transformed what once was play into display. This change, in turn, has led to more emphasis on drama and controversy surrounding sport. The late tennis champion Arthur Ashe observed that the increase in rude and boorish behavior of competitors during championship tennis matches is in part the result of huge amounts of money invested by commercial sponsors. Too much money is invested in the contestants to disqualify someone for unsportsmanlike behavior. Media experts are convinced that on-court displays of temper increase the audience of television viewers when the more temperamental players are competing. The same point has been made of league officials' tolerance for fighting in professional hockey and the increased physical contact allowed on the basketball court.

Ron Rapoport, a writer for the *Chicago Sun-Times,* suggested that sport has become more of a show than a game—just another television program. The Super Bowl halftime show, the opening ceremony of the summer Olympic games, and baseball's All Star Game are illustrations. An important distinction between play and display has to do with awareness. The true "player" loses himself in play and becomes oblivious to self and audience.[1003] To the contrary, display behavior is characterized by self-awareness and awareness of the audience. One can dunk a basketball as a way of putting the ball into the basket and scoring, or dunk the ball as a performance. Much of the behavior in the sports arena has become status display. The American preoccupation with celebrity is distorting sport. At some point, the competition becomes less of an attraction than the sensational behavior surrounding the contest. Prominent athletes' personae and rhetoric have made them the darlings of the media. As novelist John Fowles observed, "audience corrupts even more than power."

Meanwhile, the American educational system eschewed the British public school model of amateurism to emphasize elitist, spectator sports. The schools and colleges appropriated the model of professional sport: paid coaches, admission fees for spectators, commercial sponsors, etc. These features had been fully integrated into interscholastic and intercollegiate athletics by the mid-twentieth century. Amateurism has become a pretense.

College sports serve the students less than the alumni and the paying public. Some 5 percent of students participate in intercollegiate sports on large college campuses. College administrators continue to support athletics as a public relations apparatus, a device to garner support for their endowments and capital campaigns.

Likewise, children's games have been appropriated to serve an adult agenda. Educators and psychologists advise that children need to be exposed to free play, movement exploration, and low-organized games appropriate for their level of maturity. The national practice, however, has been to recruit an elite cadre of young boys and girls into highly competitive programs modeled after college and commercial sports, and under close adult direction. These structured programs show little tolerance for playfulness. The youngsters who fail to "make the team" obtain little in the way of healthy recreation as they watch from the sidelines. We accept this system as it rewards the most talented. Edward Devereux remains an unheeded prophet warning us of the "impoverishment" of children's play and its consequences. There is little doubt that well-intentioned adults are at the root of the problem. Bill Steigerwald of the *Los Angeles Times* suggested that we ban adults from Little League baseball games. But it is not likely we can keep parents and adult coaches away from youth sports arenas. Children may need supervision, and they can benefit from appropriate instruction by adults. What they also need is a new model for sport that emphasizes the experiential aspects of human movement and allows them to play an active role in determining the course of their play activities.

The writing of this book has led to a reassessment of the legacy of the Protestant ethic and the spirit of capitalism upon the future of American sport. The main issue, as I see it, is how to protect sport from cultural forces that would usurp and, ultimately, destroy its inherent spirit. The most pessimistic reading suggests that sport has been transformed into a joyless imitation of work and a marketing device for consumer capitalism. Sport may have briefly escaped the moral agenda of the Puritans and the Victorians to establish its own legitimate ethos with the flowering of pure amateurism and spontaneity. But within the encroaching hegemony of corporate capitalism, sport has capitulated to the agendas of making money and displaying status.

In a world of limited resources, where nature returns a yield only to prolonged and systematic effort, the work ethic sets the standard. This predicament may have described the reality and necessity of Colonial

America, but circumstances have changed. We no longer are struggling for our very survival in a hostile wilderness, nor are we constrained by a worldview emanating from a dogmatic Calvinism. The contemporary standard for sport needs to be based upon a holistic conception of human nature and personal development. The need exists not only to humanize human toil, but to foster human development through appropriate uses of leisure. Puritan asceticism and the Protestant work ethic have little to offer in this regard.

By the same token, we must question whether capitalism serves as an appropriate model for sport. Richard Tawney reminds us:

> At some point, human effort must satisfy criteria which are not purely economic. The distinction made by classical philosophers between liberal and servile occupations, by medieval thinkers that riches exist for man not man for riches, and by the socialists who urged that production be organized for service—all emphasized the instrumental character of economic activities by reference to an external, humanistic ideal.[1004]

However, the work ethic and the profit motive endure as the pre-eminent virtues under secularized Protestant capitalism. The Reverend F. Forrester Church suggests that our virtues can be as deadly as our sins. His point is that we are much less likely to do harm to the world because of our sins (which we are aware of) than through our virtues.[1005] This observation recalls the characterization of the Puritan as someone who carries virtue to excess. Might we conclude that the virtues in the Protestant ethic have been misapplied. To reiterate what has been stated above, the antidote to this predicament is to promote playing games and competing for inherent pleasure; stifling many of the purposive functions during play and getting into the flow; joining the game for the game's sake, with no extrinsic goal in mind; playing without awareness of self or audience; setting aside the focus of breaking records for personal glory; and instead, competing for the sense of excellence that accompanies the extension of human limits; focusing on the present and cherishing the sense of human movement; and finally, refusing to appropriate sport to the various agendas of the nonplay world. In this sense, sport can recapture a sense of the "religious," which is where we began this quest.

"Whatever the world thinks," wrote Bishop George Berkeley, "he who hath not much meditated upon...the *summum bonum* [the ultimate good] may possibly make a thriving earthworm, but will most indubitably make a sorry…statesman."[1006] The custodians of sport must reassess the contribution it makes to the ultimate good. We long for statesmen and stateswomen who can steer sport onto a new course, away from that instituted by the neo-Puritans, exploited by the capitalists, and co-opted by the technology fetishists. In this endeavor, we can recover the spirit of American sport for the twenty-first century.

Bibliography

Abeel, Erica. "Dark Secrets." *Esquire* 102/6 (June 1984): 259–65.

Adelman, Melvin. "The First Modern Sport in America: Harness Racing in New York City, 1825–1879." In *Sport in America,* edited by David Wiggins, 95–114. Champaign IL: Human Kinetics, 1995.

Ahlstrom, Sydney. *A Religious History of the American People.* New Haven: Yale University Press, 1972.

Allen, Fredrick. *Only Yesterday: An Informal History of the Nineteen Twenties.* New York: Harper & Row, 1959.

Allison, Lincoln. "Sport and Communities." In *The World & I. Washington Times,* October 1988, 613–27.

Anderson, J., et al. "Are You Better Off Now Than in 1908?" *US News & World Report* 104/21 (29 August–5 September 1988): 102–103.

Anderson, Sherwood. *Poor White.* New York: The Viking Press, 1966.

Andreski, Stanislav. "Methods and Substantive Theory in Max Weber." In *The Protestant Ethic and Modernization,* edited by Samuel N. Eisenstadt, 46–63. New York: Basic Books, 1968.

Argyle, Michael, and Benjamin Beit-Hallahmi. *The Social Psychology of Religion.* London: Routledge & Kegan Paul, 1975.

Aries, Philippe. *Centuries of Childhood: A Social History of Family Life.* Translated by R. Baldrick. New York: Knopf, 1962.

Armstrong, Lance, and Sally Jenkins. *It's Not About the Bike: My Journey Back to Life.* New York: Putnam's Sons, 2000.

Associated Press. "$10 Million-a-Year Player on Horizon." *Journal & Courier* (Lafayette IN), 26 December 1989, B3.

Associated Press. "Bulls Star Remains Top Earner." *The Clarion Ledger* (Jackson MS), 4 December 1995, C1.

Atkinson, Henry A. *The Church and the People's Play.* Boston: Pilgrim Press, 1915.

Austin, Lewis. *Saints and Samurai: The Political Culture of the American and Japanese Elites.* New Haven CT: Yale University Press, 1975.

Authers, John. "Faith in Figures Proves to Be a Big Hit." *Financial Times* 2/3 (December 2006): W5.

Back, Allan, and Daeshik Kim. "The Future Course of the Eastern Martial Arts." *Quest* 36/1 (January 1984): 7–14.

Bakan, Joel. *The Corporation: The Pathological Pursuit of Profit and Power.* New York: Free Press, 2004.

Baker, William P. "The Observance of Sunday." In *Englishmen at Rest and Play: Some Phases of English Leisure, 1558–1714,* edited by Reginald Lennard, 79–144. Oxford: The Clarendon Press, 1931.

Bale, John, and Mette Krogh Christensen, editors. *Post-Olympism? Questioning Sport in the Twenty-First Century.* Oxford, UK: Berg, 2004.

Ballparks.com. "New Yankee Stadium." http://www.ballparks.com/baseball/american/nyybpk.htm.

Baltzell, E. Digby. *The Protestant Establishment: Aristocracy and Caste in America.*

London: Secker & Warburg, 1965.

Bambery, Chris. "Marxism and Sport." *International Socialism* 73/4 (December 1996): 35–54.

Barnes, Harry E. *An Introduction to the History of Sociology.* Chicago: University of Chicago Press, 1966.

Barnes, Simon. "Poisoned Chalice of Victory." *The Times* (UK), 8 May 2006, http://www.timesonline.co.uk/article/0,,296-2170367,00.html.

Barra, Allen. "When Referee Wyatt Earp Laid Down the Law." *New York Times*, 26 November 1995, 24.

Bartlett, Arthur. *Baseball and Mr. Spalding.* New York: Farrar, Straus and Young, 1951.

Bauer, E. "Paper Reports Thumb-Twiddling by Secretaries in H.E.W. Office." *Clarion Ledger* (Jackson MS), 6 December 1979, J7.

Baym, Nina. "A Boy's Book for Adults." *New York Times Book Review*, 20 July 1986, 10.

Beamish, Rob. "Sport and the Capitalist Production Process." Unpublished paper. International Symposium on Sport, Culture, and the Modern State. Kingston, Ontario: Queens University, 1981.

Beard, George M. "Modern Civilization and American Nervousness." In *The Annals of America,* Encyclopaedia, volume 10, 480–85. Chicago: Britannica, 1968.

Becker, Howard, and Alvin Boskoff, editors. *Modern Sociological Theory in Continuity and Change.* New York: Holt, Rinehart & Winston, 1966.

Behee, John R. *Fielding Yost's Legacy to the University of Michigan.* Ann Arbor MI: Ulrich's Books, 1971.

Beisser, Arnold. *The Madness in Sports: Psychosocial Observations on Sports.* New York: Appleton-Century-Crofts, 1967.

—. "Modern Man and Sports." In *Sport & Society: An Anthology*, edited by John T. Talamini and C. Page, 85–96. Boston: Little, Brown and Co., 1973.

Bell, Daniel. *The Cultural Contradictions of Capitalism.* New York: Basic Books, 1976.

Bendix, Reinhard. *Max Weber: An Intellectual Portrait.* New York: Doubleday, 1960.

Bennett, Bruce, Maxwell Howell, and Uriel Simri. *Comparative Physical Education and Sport.* 2nd edition. Philadelphia: Lea & Febiger, 1983.

Bercovitch, Sacvan. *The Puritan Origins of the American Self.* New Haven CT: Yale University Press, 1975.

Berger, Bennett. "The Sociology of Leisure." *Industrial Relations: A Journal of Economy and Society* 1/1 (February 1962): 35–45.

Berger, Phil. *Mickey Mantle.* New York: Park Lane Press, 1998.

—. "Mike Tyson: Tales from the Dark Side." *M Inc.* 9/4 (January 1992): 69–74.

—. "Notebook," *New York Times*, 31 January 1990, http://query.nytimes.com/gst/fullpage.html?res=9C0CEED71E39F932A05752C0A966958260 (accessed 6 November 2008).

Berryman, Jack W. "The Rise of Highly Organized Sports for Preadolescent Boys." In *Children in Sport: A Contemporary Anthology*, edited by Richard Magill, Michael Ash, and Frank Smoll, 3–18. Champaign IL: Human Kinetics, 1978.

Betts, John R. *America's Sporting Heritage, 1980–1950.* Reading MA: Addison-Wesley, 1974.

—. "Mind and Body in Early American Thought." In *The American Sporting Experience: A Historical Anthology of Sport in America*, edited by Steven Riess, 61–74. New York: Leisure Press, 1984.

—. "The Technological Revolution and the Rise of Sport, 1850–1900." In *The American Sporting Experience: A Historical Anthology of Sport in America,* edited by Steven Riess, 141–57. New York: Leisure Press, 1984.

Birrell, Susan. "An Analysis of the Inter-relationships among Achievement Motivation, Athletic Participation, Academic Achievement, and Educational Aspirations." *International Journal of Sport Psychology* 8/3 (1977): 178–91.

Blanchard, Kendall, and Alyce Cheska. *The Anthropology of Sport: An Introduction.* Hadley MA: Bergin & Garvey, 1985.

Blum, Debra. "Private Association's Role in Florida Athletics Prompts Changes." *Chronicle of Higher Education*, 30 September 1992, A32.

Boekenstein, Bronwyn. "A Study of the Existence of Attributes of the Protestant Work Ethic in Leisure Participation." M.S. thesis, University of Oregon, 1976.

Boorstin, Daniel. *The Americans: The Colonial Experience.* New York: Random House, 1958.

—. *The Americans: The National Experience.* New York: Random House, 1965.

Borden, Paul. "SEC A.D.'s Surely Not Among 'Polk's Folks.'" *Clarion Ledger* (Jackson MS), 11 June 1985, D1.

Borisova, L. G., and E. P. Podalko. "Toward Classification of Motives." *International Review of Sport Sociology* 10/3, 4 (1975): 45–60.

Bourdieu, Pierre. "Programs for a Sociology of Sport." *Sociology of Sport Journal* 5/2 (June 1988): 153–61.

Boyle, Robert. *Sport—Mirror of American Life.* Boston: Little, Brown, 1963.

Brailsford, Dennis. "1787: An Eighteenth Century Sporting Year." *Research Quarterly for Exercise and Sport* 55/3 (September 1984): 217–30.

—. *Sport and Society: Elizabeth to Anne.* London: Routledge & Kegan Paul, 1969.

Bremer, Otto. "Business Is the Source of America's Values." In *American Values*, edited by David Bender, 150–54. St. Paul MN: Greenhaven Press, 1989.

Brohm, Jean Marie. *Sport—A Prison of Measured Time.* Translated by I. Fraser. London: Ink Links, 1978.

Brooks, Christine. "Sponsorship: Strictly Business." *Athletic Business* 14/2 (October 1990): 59–61.

Brooks, John. *Showing Off in America.* Boston: Little, Brown, 1981.

Brooks, Van Wyck. *America's Coming-of-Age.* New York: The Viking Press, 1930.

—. *The Wine of the Puritans.* London: Sisley's, 1908.

Brower, Jonathan. "The Professionalization of Organized Youth Sport: Social Psychological Impacts and Outcomes." *Annals of the American Academy of Political and Social Science* 445/1 (September 1979): 39–46.

Brown, Peter. *The Body and Society: Men, Women, and Sexual Renunciation in Early Christianity.* New York: Columbia University Press, 1988.

Bruskin, R. H., et al. "Leisure Time Flies." *Clarion Ledger* (Jackson MS), 23 April 1989, B1.

Budd, Adrian. "Capitalism, Sport, and Resistance; Reflections." *Culture, Sport, Society* 4/1 (Spring 2001): 1–18.

Budd, Susan. *Sociologists and Religion.* London: Collier-Macmillan, 1973.

Bueter, Robert J. "Sports, Values, and Society." *The Christian Century* 5/8 (April 1972): 389–92.

Bunyan, John. *The Pilgrim's Progress.* Norwalk CT: The Heritage Press, 1969.

Burns, Ken, and Lynn Novak, producers. *Baseball—A Film by Ken Burns.* Written by

Geoffrey C. Ward. Florentine Films, 1994.

Burrell, Sidney. "Calvinism, Capitalism, and the Middle Classes: Some Afterthoughts on an Old Problem." In *The Protestant Ethic and Modernization*, edited by Samuel N. Eisenstadt, 135–54. New York: Basic Books, 1968.

Butsch, Richard. *For Fun and Profit: The Transformation of Leisure into Consumption.* Philadelphia: Temple University Press, 1990.

Butterfield, Roger P. *The Prodigious Life of George Eastman.* New York: Time, Inc., 1954.

Cady, Edwin H. *The Big Game.* Knoxville TN: The University of Tennessee Press, 1978.

Cahn, Susan. *Coming On Strong: Gender and Sexuality in Twentieth-Century Women's Sport* (New York: Free Press, 1994) 259–78.

Caillois, Roger. *Man and the Sacred.* Glencoe IL: The Free Press, 1959.

Callahan, Raymond. *Education and the Cult of Efficiency.* Chicago: University of Chicago Press, 1962.

Campbell, Ernest Q. "Adolescent Socialization." In *Handbook of Socialization Theory and Research*, edited by David Goslin, 821–59. Chicago: Rand McNally, 1969.

Canetti, Elias. *Crowds and Power.* Translated by C. Stewart. New York: The Viking Press, 1962.

Carlson, Lewis, and John Fogarty. *Tales of Gold: An Oral History of the Summer Olympic Games.* Chicago: Contemporary Books, 1987.

Carlyle, Thomas. *Past and Present.* New York: University Press, 1977.

Carroll, John. *Puritan, Paranoid, Remissive: A Sociology of Modern Culture.* London: Routledge & Kegan Paul, 1977.

Carvajal, Doreen. "America's Cup Attracts Rich Corporate Sponsors." *International Herald Tribune,* 6 April 2007, http://www.iht.com/articles/2007/04/06/news/wbcup.php.

Cavallo, Dominick. *Muscles and Morals: Organized Playgrounds and Urban Reform, 1880–1920.* Philadelphia: University of Pennsylvania Press, 1981.

Champion, Walter T., Jr. *Sports Law in a Nutshell* (St. Paul MN: Thompson/West, 2005).

Chandler, Timothy. "Pierre de Coubertin: Le Regime Arnoldien et le Pedagogie Sportive." Paper presented at North American Society for Sport History Conference, Auburn AL, May 1996.

Chappell, Robert. "Cuba: Before and After the Wall Came Down." *The Sport Journal* 7/1 (Winter 2004): http://www.thesportjournal.org/2004Journal/Vol7-No1/chappellCuba.asp.

Cheek, Neil, and William Burch. *The Social Organization of Leisure in Human Society.* New York: Harper & Row, 1976.

Chino, Frederick. "Family Status, Protestant Ethic, and Level of Occupational Aspiration." Ph.D. dissertation, Stanford University, 1965.

Chu, Donald. *The Character of American Higher Education and Intercollegiate Sport.* Albany NY: S.U.N.Y. Press, 1989.

Clark, Beverly L., editor. *The Adventures of Tom Sawyer,* Norton Critical Edition (New York: Norton, 2006).

Clarke, John. "Pessimism Versus Populism: The Problematic Politics of Popular Culture." In *For Fun and Profit*, edited by Richard Butsch, 28–46. Philadelphia: Temple University Press, 1990.

Cleveland, Bobby. "Sanders Must Dream a Year Before BASS Masters." *Clarion Ledger* (Jackson MS), 14 July 1985, D14.

Coakley, Jay. "Beyond the Obvious: A Critical Look at Sport in the USA." In *The World & I. Washington Times*, October 1988, 589–601.

—. *Sport in Society: Issues and Controversies.* St. Louis: Mosby, 1978.

—. *Sports in Society: Issues and Controversies.* 8th edition. New York: McGraw-Hill, 2004.

Cohen, Albert K. *Deviance and Control.* Englewood Cliffs NJ: Prentice-Hall, 1966.

Cooperider, Jay. "Smart Move." *Purdue University Perspective* 22/2 (Summer 1995): 10–11.

Cox, Harvey. *The Secular City.* New York: Macmillan Co., 1966.

Cozens, Frederick, and Florence Stumpf. *Sports in American Life.* Chicago: University of Chicago Press, 1953.

Cramer, Richard B. *Joe DiMaggio: The Hero's Life.* New York: Simon & Schuster, 2000.

Crandall, Rick, and Karla Slivken. "The Importance of Measuring Leisure Attitudes." Paper presented at the National Parks and Recreation Association Conference, Miami FL, October 1978.

Cratty, Bryant. *Psychology in Contemporary Sport: Guidelines for Coaches and Athletes.* Englewood Cliffs NJ: Prentice-Hall, 1973.

Creamer, Robert. *Babe: The Legend Comes to Life.* New York: Viking, 1974.

Cronin, Mike, and Richard Holt. "The Globalization of Sport." *History Today* 15/7 (July 2003): 26–33, http://findarticles.com/p/articles/mi_hb4706/is_200307/ai_n17278634.

Cross, Gary. *A Social History of Leisure since 1600.* State College PA: Venture Publishing, 1990.

Csikszentmihalyi, Mihaly. "The Americanization of Rock Climbing." In *Play Its Role in Development and Evolution,* edited by Jerome Bruner, Alison Jolly, and Kathy Sylva, 484–88. New York: Basic Books, 1976.

Cuito, Aurora, editor. *Sports Facilities* (Barcelona, Spain: Loft Publications, 2007).

Curtis, James, and Philip White. "Toward a Better Understanding of the Sport Practices of Francophone and Anglophone Canadians." *Sociology of Sport Journal* 9/4 (1992): 403–22.

Dagavarian, Debra. *Saying It Ain't So: American Values as Revealed in Children's Baseball Stories, 1880–1950.* New York: Peter Lang, 1987.

Daniels, Bruce C. *Puritans at Play: Leisure and Recreation in Colonial New England.* New York: St. Martin's, 1995.

Davis, Arthur K. "Veblen on the Decline of the Protestant Ethic." *Social Forces* 22/3 (March 1944): 282–86.

Davis, Steve. "Is Select Soccer Worth the Shot?" *Dallas* (TX) *Morning News,* 13 June 2004, http://www.psychologyofsports.com/guest/travel.htm.

De Tocqueville, Alexis. *Democracy in America.* 1835, 1840. New York: Knopf, 1956.

De Vaya, Count Vay, and Count zu Luskod. "The Land of Mammon and Moloch." 1908. In *The Annals of America,* volume 13, 123–28. Chicago: Britannica, 1968.

Deford, Frank. "Religion in Sport." *Sports Illustrated* 53/15 (19 April 1976): 92–99.

Demerath, Nicholas J., and Phillip Hammond. *Religion in Social Context: Tradition and Transition.* New York: Random House, 1969.

Dennett, Joann, and Nancy Keogel. "Giving Athletes the Edge." In *The World & I. Washington Times,* October 1988, 162–69.

Denney, Reuel. *The Astonished Muse.* Chicago: University of Chicago Press, 1957.

Devereux, Edward C. "Backyard Versus Little League Baseball: Some Observations on the Impoverishment of Children's Games in Contemporary America." In *Sport Sociology: Contemporary Themes,* 2nd edition, edited by Andrew Yiannakis et al., 63–71. Dubuque IA: Kendall/Hunt, 1976.

Divorky, Diana. "Waterproofing Your Baby: Too Good to Be True." *Hippocrates* (May/June

1988): 28–31.

Drape, Joe. "High School Football, Under Prime-Time Lights." *New York Times*, 17 September 2006, http://www.nytimes.com/2006/09/17/sports/17highschool.html.

Dreitzel, Hans P. *Childhood and Socialization*. New York: Macmillan, 1973.

Dryden, Ken. *The Game: A Thoughtful and Provocative Look at Life in Hockey*. Toronto: Macmillan of Canada, 1983.

Dulles, Foster R. *A History of Recreation: America Learns to Play*. New York: Appleton-Century-Crofts, 1965.

Dumazedier, Joffre. *Sociology of Leisure*. New York: Elsevier, 1974.

Eaton, S. Boyd, M. Margerie Shostak, and Melvin Konner. *The Paleolithic Prescription*. New York: Harper & Row, 1988.

Edwards, Harry. "Desegregating Sexist Sport." *Intellectual Digest* 3/11 (November 1972): 82–83, 90.

—. *Sociology of Sport*. Homewood IL: Dorsey Press, 1973.

Eisenstadt, Samuel N., editor. *The Protestant Ethic and Modernization* (New York: Basic Books, 1968).

Eitzen, D. Stanley. *Fair and Foul: Beyond the Myths and Paradoxes of Sport*. Boulder CO: Rowman & Littlefield, 2003.

—. "The Myth and Reality of Elite Amateur Sport." *The World & I. Washington Times*, October 1988, 548–59.

Eitzen, D. Stanley, and George Sage. *Sociology of American Sport*. Dubuque IA: Brown, 1982.

Elkind, David. *The Hurried Child: Growing Up Too Fast, Too Soon*. Reading MA: Addison-Wesley, 1981.

Epperson, David C. "A Reassessment of Indices of Parental Influence in the Adolescent Society." *American Sociological Review* 29/1 (February 1964): 93–96.

Epstein, Edward. *Born to Skate: The Michelle Kwan Story*. New York: Ballantine Books, 1997.

Eubanks, Lon. *The Fighting Illini*. Huntsville AL: Strode Publishers, 1976.

Evensen, Bruce. *When Dempsey Fought Tunney: Heroes, Hokum, and Storytelling in the Jazz Age*. Knoxville: University of Tennessee Press, 1996.

Ewing, Martha E., et al. "Psychological Characteristics of Competitive Young Hockey Players." In *Competitive Sports for Children and Youth*, edited by Eugen Brown and Crystal Branta, 49–61. Champaign IL: Human Kinetics, 1988.

Ewing, Martha E., and Vern Seefeldt. *American Youth and Sports Participation*. West Palm Beach FL: American Footwear Association, 1990.

Fanon, Frantz. *The Wretched of the Earth*. New York: Grove Press, 1963.

Figler, Stephen. *Sport and Play in American Life*. Philadelphia: Saunders, 1981.

Filene, Peter. "Manhood in the Twenties: Was It So Great to Be Gatsby?" *Ms.* 11/12 (June 1974): 12–18.

Fine, Gary. "Sport as Play." *The World & I. Washington Times*, October 1988, 643–55.

Finney, Craig. "NESRA Conference Addressed Stress and Recreation." *Corporate Fitness & Recreation* (October/November 1984): 14–15.

Flint, William, and D. Stanley Eitzen. "Professional Sports Team Ownership and Entrepreneurial Capitalism." *Sociology of Sport Journal* 4/1 (March 1987): 17–27.

Flynn, George F. *Vince Lombardi on Football*. New York: Van Nostrand, 1981.

Foer, Franklin. *How Soccer Explains the World*. New York: Harper Collins, 2004.

Franklin, Raymond S. *American Capitalism: Two Visions.* New York: Random House, 1977.

Fredericksen, Linwood. "Feast and Festival." In *Encyclopaedia Britannica*, volume 7, 202. Chicago: Britannica, 1974.

Frey, James H. "Book Review. *The Big Game,* by Edwin H. Cady." *The Annals of the American Academy of Political and Social Science* 445/1 (September 1979): 190–91.

Friedman, Sally. *Swimming the Channel.* New York: FSG, 1996.

Friedman, Thomas L. *The World Is Flat: A Brief History of the Twenty-First Century.* New York: Farrar, Straus & Giroux, 2006.

Fulcher, James. *Capitalism: A Very Short Introduction.* Oxford, UK: Oxford University Press, 2004.

Fullerton, Kemper. "Calvinism and Capitalism: An Explanation of the Weber Thesis." In *Protestantism, Capitalism, and Social Science,* edited by Robert Green, 8–31. Lexington MA: Heath, 1973.

Fulton, William. "Politicians Who Chase After Sports Franchises May Get Less than They Pay For." *Governing* 1/6 (March 1988): 34–40.

Furst, Terry. "Social Change and the Commercialization of Professional Sports." *International Review for the Sociology of Sport* 6 (March 1971): 153–73.

Galbraith, John K. "What Tact the Press Showed!" *New York Times,* 22 December 1987, http://query.nytimes.com/gst/fullpage.html?res=9B0DE0DD1F3BF931A15751C1A9619 48260&sec=&spon=&pagewanted=1.

Ganster, D. C. "Protestant Ethic and Performance: A Re-examination." *Psychological Reports* 48 (1981): 335–38.

Geldbach, Erich. *Sport und Protestantismus: Geschichte einer Begegnung.* Wuppertal, Germany: Theologischer Verlag R. Brockhaus, 1975.

George, Charles, and Katherine George. "Protestantism and Capitalism in Pre-revolutionary England." In *Church History* 27 (1958): 351–71.

Gerber, Ellen. *Innovators and Institutions in Physical Education.* Philadelphia: Lea & Febiger, 1971.

Germani, Gino. "Secularization, Modernization, and Economic Development." In *The Protestant Ethic and Modernization*, edited by Samuel N. Eisenstadt, 343–66. New York: Basic Books: New York, 1968.

Gilder, George. "Christianity and Capitalism Are Complementary." In *American Values: Opposing Viewpoints*, edited by David Bender, 140–44. St. Paul MN: Greenhaven Press, 1989.

Godbey, Geoffrey, and Stanley Parker. *Leisure Studies and Services: An Overview.* Philadelphia: Saunders, 1976.

Goffman, Erving. *Behavior in Public Places.* New York: The Free Press, 1964.

Goldman, Robert, and John Wilson. "The Rationalization of Leisure." *Politics & Society* 7/2 (June 1977): 157–87.

Goldstein, Bernice. "The Changing Protestant Ethic: Rural Patterns in Health, Work, and Leisure." Ph.D. dissertation, Purdue University, 1959.

Gooding, Judson. "The Tennis Industry." *Fortune* 87/6 (June 1973): 124–33.

Goodman, Matthew. "Bowling for Dollars." *Sports Today* (March 1989): n.p.

Gould, Julius, and William Kolb. A *Dictionary of the Social Sciences.* New York: The Free Press, 1964.

Greeley, Andrew. "The Protestant Ethic: Time for a Moratorium." *Sociological Analysis* 25/1 (Spring 1964): 20–33.

Green, Tim. *The Dark Side of the Game: My Life in the NFL.* New York: Warner Books, 1996.

Greenberg, Clement. "Work and Leisure under Industrialism." In *Mass Leisure,* edited by Eric Larrabee and Rolf Meyerson, 38–43. Glencoe IL: The Free Press, 1958.

Greenberg, Jerald. "Equity, Equality, and the Protestant Ethic: Allocating Rewards Following Fair and Unfair Competition." *Journal of Experimental and Social Psychology* 14/2 (1978a): 217–26.

—. "Protestant Ethic Endorsement and Attitudes Toward Commuting to Work Among Mass Transit Riders." *Journal of Applied Psychology* 63/6 (1978b): 755–58.

—. "The Protestant Work Ethic and Reactions to Negative Performance Evaluations on a Laboratory Task." *Journal of Applied Psychology* 62/6 (December 1977): 682–90.

Greene, David, and Mark Lepper. "How to Turn Play into Work." *Psychology Today* 8/9 (September 1974): 49–54.

Greenhouse, Steven. "Americans' International Lead in Hours Worked Grew in 90s, Report Shows." *New York Times,* 1 September 2001, 8, http://query.nytimes.com/gst/fullpage.html?res=9A0CE5D91130F932A3575AC0A9679 C8B63 (accessed 25 August 2009).

Grella, George. "Baseball and the American Dream." In *Sport Inside Out: Readings in Literature and Philosophy,* edited by David Vanderwerken and Spencer Wertz, 267–79. Fort Worth: Texas Christian University, 1985.

Grenier, Richard. "Olympic Myths." *National Review* 48/14 (29 July 1996): 52–53.

Greven, Philip. *The Protestant Temperament: Patterns of Child-Rearing, Religious Experience, and the Self in Early America.* New York: Knopf, 1977.

Groos, Karl. *The Play of Man.* New York: Appleton, 1901.

Gruneau, Richard. *Class, Sports, and Social Development.* Amherst: University of Massachusetts Press, 1983.

—. "Freedom and Constraint: The Paradoxes of Play, Games, and Sports." *Journal of Sport History* 7/3 (Winter 1980): 68–86, http://216.239.51.104/search?q=cache:TQJ5Ei1op74J:www.aafla.org/SportsLibrary/JSH/ JSH1980/JSH0703/jsh0703e.pdf.

Guttmann, Allen. *From Ritual to Record: The Nature of Modern Sports.* New York: Columbia University Press, 1978.

—. *A Whole New Ball Game: An Interpretation of American Sports.* Chapel Hill: University of North Carolina Press, 1988.

Haley, Bruce. "Sports and the Victorian World." *Western Humanities Review* 22/2 (Spring 1968): 115–25.

Halmos, Paul. "The Ideology of Privacy and Reserve." In *Mass Leisure,* edited by Eric Larrabee and Rolf Meyerson, 125–36. Glencoe Press IL: The Free Press, 1958.

Hammond, Phillip, and Kirk Williams. "The Protestant Ethic Thesis: A Social-Psychological Assessment." *Social Forces* 54/3 (March 1976): 579–89.

Hardy, Stephen. "Adopted by All the Leading Clubs: Sporting Goods and the Shaping of Leisure, 1800–1900." In *For Fun and Profit,* edited by Richard Butsch, 71–101. Philadelphia: Temple University Press, 1990.

Harris, Janet C. "Play and Enjoyment: Perspectives and Implications." *Quest* 29/1 (Winter 1978): 60–72.

Harris, Louis. "Prophets Wrong: Leisure Time Dwindling." *Journal & Courier* (Lafayette IN), 29 December 1985, B2.

Hart-Nibbrig, Nand. "Corporate Athleticism: An Inquiry into the Political Economy of College Sports." *Proceedings, NAPEHE* 5 (1984): 11–20.

Harvey, Jean, Alan Law, and Michael Cantelon. "North American Professional Team Sport Franchises Ownership Patterns and Global Entertainment Conglomerates." *Sociology of Sport Journal* 18/4 (December 2001): 435–57.

"Health Craze Tricks US into Faith in Immortality." *Clarion Ledger/Jackson* (MS) *Daily News*, 14 May 1989, C2.

Heinemann, Klaus. "Unemployment, Personality, and Involvement in Sport." *Sociology of Sport Journal* 2/2 (June 1985): 157–63.

Hemingway, Ernest. *Death in the Afternoon.* New York: Scribner, 1932.

Hernandez, Keith, and Mike Bryan. *If at First: A Season with the Mets.* New York: McGraw Hill, 1986.

Higginson, Thomas W. "Saints and Their Bodies." *Atlantic Monthly* 1 (March 1858): 582–95.

Higgs, Robert J. "Muscular Christianity, Holy Play, and Spiritual Exercises: Confusion about Christ in Sports and Religion." *Arete* 1/1 (Fall 1983): 59–85.

Hiner, N. Ray. "The Cry of Sodom Enquired into: Educational Analysis in Seventeenth-Century New England." *History of Education Quarterly* 13/1 (Spring 1973): 3–22.

Hoberman, John. *Mortal Engines: The Science of Performance and the Dehumanization of Sport.* New York: The Free Press, 1992.

Hoch, Paul. *Rip Off the Big Game: The Exploitation of Sports by the Power Elite.* New York: Doubleday, 1972.

Hoffman, Shirl J., editor. *Sport and Religion.* Champaign IL: Human Kinetics, 1992.

Hofstadter, Richard. *The Age of Reform.* New York: Knopf, 1956.

Hogan, William. "Sin and Sports." In *Motivations in Play, Games, and Sports*, edited by Ralph Slovenko and James Knight, 121–47. Springfield IL: Chas. Thomas, 1967.

Hollander, Zander, and Paul Zimmerman. *Football Lingo.* New York: Norton, 1967.

Hoover, Dwight W. "The Division of Leisure." *The Social Change Report* 2/1. Muncie IN: The Center for Middletown Studies, 1987, 1–15.

Horney, Karen. *The Neurotic Personality of Our Time.* New York: Norton, 1937.

Houlihan, Barrie. *Sport, Policy & Politics: A Comparative Analysis.* London: Routledge, 1997.

Howell, Jeremy. "A Revolution in Motion: Advertising and the Politics of Nostalgia." *Sociology of Sport Journal* 8/3 (September 1991): 258–71.

Hruby, Patrick. "Beer and Sports, So Happy Together." *Washington Times,* 17 June 2003, http://www.washtimes.com/sports/20030617-124535-9205r.htm.

Hughes, H. Stuart. "Weber's Search for Rationality in Western Society." In *Protestantism, Capitalism, and Social Science,* edited by Robert Green, 150–69. Lexington MA: Heath, 1973.

Hughes, Thomas. *Tom Brown at Oxford.* New York: Hurst, 1885.

Huizinga, Johan. *Homo Ludens: A Study of the Play Element in Culture.* 7th edition. Boston: Beacon Press, 1968.

Hurlock, Elizabeth B. *Child Development.* New York: McGraw Hill, 1964.

Ingham, Alan G. "American Sport in Transition: The Maturation of Industrial Capitalism and Its Impact upon Sport." Ph.D. dissertation, University of Massachusetts, 1978.

—. "From Public Issue to Personal Trouble: Well-Being and the Fiscal Crisis of the State." *Sociology of Sport Journal* 2/1 (March 1985): 43–55.

Isaacs, Neil D. *Jock Culture, USA.* New York: Norton, 1978.

Iso-Ahola, Seppo. *The Social Psychology of Leisure and Recreation.* Dubuque IA: Brown, 1980.

Iso-Ahola, Seppo, and Kevin Buttimer. "The Emergence of Work and Leisure Ethic from Early Adolescence to Early Adulthood." *Journal of Leisure Research* 13/4 (Fourth Quarter 1981): 282–88.

Jable, J. Thomas. "The English Puritans—Suppressors of Sport and Amusement?" *Canadian Journal of History of Sport and Physical and Physical Education* 7/5 (May 1976): 33–40.

—. "The Public Schools Athletic League of New York City: Organized Athletics for City Schoolchildren, 1903–1914." In *The American Sporting Experience: A Historical Anthology of Sport in America,* edited by Steven Riess, 219–38. New York: Leisure Press, 1984.

Jaeger, Werner. *Paideia: The Ideals of Greek Culture.* Volume 2. New York: Oxford University Press, 1943.

Jhally, Sut. "Media Sports, Culture, and Power: Critical Issues in the Communication of Sport." In *Media, Sports, and Society: Research on the Communication of Sport,* edited by Lawrence A. Wenner, 70–93. Beverly Hills California: Sage Publications, 1989.

Jordan, Pat. *A False Spring.* New York: Dodd, Mead & Co., 1975.

Kakar, Sudhir. *Frederick Taylor: A Study in Personality and Innovation.* Boston: M.I.T. Press, 1970.

Kando, Thomas, and Worth Summers. "The Impact of Work on Leisure: Toward a Paradigm and Research Strategy." In *Sociology of Leisure,* edited by Theodore Johannis, Jr. and C. Neil Bull, 310–27. Beverly Hills CA: Sage Publications, 1971.

Kaplan, H. Roy. "The Convergence of Work, Sport, and Gambling in America." *The Annals of the Academy of Political and Social Science* 445/1 (September 1979): 24–38.

Katz, Elihu, and Michael Gurevitch. *The Secularization of Leisure: Culture and Communication in Israel.* London: Faber & Faber, 1976.

Kelly, Colin C. "Socialization into Sport among Male Adolescents from Canada, England, and the United States." M.S. thesis, University of Wisconsin, 1970.

Kenyon, Gerald, and Barry McPherson. "An Approach to the Study of Sport Socialization." *International Review of Sport Sociology* 9/1 (March 1974): 127–39.

—. "Becoming Involved in Physical Activity and Sport: A Process of Socialization." In *Physical Activity: Human Growth and Development,* edited by G. Lawrence Rarick, 303–32. New York: Academic Press, 1973.

Kerr, Walter. *The Decline of Pleasure.* New York: Time Inc., 1966.

Kett, Joseph. *Rites of Passage: Adolescence in America 1790 to the Present.* New York: Basic Books, 1977.

Kiester, Ed, Jr. "They'll Help Organize Your Leisure Time." *Parade* (25 February 1979): 24–27.

King, Alan J., and C. E. Angi. "The Hockey Playing Student." *Journal of the Canadian Association for Health, Physical Education, and Recreation* 35/10 (October/November 1968): 25–28.

Kirkpatrick, T. "Running Makes Imprint on Our Language, Commerce." *Clarion Ledger* (Jackson MS), 17 September 1978, G2.

Kliever, Lonnie D. "God and Games in Modern Culture." In *The World & I. Washington Times,* October 1988, 561–72.

Kluckhohn, Clyde. "Have There Been Discernible Shifts in American Values During the Past

Generation?" In *The American Style: Essays in Value and Performance*, edited by Elting E. Morison, 145–217. New York: Harper, 1958.

Knobler, Mike. "SEC Makes Big Bucks Off Name: Conference Slices Pie Pretty Evenly." *Clarion Ledger* (Jackson MS), 22 October 1995, D8.

Knoppers, Annelies, and Jayne Schuiteman. "Winning Is Not the Only Thing." *Sociology of Sport Journal* 3/1 (February 1986): 43–56.

Knox, Chuck, and Bill Plaschke. *Hard Knox: The Life of an NFL Coach*. San Diego: Harcourt Brace Jovanovich, 1988.

Koch, James, and Wilbert Leonard II. "The NCAA: A Socio-economic Analysis: The Development of the College Sports Cartel from Social Movement to Formal Organization." *American Journal of Economics and Sociology* 37/3 (July 1978): 225–39.

Kohn, Melvin L. *Class and Conformity: A Study in Values*. Homewood IL: Dorsey, 1969.

—. "Social Class and Parent-Child Relationships: an Interpretation." *American Journal of Sociology* 68/1 (January 1963): 471–80.

Koppett, Leonard. *Koppett's Concise History of Major League Baseball*. New York: Carroll & Graf, 2004.

—. *Sports Illusion, Sports Reality: A Reporter's View of Sports, Journalism, and Society*. 2nd edition. Champaign IL: University of Illinois Press, 1994.

Kowet, Don. *The Rich Who Own Sports*. New York: Random House, 1977.

Kram, Mark. "Religion in Athletics: Touchy Subject." *Clarion Ledger* (Jackson MS), 19 November 1988, C1, C7.

Kramer, Jerry. *Instant Replay: The Green Bay Diary of Jerry Kramer*. Edited by Dick Schaap. New York: New American Library, 1968.

Kraus, Richard. "Changing Views of Tomorrow's Leisure." *Journal of Physical Education, Recreation & Dance* 67/8 (August 1988): 83–87.

Krauthammer, Charles. "The Appeal of Ordeal." *Time* 123/20 (14 May 1984): 93–94.

Ladd, Tony, and James A. Mathisen. *Muscular Christianity: Evangelical Protestants and the Development of American Sport*. Grand Rapids MI: Baker Books, 1999.

Larrabee, Eric, and Rolf Meyersohn, editors. *Mass Leisure*. Glencoe IL: The Free Press, 1958.

Lasch, Christopher. "The Corruption of Sports." *New York Review of Books* 24/7 (April 1977): 24–30.

—. *The Culture of Narcissism: American Life in an Age of Diminishing Expectations*. New York: Norton, 1978.

Lawton, James. "Fallen Hero: How We're All Being Cheated." *Belfast* (NIR) *Telegraph*, 29 June 2006, http://www.belfasttelegraph.co.uk/.

Lee, Mabel. *A History of Physical Education and Sports in the USA*. New York: John Wiley & Sons, 1983.

Lee, Robert. *Religion and Leisure in America*. New York: Abingdon Press, 1964.

Lenk, Hans. *Social Philosophy of Athletics*. Champaign IL: Stipes, 1979.

Lenski, Gerhard. *The Religious Factor: A Sociological Study of Religion's Impact on Politics, Economics, and Family Life*. Garden City NY: Doubleday, 1961.

Leonard, Fred. *A Guide to the History of Physical Education*. Philadelphia: Lea & Febiger, 1947.

Leonard, George. "Life Skills." *Esquire* 101/5 (May 1984): 149–52.

Lerner, Daniel. "Comfort and Fun: Morality in a Nice Society." *The American Scholar* 27/2 (Spring 1958): 153–65.

Lerner, Max. *America as a Civilization: Life and Thought in the United States Today.* New York: Simon and Schuster, 1957.

"Let's Make a Deal." *The Clarion Ledger* (Jackson MS), 1 July 1989, C1.

Levine, Robert. *Culture, Behavior, and Personality.* Chicago: Aldine, 1973.

—. "Culture, Personality, and Socialization: An Evolutionary View." In *Handbook of Socialization and Research,* edited by David A. Goslin, 791–820. Chicago: Rand McNally, 1969.

Levinson, David, and Karen Christensen, editors. *Encyclopedia of World Sport: From Ancient Times to the Present.* New York: Oxford University Press, 1999.

Lewis, Guy. "The Muscular Christianity Movement." *Journal of Health, Physical Education & Recreation* 45/5 (May 1966): 27–28, 42.

Linder, Staffan. *The Harried Leisure Class.* New York: Columbia University Press, 1970.

Lipset, Seymour. *The First New Nation: The United States in Historical and Comparative Perspective.* New York: Doubleday, 1967.

Lipsky, Richard. *How We Play the Game: Why Sports Dominate American Life.* Boston: Beacon Press, 1981.

Lipsyte, Robert. "Varsity Syndrome: The Unkindest Cut." *The Annals of the American Academy of Political and Social Science* 445/1 (September 1979): 15–23.

Looney, Douglas S. "Bred to Be a Superstar." *Sports Illustrated* 68/8 (22 February 1988): 56–58.

Loubser, Jan. "Calvinism, Equality, and Inclusion: The Case of Afrikaner Calvinism." In *The Protestant Ethic and Modernization,* edited by Samuel N. Eisenstadt, 343–67. New York: Basic Books, 1968.

Loy, John. "The Cultural System of Sport." *Quest* 29/4 (Winter 1978): 60–72.

—. "The Nature of Sport: A Definitional Effort." *Quest* 10/2 (May 1968): 1–15.

—. "Sociological Analysis of Sport." In *Physical Education: An Inter-disciplinary Approach,* edited by Robert Singer et al., 208–14. New York: Macmillan, 1972.

Loy, John, Barry McPherson, and Gerald Kenyon. *Sport and Social Systems.* Reading MA: Addison-Wesley, 1978.

"L.S.U. Athletics Hands Over $2 Million to Academics." *The Clarion Ledger* (Jackson MS), 1 July 1989, C3.

Lucas, John. "Olympic Changes: Dollars and Sense." *Online NewsHour* (23 July 1996) http:/www.pbs.org/newshour/forum/july96/Olympics_7-23.html (accessed 1 March 2009).

Lueschen, Günther. "The Interdependence of Sport and Culture." *International Review of Sport Sociology* 2/1 (1967) 127–42.

—. "Social Stratification and Social Mobility Among Young Sportsmen." In *Sport, Culture, and Society,* edited by John W. Loy and Gerald Kenyon, 258–76. London: Collier-Macmillan, 1969.

Luethy, Herbert. "Once Again: Calvinism and Capitalism." In *The Protestant Ethic and Modernization,* edited by Samuel N. Eisenstadt, 87–108. New York: Basic Books, 1968.

Maccoby, Eleanor. "The Development of Moral Values and Behavior in Childhood." In *Socialization and Society,* edited by John Calusen, 227–69. Boston: Little, Brown, 1968.

Maccoby, Michael. *The Gamesman: The New Corporate Leaders.* New York: Simon and Schuster, 1976.

MacDonald, A. P., Jr. "More on the Protestant Ethic." *Journal of Consulting and Clinical Psychology* 39/1 (February 1972): 116–22.

Malamud, Bernard. *The Natural.* New York: Farrar, Straus & Giroux, 1980.

Mangan, J. A. *Athletics in the Victorian and Edwardian Public School.* Cambridge: Cambridge University Press, 1981.

Mann, Thomas. *The Magic Mountain.* 1927. Translated by Helen T. Lowe-Porter. New York: Knopf, 1985.

Mantel, Richard, and Lee Vander Velden. "The Relationship Between the Professionalization of Attitude toward Play of Pre-Adolescent Boys and Participation in Organized Sports." In *Sport and American Society: Selected Readings,* edited by George Sage, 172–78. Reading MA: Addison-Wesley, 1974.

Maraniss, David. *Rome 1960: The Olympics That Changed the World* (New York: Simon & Schuster, 2008).

Marshall, Gordon. *In Search of the Spirit of Capitalism: An Essay on Max Weber's Protestant Ethic Thesis.* New York: Columbia University Press, 1982.

Martens, Rainer. *Joy and Sadness in Children's Sports.* Champaign IL: Human Kinetics, 1978.

—. *Sociology Psychology and Physical Activity.* New York: Harper & Row, 1975.

Martin, Brian. "Design Flaws of the Olympics." *Social Alternatives* 19/2 (April 2000): 19–23.

Martin, David. *A General Theory of Secularization.* New York: Harper & Row, 1978.

Marty, Martin. *Protestantism.* New York: Holt, Rinehart & Winston, 1972.

Marx, Karl. *Das Kapital.* Chicago: Britannica, 1952.

Mather, C. (1701), Cotton. "A Christian at His Calling." In *The American Gospel of Success: Individualism and Beyond,* edited by Moses Rischen, 23–30. New York: Franklin Watts, 1974.

Mayo, James M. *The American Country Club: Its Origins and Development.* Piscataway NJ: Rutgers University Press, 1998.

McClelland, David. *The Achieving Society.* New York: Macmillan, 1961.

McMurtry, John. "The Illusions of a Football Fan: A Reply to Michalos." In *Sport Inside Out: Readings in Literature and Philosophy,* edited by David Vanderwerken and Spencer Wertz, 241–44. Fort Worth: Texas Christian University Press, 1985.

McNeill, John T. *The History and Character of Calvinism.* London: Oxford University Press, 1954.

—, editor. *On the Christian Faith: Selections from the Institutes, Commentaries, and Tracts of John Calvin.* Indianapolis IN: Bobbs-Merrill, 1957.

McPherson, Barry. "The Child in Competitive Sport: Influence of the Social Milieu." In *Children in Sport: A Contemporary Anthology,* edited by Richard Magill, Michael Ash, and Frank Smoll, 219–49. Champaign IL: Human Kinetics, 1978.

McPherson, Barry, James Curtis, and John Loy. *The Social Significance of Sport: An Introduction to the Sociology of Sport.* Champaign IL: Human Kinetics, 1989.

Mead, George. *Mind, Self, and Society.* Chicago: University of Chicago Press, 1934.

Mead, Margaret. *And Keep Your Powder Dry: An Anthropologist Looks at America.* New York: Morrow, 1965.

—. "The Pattern of Leisure in Contemporary American Culture." In *Mass Leisure,* edited by Eric Larrabee and Rolf Meyerson, 10–15. Glencoe IL: The Free Press, 1958.

Means, Richard. "American Protestantism and Max Weber's Protestant Ethic." *Religious Education* 60/2 (March/April 1965): 90–98.

Meggyesy, Dave. *Out of Their League.* Berkeley CA: Ramparts Press, 1970.

Mehl, Roger. *The Sociology of Protestantism*. Translated by James H. Farley. Philadelphia: The Westminster Press, 1970.

Mencken, Henry L. "Puritanism as a Literary Force." In *A Book of Prefaces*, 99–136. London: Jonathan Cape, 1922.

Merton, Robert K. *Science, Technology & Society in Seventeenth Century England*. New York: Howard Fertig, 1970.

—. "Social Structure and Anomie." In *Approaches to Deviance: Theories, Concepts, and Research Findings*, edited by Mark Lefton, James Skipper, and Charles McCaghy, 34–39. New York: Appleton-Century-Crofts, 1968a.

—. *Social Theory and Social Structure*. New York: The Free Press, 1968b.

Messenger, Christian. *Sport and the Spirit of Play in American Fiction: Hawthorne to Faulkner*. New York: Columbia University Press, 1981.

Meyer, Heinz. "Puritanism and Physical Training: Ideological and Political Accents in the Christian Interpretation of Sport." *International Review of Sport Sociology* 8/1 (March 1973): 37–51.

Miah, Andy. "Be Very Afraid: Cyborg Athletes, Transhuman Ideals & Posthumanity." *Journal of Evolution and Technology* 13/2 (October 2003) http://jetpress.org/volume13/miah.htm.

Michener, James A. *Sports in America*. New York: Random House, 1976.

Miller, David L. *Gods and Games: Toward a Theology of Play*. New York: The World Publishing Co., 1970.

Miller, Perry. *The New England Mind: From Colony to Province*. Cambridge MA: Harvard University Press, 1962.

Miller, Stephen. "The Playful, the Crazy, and the Nature of Pretense." *The Anthropological Study of Human Play* 60/3, edited by Edward Norbeck. Houston: Rice University Studies. (Summer 1974): 31–51.

Milton, Brian. "Sport as Functional Equivalent of Religion." M.S. thesis, University of Wisconsin, 1972.

Milverstadt, Fred. "Colleges Courting Corporate Sponsors." *Athletic Business* 13/3 (March 1989): 22–27.

Mirels, Herbert, and James Garrett. "The Protestant Ethic as a Personality Variable." *Journal of Counseling and Clinical Psychology* 36/1 (1971): 40–44.

Mitzman, Arthur. "Max Weber." In *Encyclopaedia Britannica*, volume 19, 714–17. Chicago: Britannica, 1974.

Miyakawa, T. Scott. *Protestants and Pioneers: Individualism and Conformity on the American Frontier*. Chicago: University of Chicago Press, 1964.

Moore, Raymond, and Dorothy Moore. *School Can Wait*. Provo UT: Brigham Young University Press, 1979.

"More Than a Game" (telecast), narrator Frank Gifford. New York: Arts and Entertainment Network, May 1992.

Morgan, Edmund S. *Visible Saints: The History of a Puritan Idea*. Ithaca NY: Cornell University Press, 1963.

Morgan, William J. "'Radical' Social Theory of Sport: A Critique and a Conceptual Emendation." *Sociology of Sport Journal* 2/1 (March 1985): 56–71.

Morone, James A. *Hellfire Nation: The Politics of Sin in American History*. New Haven: Yale University Press, 2003.

Moyers, Bill. *A World of Ideas*. Edited by B. S. Flowers. New York: Doubleday, 1989.

Mrozek, Donald J. *Sport and American Mentality, 1880–1910.* Knoxville: University of Tennessee Press, 1983.

Muir, Donal. "Club Tennis: A Case Study in Taking Leisure Very Seriously." *Sociology of Sport Journal* 8/1 (March 1991): 70–78.

Mumford, Lewis. *Technics and Civilization.* New York: Harcourt, Brace, 1934.

Murdock, Graham. "Education, Culture, and the Myth of Classlessness." In *Work and Leisure,* edited by John Haworth and Michael Smith, 88–104. Princeton NJ: Princeton Book Co., 1976.

Murphy, Betty S. "The Commercial Republic and the Dignity of Work." *National Forum* 64/4 (Fall 1984): 49–52.

Muscatine, A. "Tobacco Tempest: Anti-Smoking Movement Finds Deep Roots Tying Sports, Industry." *Commercial Appeal* (Memphis TN), 12 May 1991, B1.

Myrdal, Gunnar. *An American Dilemma: The Negro Problem and Modern Democracy.* New York: Harper & Row, 1962.

Nef, John. *Cultural Foundations of Industrial Civilization.* New York: Harper & Row, 1960.

Neider, Charles, editor. *The Complete Tales of Washington Irving.* New York: Doubleday, 1975.

Nelson, Benjamin. "Weber's Protestant Ethic: Its Origins, Wanderings, and Foreseeable Futures." In *Beyond the Classics? Essays in the Scientific Study of Religion,* edited by Charles Glock and Phillip Hammond, 71–130. New York: Harper & Row, 1973.

Neulinger, John. *The Psychology of Leisure.* Springfield IL: Thomas, 1974.

Newcombe, Jack. *The Best of the Athletic Boys: The White Man's Impact on Jim Thorpe.* New York: Doubleday, 1975.

Nichols, Thomas L. "Work and Play in America." 1864. In *The Annals of America*, volume 9, 537–42. Chicago: Britannica, 1968.

Niebuhr, H. Richard. "The Captive Church." In *The Annals of America*, volume 15, 340–44. Chicago: Britannica, 1968.

Nietzsche, Friedrich. *On the Genealogy of Morals.* Translated by Walter Kaufmann. New York: Random House, 1969.

Nixon, Howard L. "The Commercialization and Organizational Development of Modern Sport." *International Review of Sport Sociology* 9/2 (June 1974): 107–35.

—. "A Social Network Analysis of Influences on Athletes to Play with Pain and Injuries." *Journal of Sport and Social Issues* 16/2 (September 1992): 127–35.

Novak, Michael. *The Joy of Sports.* New York: Basic Books, 1976.

Nyerges, Christopher. "Running to Olympus." In *Core Concepts of Health*, edited by Paul Insel and Walton Roth, 302. Palo Alto CA: Mayfield, 1985.

Ogilvie, Bruce. "The Child Athlete: Psychological Implications of Participation in Sport." *The Annals of the American Academy of Political and Social Science* 445/1 (September 1979): 47–58.

Ogilvie, Bruce, and Thomas Tutko. "If You Want to Build Character, Try Something Else." *Psychology Today* 5/10 (October 1971): 61–63.

Olmstead, Clifton. *Religion in America: Past and Present.* Englewood Cliffs NJ: Prentice-Hall, 1961.

Oppliger, Robert A., et al. "Grappling with Weight Cutting." *The Physician and Sportsmedicine* 23/3 (October 1995): 69–78.

Orlean, Susan. "Shoot the Moon." *The New Yorker* 69/5 (22 March 1993): 74–85.

Orlick, Terrance D. "A Socio-psychological Analysis of Early Sports Participation." Ph.D.

dissertation, University of Alberta, 1972.

Osterhoudt, Robert G. *The Philosophy of Sport: A Collection of Original Essays.* Springfield IL: Thomas, 1973.

Overman, Steven J. *The Influence of the Protestant Ethic on Sport and Recreation.* Aldershot, UK: Avebury, 1997.

—. "Perceived Protestant Ethic Endorsement in Parents and Motivation for and Extent of Participation in Organized Sport by High School Seniors." M.A. thesis, Jackson State University, 1979.

—. "The Student in the Medieval University." Ph.D. dissertation, Washington State University, 1971.

—. "Work and Play in America: Three Centuries of Commentary." *The Physical Educator* 40/4 (December 1983): 184–90.

"The Packers." *Commercial Appeal* (Memphis TN), 12 July 1992, B1.

Park, Roberta. "Too Important to Trust to the Children: The Search for Freedom and Order in Children's Play, 1900–1917." In *The Paradoxes of Play*, edited by John Loy, 96–104. West Point NY: Leisure Press, 1982.

Parker, Stanley. *The Future of Work and Leisure.* New York: Praeger, 1971.

—. *The Sociology of Leisure.* New York: International Publications Service, 1976.

Parsons, Talcott. "Belief, Unbelief, and Disbelief." In *The Culture of Unbelief*, edited by Rocco Caporale and Antonio Grumelli, 207–46. Berkeley: University of California Press, 1971.

—. "Max Weber's Analysis of Capitalism and Modern Institutions." In *An Introduction to the History of Sociology*, edited by Harry E. Barnes, 287–308. Chicago: University of Chicago Press, 1948.

—. *The Structure of Social Action.* New York: The Free Press, 1937.

Paxson, Frederic L. "The Rise of Sport." *The Mississippi Valley Historical Review* 4/2 (September 1917): 143–68.

Peele, Stanton. *Diseasing of America: Addiction Treatment Out of Control.* Lexington MA: Lexington Books, 1989.

Peppard, Victor E. "The Soviet Critique of Sport and Physical Culture." *Quest* 34/1 (January 1982): 23–33.

Perry, Ralph Barton. *Puritanism and Democracy.* New York: Vanguard, 1944.

Pirsig, Robert M. *Lila: An Inquiry into Morals.* New York: Bantam, 1991.

Poggi, Gianfranco. *Calvinism and the Capitalist Spirit: Max Weber's Protestant Ethic.* Amherst: University of Massachusetts Press, 1983.

Polanyi, Karl. *The Great Transformation.* New York: Rinehart, 1944.

Polsky, Ned. *Hustlers, Beats, and Others.* Chicago: Aldine, 1967.

Ponomaryov, N. I. *Sport and Society.* Translated by James Riordan. Moscow: Izdatelstvo Fizkul'tura i Sport, 1981.

Pope, S. W. *Patriotic Games: Sporting Traditions in the American Imagination, 1876–1926.* New York: Oxford University Press, 1997.

Postrel, Virginia. *The Future and Its Enemies.* New York: Simon & Schuster, 1999.

Price, Joseph L. *From Season to Season: Sports as American Religion.* Macon GA: Mercer University Press, 2001.

Purdy, Dean. "For Whom Sport Tolls: Players, Owners, and Fans." In *The World & I. Washington Times*, October 1988, 573–87.

Ralbovsky, Martin. *Lords of the Locker Room: The American Way of Coaching and Its Effect on Youth.* New York: Peter H. Wyden, 1974.

Redlich, Fritz. "The Business Leader as a 'Daimonic Figure.'" *The American Journal of Economics and Sociology* 12/2 (April 1953): 289–99.

Rieff, Philip. *The Triumph of the Therapeutic: Uses of Faith after Freud.* New York: Harper & Row, 1968.

Riesman, David. *Individualism Reconsidered.* New York: The Free Press, 1954.

—. "Leisure and Work in Post-industrial Society." In *Mass Leisure,* edited by Eric Larrabee and Rolf Meyersohn, 363–85. Glencoe IL: The Free Press, 1958.

—. *The Lonely Crowd: A Study of the Changing American Character.* New Haven CT: Yale University Press, 1950.

—. "The Saving Remnant: An Examination of Character Structure." In *Years of the Modern: An American Appraisal,* edited by John W. Chase, 115–47. New York: Longmans, Green & Co., 1949.

Riess, Steven A., editor. *The American Sporting Experience: A Historical Anthology of Sport in America.* New York: Leisure Press, 1984.

Rigauer, Bero. *Sport and Work.* Translated by Allen Guttmann. New York: Columbia University Press, 1981.

Riggs, Bobby. *Court Hustler.* Philadelphia: J. B. Lippincott Co., 1973.

Rischen, Moses, editor. *The American Gospel of Success: Individualism and Beyond.* New York: Franklin Watts, 1974.

Ritchie, Ian. "Book Review, *Genetically Modified Athletes: Biomedical Effects, Gene Doping, and Sport* by Andy Miah." *Sociology of Sport Journal* 22/2 (June 2005): 239–41.

Ritchie, Oscar, and Marvin Koller. *Sociology of Childhood.* New York: Appleton-Century-Crofts, 1978.

Ritzer, George, and Todd Stillman. "The Postmodern Ballpark as a Leisure Setting: Enchantment and Simulated De-McDonaldization." *Leisure Studies* 23/2 (April 2001): 99–113.

Robbins, Liz. "Tennis; Official and Players Wary of Heat Illness." *New York Times,* 2 September 2001, http://query.nytimes.com/gst/fullpage.html?res=9807E5DD1F30F931A3575AC0A9679C 8B63.

Roberts, John, and Brian Sutton-Smith. "Child Training and Game Involvement." *Ethnology* 1/2 (July 1962): 166–85.

Roberts, Randy, and James Olson. *Winning Is the Only Thing.* Baltimore: The Johns Hopkins University Press, 1989.

Rockefeller, David. "America Must Stress the Value of Work." In *American Values,* edited by David Bender, 204–208. St. Paul MN: Greenhaven Press, 1984.

Rodgers, Daniel T. *The Work Ethic in Industrial America, 1850–1920.* Chicago: University of Chicago Press, 1978.

Romanowski, Bill, Adam Scheffter, and Phil Towle. *Romo: My Life on the Edge.* New York: William Morrow, 2005.

Rose, Arnold, editor. *Human Behavior and Social Processes: An Interactionist Approach.* Boston: Houghton Mifflin, 1962.

Rotenberg, Mordechai. *Damnation and Deviance: The Protestant Ethic and the Spirit of Failure* New York: Free Press, 1978.

Ruhl, J. K. "Puritanism and Sport—the Classical and Scriptural Heritage of Several Principles in the Modern Conception of Sport." In *Sport and Religion: The History of*

Sport and the Physical Education in the Iberian Cultures, 183–91. Lisbon: Instituto Nacional Dos Desportos, 1981.

Ryan, Joan. *Little Girls in Pretty Boxes.* New York: Doubleday, 1995.

Sack, Allen. "The Underground Economy of College Football." *Sociology of Sport Journal* 13/1 (March 1991): 1–15.

Sadler, William. "Competition Out of Bounds: Sport in American Life." *Quest* 19/1 (January 1973): 124–32.

Sage, George. "American Values and Sport: Formation of a Bureaucratic Personality." *Journal of Physical Education and Recreation* 49/8 (October 1978): 8.

—. "The Coach as Management: Organizational Leadership in American Sport." *Quest* 19/1 (Winter 1973): 35–40.

—. "Socialization and Sport." In *Sport and American Society: Selected Readings*, edited by George Sage, 133–42. Reading MA: Addison-Wesley, 1974a.

—. "Socialization of Coaches: Antecedents to Coaches' Beliefs and Behaviors." *Proceedings, National College Physical Education Association for Men* 79 (January 1975): 124–32.

—. "Sports Participation as a Builder of Character." In *The World & I. Washington Times*, October 1988, 629–41.

—. "Value Orientations of American College Coaches Compared to Those of Male College Students and Businessmen." In *Sport and American Society: Selected Readings,* edited by George Sage, 187–228. Reading, MA: Addison-Wesley, 1974b.

Salvino, Carmen, and Frederick Klein. *Fast Lanes.* Chicago: Bonus Books, 1988.

Santayana, George. *The Last Puritan: A Memoir in the Form of a Novel.* New York: Scribner, 1936.

Scanlon, Tara K. "Antecedents of Competitiveness." In *Children in Sport: A Contemporary Anthology,* edited by Richard Magill, Michael Ash, and Frank Smoll, 53–75. Champaign IL: Human Kinetics, 1978.

Scanlon, Tara K., and Rebecca Lewthwaite. "From Stress to Enjoyment: Parental and Coach Influences on Young Participants." In *Competitive Sports for Children and Youth*, edited by Eugene Brown and Crystal Branta, 63–73. Champaign IL: Human Kinetics, 1988.

Schaaf, Phil. *Sports Inc: 100 Years of Sports Business.* Amherst NY: Prometheus Books, 2004.

Schilling, A. "Lazy Days of Summer Can Be Filled with Variety of Fun." *Sunday Post* (Vicksburg MS), 17 July 1988, B2.

Schloz, Rudiger. "Problems and Trends in Protestant Theology." In *The Scientific View of Sport: Perspectives, Aspects, Issues*, edited by Ommo Grupe et al., 81–98. New York: Springer-Verlag, 1972.

Schmitz, Kenneth. "Sport and Play: Suspension of the Ordinary." In *Philosophic Inquiry in Sport,* edited by William Morgan and Klaus Meier, 29–38. Champaign IL: Human Kinetics, 1988.

Schor, Juliet B. *The Overworked American.* New York: Basic Books, 1992.

Scott, Harvey A. "Self, Coach, and Team: A Theoretical and Empirical Application of the Social Interactionist Perspective to Teenage Sports Candidacy and Participation." Ph.D. dissertation, University of Alberta, 1973.

Scully, Gerald W. *The Business of Major League Baseball.* Chicago: University of Chicago Press, 1989.

Selznick, David O. "Hollywood's Favorite Son." *M Inc.* (July 1991): 64–71.

Shaughnessy, James D., editor. *The Roots of Ritual*. Grand Rapids MI: Eerdmans, 1973.

Sherman, Stuart P. *Points of View*. New York: Scribner, 1924.

Shermer, Michael. "Blood, Sweat, and Fears." *Skeptic Magazine* 8/1 (January 2000): 44.

Shipnuck, Alan. "Does Power Corrupt?" *Sports Illustrated* 105/9 (4 September 2006): 32–33.

Shore, K. "After-School Overload." *Clarion Ledger* (Jackson MS), 3 March 1991, E5.

Shurr, William H. *Rappaccini's Children: American Writers in a Calvinist World*. Lexington: University of Kentucky Press, 1981.

Simon, Julie, and Frank Smoll. "An Instrument for Assessing Children's Attitudes Toward Physical Activity." *Research Quarterly* 47/4 (December 1974): 407–15.

Simon, Robert L. *Fair Play: Sports, Values & Society*. Boulder CO: Westview Press, 1991.

Simonnot, Philippe. *Homo Sportivus: Sport, Capitalisme et Religion*. Paris: Gallimard, 1988.

Slusher, Howard. *Man, Sport, and Existence: A Critical Analysis*. Philadelphia: Lea & Febiger, 1967.

Smith, Kelly. "Valuing Professional Sports Franchises: An Econometric Approach." *About.com:Economics*. 2004. http://economics.about.com/library/weekly/ae043004g.htm.

Smith, Michael D. "Social Learning of Violence in Minor Hockey." In *Psychological Perspectives in Youth Sports*, edited by Frank Smoll and Ronald Smith, 91–106. Washington: Hemisphere Publishing, 1978.

Smith, Page. *Dissenting Opinions*. San Francisco: North Point Press, 1984.

Smith, Ronald. "History of Amateurism in Men's Intercollegiate Athletics: The Continuance of a 19th-Century Anachronism in America." *Quest* 45/4 (November 1993): 430–47.

Snyder, Eldon, and Elmer Spreitzer. "Correlates of Sport Participation Among Adolescent Girls." *Research Quarterly* 47/4 (December 1976): 804–809.

—. "Family Influence and Involvement in Sports." *Research Quarterly* 44/3 (October 1973): 248–55.

—. "Orientation Toward Work and Leisure as Predictors of Sports Involvement." *Research Quarterly* 45/4 (December 1974): 398–406.

Sobol, Ken. *Babe Ruth and the American Dream*. New York: Random House, 1974.

Soell, Georg. "Sport in Catholic Theology in the 20th Century." In *The Scientific View of Sport: Perspectives, Aspects, Issues*, edited by Ommo Grupe et al., 61–75. New York: Springer-Verlag, 1972.

Sokolove, Michael. *Hustle: The Myth, Life, and Lies of Pete Rose*. New York: Simon & Schuster, 1990.

Soule, George. *Economic Forces in American History*. New York: William Sloane, 1952.

Spalding, James C. "Puritanism." In *Encyclopaedia Britannica*, volume 15, 304–308. Chicago: Britannica, 1974.

Sperber, Murray A. "The College Coach as Entrepreneur." *Academe* 73/4 (July/August 1987): 30–33.

Spitz, Lewis. "Reformation." In *Dictionary of the History of Ideas*, edited by Philip Wiener, volume 4, 60–68. New York: Scribner, 1973.

Spurr, Frederick C. *The Christian Use of Leisure*. London: Kingsgate, 1935.

Staudohar, Paul. *The Sports Industry and Collective Bargaining*. Ithaca NY: I.L.R. Press, 1989.

Steinbeck, John. "Then My Arm Glassed Up." *Sports Illustrated* 23/24 (20 December 1965): 99–102.

Stern, W. "Play." In *A Treasury of Philosophy*, edited by Dagobert Runes, volume 2, 1144–46. New York: Grollier, 1955.

Stone, Gregory. "American Sports: Play and Display." In *Sport & Society: An Anthology,* edited by John T. Talamini and C. Page, 83–100. Boston: Little, Brown, 1973.

Stone, Gregory, and Harvey Farberman, editors. *Social Psychology Through Symbolic Interaction.* Waltham MA: Xerox, 1970.

Stossel, Scott. "The Tragedy of '04." *Boston Globe,* 28 August 2005, http://www.boston.com/sports/baseball/redsox/articles/2005/08/28/the_tragedy_of_04/.

Stracher, Cameron. "The Endless Summer." *Wall Street Journal,* 3 September 2004, W13.

Street, Lloyd. "Game Forms in the Factory Group." *Berkeley Publications in Society & Institutions* 4/1 (1958): 44–55.

Struna, Nancy. "Puritans and Sport: The Irretrievable Tide of Change." *Journal of Sport History* 4/1 (Spring 1977a): 1–21.

—. "Sport and Societal Values: Massachusetts Bay." *Quest* 27/4 (Winter 1977b): 38–46.

Stump, Al. *Cobb: The Life and Times of the Meanest Man Who Ever Played Baseball.* Chapel Hill NC: Algonquin Books, 1994.

Susman, Warren. "Piety, Profits, and Play." In *Men, Women, and Issues in American History,* edited by Howard Quint and Milton Cantor, volume 2, 202–27. Homewood IL: Dorsey, 1980.

Sutton, Francis X. "The Motivations and Rewards of the Business Executive." In *The American Business Creed,* edited by Francis X. Sutton et al., 99–107. New York: Shocken Books, 1956.

Sutton-Smith, Brian, John Roberts, and Robert Kozelka. "Game Involvement in Adults." In *Contemporary Readings in Sport Psychology,* edited by William Morgan, 375–82. Springfield IL: Thomas, 1970.

Swanson, Richard. "The Acceptance and Influence of Play in American Protestantism." *Quest* 11/4 (December 1968): 58–70.

Talbott, Strobe. "How *Tout le Monde* Missed the Story." *Time* 138/17 (28 October 1991): 74.

Tausky, Curt. "Meanings of Work Among Blue-Collar Men." *Pacific Sociological Review* 12/1 (Spring 1969): 49–55.

Tawney, Richard. *Religion and the Rise of Capitalism.* Gloucester MA: Peter Smith, 1962.

Teich, Mark, and Pamela Weintraub. "Ultrasport." *Omni* 7/11 (August 1985): 39–44, 96–103.

Theobald, William. "All Work Makes Jack an Executive." *Perspective: Purdue University Alumni Newsletter* (July 1984): 6.

Tozer, Malcolm. "Charles Kingsley and the 'Muscular Christian' Ideal of Manliness." *Physical Education Review* 8/1 (Spring 1985): 5–40.

Troeltsch, Ernst. *The Social Teachings of the Christian Churches.* 2 volumes. New York: Harper & Row, 1960.

Tunis, John R. *The American Way of Sport.* New York: Duell, Sloan, and Pearce, 1958.

Turner, Victor. "Liminal to Liminoid in Play, Flow, and Ritual: An Essay in Comparative Symbology." In *The Anthropological Study of Human Play* 60/3, edited by Edward Norbeck. Houston: Rice University Studies. (December 1974): 53–92.

The TV Viewers Guide to the 1984 Olympic Games. New York: Pindar Press, 1984.

Umphlett, Wiley. *The Sporting Myth and the American Experience: Studies in Contemporary Fiction.* Lewisburg PA: Bucknell University Press, 1975.

Van den Berghe, Pierre. *Race and Racism: A Cultural Perspective.* New York: Wiley, 1967.

Veblen, Thorstein. "The Case of America: The Self-Made Man." In *Absentee Ownership and Business Enterprise in Recent Times,* edited by Thorstein Veblen, 119–65. New York: Huebsch, 1923.

—. *The Theory of the Leisure Class.* Minerva Press edition. New York: Funk & Wagnalls, 1899.

Veysey, Laurence. *The Emergence of the American University* (Chicago: University of Chicago Press, 1970).

"'Virtual Reality' Networks Link Worlds." *Clarion Ledger* (Jackson MS), 1 April 1992, B8.

Voeller, Edward. *Sport Climbing.* Mankato MN: Capstone Press, 2000.

Voigt, David Q. *America Through Baseball.* Chicago: Nelson Hall, 1976.

Voobus, Arthur. "Asceticism." In *Encyclopaedia Britannica*, volume 2, 135–37. Chicago: Britannica, 1974.

Wagenheim, Kal. *Clemente!* New York: Praeger Publishers, 1973.

Wagner, Helmut. "The Protestant Ethic: A Mid-Twentieth Century View." *Sociological Analysis* 25/1 (Spring 1964): 34–41.

Walker, Amasa. "Wealth and the Division of Labor." 1866. In *The Annals of America*, volume 10, 66–73. Chicago: Britannica, 1968.

Walzer, Michael. "Puritanism as a Revolutionary Ideology." In *The Protestant Ethic and Modernization*, edited by Samuel N. Eisenstadt, 109–34. New York: Basic Books, 1968.

—. *The Revolution of the Saints: A Study in the Origins of Radical Politics.* Cambridge MA: Harvard University Press, 1965.

Wartella, Ellen, and Sharon Mazzarella. "A Historical Comparison of Children's Use of Leisure Time." In *For Fun and Profit,* edited by Richard Butsch, 173–94. Philadelphia: Temple University Press, 1990.

Watkins, Billy. "What Polk Is All About." *Clarion Ledger/Jackson* (MS) *Daily News*, 17 April 1988, D1.

Watson, Geoffrey. "Game Interaction in Little League Baseball and Family Organization." Ph.D. dissertation, University of Illinois, 1973.

Watson, Goodwin. *Social Psychology: Issues and Insights.* Philadelphia: Lippincott, 1966.

Wattenberg, Ben J. "Do Americans Believe in Anything Anymore?" *Esquire* 102/5 (November 1984): 78–89.

Weaver, Robert B. *Amusements and Sports in American Life.* New York: Greenwood Press, 1968.

Webb, Harry. "Professionalization of Attitudes toward Play Among Adolescents." In *Aspects of Contemporary Sport Sociology,* edited by Gerald Kenyon, 161–78. Chicago: The Athletic Institute, 1969.

Weber, Max. *Essay on Sociology.* Translated by Hans Gerth and C. Wright Mills. New York: Oxford University Press, 1958b.

—. *The Protestant Ethic and the Spirit of Capitalism.* Translated by Talcott Parsons. New York: Scribner, 1958a.

—. *The Theory of Social and Economic Organization.* Translated by A. M. Henderson and Talcott Parsons. New York: Free Press, 1947.

Wegener, Albert B. *Church and Community Recreation.* New York: Macmillan, 1924.

Weiss, Maureen R., V. M. Wiese, and K. A. Kline. "Head over Heels with Success: The Relationship Between Self-Efficacy and Performance in Competitive Young Gymnasts." *Journal of Sport & Exercise Psychology* 11/4 (December 1989): 444–51.

Whan, Vorin E., Jr. *A Soldier Speaks: Public Papers and Speeches of General of the Army Douglas MacArthur.* New York: Praeger, 1965.

Whitney, Caspar. "Evolution of the Country Club." 1894. In *The Annals of America*, volume 11, 555–57. Chicago: Britannica, 1968.

Whitson, David. "Sport and Hegemony: On the Construction of the Dominant Culture." *Sociology of Sport Journal* l/1 (March 1984): 64–78.

Whyte, William H. *The Organization Man.* Garden City NY: Doubleday, 1956.

Wieberg, Steve. "For Players' Parents, Few Perks from NCAA." *USA Today* (30 March 1–April 2007): 1–2.

Williams, Robin M. *American Society: A Sociological Interpretation* (New York: Knopf, 1970).

Willison, George F. *Saints and Strangers.* Chicago: Time-Life Books, 1964.

Wilson, R. "Pay Attention, Football Dads." *Jackson* (MS) *Daily News*, 10 December 1986, D7.

Wohl, Andrzej. "Competitive Sport and Its Social Functions." *International Review of Sport Sociology* 5/1 (March 1970): 117–32.

—. "Prognostic Models of Sport in Socialist Countries on the Background of Changes in Sport in Peoples' Poland." *International Review of Sport Sociology* 6/1 (March 1971): 17–47.

Wolfenstein, Martha. "The Emergence of Fun Morality." In *Mass Leisure*, edited by Eric Larrabee and Rolf Meyerson, 86–97. Glencoe IL: The Free Press, 1958.

Wood, Chris. "The Perils of Doping." *Maclean's* 105/30 (27 July 1992): 48–53.

Woodruff, Everett. "Steam Power." In *Encyclopaedia Britannica*, volume 17, 624–33. Chicago: Britannica, 1974.

Woodward, S. "Focus, Funding Top Items on Organization's Agenda." *USA Today* (11 November 1988): C3.

Yagoda, Ben. "Fitness Without Tears." *Esquire* 101/2 (August 1983): 31–32.

Yang, C. K. "Introduction." In Max Weber, *The Religion of China,* i–xviii. New York: The Free Press, 1951.

Yarbrough, Richard. *And They Call Them Games.* Atlanta: Mercer University Press, 2000.

Zamiatin, Yevgeny. *We.* Translated by Gregory Zilboorg. New York: Dutton, 1952.

Zirin, Dave. "Varsity Ruse: High School Football Today." *Edge of Sports*, 27 August 2006, http://www.edgeofsports.com/2006-08-27-197/index.html.

Notes

[1] Max Weber, *The Protestant Ethic and the Spirit of Capitalism*, trans. Talcott Parsons (New York: Scribner, 1958a).

[2] Quoted in Gordon Marshall, *In Search of the Spirit of Capitalism: An Essay on Max Weber's Protestant Ethic Thesis* (New York: Columbia University Press, 1982) 151.

[3] Gianfranco Poggi, *Calvinism and the Capitalist Spirit: Max Weber's Protestant Ethic* (Amherst: University of Massachusetts Press, 1983) 55.

[4] Marshall, *In Search of the Spirit of Capitalism*, 100, 161.

[5] Gino Germani, "Secularization, Modernization, and Economic Development," in *The Protestant Ethic and Modernization*, ed. Samuel N. Eisenstadt (New York: Basic Books: New York, 1968) 345; Talcott Parsons, "Belief, Unbelief, and Disbelief," in *The Culture of Unbelief*, eds. Rocco Caporale and Antonio Grumelli (Berkeley: University of California Press, 1971) 207–35; Lonnie D. Kliever, "God and Games in Modern Culture," in *The World & I, Washington Times,* October 1988, 561–72.

[6] Parsons, "Belief, Unbelief, and Disbelief," 243.

[7] Kliever, "God and Games in Modern Culture," 565; Roger Mehl, *The Sociology of Protestantism*, trans. James H. Farley (Philadelphia: Westminster Press, 1970) 208.

[8] Talcott Parsons, "Max Weber's Analysis of Capitalism and Modern Institutions," in *An Introduction to the History of Sociology*, ed. Harry E. Barnes (Chicago: University of Chicago Press, 1948) 256.

[9] Bennett Berger, "The Sociology of Leisure," *Industrial Relations: A Journal of Economy and Society* 1/1 (February 1962): 45.

[10] Leonard Koppett, *Sports Illusion, Sports Reality: A Reporter's View of Sports, Journalism, and Society*, 2nd ed. (Champaign IL: University of Illinois Press, 1994) 173, 191.

[11] Robert K. Merton, *Science, Technology & Society in Seventeenth Century England* (New York: Howard Fertig, 1970).

[12] Thorstein Veblen, *The Theory of the Leisure Class,* Minerva Press ed. (New York: Funk & Wagnalls, 1899) 211.

[13] Merton, *Science, Technology & Society.*

[14] David McClelland, *The Achieving Society* (New York: Macmillan, 1961) 16–17, 391.

[15] John Neulinger, *The Psychology of Leisure* (Springfield IL: Thomas, 1974) 101.

[16] Harry Edwards, "Desegregating Sexist Sport," *Intellectual Digest* 3/1 (November 1972): 90.

[17] Günther Lueschen, "The Interdependence of Sport and Culture," in *International Review of Sport Sociology* 2/1 (1967): 127–42.

[18] D. Stanley Eitzen and George Sage, *Sociology of American Sport* (Dubuque IA: Brown, 1982) 156.

[19] The theme of sport as religion is explored in Shirl J. Hoffman, ed., *Sport and Religion* (Champaign IL: Human Kinetics, 1992); for a functionalist view, see Brian Milton, "Sport as Functional Equivalent of Religion" (M.S. thesis, University of Wisconsin, 1972). See also Jay Coakley, *Sports in Society: Issues and Controversies*. 8th ed. (New York: McGraw-Hill, 2004) 532–34.

[20] See Kendall Blanchard and Alyce Cheska, *The Anthropology of Sport: An Introduction* (Hadley MA: Bergin & Garvey, 1985).

[21] Linwood Fredericksen, "Feast and Festival," in *Encyclopaedia Britannica*, vol. 7 (Chicago: Britannica, 1974) 202; A bucolic version of this theme appears in a monologue by the American comedian Andy Griffith titled, "What It Was, Was Football," http://www.youtube.com/watch?v=aKSo7QO7ceo (accessed 9 November 2009).

[22] Michael Novak, *The Joy of Sports* (New York: Basic Books, 1976) 19–24, 31, 284; Howard Slusher, *Man, Sport and Existence: A Critical Analysis* (Philadelphia: Lea & Febiger, 1967) 10, 121–29.

[23] Ibid.

[24] Thorstein Veblen, *The Theory of the Leisure Class,* Minerva Press ed. (New York: Funk & Wagnalls, 1899) 186, 227, 230–35; Georg Soell, "Sport in Catholic Theology in the 20th Century," in *The Scientific View of Sport: Perspectives, Aspects, Issues,* ed. Ommo Grupe et al. (New York: Springer-Verlag, 1972) 71.

[25] Michael Shermer, "Blood, Sweat and Fears," *Skeptic Magazine* 8/1 (January 2000): 44.

[26] Joseph Price, "The Super Bowl as Religious Festival," in Hoffman, *Sport and Religion*, 13–15; Joseph Price, *From Season to Season: Sports as American Religion* (Macon GA: Mercer University Press, 2001).

[27] Johan Huizinga, *Homo Ludens: A Study of the Play Element in Culture*, 7th ed. (Boston: Beacon Press, 1968) 197.

[28] Robert J. Higgs, "Muscular Christianity, Holy Play and Spiritual Exercises: Confusion about Christ in Sports and Religion," *Arete* 1/1 (Fall 1983): 81.

[29] Allen Guttmann, *From Ritual to Record: The Nature of Modern Sports* (New York: Columbia University Press, 1978) 54–55.

[30] See Ernst Fischer, *How to Read Karl Marx* (New York: Monthly Review Press, 1996).

[31] See Bambery, "Marxism and Sport," *International Socialism* 73/4 (December 1996): 35–54; Paul Hoch, *Rip Off the Big Game: The Exploitation of Sports by the Power Elite* (New York: Doubleday, 1972) 36–45.

[32] Richard Gruneau, *Class, Sports and Social Development* (Amherst: University of Massachusetts Press, 1983) 9.

[33] Quoted in Marshall, *In Search of the Spirit of Capitalism, 151.*

[34] John Loy, "The Cultural System of Sport," *Quest* 29/4 (Winter 1978): 78.

[35] Guttmann, *From Ritual to Record, 79–80.*

[36] Christopher Lasch, *The Culture of Narcissism: American Life in an Age of Diminishing Expectations* (New York: Norton, 1978) 115.

[37] Heinz Meyer, "Puritanism and Physical Training: Ideological and Political Accents in the Christian Interpretation of Sport," *International Review of Sport Sociology* 8/1 (March 1973): 37–51.

[38] George Sage, "American Values and Sport: Formation of a Bureaucratic Personality," *Journal of Physical Education and Recreation* 49/8 (October 1978): 10; John McMurtry, "The Illusions of a Football Fan: A Reply to Michalos," in *Sport Inside Out: Readings in Literature and Philosophy*, eds. David Vanderwerken and Spencer Wertz (Fort Worth: Texas Christian University Press, 1985) 241–44.

[39] McMurtry, "The Illusions of a Football Fan," 241.

[40] Weber, *The Protestant Ethic*, chapter 2.

[41] Novak, *The Joy of Sports*, 18*ff.*

[42] Brian Martin, "Design Flaws of the Olympics," *Social Alternatives* 19/2 (April 2000): 20.

[43] Ibid.

[44] See Philippe Simonnot, *Homo Sportivus: Sport, Capitalisme et Religion* (Paris: Gallimard, 1988), and John Bale and Mette Krogh Christensen, eds., *Post-Olympism? Questioning Sport in the Twenty-First Century* (Oxford, UK: Berg, 2004) 148–49.

[45] Quoted in Simonnot, *Homo Sportivus,* 84.

[46] Blanchard and Cheska, *The Anthropology of Sport,* 35, 55.

[47] See Hoffman, *Sport and Religion*; Novak, *The Joy of Sports*; Robert Higgs, *God in the Stadium: Sport and Religion in America* (Lexington KY: University of Kentucky Press, 1995).

[48] Notably Allen Guttmann, *A Whole New Ball Game: An Interpretation of American Sports* (Chapel Hill: University of North Carolina Press, 1988); Eitzen and Sage, *Sociology of American Sport*; and Harry Edwards, *Sociology of Sport* (Homewood IL: Dorsey Press, 1973).

[49] Sydney Ahlstrom, *A Religious History of the American People* (New Haven: Yale University Press, 1972) 25; Lewis Spitz, "Reformation," in *Dictionary of the History of Ideas*, ed. Philip Wiener, vol. 4 (New York: Scribners, 1973) 60.

[50] T. Scott Miyakawa, *Protestants and Pioneers: Individualism and Conformity on the American Frontier* (Chicago: University of Chicago Press, 1964) 78. See also Michael Walzer, *The Revolution of the Saints: A Study in the Origins of Radical Politics* (Cambridge MA: Harvard University Press, 1965).

[51] See Roger Mehl, *The Sociology of Protestantism*, trans. James H. Farley (Philadelphia: Westminster Press, 1970); Talcott Parsons, *The Structure of Social Action* (New York: The Free Press, 1937) 524, 571.

[52] Mehl, *The Sociology of Protestantism,* 109–20; Phillip Hammond and Kirk Williams, "The Protestant Ethic Thesis: A Social-psychological Assessment," *Social Forces* 54/3 (March 1976): 579–80. See also Walzer, *The Revolution of the Saints,* 218*ff.*

[53] John T. McNeill, *The History and Character of Calvinism* (London: Oxford University Press, 1954) xiii; Herbert Luethy, "Once Again: Calvinism and Capitalism," in *The Protestant Ethic and Modernization,* ed. Samuel N. Eisenstadt (New York: Basic Books, 1968) 103–105.

[54] McNeill, *The History and Character of Calvinism,* 201*ff.*; Calvin quoted, 233.

[55] Kemper Fullerton, "Calvinism and Capitalism: An Explanation of the Weber Thesis," in *Protestantism, Capitalism, and Social Science,* ed. Robert Green (Lexington MA: Heath, 1973) 23.

[56] John Carroll, *Puritan, Paranoid, Remissive: A Sociology of Modern Culture* (London: Routledge & Kegan Paul, 1977) 3–4; John T. McNeill, ed., *On the Christian Faith: Selections From the Institutes, Commentaries and Tracts of John Calvin* (Indianapolis IN: Bobbs-Merrill, 1957) 42–43; Max Weber, *The Protestant Ethic and the Spirit of Capitalism,* trans. Talcott Parsons (New York: Scribner, 1958a) 98.

[57] Carroll, *Puritan, Paranoid, Remissive,* 127.

[58] Parsons, *The Structure of Social Action*, 524.

[59] Ibid., 525; McNeill, *The History and Character of Calvinism*, 222–23.

[60] Charles George and Katherine George, "Protestantism and Capitalism in Pre-revolutionary England," in *Church History* 27 (1958): 351–71; Fullerton, "Calvinism and Capitalism," 10–14; Gordon Marshall, *In Search of the Spirit of Capitalism: An Essay on Max Weber's Protestant Ethic Thesis* (New York: Columbia University Press, 1982) 72, 80.

[61] Weber, *The Protestant Ethic*, 2.

[62] Quoted in McNeill, *On the Christian Faith*, 81.

[63] In Moses Rischen, ed., *The American Gospel of Success: Individualism and Beyond* (New York: Franklin Watts, 1974) 22–23.

[64] See McNeill, *On the Christian Faith*; Richard Tawney, *Religion and the Rise of Capitalism* (Gloucester MA: Peter Smith, 1962) 240; Marshall, *In Search of the Spirit of Capitalism*, 92–93.

[65] Ernst Troeltsch, *The Social Teachings of the Christian Churches*, 2 vols. (New York: Harper & Row, 1960) 607–11; Walzer, *The Revolution of the Saints*, 215–18; Fullerton, "Calvinism and Capitalism," 14–15.

[66] Mordechai Rotenberg, *Damnation and Deviance: The Protestant Ethic and the Spirit of Failure* (New York: Free Press, 1978) 10–11.

[67] Marshall, *In Search of the Spirit of Capitalism*, 78, 101; Weber, *The Protestant Ethic*, 112–15; Walzer, *The Revolution of the Saints*, 214.

[68] In McNeill, *On the Christian Faith*, 72.

[69] Jan Loubser, "Calvinism, Equality, and Inclusion: The Case of Afrikaner Calvinism," in *The Protestant Ethic and Modernization,* ed. Samuel N. Eisenstadt (New York: Basic Books, 1968) 372; Troeltsch, *The Social Teachings of the Christian Churches*, 602.

[70] Van Wyck Brooks, *The Wine of the Puritans* (London: Sisley's, 1908) 56.

[71] John Bunyan, *The Pilgrim's Progress* (Norwalk CT: The Heritage Press, 1969) 37.

[72] Troeltsch, *The Social Teachings of the Christian Churches*, 611.

[73] Tawney, *Religion and the Rise of Capitalism*, 117; McNeill, *The History and Character of Calvinism*, 165.

[74] Bruce C. Daniels, *Puritans at Play: Leisure and Recreation in Colonial New England* (New York: St. Martin's, 1995) 176–81; McNeill, *The History and Character of Calvinism*, 166, 195.

[75] Miyakawa, *Protestants and Pioneers*, 79; Daniel Bell, *The Cultural Contradictions of Capitalism* (New York: Basic Books, 1976) 61.

[76] Weber, *The Protestant Ethic*, 105; Parsons, *The Structure of Social Action*, 523; Tawney, *Religion and the Rise of Capitalism*, 228.

[77] Parsons, *The Structure of Social Action*, 523; Walzer, *The Revolution of the Saints*, 169.

[78] See Carroll, *Puritan, Paranoid, Remissive*, 3–11.

[79] The concepts of Puritanism and Calvinism can be kept distinct in their earliest incarnations in the sixteenth century. After that, particularly on the American scene, Puritanism is the most generic description for the culture that evolved, while Calvin remained the dominant figure. Critics generally agree about the set of primary forces that have molded American culture. Whether it should be called "Puritanism" or "Calvinism" need not be pressed too sharply. The terms "Puritanism" and "Calvinism" will be used interchangeably

by this author. See William H. Shurr, *Rappaccini's Children: American Writers in a Calvinist World* (Lexington: University of Kentucky Press, 1981) 12–13.

[80] Tawney, *Religion and the Rise of Capitalism*, 203; Michael Walzer, "Puritanism as a Revolutionary Ideology," in *The Protestant Ethic and Modernization*, ed. Samuel N. Eisenstadt (New York: Basic Books, 1968) 119; Martin Marty, *Protestantism* (New York: Holt, Rinehart & Winston, 1972) 31–33.

[81] Ralph B. Perry, *Puritanism and Democracy* (New York: Vanguard, 1944) 245, 255–57, 263–68.

[82] In James A. Morone, *Hellfire Nation: The Politics of Sin in American History* (New Haven: Yale University Press, 2003) 127.

[83] John Carroll, *Puritan, Paranoid, Remissive*, 6–11.

[84] Ibid. See also Walzer, *The Revolution of the Saints*, 308.

[85] Loubser, "Calvinism, Equality, and Inclusion," 373, 377; Tawney, *Religion and the Rise of Capitalism*, 230; Walzer, "Puritanism as a Revolutionary Ideology," 307; Ahlstrom, *A Religious History of the American People*, 80.

[86] Walzer, "Puritanism as a Revolutionary Ideology," 126; Marshall, *In Search of the Spirit of Capitalism*, 79; Dennis Brailsford, *Sport and Society: Elizabeth to Anne* (London: Routledge & Kegan Paul, 1969) 141.

[87] Bell, *The Cultural Contradictions of Capitalism*, 57–60; Joseph Kett, *Rites of Passage: Adolescence in America 1790 to the Present* (New York: Basic Books, 1977) 47, 56; Philip Greven, *The Protestant Temperament: Patterns of Child-Rearing, Religious Experience, and the Self in Early America* (New York: Knopf, 1977) 146.

[88] Ahlstrom, *A Religious History of the American People*, 146; Perry, *Puritanism and Democracy,* 107, 245.

[89] Greven, *The Protestant Temperament*, 227; William H. Shurr, *Rappaccini's Children: American Writers in a Calvinist World* (Lexington: University of Kentucky Press, 1981) 6–8.

[90] Max Lerner, *America as a Civilization: Life and Thought in the United States Today* (New York: Simon and Schuster, 1957) 471.

[91] Nancy Struna, "Puritans and Sport: The Irretrievable Tide of Change," *Journal of Sport History* 4/1 (Spring 1977a): 6.

[92] See Edmund S. Morgan, *Visible Saints: The History of a Puritan Idea* (Ithaca NY: Cornell University Press, 1963).

[93] Tawney, *Religion and the Rise of Capitalism*, 229; Brooks, *The Wine of the Puritans*, 14–15.

[94] Tawney, *Religion and the Rise of Capitalism*, 201, 230; Walzer, *The Revolution of the Saints*, 148.

[95] Sacvan Bercovitch, *The Puritan Origins of the American Self* (New Haven CT: Yale University Press, 1975) 21; George and George, "Protestantism and Capitalism in Pre-revolutionary England," 351–71.

[96] Perry, *Puritanism and Democracy*, 297–98; Tawney, *Religion and the Rise of Capitalism*, 211.

[97] Heinz Meyer, "Puritanism and Physical Training: Ideological and Political Accents in the Christian Interpretation of Sport," *International Review of Sport Sociology* 8/1 (March 1973): 40.

[98] Shurr, *Rappaccini's Children*, 16, 31.

[99] Carroll, *Puritan, Paranoid, Remissive*, 22ff.

[100] Erich Geldbach, *Sport und Protestantismus: Geschichte einer Begegnung* (Wuppertal, Germany: Theologischer Verlag R. Brockhaus, 1975) 47.

[101] Brailsford, *Sport and Society*; Struna, "Puritans and Sport," 1–21; Nancy Struna, "Sport and Societal Values: Massachusetts Bay," *Quest* 27/4 (Winter 1977b): 38–46; Geldbach, *Sport und Protestantismus*, chapters 3–4.

[102] In Brailsford, *Sport and Society*, 97.

[103] Ibid., 144; Geldbach, *Sport und Protestantismus*, 56–57.

[104] Quoted in Geldbach, *Sport und Protestantismus*, 48.

[105] In Brailsford, *Sport and Society*, 144–47.

[106] Quoted in J. K. Ruhl, "Puritanism and Sport—the Classical and Scriptural Heritage of Several Principles in the Modern Conception of Sport," *Sport and Religion: The History of Sport and the Physical Education in the Iberian Cultures* (Lisbon: Instituto Nacional Dos Desportos, 1981) 304.

[107] In Geldbach, *Sport und Protestantismus*, 49–51.

[108] Brailsford, *Sport and Society*, 127–30.

[109] Geldbach, *Sport und Protestantismus*, 51–52.

[110] Brailsford, *Sport and Society*, 140–44; Rudiger Schloz, "Problems and Trends in Protestant Theology," in *The Scientific View of Sport: Perspectives, Aspects, Issues*, ed. Ommo Grupe et al. (New York: Springer-Verlag, 1972) 87.

[111] Brailsford, *Sport and Society*, 132–33.

[112] Foster R. Dulles, *A History of Recreation: America Learns to Play* (New York: Appleton-Century-Crofts, 1965) 9–10.

[113] Reprinted in Steven A. Riess, ed., *The American Sporting Experience: A Historical Anthology of Sport in America* (New York: Leisure Press, 1984) 12–14.

[114] J. Thomas Jable, "The English Puritans—Suppressors of Sport and Amusement?" *Canadian Journal of History of Sport and Physical and Physical Education* 7/5 (May 1976): 39; Weber, *The Protestant Ethic*, 166–67; Dulles, *A History of Recreation*, 12.

[115] McNeill, *The History and Character of Calvinism*, 337; James C. Spalding, "Puritanism," *Encyclopaedia Britannica*, vol. 15 (Chicago: Britannica, 1974) 306–307; Ahlstrom, *A Religious History of the American People*, 124.

[116] Clifton Olmstead, *Religion in America: Past and Present* (Englewood Cliffs NJ: Prentice-Hall, 1961) 24.

[117] Dulles, *A History of Recreation*, 12–13.

[118] Ibid., 4–5.

[119] Ibid., 4–6, 13; Olmstead, *Religion in America*, 24.

[120] Struna, "Sport and Societal Values," 5–7.

[121] Charles Neider, ed., *The Complete Tales of Washington Irving* (New York: Doubleday, 1975); Christian Messenger, *Sport and the Spirit of Play in American Fiction: Hawthorne to Faulkner* (New York: Columbia University Press, 1981) 39–44.

[122] See George F. Willison, *Saints and Strangers* (Chicago: Time-Life Books, 1964); Dulles, *A History of Recreation*, 16, 19.

[123] Bell, *The Cultural Contradictions of Capitalism*, 57. See Struna, "Sport and Societal Values," 38–46.

[124] Daniel Boorstin, *The Americans: The Colonial Experience* (New York: Random House, 1958) 28; Struna, "Puritans and Sport," 14–18.

[125] In Struna, "Sport and Societal Values," 5–7.

[126] Meyer, "Puritanism and Physical Training," 39–43. See Struna, "Puritans and Sport," 1–21, and "Sport and Societal Values," 38–46.

[127] See Struna, "Puritans and Sport," 1-21; Geldbach, *Sport und Protestantismus*, 48–49.

[128] Struna, "Puritans and Sport," 2, 7–14; Struna, "Sport and Societal Values," 40.

[129] See Daniels, *Puritans at Play*, 17–19, for a discussion of Colman's views.

[130] Brailsford, *Sport and Society*, 141.

[131] Geldbach, *Sport und Protestantismus,* 35–58.

[132] Jable, "The English Puritans—Suppressors of Sport and Amusement?" 33–40.

[133] Messenger, *Sport and the Spirit of Play in American Fiction*, 312.

[134] Olmstead, *Religion in America*, 46; Dulles, *A History of Recreation*, 86–90; Ahlstrom, *A Religious History of the American People*, 236–39.

[135] Max Weber, *The Protestant Ethic and the Spirit of Capitalism*, trans. Talcott Parsons (New York: Scribner, 1958a) chapter 2.

[136] C. K. Yang, "Introduction," in Max Weber's *The Religion of China* (New York: The Free Press, 1951) xv.

[137] See Howard Becker and Alvin Boskoff, eds., *Modern Sociological Theory in Continuity and Change* (New York: Holt, Rinehart & Winston: 1966) 478–79 for reference to Sombart and Sorokin; Gordon Marshall, *In Search of the Spirit of Capitalism: An Essay on Max Weber's Protestant Ethic Thesis* (New York: Columbia University Press, 1982).

[138] Weber, *The Protestant Ethic*, chapter 2.

[139] Ibid., 120–22.

[140] Ibid., 156–60.

[141] Ibid., 62; Max Lerner, *America as a Civilization: Life and Thought in the United States Today* (New York: Simon and Schuster, 1957) 46; Marshall, *In Search of the Spirit of Capitalism,* 129.

[142] Marshall, *In Search of the Spirit of Capitalism*, 145, 155.

[143] Michael Walzer, *The Revolution of the Saints: A Study in the Origins of Radical Politics* (Cambridge MA: Harvard University Press, 1965) 303*ff.*

[144] Max Weber, *Essay on Sociology,* trans. Hans Gerth and C. Wright Mills (New York: Oxford University Press, 1958b) 321; Kemper Fullerton, "Calvinism and Capitalism: An Explanation of the Weber Thesis," in *Protestantism, Capitalism, and Social Science,* ed. Robert Green (Lexington MA: Heath, 1973) 29.

[145] James Fulcher, *Capitalism: A Very Short Introduction* (Oxford, UK: Oxford University Press, 2004) 2, 37; Richard Tawney, *Religion and the Rise of Capitalism* (Gloucester MA: Peter Smith, 1962) 57*ff.*

[146] Fulcher, *Capitalism*, 3–9.

[147] Ibid., 3–9, 107–108.

[148] See John R. Betts, "The Technological Revolution and the Rise of Sport, 1850–1900," in *The American Sporting Experience: A Historical Anthology of Sport in America,* ed. Steven Riess (New York: Leisure Press, 1984) 141–57, for a description of the American experience.

[149] Fulcher, *Capitalism*, 9–21, 39–42.

[150] Ibid., 66–68.

[151] Joel Bakan, *The Corporation: The Pathological Pursuit of Profit and Power* (New York: Free Press, 2004) 6, 10–14.

[152] Alexis de Tocqueville, *Democracy in America*, 1835, 1840 (New York: Knopf, 1956) 213–17*ff.*

[153] David McClelland, *The Achieving Society* (New York: Macmillan, 1961) 207.

[154] Gianfranco Poggi, *Calvinism and the Capitalist Spirit: Max Weber's Protestant Ethic* (Amherst: University of Massachusetts Press, 1983) 47; Gino Germani, "Secularization, Modernization, and Economic Development," in *The Protestant Ethic and Modernization*, ed. Samuel N. Eisenstadt (New York: Basic Books: New York, 1968) 351.

[155] Tawney, *Religion and the Rise of Capitalism*, 245.

[156] Weber, *The Protestant Ethic*, xiii–xvii. See also the section on Marx and Weber in chapter 6 of Gordon Marshall, *In Search of the Spirit of Capitalism: An Essay on Max Weber's Protestant Ethic Thesis* (New York: Columbia University Press, 1982) 55–68.

[157] Tawney, *Religion and the Rise of Capitalism*, 32–37, 81, 92. See also Kemper Fullerton, "Calvinism and Capitalism: An Explanation of the Weber Thesis," in *Protestantism, Capitalism, and Social Science,* ed. Robert Green (Lexington MA: Heath, 1973) 8–31.

[158] Tawney, *Religion and the Rise of Capitalism*, 221, 239, 246–49; Michael Walzer, *The Revolution of the Saints: A Study in the Origins of Radical Politics* (Cambridge MA: Harvard University Press, 1965) 212.

[159] Tawney, *Religion and the Rise of Capitalism*, 280.

[160] Fullerton, "Calvinism and Capitalism," 8–9; Tawney, *Religion and the Rise of Capitalism*, 107–108, 213–23.

[161] Quoted in James A. Morone, *Hellfire Nation: The Politics of Sin in American History* (New Haven: Yale University Press, 2003) 493.

[162] Poggi, *Calvinism and the Capitalist Spirit*, 40–41. See also Weber, *The Protestant Ethic,* chapter 2.

[163] Robin M. Williams, *American Society: A Sociological Interpretation* (New York: Knopf, 1970) 370; Marshall, *In Search of the Spirit of Capitalism*, 64–65. See also Gerhard Lenski, *The Religious Factor: A Sociological Study of Religion's Impact on Politics, Economics, and Family Life* (Garden City NY: Doubleday, 1961).

[164] John K. Galbraith, "What Tact the Press Showed!" *New York Times*, 22 December 1987. http://www.nytimes.com/1987/12/22/opinion/what-tact-the-press-showed.html.

[165] Quoted in *American Values: Opposing Viewpoints*, ed. David Bender (St. Paul MN: Greenhaven Press, 1984) 140.

[166] Ibid., 140–44.

[167] Karl Polanyi, *The Great Transformation* (New York: Rinehart, 1944) 133.

[168] George Soule, *Economic Forces in American History* (New York: William Sloane, 1952) 41–43.

[169] Ibid. See also Tawney, *Religion and the Rise of Capitalism*, 233–34, for the European legacy.

[170] Thorstein Veblen, "The Case of America: The Self-Made Man," in *Absentee Ownership and Business Enterprise in Recent Times,* ed. Thorstein Veblen (New York:

Huebsch, 1923) 119*ff.*; Richard Hofstadter, *The Age of Reform* (New York: Knopf, 1956) 24, 36.

[171] Poggi, *Calvinism and the Capitalist Spirit*, 32.

[172] Daniel Boorstin, *The Americans: The National Experience* (New York: Random House, 1965) 115–23.

[173] Van Wyck Brooks, *The Wine of the Puritans* (London: Sisley's, 1908) 19.

[174] Peter Filene, "Manhood in the Twenties: Was It So Great to Be Gatsby?" *Ms.* 11/12 (June 1974) 12–18.

[175] Nichols, "Work and Play in America," 541.

[176] Juliet B. Schor, *The Overworked American* (New York: Basic Books, 1992) 112.

[177] Thomas L. Nichols, "Work and Play in America," 1864, in *The Annals of America*, vol. 9 (Chicago: Britannica, 1968) 541; H. Richard Niebuhr, "The Captive Church," *The Annals of America*, vol. 15 (Chicago: Britannica, 1968) 341–44.

[178] Otto Bremer, "Business Is the Source of America's Values," in *American Values*, ed. David Bender (St. Paul MN: Greenhaven Press, 1984) 150–54.

[179] Benjamin Nelson, "Weber's Protestant Ethic: Its Origins, Wanderings, and Foreseeable Futures," in *Beyond the Classics? Essays in the Scientific Study of Religion,* eds. Charles Glock and Phillip Hammond (New York: Harper & Row, 1973) 80.

[180] Herbert Mirels and James Garrett, "The Protestant Ethic as a Personality Variable," *Journal of Counseling and Clinical Psychology* 36/1 (1971): 40–44.

[181] A. P. MacDonald, Jr., "More on the Protestant Ethic," *Journal of Consulting and Clinical Psychology* 39/1 (February 1972): 116–22.

[182] Jerald Greenberg, "The Protestant Work Ethic and Reactions to Negative Performance Evaluations on a Laboratory Task," *Journal of Applied Psychology* 62/6 (December 1977): 682–90; Jerald Greenberg, "Equity, Equality, and the Protestant Ethic: Allocating Rewards Following Fair and Unfair Competition," *Journal of Experimental and Social Psychology* 14/2 (1978a): 217–26; Jerald Greenberg, "Protestant Ethic Endorsement and Attitudes Toward Commuting to Work Among Mass Transit Riders," *Journal of Applied Psychology* 63/6 (1978b): 755–58.

[183] Frederick Chino, "Family Status, Protestant Ethic and Level of Occupational Aspiration" (Ph.D. diss., Stanford University, 1965).

[184] Yang, "Introduction," i–xviii.

[185] Bernice Goldstein, "The Changing Protestant Ethic: Rural Patterns in Health, Work, and Leisure" (Ph.D. diss., Purdue University, 1959).

[186] Ernst Troeltsch, *The Social Teachings of the Christian Churches*, 2 vols. (New York: Harper & Row, 1960).

[187] T. Scott Miyakawa, *Protestants and Pioneers: Individualism and Conformity on the American Frontier* (Chicago: University of Chicago Press, 1964).

[188] Helmut Wagner, "The Protestant Ethic: A Mid-twentieth Century View," *Sociological Analysis* XXV/1 (Spring 1964): 34–41.

[189] Chino, "Family Status."

[190] Seymour Lipset, *The First New Nation: The United States in Historical and Comparative Perspective* (New York: Doubleday, 1967).

[191] Daniel Bell, *The Cultural Contradictions of Capitalism* (New York: Basic Books, 1976).

[192] Bronwyn Boekenstein, "A Study of the Existence of Attributes of the Protestant Work Ethic in Leisure Participation" (M.S. thesis, University of Oregon, 1976).

[193] Greenberg, "Protestant Ethic Endorsement," 755–58.

[194] Mordechai Rotenberg, *Damnation and Deviance: The Protestant Ethic and the Spirit of Failure* (New York: Free Press, 1978) 94, 146–48.

[195] Werner Jaeger, *Paideia: The Ideals of Greek Culture*, vol. 2 (New York: Oxford University Press, 1943) 53; Peter Brown, *The Body and Society: Men, Women and Sexual Renunciation in Early Christianity* (New York: Columbia University Press, 1988) 37–38.

[196] Arthur Voobus, "Asceticism," *Encyclopaedia Britannica*, vol. 2 (Chicago: Britannica, 1974) 135–37. See also Brown, *The Body and Society*.

[197] Brown, *The Body and Society*, 222, 249; Fred Leonard, *A Guide to the History of Physical Education* (Philadelphia: Lea & Febiger, 1947) 37–39.

[198] Miyakawa, *Protestants and Pioneers*, 77–78.

[199] Fullerton, "Calvinism and Capitalism, 15; Roger Mehl, *The Sociology of Protestantism,* trans. James H. Farley (Philadelphia: Westminster Press, 1970) 120; David Martin, *A General Theory of Secularization* (New York: Harper & Row, 1978) 61.

[200] In Walzer, *The Revolution of the Saints*, 166.

[201] Max Weber, *The Theory of Social and Economic Organization*, trans. A. M. Henderson and Talcott Parsons (New York: Free Press, 1947) 80; Weber, *Essay on Sociology*, 325; Richard Tawney, *Religion and the Rise of Capitalism* (Gloucester MA: Peter Smith, 1962) 242; Gianfranco Poggi, *Calvinism and the Capitalist Spirit: Max Weber's Protestant Ethic* (Amherst: University of Massachusetts Press, 1983) 64.

[202] Walzer, *The Revolution of the Saints*, 85.

[203] Weber, *The Protestant Ethic*, 136; Poggi, *Calvinism and the Capitalist Spirit*, 64.

[204] Poggi, *Calvinism and the Capitalist Spirit*, 76–77.

[205] Both quoted in Walzer, *The Revolution of the Saints*, 166, 285.

[206] Ibid., 285–87.

[207] Poggi, *Calvinism and the Capitalist Spirit*, 68.

[208] Ralph B. Perry, *Puritanism and Democracy* (New York: Vanguard, 1944) 247; Clifton Olmstead, *Religion in America: Past and Present* (Englewood Cliffs NJ: Prentice-Hall, 1961) 116; Foster R. Dulles, *A History of Recreation: America Learns to Play* (New York: Appleton-Century-Crofts, 1965) 13.

[209] Weber, *The Protestant Ethic*, 163*ff.*; Fullerton, "Calvinism and Capitalism," 22–23.

[210] Arnold Rose, ed., *Human Behavior and Social Processes: An Interactionist Approach* (Boston: Houghton Mifflin, 1962) 501.

[211] Walzer, *The Revolution of the Saints*, 168.

[212] See Roger Caillois, *Man and the Sacred* (Glencoe IL: The Free Press, 1959).

[213] George Santayana, *The Last Puritan: A Memoir in the Form of a Novel* (New York: Scribner, 1936) 371.

[214] William Hogan, "Sin and Sports," in *Motivations in Play, Games, and Sports*, eds. Ralph Slovenko and James Knight (Springfield IL: Chas. Thomas, 1967) 121; Joseph Kett, *Rites of Passage: Adolescence in America 1790 to the Present* (New York: Basic Books, 1977) 232.

[215] David McClelland, *The Achieving Society* (New York: Macmillan, 1961) 329.

[216] See Max Weber, *The Theory of Social and Economic Organization*, trans. A. M.

Henderson and Talcott Parsons (New York: Free Press, 1947); Weber, *The Protestant Ethic,* 75–78.

[217] N. J. Demerath and Phillip Hammond, *Religion in Social Context: Tradition and Transition* (New York: Random House, 1969) 120.

[218] Weber, *The Theory of Social and Economic Organization*, 80.

[219] Walzer, *The Revolution of the Saints*, 275–76.

[220] Robert Goldman and John Wilson, "The Rationalization of Leisure," *Politics & Society* 7/2 (June 1977): 159, 164.

[221] Adam Smith, *The Wealth of Nations* (New York: Modern Library, 1937); Daniel T. Rodgers, *The Work Ethic in Industrial America, 1850–1920* (Chicago: University of Chicago Press, 1978) 53–57.

[222] Sudhir Kakar, *Frederick Taylor: A Study in Personality and Innovation* (Boston: M.I.T. Press, 1970) 10–20.

[223] Robert K. Merton, *Science, Technology & Society in Seventeenth Century England* (New York: Howard Fertig, 1970) 61–63.

[224] H. Richard Niebuhr, "The Captive Church," *The Annals of America*, vol. 15 (Chicago: Britannica, 1968) 344.

[225] Merton, *Science, Technology & Society*, 90.

[226] Quoted in Tawney, *Religion and the Rise of Capitalism*, 250.

[227] Ibid.; John Nef, *Cultural Foundations of Industrial Civilization* (New York: Harper & Row, 1960) 7–11, 33, 50–64.

[228] Thorstein Veblen, *The Theory of the Leisure Class,* Minerva Press ed. (New York: Funk & Wagnalls, 1899) 238; H. Stuart Hughes, "Weber's Search for Rationality in Western Society," in *Protestantism, Capitalism, and Social Science,* ed. Robert Green (Lexington MA: Heath, 1973) 166.

[229] Friedrich Nietzsche, *On the Genealogy of Morals*, trans. Walter Kaufmann (New York: Random House, 1969) 97.

[230] Lerner, *America as a Civilization*, 70.

[231] Charles George and Katherine George, "Protestantism and Capitalism in Pre-revolutionary England," in *Church History* 27 (1958): 351–71; Staffan Linder, *The Harried Leisure Class* (New York: Columbia University Press, 1970) 27.

[232] Frederick C. Spurr, *The Christian Use of Leisure* (London: Kingsgate, 1935) 18.

[233] Donald Chu, *The Character of American Higher Education and Intercollegiate Sport* (Albany NY: S.U.N.Y. Press, 1989) 61.

[234] Demerath and Hammond, *Religion in Social Context*, 173–75; Poggi, *Calvinism and the Capitalist Spirit*, 45–46.

[235] Poggi, *Calvinism and the Capitalist Spirit*, 46.

[236] Quoted in David L. Miller, *Gods and Games: Toward a Theology of Play* (New York: The World Publishing Co., 1970) 174.

[237] Fullerton, "Calvinism and Capitalism," 31; Peter Filene, "Manhood in the Twenties: Was It So Great to Be Gatsby?" *Ms.* 11/12 (June 1974) 12–18.

[238] Demerath and Hammond, *Religion in Social Context*, 173–75.

[239] Van Wyck Brooks, *America's Coming-of-Age* (New York: Viking Press, 1930) 53; Robin M. Williams, *American Society: A Sociological Interpretation* (New York: Knopf, 1970) 461.

[240] Van Wyck Brooks, *The Wine of the Puritans* (London: Sisley's, 1908) 20.

[241] Tawney, *Religion and the Rise of Capitalism*, 285.

[242] Pierre Van den Berghe, *Race and Racism: A Cultural Perspective* (New York: Wiley, 1967) 124–25.

[243] See Weber, *The Protestant Ethic*; McClelland, *The Achieving Society*, 39, 43, 70.

[244] See Rotenberg, *Damnation and Deviance*.

[245] Perry, *Puritanism and Democracy*, 318–19; Philip Greven, *The Protestant Temperament: Patterns of Child-Rearing, Religious Experience, and the Self in Early America* (New York: Knopf, 1977) 220.

[246] In John T. McNeill, *The History and Character of Calvinism* (London: Oxford University Press, 1954) 421.

[247] Moses Rischen, ed., *The American Gospel of Success: Individualism and Beyond* (New York: Franklin Watts, 1974) 21.

[248] Fullerton, "Calvinism and Capitalism," 27–29; Williams, *American Society*, 457.

[249] See McClelland, *The Achieving Society*; Demerath and Hammond, *Religion in Social Context*, 86.

[250] Perry, *Puritanism and Democracy*, 297–98;

[251] McClelland, *The Achieving Society,* chapter 9; Tara K. Scanlon, "Antecedents of Competitiveness," in *Children in Sport: A Contemporary Anthology*, eds. Richard Magill, Michael Ash, and Frank Smoll (Champaign IL: Human Kinetics, 1978) 55–59, 70.

[252] McClelland, *The Achieving Society*, 39, 43, 70; Miyakawa, *Protestants and Pioneers*, 233. See also Gerhard Lenski, *The Religious Factor: A Sociological Study of Religion's Impact on Politics, Economics, and Family Life* (Garden City NY: Doubleday, 1961).

[253] Veblen, *The Theory of the Leisure Class*, 34.

[254] In Nancy Struna, "Puritans and Sport: The Irretrievable Tide of Change," *Journal of Sport History* 4/1 (Spring 1977a): 6.

[255] Thorstein Veblen, "The Case of America: The Self-Made Man," in *Absentee Ownership and Business Enterprise in Recent Times,* ed. Thorstein Veblen (New York: Huebsch, 1923) 119.

[256] In Morone, *Hellfire Nation*, 16.

[257] Rotenberg, *Damnation and Deviance*, 5, 31.

[258] Morgan, *Visible Saints*, 106; Perry, *Puritanism and Democracy*, 327; Walzer, *The Revolution of the Saints*, 222–23; Poggi, *Calvinism and the Capitalist Spirit*, 76–77.

[259] Morgan, *Visible Saints*, 116–17.

[260] Weber, *Essay on Sociology*, 316.

[261] Elias Canetti, *Crowds and Power,* trans. C. Stewart (New York: Viking Press, 1962) 296–97.

[262] Santayana, *The Last Puritan*, 452.

[263] See Talcott Parsons, "Belief, Unbelief, and Disbelief," in *The Culture of Unbelief,* eds. Rocco Caporale and Antonio Grumelli (Berkeley: University of California Press, 1971) 207–245; Rotenberg, *Damnation and Deviance*, 97.

[264] Paul Halmos, "The Ideology of Privacy and Reserve," in *Mass Leisure*, eds. Eric Larrabee and Rolf Meyerson (Glencoe Press IL: Free Press, 1958) 126; Tawney, *Religion*

and the Rise of Capitalism, 212–26; Miyakawa, *Protestants and Pioneers*, 79.

[265] Bell, *The Cultural Contradictions of Capitalism*, 16.

[266] Tawney, *Religion and the Rise of Capitalism*, 229.

[267] Ibid., 212, 229.

[268] Perry, *Puritanism and Democracy*, 327, 332, 359–61; Walzer, *The Revolution of the Saints*, 315; Fullerton, "Calvinism and Capitalism," 17.

[269] Weber, *Essay on Sociology*, 321; McClelland, *The Achieving Society*, 367; Sacvan Bercovitch, *The Puritan Origins of the American Self* (New Haven CT: Yale University Press, 1975) 16–19. See also Philip Greven, *The Protestant Temperament: Patterns of Child-Rearing, Religious Experience, and the Self in Early America* (New York: Knopf, 1977).

[270] Talcott Parsons, *The Structure of Social Action* (New York: Free Press, 1937) 570; Martin, *A General Theory*, 6–8.

[271] Tawney, *Religion and the Rise of Capitalism*, 230. See Rischen, *The American Gospel of Success,* 67–89.

[272] McNeill, *The History and Character of Calvinism*, 222.

[273] Halmos, "The Ideology of Privacy and Reserve," 125–26; Bercovitch, *The Puritan Origins of the American Self*, 20.

[274] Karl Polanyi, *The Great Transformation* (New York: Rinehart, 1944) 163.

[275] Yang, "Introduction," xvii; Goldman and Wilson, "The Rationalization of Leisure," 173.

[276] Poggi, *Calvinism and the Capitalist Spirit*, 45–46, 73.

[277] Tawney, *Religion and the Rise of Capitalism*, 266.

[278] Yevgeny Zamiatin, *We*, trans. Gregory Zilboorg (New York: Dutton, 1952) 183.

[279] Victor Turner, "Liminal to Liminoid in Play, Flow, and Ritual: An Essay in Comparative Symbology," in *The Anthropological Study of Human Play* 60/3, ed. Edward Norbeck (Houston: Rice University Studies, 1974) 62–63; Neil Cheek and William Burch, *The Social Organization of Leisure in Human Society* (New York: Harper & Row, 1976) 84–85.

[280] Clement Greenberg, "Work and Leisure under Industrialism," *Mass Leisure*, eds. Eric Larrabee and Rolf Meyerson (Glencoe IL: Free Press, 1958) 38–39; S. Boyd Eaton, Margerie Shostak, and Melvin Konner, *The Paleolithic Prescription* (New York: Harper & Row, 1988) 32, 178–79.

[281] Kakar, *Frederick Taylor*, 75–76.

[282] Juliet B. Schor, *The Overworked American* (New York: Basic Books, 1992) 44–47.

[283] Tawney, *Religion and the Rise of Capitalism*, 230.

[284] In Walzer, *The Revolution of the Saints*, 210–11.

[285] "Bartlett's Familiar Quotations," http://www.onlineliterature.com/quotes/quotation_search.php?author=Rudyard%20Kipling (accessed 10 September 2009).

[286] See Weber, *The Protestant Ethic.*

[287] Tawney, *Religion and the Rise of Capitalism*, 230, 245, 265–70; Fullerton, "Calvinism and Capitalism," 14–15.

[288] Tawney, *Religion and the Rise of Capitalism*, 242; Walzer, *The Revolution of the Saints*, 219.

[289] Tawney, *Religion and the Rise of Capitalism*, 109.

[290] Thomas Carlyle, *Past and Present* (New York: University Press, 1977) chapter 3.

[291] In Kakar, *Frederick Taylor*, 85.

[292] Rodgers, *The Work Ethic in Industrial America*, 7.

[293] Spurr, *The Christian Use of Leisure*, 15.

[294] Reinhard Bendix, *Max Weber: An Intellectual Portrait* (New York: Doubleday, 1960) 87.

[295] Thomas Mann, *The Magic Mountain*, 1927, trans. Helen T. Lowe-Porter (New York: Knopf, 1985) 34.

[296] See Harvey Cox, *The Secular City* (New York: Macmillan Co., 1966) 15–32.

[297] Poggi, *Calvinism and the Capitalist Spirit*, 67.

[298] Page Smith, *Dissenting Opinions* (San Francisco: North Point Press, 1984) 18; Marshall, *In Search of the Spirit of Capitalism*, 76.

[299] In H. Roy Kaplan, "The Convergence of Work, Sport, and Gambling in America," *The Annals of the Academy of Political and Social Science* 445/1 (September 1979): 27.

[300] Marshall, *In Search of the Spirit of Capitalism*, 94.

[301] Mann, *The Magic Mountain*, 243.

[302] In Wiley Umphlett, *The Sporting Myth and the American Experience: Studies in Contemporary Fiction (*Lewisburg PA: Bucknell University Press, 1975) 35.

[303] Gary Cross, *A Social History of Leisure since 1600* (State College PA: Venture Publishing, 1990) 7; Margaret Mead, "The Pattern of Leisure in Contemporary American Culture," in *Mass Leisure,* eds. Eric Larrabee and Rolf Meyerson (Glencoe IL: Free Press, 1958) 10–11.

[304] Linder, *The Harried Leisure Class.*

[305] Schor, *The Overworked American*, 51.

[306] Linder, *The Harried Leisure Class*, 13–15. See also Stanley Parker, *The Future of Work and Leisure* (New York: Praeger, 1971).

[307] Elihu Katz and Michael Gurevitch, *The Secularization of Leisure: Culture and Communication in Israel* (London: Faber & Faber, 1976) 76; Linder, *The Harried Leisure Class*, 145.

[308] Robert Lee, *Religion and Leisure in America* (New York: Abingdon Press, 1964) 209.

[309] E. P. Thompson in Schor, *The Overworked American*, 49–50.

[310] George M. Beard, "Modern Civilization and American Nervousness," in *The Annals of America,* vol. 10 (Chicago: Britannica, 1968) 481; Rodgers, *The Work Ethic in Industrial America,* 18.

[311] Linder, *The Harried Leisure Class*, 8, 53, 67, 143; E. P. Thompson in Schor, *The Overworked American*, xvii.

[312] Bennett Berger, "The Sociology of Leisure," *Industrial Relations: A Journal of Economy and Society* 1/1 (February 1962): 38; Lee, *Religion and Leisure in America*, 27.

[313] Ken Dryden, *The Game: A Thoughtful and Provocative Look at Life in Hockey* (Toronto: Macmillan of Canada, 1983) 18–19.

[314] Ibid.

[315] In John T. McNeill, ed., *On the Christian Faith: Selections From the Institutes, Commentaries and Tracts of John Calvin* (Indianapolis IN: Bobbs-Merrill, 1957) 72.

[316] McClelland, *The Achieving Society*, 123.

[317] Michael Novak, *The Joy of Sports* (New York: Basic Books, 1976) 218.

[318] Beard, "Modern Civilization and American Nervousness," 485–86.

[319] In Miller, *Gods and Games*, 35.

[320] George Goodwin, *Auto-Machia* (London: Edward Blount, 1607) 138.

[321] Van Wyck Brooks, *The Wine of the Puritans* (London: Sisley's, 1908) 16; Van Wyck Brooks, *America's Coming-of-Age* (New York: Viking Press, 1930) 8.

[322] Quoted in Walter Kerr, *The Decline of Pleasure* (New York: Time Inc., 1966) xx.

[323] Weber, *The Protestant Ethic,* 50–55*ff.*; Sacvan Bercovitch, *The Puritan Origins of the American Self* (New Haven CT: Yale University Press, 1975) 108, 185.

[324] See John T. McNeill, *The History and Character of Calvinism* (London: Oxford University Press, 1954), and Ralph B. Perry, *Puritanism and Democracy* (New York: Vanguard, 1944) 349–57.

[325] Ibid.

[326] Alexis de Tocqueville, *Democracy in America*, 1835, 1840, volume 2 (New York: Knopf, 1956) chapter 6.

[327] Clifton Olmstead, *Religion in America: Past and Present* (Englewood Cliffs NJ: Prentice-Hall, 1961) 109.

[328] Arthur Bartlett, *Baseball and Mr. Spalding* (New York: Farrar, Straus and Young, 1951) 95; Allen Bodner, *When Boxing Was a Jewish Sport* (Westport CT: Praeger, 1997) 129–30; Neil Cheek and William Burch, *The Social Organization of Leisure in Human Society* (New York: Harper & Row, 1976) 85.

[329] Seymour Lipset, *The First New Nation: The United States in Historical and Comparative Perspective* (New York: Doubleday, 1967) 183; Joseph Kett, *Rites of Passage: Adolescence in America 1790 to the Present* (New York: Basic Books, 1977) 73, 85, 192. See also Tony Ladd and James A. Mathisen, *Muscular Christianity: Evangelical Protestants and the Development of American Sport* (Grand Rapids MI: Baker Books, 1999).

[330] Daniel Bell, *The Cultural Contradictions of Capitalism* (New York: Basic Books, 1976) 63–65; Daniel T. Rodgers, *The Work Ethic in Industrial America, 1850–1920* (Chicago: University of Chicago Press, 1978) 16; Richard Hofstadter, *The Age of Reform* (New York: Knopf, 1956) 203. See also James A. Morone, *Hellfire Nation: The Politics of Sin in American History* (New Haven: Yale University Press, 2003).

[331] Hofstadter, *The Age of Reform*, 3, 145–52, 203, 318.

[332] Reuel Denney, *The Astonished Muse* (Chicago: University of Chicago Press, 1957) 113–15; E. Digby Baltzell, *The Protestant Establishment: Aristocracy and Caste in America* (London: Secker & Warburg, 1965) 12.

[333] Olmstead, *Religion in America*, 140.

[334] Henry L. Mencken, "Puritanism as a Literary Force," in *A Book of Prefaces* (London: Jonathan Cape, 1922) 198.

[335] Morone, *Hellfire Nation*, 9.

[336] T. Scott Miyakawa, *Protestants and Pioneers: Individualism and Conformity on the American Frontier* (Chicago: University of Chicago Press, 1964) 213.

[337] Daniel Boorstin, *The Americans: The Colonial Experience* (New York: Random House, 1958) 17, 311; Susan Budd, *Sociologists and Religion* (London: Collier-Macmillan, 1973) 6–7; Brooks, *America's Coming-of-Age*, 8; Bell, *The Cultural Contradictions of*

Capitalism, 57.

[338] Hofstadter, *The Age of Reform*, 150; Nicholas J. Demerath and Phillip Hammond, *Religion in Social Context: Tradition and Transition* (New York: Random House, 1969) 84, 122, 180. See also James A. Mathisen, "From Civil Religion to Folk Religion," in Shirl J. Hoffman, ed., *Sport and Religion* (Champaign IL: Human Kinetics, 1992) 19–21.

[339] Michael Argyle and Benjamin Beit-Hallahmi, *The Social Psychology of Religion* (London: Routledge & Kegan Paul, 1975) 27.

[340] Talcott Parsons, "Belief, Unbelief, and Disbelief," in *The Culture of Unbelief*, eds. Rocco Caporale and Antonio Grumelli (Berkeley: University of California Press, 1971) 217.

[341] Quoted in Ladd and Mathisen, *Muscular Christianity*, 144.

[342] Bell, *The Cultural Contradictions of Capitalism*, 55; Raymond S. Franklin, *American Capitalism: Two Visions* (New York: Random House, 1977) 185–86; Perry, *Puritanism and Democracy*, 297–98.

[343] Melvin L. Kohn, "Social Class and Parent-Child Relationships: an Interpretation," *American Journal of Sociology* 68/1 (January 1963): 471–80; Graham Murdock, "Education, Culture and the Myth of Classlessness," in *Work and Leisure*, eds. John Haworth and Michael Smith (Princeton NJ: Princeton Book Co., 1976) 128; Kett, *Rites of Passage*, 129, 167, 243. See also Melvin L. Kohn, *Class and Conformity: A Study in Values* (Homewood IL: Dorsey, 1969).

[344] Daniel Lerner, "Comfort and Fun: Morality in a Nice Society," *The American Scholar* 27/2 (Spring 1958): 157; David McClelland, *The Achieving Society* (New York: Macmillan, 1961) 253; Frederick Chino, "Family Status, Protestant Ethic and Level of Occupational Aspiration" (Ph.D. diss., Stanford University, 1965) 14–17; Kohn, *Class and Conformity*, 19–21.

[345] John Brooks, *Showing Off in America* (Boston: Little, Brown, 1981) 66.

[346] Veblen, *The Theory of the Leisure Class,* 17–26; Robert Goldman and John Wilson, "The Rationalization of Leisure," *Politics & Society* 7/2 (June 1977): 165.

[347] Veblen, *The Theory of the Leisure Class*, 2, 32, 35, 74.

[348] Clement Greenberg, "Work and Leisure under Industrialism," in *Mass Leisure*, eds. Eric Larrabee and Rolf Meyerson (Glencoe IL: Free Press, 1958) 40.

[349] Richard Tawney, *Religion and the Rise of Capitalism* (Gloucester MA: Peter Smith, 1962) 202.

[350] Morone, *Hellfire Nation*, 4.

[351] See Lewis Austin, *Saints and Samurai: The Political Culture of the American and Japanese Elites* (New Haven CT: Yale University Press, 1975).

[352] See Morone, *Hellfire Nation*, 281–317.

[353] See Stanton Peele, *Diseasing of America: Addiction Treatment Out of Control* (Lexington MA: Lexington Books, 1989).

[354] Warren Susman, "Piety, Profits and Play," in *Men, Women, and Issues in American History,* eds. Howard Quint and Milton Cantor, vol. 2 (Homewood IL: Dorsey, 1980) 203; Philip Rieff, *The Triumph of the Therapeutic: Uses of Faith after Freud* (New York: Harper & Row, 1968); Stanley Parker, *The Future of Work and Leisure* (New York: Praeger, 1971) 7.

[355] Daniel Boorstin, *The Americans: The National Experience* (New York: Random House, 1965) 51.

[356] Nancy Struna, "Puritans and Sport: The Irretrievable Tide of Change," *Journal of Sport History* 4/1 (Spring 1977a): 1–21.

[357] See Perry, *Puritanism and Democracy,* 438–64.

[358] Fritz Redlich, "The Business Leader as a 'Daimonic Figure,'" *The American Journal of Economics and Sociology* 12/2 (April 1953): 289–99; Rodgers, *The Work Ethic in Industrial America,* 126.

[359] Max Lerner, *America as a Civilization: Life and Thought in the United States Today* (New York: Simon and Schuster, 1957) 49.

[360] Gunnar Myrdal, *An American Dilemma: The Negro Problem and Modern Democracy* (New York: Harper & Row, 1962) 210.

[361] Quoted in Bill Moyers, *A World of Ideas,* ed. B. S. Flowers (New York: Doubleday, 1989) 119.

[362] David Riesman, *The Lonely Crowd: A Study of the Changing American Character* (New Haven CT: Yale University Press, 1950).

[363] Ernst Troeltsch, *The Social Teachings of the Christian Churches,* 2 vols. (New York: Harper & Row, 1960) 602; Michael Walzer, *The Revolution of the Saints: A Study in the Origins of Radical Politics* (Cambridge MA: Harvard University Press, 1965) 29, 221–22.

[364] Walzer, *The Revolution of the Saints,* 122.

[365] See de Tocqueville, *Democracy in America,* volume 2, chapter 5.

[366] Morone, *Hellfire Nation,* 5.

[367] Ibid., 5; Sydney Ahlstrom, *A Religious History of the American People* (New Haven: Yale University Press, 1972) 387.

[368] In Lipset, *The First New Nation,* 182–83.

[369] Margaret Mead, *And Keep Your Powder Dry: An Anthropologist Looks at America* (New York: Morrow, 1965) 35–36; Max Weber, *Essay on Sociology,* trans. Hans Gerth and C. Wright Mills (New York: Oxford University Press, 1958b) 310.

[370] Kett, *Rites of Passage,* 31–39, 173, 184–94, 222, 250–53.

[371] John R. Tunis, *The American Way of Sport* (New York: Duell, Sloan and Pearce, 1958) 103.

[372] Myrdal, *An American Dilemma,* 210; Lipset, *The First New Nation,* 115, 232.

[373] Quoted in Walzer, *The Revolution of the Saints,* 157.

[374] Bercovitch, *The Puritan Origins of the American Self,* 185.

[375] Tawney, *Religion and the Rise of Capitalism,* 230, 259–64; Mead, *And Keep Your Powder Dry,* 65, 195; Austin, *Saints and Samurai,* 115; Kett, *Rites of Passage,* 45, 170.

[376] Albert K. Cohen, *Deviance and Control* (Englewood Cliffs NJ: Prentice-Hall, 1966) 65; Robin M. Williams, *American Society: A Sociological Interpretation* (New York: Knopf, 1970) 454; Bercovitch, *The Puritan Origins of the American Self,* 185; Wiley Umphlett, *The Sporting Myth and the American Experience: Studies in Contemporary Fiction* (Lewisburg PA: Bucknell University Press, 1975) 36.

[377] Thomas L. Nichols, "Work and Play in America," 1864, in *The Annals of America,* vol. 9 (Chicago: Britannica, 1968) 541.

[378] McClelland, *The Achieving Society,* 104, 227.

[379] Austin, *Saints and Samurai,* 113; Umphlett, *The Sporting Myth and the American Experience,* 34; Christopher Lasch, *The Culture of Narcissism: American Life in an Age of Diminishing Expectations* (New York: Norton, 1978) 56.

[380] Barton in Moses Rischen, ed., *The American Gospel of Success: Individualism and Beyond* (New York: Franklin Watts, 1974) 415–18; Susman, "Piety, Profits and Play," 203.

[381] Lerner, *America as a Civilization,* 252; Bell, *The Cultural Contradictions of Capitalism,* 70.

[382] Brooks, *The Wine of the Puritans,* 92; Arthur K. Davis, "Veblen on the Decline of the Protestant Ethic," *Social Forces* 22/3 (March 1944): 286; Reinhard Bendix, *Max Weber: An Intellectual Portrait* (New York: Doubleday, 1960) 32.

[383] Goldman and Wilson, "The Rationalization of Leisure," 173.

[384] Mead, *And Keep Your Powder Dry,* 264.

[385] Quoted in Moyers, *A World of Ideas,* 63.

[386] Denney, *The Astonished Muse,* 113–14; Beecher is quoted in Rodgers, *The Work Ethic in Industrial America,* 101.

[387] *Good News for Modern Man: The New Testament in Today's English Version* (New York: American Bible Society, 1972) 415.

[388] Perry, *Puritanism and Democracy,* 246, 255; Karen Horney, *The Neurotic Personality of Our Time* (New York: Norton, 1937) 188; Richard Lipsky, *How We Play the Game: Why Sports Dominate American Life* (Boston: Beacon Press, 1981) 124.

[389] Veblen, *The Theory of the Leisure Class, 163ff.*

[390] Sudhir Kakar, *Frederick Taylor: A Study in Personality and Innovation* (Boston: M.I.T. Press, 1970) 17.

[391] Ibid., 25.

[392] Brooks, *America's Coming-of-Age,* 18; Paul Staudohar, *The Sports Industry and Collective Bargaining* (Ithaca NY: I.L.R. Press, 1989) 177.

[393] Michael Maccoby, *The Gamesman: The New Corporate Leaders* (New York: Simon and Schuster, 1976) 69; Veblen, "The Case of America: The Self-Made Man," 119*ff.*

[394] Horney, *The Neurotic Personality of Our Time,* 188–92.

[395] Quoted in Perry, *Puritanism and Democracy,* 60.

[396] See Bell, *The Cultural Contradictions of Capitalism.*

[397] M. Lerner, *America as a Civilization,* 252, 269; Veblen, *The Theory of the Leisure Class,* 19.

[398] "George Eastman—the Man: About His Life," http://www.kodak.com/US/en/corp/kodakHistory/eastmanTheMan.shtml (accessed 3 April 2008).

[399] Michael Walzer, *The Revolution of the Saints: A Study in the Origins of Radical Politics* (Cambridge MA: Harvard University Press, 1965) 303–304.

[400] Gianfranco Poggi, *Calvinism and the Capitalist Spirit: Max Weber's Protestant Ethic* (Amherst: University of Massachusetts Press, 1983) 41.

[401] Max Lerner, *America as a Civilization: Life and Thought in the United States Today* (New York: Simon and Schuster, 1957) 238.

[402] Daniel T. Rodgers, *The Work Ethic in Industrial America, 1850–1920* (Chicago: University of Chicago Press, 1978) 10–14.

[403] Ibid., 9–14, 54–55, 111; Ralph B. Perry, *Puritanism and Democracy* (New York: Vanguard, 1944) 308.

[404] Rodgers, *The Work Ethic in Industrial America,* 9; Lerner, *America as a Civilization,* 50.

[405] Alexis de Tocqueville, *Democracy in America,* vol. 2, 1835, 1840 (New York: Knopf, 1956) chapter 18.

[406] Juliet B. Schor, *The Overworked American* (New York: Basic Books, 1992) 6, 43, 60.

[407] Rodgers, *The Work Ethic in Industrial America*, 105–108.

[408] Ibid.; Dulles, *A History of Recreation*, 90–91.

[409] In Foster R. Dulles, *A History of Recreation: America Learns to Play* (New York: Appleton-Century-Crofts, 1965) 86.

[410] Rodgers, *The Work Ethic in Industrial America*, 83–87, 90.

[411] Quoted in Christian Messenger, *Sport and the Spirit of Play in American Fiction: Hawthorne to Faulkner* (New York: Columbia University Press, 1981) 165.

[412] Johan Huizinga, *Homo Ludens: A Study of the Play Element in Culture*, 7th ed. (Boston: Beacon Press, 1968) 192; Rodgers, *The Work Ethic in Industrial America*, 79.

[413] Robert Lee, *Religion and Leisure in America* (New York: Abingdon Press, 1964) 40.

[414] Van Wyck Brooks, *America's Coming-of-Age* (New York: Viking Press, 1930) 18.

[415] Count Vay de Vaya and Count zu Luskod, "The Land of Mammon and Moloch," 1908, in *The Annals of America*, vol. 13 (Chicago: Britannica, 1968) 126.

[416] Perry, *Puritanism and Democracy*, 313.

[417] In Peter Filene, "Manhood in the Twenties: Was It So Great to Be Gatsby?" *Ms.* 11/12 (June 1974) 12–18.

[418] Lewis Austin, *Saints and Samurai: The Political Culture of the American and Japanese Elites* (New Haven CT: Yale University Press, 1975) 115.

[419] William Theobald, "All Work Makes Jack an Executive," *Perspective: Purdue University Alumni Newsletter* (July 1984): 6.

[420] Richard Kraus, "Changing Views of Tomorrow's Leisure," *Journal of Physical Education, Recreation & Dance* 67/8 (August 1988): 83.

[421] David Rockefeller, "America Must Stress the Value of Work," in *American Values,* ed. David Bender (St. Paul MN: Greenhaven Press, 1984) 206.

[422] David Riesman, "Leisure and Work in Post-industrial Society," in *Mass Leisure*, eds. Eric Larrabee and Rolf Meyersohn (Glencoe IL: Free Press, 1958) 374–77.

[423] Ibid.

[424] Reported in Staffan Linder, *The Harried Leisure Class* (New York: Columbia University Press, 1970) 136.

[425] Seppo Iso-Ahola, *The Social Psychology of Leisure and Recreation* (Dubuque IA: Brown, 1980) 370; Lee, *Religion and Leisure in America*, 40.

[426] Riesman, "Leisure and Work in Post-industrial Society," 369–74.

[427] Steven Greenhouse, "Americans' International Lead in Hours Worked Grew in 90s, Report Shows," *New York Times,* 1 September 2001, 8, http://query.nytimes.com/gst/fullpage.html?res=9A0CE5D91130F932A3575AC0A9679C8B 63 (accessed 25 August 2009); Kraus, "Changing Views of Tomorrow's Leisure," 83–85.

[428] Schor, *The Overworked American*, 8, 24–25, 87*ff.*

[429] Dwight W. Hoover, "The Division of Leisure," *The Social Change Report* 1/1 (Muncie IN: The Center for Middletown Studies, 1987).

[430] See Gerhard Lenski, *The Religious Factor: A Sociological Study of Religion's*

Impact on Politics, Economics, and Family Life (Garden City NY: Doubleday, 1961); David McClelland, *The Achieving Society* (New York: Macmillan, 1961) 358–64.

[431] In Riesman, "Leisure and Work in Post-industrial Society," 377.

[432] In David Whitson, "Sport and Hegemony: On the Construction of the Dominant Culture," *Sociology of Sport Journal* l/1 (March 1984): 69.

[433] Erica Abeel, "Dark Secrets," *Esquire* 102/6 (June 1984): 259–60.

[434] Daniel Bell, *The Cultural Contradictions of Capitalism* (New York: Basic Books, 1976) 156; Stanley Parker, *The Future of Work and Leisure* (New York: Praeger, 1971) 44–48, 53.

[435] David Riesman, *Individualism Reconsidered* (New York: Free Press, 1954) 332; Melvin L. Kohn, "Social Class and Parent-Child Relationships: an Interpretation," *American Journal of Sociology* 68/1 (January 1963): 194.

[436] Polanyi, *The Great Transformation*, 163; Franklin, *American Capitalism*, 138; Bennett Berger, "The Sociology of Leisure," *Industrial Relations: A Journal of Economy and Society* 1/1 (February 1962): 38–39; Rodgers, *The Work Ethic in Industrial America*, 26–37.

[437] Rigaeur, *Sport and Work*, 44; H. Stuart Hughes, "Weber's Search for Rationality in Western Society," in *Protestantism, Capitalism, and Social Science*, ed. Robert Green (Lexington MA: Heath, 1973) 151; Howard L. Nixon, "The Commercialization and Organizational Development of Modern Sport," *International Review of Sport Sociology* 9/2 (June 1974): 8–10.

[438] Quoted in Barnes, *An Introduction to the History of Sociology*, 95.

[439] Goldman and Wilson, "The Rationalization of Leisure," 159; Hofstadter, *The Age of Reform*, 220.

[440] See Filene, "Manhood in the Twenties: Was It So Great to Be Gatsby?" 12–18.

[441] E. Bauer, "Paper Reports Thumb-Twiddling by Secretaries in H.E.W. Office," *Clarion Ledger* (Jackson MS), 6 December 1979, J7.

[442] Parker, *The Future of Work and Leisure*, 44–50, 53; Iso-Ahola, *The Social Psychology of Leisure and Recreation*, 366.

[443] Parker, *The Future of Work and Leisure,* 44–50.

[444] D. C. Ganster, "Protestant Ethic and Performance: A Re-examination," *Psychological Reports* 48 (1981): 335–38.

[445] Rigauer, *Sport and Work*, 38–39.

[446] Bennett Berger, "The Sociology of Leisure," 39.

[447] See Margaret Mead, "The Pattern of Leisure in Contemporary American Culture," in *Mass Leisure,* eds. Eric Larrabee and Rolf Meyerson (Glencoe IL: Free Press, 1958) 10–15; Whyte, *The Organization Man.*

[448] Parker, *The Future of Work and Leisure*, 69; Berger, "The Sociology of Leisure," 36–44; Bell, *The Cultural Contradictions of Capitalism*, 55.

[449] Lloyd Street, "Game Forms in the Factory Group," *Berkeley Publications in Society & Institutions* 4/1 (1958): 44–55.

[450] Paul Hoch, *Rip Off the Big Game: The Exploitation of Sports by the Power Elite* (New York: Doubleday, 1972) 20; John Loy, Barry McPherson, and Gerald Kenyon, *Sport and Social Systems* (Reading MA: Addison-Wesley, 1978) 301.

[451] Reuel Denney, *The Astonished Muse* (Chicago: University of Chicago Press, 1957) 6–7; Goldman and Wilson, "The Rationalization of Leisure," 158.

[452] Toynbee quoted in John R. Betts, *America's Sporting Heritage, 1980–1950* (Reading MA: Addison-Wesley, 1974) 320; Lewis Mumford, *Technics and Civilization* (New York: Harcourt, Brace, 1934) 304.

[453] Veblen, *The Theory of the Leisure Class.*

[454] Christopher Lasch, "The Corruption of Sports," *New York Review of Books* 24/7 (April 1977): 24.

[455] Thomas Kando and Worth Summers, "The Impact of Work on Leisure: Toward a Paradigm and Research Strategy," in *Sociology of Leisure*, eds. Theodore Johannis, Jr. and C. Neil Bull (Beverly Hills CA: Sage Publications, 1971) 75; Greenberg, "Work and Leisure under Industrialism," 39; Iso-Ahola, *The Social Psychology of Leisure and Recreation*, 366–67.

[456] Carroll, *Puritan, Paranoid, Remissive: A Sociology of Modern Culture*, 45.

[457] Lasch, "The Corruption of Sports," 24; Rigauer, *Sport and Work*, 88.

[458] See Rainer Martens, *Sociology Psychology and Physical Activity* (New York: Harper & Row, 1975); Lee, *Religion and Leisure in America*, 214.

[459] Berger, "The Sociology of Leisure," 41–44; Dulles, *A History of Recreation: America Learns to Play*, 187.

[460] Berger, "The Sociology of Leisure," 41–44.

[461] Richard Gruneau, *Class, Sports and Social Development* (Amherst: University of Massachusetts Press, 1983) 35.

[462] See Betts, *America's Sporting Heritage*; Kando and Summers, "The Impact of Work on Leisure," 210–27.

[463] Denney, *The Astonished Muse*, 111.

[464] Mumford, *Technics and Civilization,* 185–87.

[465] Mead, "The Pattern of Leisure in Contemporary American Culture," 11; Goldman and Wilson, "The Rationalization of Leisure," 187; Carroll, *Puritan, Paranoid, Remissive: A Sociology of Modern Culture*, 23–38.

[466] John R. Betts, "The Technological Revolution and the Rise of Sport, 1850–1900," in *The American Sporting Experience: A Historical Anthology of Sport in America,* ed. Steven Riess (New York: Leisure Press, 1984) 155–57.

[467] Goldman and Wilson, "The Rationalization of Leisure," 157, 161–63, 168–70.

[468] Ibid. Also Frederick Cozens and Florence Stumpf, *Sports in American Life* (Chicago: University of Chicago Press, 1953) 61.

[469] Victor Turner, "Liminal to Liminoid in Play, Flow, and Ritual: A Essay in Comparative Symbology," in *The Anthropological Study of Human Play* 60/3*,* ed. Edward Norbeck (Houston: Rice University Studies, 1974) 90.

[470] Goldman and Wilson, "The Rationalization of Leisure," 168; Rodgers, *The Work Ethic in Industrial America*, 88.

[471] See Street, "Game Forms in the Factory Group," 44–55; Goldman and Wilson, "The Rationalization of Leisure," 168.

[472] Street, "Game Forms in the Factory Group," 46–53; Goldman and Wilson, "The Rationalization of Leisure," 157–67; Whitson, "Sport and Hegemony: On the Construction of the Dominant Culture," 69.

[473] Craig Finney, "NESRA Conference Addressed Stress and Recreation," *Corporate Fitness & Recreation* (October/November 1984): 14–15; Brohm, *Sport—A Prison of Measured Time* (London: Ink Links, 1978) 89–94; Kendall Blanchard and Alyce Cheska, *The Anthropology of Sport: An Introduction* (Hadley MA: Bergin & Garvey, 1985) 44–46; Cozens and Stumpf, *Sports in American Life*, 61; Street, "Game Forms in the Factory Group," 46–53.

[474] Betts, *America's Sporting Heritage,* 96–98; Leonard Koppett, *Koppett's Concise History of Major League Baseball* (New York: Carroll & Graf, 2004) 8; Hoch, *Rip Off the Big Game*, 34; Arthur Bartlett, *Baseball and Mr. Spalding* (New York: Farrar, Straus and Young, 1951) 51–52; Ken Burns and Lynn Novak, producers, *Baseball—A Film by Ken Burns*, vol. 3, writer Geoffrey C. Ward (Florentine Films, 1994). See Susan Cahn, *Coming on Strong* (New York: Free Press, 1994), for a chronicle of the working woman's sport.

[475] Dulles, *A History of Recreation: America Learns to Play*, 189; Bartlett, *Baseball and Mr. Spalding*, 51; Goldman and Wilson, "The Rationalization of Leisure," 179–81; Richard B. Cramer, *Joe DiMaggio: The Hero's Life* (New York: Simon & Schuster, 2000) 29–30.

[476] Betts, *America's Sporting Heritage*, 270; Don Kowet, *The Rich Who Own Sports* (New York: Random House, 1977) 33; Lon Eubanks, *The Fighting Illini* (Huntsville AL: Strode Publishers, 1976) 68–69; "The Packers," *Commercial Appeal* (Memphis TN), 12 July 1992, B1.

[477] Betts, *America's Sporting Heritage,* 308.

[478] The author worked for National Homes Corporation in the early 1960s when they were hiring former high-school and college ballplayers, and competing against the Phillips Oilers and other semi-pro basketball teams.

[479] John Loy, "The Nature of Sport: A Definitional Effort," *Quest* 10/2 (May 1968): 1–15. The relationship between sport and religious institutions is discussed below, and the relationship with commercial institutions in chapter 12.

[480] Ibid. See also James Koch and Wilbert Leonard II, "The NCAA: A Socio-economic Analysis: The Development of the College Sports Cartel from Social Movement to Formal Organization," *American Journal of Economics and Sociology* 37/3 (July 1978): 228; Richard Gruneau, *Class, Sports and Social Development* (Amherst: University of Massachusetts Press, 1983) 59.

[481] Melvin Adelman, "The First Modern Sport in America: Harness Racing in New York City, 1825–1879," in *Sport in America,* ed. David Wiggins (Champaign IL: Human Kinetics, 1995) 105.

[482] See Foster R. Dulles, *A History of Recreation: America Learns to Play* (New York: Appleton-Century-Crofts, 1965); John R. Betts, *America's Sporting Heritage, 1980–1950* (Reading MA: Addison-Wesley, 1974) 92–129; Barrie Houlihan, *Sport, Policy & Politics: A Comparative Analysis* (London: Routledge, 1997) 1*ff.*

[483] Dennis Brailsford, "1787: An Eighteenth Century Sporting Year," *Research Quarterly for Exercise and Sport* 55/3 (September 1984): 217; Arthur Bartlett, *Baseball and Mr. Spalding* (New York: Farrar, Straus and Young, 1951): 12–17, 82; Dulles, *A History of Recreation*, 186; Adelman, "The First Modern Sport in America," 95–114; Bruce Bennett, Maxwell Howell, and Uriel Simri, *Comparative Physical Education and Sport,* 2nd ed. (Philadelphia: Lea & Febiger, 1983) 111; Houlihan, *Sport, Policy & Politics*, 56.

[484] Adelman, "The First Modern Sport in America," 95–114; Gary Cross, *A Social History of Leisure since 1600* (State College PA: Venture Publishing, 1990) 172.

[485] Roberta Park, "Too Important to Trust to the Children: The Search for Freedom and Order in Children's Play, 1900–1917," in *The Paradoxes of Play*, ed. John Loy (West Point NY: Leisure Press, 1982) 96; Allen Guttmann, *A Whole New Ball Game: An Interpretation of American Sports* (Chapel Hill: University of North Carolina Press, 1988) 82–83, 91. See also Jonathan Brower, "The Professionalization of Organized Youth Sport: Social Psychological Impacts and Outcomes," *Annals of the American Academy of Political and Social Science* 445/1 (September 1979): 39–46.

[486] Rainer Martens, *Joy and Sadness in Children's Sports* (Champaign IL: Human Kinetics, 1978) 6; J. Thomas Jable, "The Public Schools Athletic League of New York City: Organized Athletics for City Schoolchildren, 1903–1914," in *The American Sporting Experience: A Historical Anthology of Sport in America*, ed. Steven Riess (New York: Leisure Press, 1984) 234; Cross, *A Social History of Leisure*, 144.

[487] Frederick Cozens and Florence Stumpf, *Sports in American Life* (Chicago: University of Chicago Press, 1953) 74; Dominick Cavallo, *Muscles and Morals: Organized Playgrounds and Urban Reform, 1880–1920* (Philadelphia: University of Pennsylvania Press, 1981) 84.

[488] Donald J. Mrozek, *Sport and American Mentality, 1880–1910* (Knoxville: University of Tennessee Press, 1983) 100; Jay Cooperider, "Smart Move," *Purdue University Perspective* 22/2 (Summer 1995): 10–11.

[489] See Donald Chu, *The Character of American Higher Education and Intercollegiate Sport* (Albany NY: S.U.N.Y. Press, 1989) 131–35.

[490] Bartlett, *Baseball and Mr. Spalding*; Randy Roberts and James Olson, *Winning Is the Only Thing* (Baltimore: Johns Hopkins University Press, 1989) 50–51. See also Levinson and Christensen, *Encyclopedia of World Sport, passim*.

[491] See David Levinson and Karen Christensen, eds., *Encyclopedia of World Sport: From Ancient Times to the Present* (New York: Oxford University Press, 1999) *passim*.

[492] George Sage, "American Values and Sport: Formation of a Bureaucratic Personality," *Journal of Physical Education and Recreation* 49/8 (October 1978): 8.

[493] Gruneau, *Class, Sports, and Social Development*, 12.

[494] See John R. Betts, "The Technological Revolution and the Rise of Sport, 1850–1900," in *The American Sporting Experience: A Historical Anthology of Sport in America*, ed. Steven Riess (New York: Leisure Press, 1984) 141–57; See also Frederic L. Paxson, "The Rise of Sport," *Mississippi Valley Historical Review* 4/2 (September 1917): 143–68.

[495] Betts, *America's Sporting Heritage*, 142; Reuel Denney, *The Astonished Muse* (Chicago: University of Chicago Press, 1957) 126.

[496] James M. Mayo, *The American Country Club: Its Origins and Development* (Piscataway NJ: Rutgers University Press, 1998) 63*ff.*; Betts, *America's Sporting Heritage*, 262; Caspar Whitney, "Evolution of the Country Club," 1894, in *The Annals of America*, vol. 11 (Chicago: Britannica, 1968) 555–57; Howard L. Nixon, "The Commercialization and Organizational Development of Modern Sport," *International Review of Sport Sociology* 9/2 (June 1974): 116.

[497] Guttmann, *A Whole New Ball Game*, 55–57; Robert Boyle, *Sport—Mirror of American Life* (Boston: Little, Brown, 1963) 90; Donald J. Mrozek, *Sport and American*

Mentality, 1880–1910 (Knoxville: University of Tennessee Press, 1983) 118, 127; Thorstein Veblen, *The Theory of the Leisure Class,* Minerva Press ed. (New York: Funk & Wagnalls, 1899) chapter 10.

[498] Guttmann, *A Whole New Ball Game,* 146; Günther Lueschen, "Social Stratification and Social Mobility Among Young Sportsmen," in *Sport, Culture, and Society,* eds. John W. Loy and Gerald Kenyon (London: Collier-Macmillan, 1969) 268; Cavallo, *Muscles and Morals,* 21; Mrozek, *Sport and American Mentality,* 103.

[499] Betts, *America's Sporting Heritage,* 160–69; Steven A. Riess, ed., *The American Sporting Experience: A Historical Anthology of Sport in America* (New York: Leisure Press, 1984) 139; Paul Hoch, *Rip Off the Big Game: The Exploitation of Sports by the Power Elite* (New York: Doubleday, 1972) 32.

[500] Denney, *The Astonished Muse,* 104*ff.*

[501] See Bartlett, *Baseball and Mr. Spalding,* chapter 7; Hoch, *Rip Off the Big Game,* 20, 34.

[502] Mrozek, *Sport and American Mentality,* 103*ff.*; Riess, *The American Sporting Experience,* 217.

[503] Dwight W. Hoover, "The Division of Leisure," *The Social Change Report* 1/1 (Muncie IN: The Center for Middletown Studies, 1987) 1–15.

[504] John Roberts and Brian Sutton-Smith, "Child Training and Game Involvement," *Ethnology* 1/2 (July 1962): 172.

[505] Lueschen, "Social Stratification and Social Mobility Among Young Sportsmen," 274; John Loy, "Sociological Analysis of Sport," in *Physical Education: An Interdisciplinary Approach,* ed. Robert Singer et al. (New York: Macmillan, 1972) 214.

[506] David Riesman, *Individualism Reconsidered* (New York: Free Press, 1954) 208, 333; Bero Rigauer, *Sport and Work,* trans. Allen Guttmann (New York: Columbia University Press, 1981) 99; Geoffrey Godbey and Stanley Parker, *Leisure Studies and Services: An Overview* (Philadelphia: Saunders, 1976) 36.

[507] Melvin L. Kohn, *Class and Conformity: A Study in Values* (Homewood IL: Dorsey, 1969) 117; Geoffrey Watson, "Game Interaction in Little League Baseball and Family Organization" (Ph.D. diss., University of Illinois, 1973) 279–80.

[508] See Paul Halmos, "The Ideology of Privacy and Reserve," in *Mass Leisure,* eds. Eric Larrabee and Rolf Meyerson (Glencoe Press IL: Free Press, 1958) 125–36. See also Betts, *America's Sporting Heritage.*

[509] Max Lerner, *America as a Civilization: Life and Thought in the United States Today* (New York: Simon and Schuster, 1957) 819; See also Betts, *America's Sporting Heritage.*

[510] Quoted in Michael Novak, *The Joy of Sports* (New York: Basic Books, 1976) 301.

[511] John R. Tunis, *The American Way of Sport* (New York: Duell, Sloan and Pearce, 1958) 18.

[512] Guy Lewis, "The Muscular Christianity Movement," *Journal of Health, Physical Education & Recreation* 45/5 (May 1966): 28; Richard Swanson, "The Acceptance and Influence of Play in American Protestantism," *Quest* 11/1 (December 1968): 58; Christian Messenger, *Sport and the Spirit of Play in American Fiction: Hawthorne to Faulkner* (New York: Columbia University Press, 1981) 97.

[513] Lonnie D. Kliever, "God and Games in Modern Culture," in *The World & I, Washington Times,* October 1988, 565; republished in *From Season to Season: Sport as*

American Religion, ed. Joe Price (Macon GA: Mercer University Press, 2004) 39–48.

[514] Lewis, "The Muscular Christianity Movement," 28; Swanson, "The Acceptance and Influence of Play in American Protestantism," 65–66; Cozens and Stumpf, *Sports in American Life*, 95–96. See also Joseph Kett, *Rites of Passage: Adolescence in America 1790 to the Present* (New York: Basic Books, 1977), and Thomas W. Higginson, "Saints and Their Bodies," *Atlantic Monthly* 1 (March 1858): 582–95.

[515] Mrozek, *Sport and American Mentality*, 4, 12.

[516] Betts, *America's Sporting Heritage,*180; Kett, *Rites of Passage*, 31–39, 184–94, 250–53; D. Stanley Eitzen and George Sage, *Sociology of American Sport* (Dubuque IA: Brown, 1982) 150.

[517] Erich Geldbach, *Sport und Protestantismus: Geschichte einer Begegnung* (Wuppertal, Germany: Theologischer Verlag R. Brockhaus, 1975) 178–86.

[518] Geldbach, *Sport und Protestantismus,* 182; Rudiger Schloz, "Problems and Trends in Protestant Theology," in *The Scientific View of Sport: Perspectives, Aspects, Issues*, eds. Ommo Grupe et al. (New York: Springer-Verlag, 1972) 87.

[519] Geldbach, *Sport und Protestantismus*, 184–86.

[520] Cozens and Stumpf, *Sports in American Life*, 102; John Loy, Barry McPherson, and Gerald Kenyon, *Sport and Social Systems* (Reading MA: Addison-Wesley, 1978) 301; Albert B. Wegener, *Church and Community Recreation* (New York: Macmillan, 1924) 45; William Hogan, "Sin and Sports," in *Motivations in Play, Games, and Sports*, eds. Ralph Slovenko and James Knight (Springfield IL: Chas. Thomas, 1967) 135. See also Tony Ladd and James A. Mathisen, *Muscular Christianity: Evangelical Protestants and the Development of American Sport* (Grand Rapids MI: Baker Books, 1999).

[521] Swanson, "The Acceptance and Influence of Play in American Protestantism," 58–60; Ladd and Mathisen, *Muscular Christianity*, 196–97; Eitzen and Sage, *Sociology of American Sport*, 141.

[522] In Nicholas J. Demerath and Phillip Hammond, *Religion in Social Context: Tradition and Transition* (New York: Random House, 1969) 182.

[523] Robert J. Higgs, "Muscular Christianity, Holy Play and Spiritual Exercises: Confusion about Christ in Sports and Religion," *Arete* 1/1 (Fall 1983): 62; Frank Deford, "Religion in Sport," *Sports Illustrated* 53/15 (19 April 1976): 92–99.

[524] Mark Kram, "Religion in Athletics: Touchy Subject," *Clarion Ledger* (Jackson MS), 19 November 1988, C1–7.

[525] Ibid. See also Hogan, "Sin and Sports," 139; Bennett et al., *Comparative Physical Education and Sport*, 224; Hoch, *Rip Off the Big Game*, 21; Deford, "Religion in Sport," 92–99; Eitzen and Sage, *Sociology of American Sport*, 153.

[526] Geldbach, *Sport und Protestantismus*, 15*ff.* See also Ladd and Mathisen, *Muscular Christianity*, and for a broader perspective, Sydney Ahlstrom, *A Religious History of the American People* (New Haven: Yale University Press, 1972).

[527] Mrozek, *Sport and American Mentality*, 168, 192–94.

[528] Higgs, "Muscular Christianity," 67; Kingsley quoted in Malcolm Tozer, "Charles Kingsley and the 'Muscular Christian' Ideal of Manliness," *Physical Education Review* 8/1 (Spring 1985): 37.

[529] Bruce Haley, "Sports and the Victorian World," *Western Humanities Review* 22/2 (Spring 1968): 115–17, 124; quote in Tozer, "Charles Kingsley and the 'Muscular

---

Christian,'" 37; Thomas Hughes, *Tom Brown at Oxford* (New York: Hurst, 1885) 118.

[530] Hughes, *Tom Brown at Oxford*, 119.

[531] Ladd and Mathisen, *Muscular Christianity*, 16.

[532] Riess, *The American Sporting Experience*, 59; Allen Guttmann, *From Ritual to Record: The Nature of Modern Sports* (New York: Columbia University Press, 1978) 74.

[533] Wegener, *Church and Community Recreation*, 15; Cavallo, *Muscles and Morals*, 33, 81; Philippe Aries, *Centuries of Childhood: A Social History of Family Life*, trans. R. Baldrick (New York: Knopf, 1962) 82.

[534] Quoted in Ladd and Mathisen, *Muscular Christianity*, 57.

[535] Cavallo, *Muscles and Morals*, 59–60.

[536] Robert J. Higgs, "Muscular Christianity: Holy Play, and Spiritual Exercises," in Shirl J. Hoffman, ed., *Sport and Religion* (Champaign IL: Human Kinetics, 1992) 100–101; Ladd and Mathisen, *Muscular Christianity*, 20, 79–80.

[537] Ladd and Mathisen, *Muscular Christianity*, 100–102, 149.

[538] Scott Stossel, "The Tragedy of '04," *Boston Globe*, 28 August 2005, http://www.boston.com/sports/baseball/redsox/articles/2005/08/28/the_tragedy_of_04 (accessed 3 November 2008).

[539] Harry Edwards, *Sociology of Sport* (Homewood IL: Dorsey Press, 1973); Bruce Ogilvie and Thomas Tutko, "If You Want to Build Character, Try Something Else," *Psychology Today* 5/10 (October 1971): 61; John Loy, Barry McPherson, and Gerald Kenyon, *Sport and Social Systems* (Reading MA: Addison-Wesley, 1978) 381.

[540] D. Stanley Eitzen and George Sage, *Sociology of American Sport* (Dubuque IA: Brown, 1982) 157–59.

[541] Arthur Bartlett, *Baseball and Mr. Spalding* (New York: Farrar, Straus and Young, 1951) 137*ff*.

[542] Ibid., 167–68.

[543] Ibid., 128; Patrick Hruby, "Beer and Sports, So Happy Together," *Washington Times,* 17 June 2003, http://www.washtimes.com/sports/20030617-124535-9205r.htm (accessed 24 January 2009).

[544] Debra Dagavarian, *Saying It Ain't So: American Values as Revealed in Children's Baseball Stories, 1880–1950* (New York: Peter Lang, 1987) 108; Roberta Park, "Too Important to Trust to the Children: The Search for Freedom and Order in Children's Play, 1900–1917," in *The Paradoxes of Play*, ed. John Loy (West Point NY: Leisure Press, 1982) 102.

[545] Chuck Knox and Bill Plaschke, *Hard Knox: The Life of an NFL Coach* (San Diego: Harcourt Brace Jovanovich, 1988) 244.

[546] See Robert Creamer, *Babe: The Legend Comes to Life* (New York: Viking, 1974); Jerry Kramer, *Instant Replay: The Green Bay Diary of Jerry Kramer,* ed. Dick Schaap (New York: New American Library, 1968) 27–32.

[547] Phil Berger, *Mickey Mantle* (New York: Park Lane Press, 1998) 86–87.

[548] Heinz Meyer, "Puritanism and Physical Training: Ideological and Political Accents in the Christian Interpretation of Sport," *International Review of Sport Sociology* 8/1 (March 1973): 41; Erich Geldbach, *Sport und Protestantismus: Geschichte einer Begegnung* (Wuppertal, Germany: Theologischer Verlag R. Brockhaus, 1975) 46, 184.

[549] Bruce Haley, "Sports and the Victorian World," *Western Humanities Review* 22/2

(Spring 1968), 124; Meyer, "Puritanism and Physical Training," 43; Pierre Bourdieu, "Programs for a Sociology of Sport," *Sociology of Sport Journal* 5/2 (June 1988): 161; Donald J. Mrozek, *Sport and American Mentality, 1880–1910* (Knoxville: University of Tennessee Press, 1983) 230.

[550] Georg Soell, "Sport in Catholic Theology in the 20th Century," in *The Scientific View of Sport: Perspectives, Aspects, Issues,* ed. Ommo Grupe et al. (New York: Springer-Verlag, 1972) 62–63; Meyer, "Puritanism and Physical Training," 41.

[551] Phil Schaaf, *Sports Inc: 100 Years of Sports Business* (Amherst NY: Prometheus Books, 2004) 278.

[552] See John Feinstein, *A Season on the Brink: A Year with Bobby Knight and the Indiana Hoosiers* (New York: Simon & Schuster, 1989).

[553] Henry A. Atkinson, *The Church and the People's Play* (Boston: Pilgrim Press, 1915) 18.

[554] Brailsford, *Sport and Society: Elizabeth to Anne,* 154.

[555] Lance Armstrong and Sally Jenkins, *It's Not About the Bike: My Journey Back to Life* (New York: Putnam's Sons, 2000) 88, 220.

[556] Kramer, *Instant Replay,* 221*ff.* See also Ed Gruver, *The Ice Bowl: The Cold Truth About Football's Most Unforgettable Game* (Ithaca NY: McBooks Press, 2005).

[557] Liz Robbins, "Tennis; Official and Players Wary of Heat Illness," *New York Times,* 2 September 2001, http://query.nytimes.com/gst/fullpage.html?res=9807E5DD1F30F931A3575AC0A9679C8B 63 (accessed 16 July 2007).

[558] Wiley Umphlett, *The Sporting Myth and the American Experience: Studies in Contemporary Fiction (*Lewisburg PA: Bucknell University Press, 1975) 33–34; Ned Polsky, *Hustlers, Beats and Others* (Chicago: Aldine, 1967).

[559] Ben Yagoda, "Fitness Without Tears," *Esquire* 10/2 (August 1983): 31.

[560] Charles Krauthammer, "The Appeal of Ordeal," *Time* 123/20 (14 May 1984): 93–94.

[561] Chris Wood, "The Perils of Doping," *Maclean's* 105/30 (27 July 1992): 48–53.

[562] Bill Romanowski with Adam Scheffter and Phil Towle, *Romo: My Life on the Edge* (New York: William Morrow, 2005) 33, 38.

[563] Dave Meggyesy, *Out of Their League* (Berkeley CA: Ramparts Press, 1970) 169.

[564] Romanowski, *Romo: My Life on the Edge,* 65.

[565] Meggyesy, *Out of Their League,* 182–83.

[566] Pat Jordan, *A False Spring* (New York: Dodd, Mead & Co. 1975) 180–81.

[567] In Albert B. Wegener, *Church and Community Recreation* (New York: Macmillan, 1924) 4.

[568] Mrozek, *Sport and American Mentality,* 23–35, 147.

[569] Christian Messenger, *Sport and the Spirit of Play in American Fiction: Hawthorne to Faulkner* (New York: Columbia University Press, 1981) 261.

[570] Bernard Malamud, *The Natural* (New York: Farrar, Straus & Giroux, 1980).

[571] Walter Kerr, *The Decline of Pleasure* (New York: Time Inc., 1966) 27, 31.

[572] George Santayana, *The Last Puritan: A Memoir in the Form of a Novel* (New York: Scribner, 1936) 394, 420.

[573] Gary Fine, "Sport as Play," in *The World & I, Washington Times,* October 1988,

---

650. See also Mrozek, *Sport and American Mentality,* 189–202.

[574] Ralph Barton Perry, *Puritanism and Democracy* (New York: Vanguard, 1944) 255–56, 263.

[575] Stephen Hardy, "Adopted by All the Leading Clubs: Sporting Goods and the Shaping of Leisure, 1800–1900," in *For Fun and Profit,* ed. Richard Butsch (Philadelphia: Temple University Press, 1990) 71.

[576] Howard L. Nixon, "The Commercialization and Organizational Development of Modern Sport," *International Review of Sport Sociology* 9/2 (June1974): 113–14; Bero Rigauer, *Sport and Work,* trans. Allen Guttmann (New York: Columbia University Press, 1981) 24–25.

[577] William J. Morgan, "'Radical' Social Theory of Sport: A Critique and a Conceptual Emendation," *Sociology of Sport Journal* 2/1 (March 1985): 66.

[578] Dagavarian, *Saying It Ain't So,* 63.

[579] Sudhir Kakar, *Frederick Taylor: A Study in Personality and Innovation* (Boston: M.I.T. Press, 1970) 18.

[580] Ibid., 168.

[581] Allen Guttmann, *A Whole New Ball Game: An Interpretation of American Sports* (Chapel Hill: University of North Carolina Press, 1988) 72.

[582] Rigauer, *Sport and Work,* xiv; Robert Goldman and John Wilson, "The Rationalization of Leisure," *Politics & Society* 7/2 (June 1977): 169, 185; Morgan, "'Radical' Social Theory of Sport," 66.

[583] Mrozek, *Sport and American Mentality,* 68–73, 102, 169, 195, 201.

[584] Rigauer, *Sport and Work,* 54.

[585] Tony Ladd and James A. Mathisen, *Muscular Christianity: Evangelical Protestants and the Development of American Sport* (Grand Rapids MI: Baker Books, 1999) 64–65. See also Mrozek, *Sport and American Mentality,* and Betts, *America's Sporting Heritage.*

[586] Bartlett, *Baseball and Mr. Spalding,* 161; Mrozek, *Sport and American Mentality,* 90; John R. Behee, *Fielding Yost's Legacy to the University of Michigan* (Ann Arbor MI: Ulrich's Books, 1971).

[587] Christopher Lasch, "The Corruption of Sports," *New York Review of Books* 24/7 (April 1977): 29.

[588] Rigauer, *Sport and Work,* 30–31.

[589] Mrozek, *Sport and American Mentality,* 75–90, 195. For Rickey's contribution, see Ken Burns and Lynn Novak, producers, *Baseball—A Film by Ken Burns,* vol. 3, writer Geoffrey C. Ward (Florentine Films, 1994).

[590] John R. Tunis, *The American Way of Sport* (New York: Duell, Sloan and Pearce, 1958) 56.

[591] See Reuel Denney, *The Astonished Muse* (Chicago: University of Chicago Press, 1957).

[592] Rigauer, *Sport and Work,* xv; Eitzen and Sage, *Sociology of American* Sport, 160.

[593] Regarding the athletic program at Carlisle College, see Jack Newcombe, *The Best of the Athletic Boys: The White Man's Impact on Jim Thorpe* (New York: Doubleday, 1975) chapters 3–4; Mrozek, *Sport and American Mentality,* 82–94.

[594] Neil D. Isaacs, *Jock Culture, USA* (New York: Norton, 1978) 169; Behee, *Fielding Yost's Legacy to the University of Michigan.*

[595] See Donald Chu, *The Character of American Higher Education and Intercollegiate Sport* (Albany NY: S.U.N.Y. Press, 1989) 106–108.

[596] Don Kowet, *The Rich Who Own Sports* (New York: Random House, 1977) 90–92.

[597] John Authers, "Faith in Figures Proves to Be a Big Hit," *Financial Times* 2/3 (December 2006): W5. See also Michael Lewis, *Moneyball: The Art of Winning an Unfair Game* (New York: Norton, 2003).

[598] Mrozek, *Sport and American Mentality*, 100, 212. See also Reuel Denney, *The Astonished Muse*, and Betts, *America's Sporting Heritage*, 217.

[599] Hardy, "Adopted by All the Leading Clubs," 97–98.

[600] Foster R. Dulles, *A History of Recreation: America Learns to Play* (New York: Appleton-Century-Crofts, 1965) 186.

[601] Quoted in Mrozek, *Sport and American Mentality*, 172.

[602] See Denney, *The Astonished Muse.*

[603] Ibid.

[604] Ibid., 114–16.

[605] Terry Furst, "Social Change and the Commercialization of Professional Sports," *International Review for the Sociology of Sport* 6 (March 1971): 163; Denney, *The Astonished Muse*, 114–16. .

[606] Bartlett, *Baseball and Mr. Spalding*, 200; Leonard Koppett, *Koppett's Concise History of Major League Baseball* (New York: Carroll & Graf, 2004) 121.

[607] Mihaly Csikszentmihalyi, "The Americanization of Rock Climbing," in *Play Its Role in Development and Evolution,* eds. Jerome Bruner, Alison Jolly, and Kathy Sylva (New York: Basic Books, 1976) 485–87; Peter Donnelly, "Rock Climbing," in David Levinson and Karen Christensen, eds., *Encyclopedia of World Sport: From Ancient Times to the Present* (New York: Oxford University Press, 1999) 326; see also Edward Voeller, *Sport Climbing* (Mankato MN: Capstone Press, 2000).

[608] David Whitson, "Sport and Hegemony: On the Construction of the Dominant Culture," *Sociology of Sport Journal* l/1 (March 1984): 73; Jay Coakley, "Beyond the Obvious: A Critical Look at Sport in the USA," in *The World & I, Washington Times*, October 1988, 599.

[609] Andrzej Wohl, "Competitive Sport and Its Social Functions," *International Review of Sport Sociology* 5/1 (March 1970): 123.

[610] See Guttmann, *From Ritual to Record*, 47–51.

[611] Rigauer, *Sport and Work*, xiv, 37, 59.

[612] Warren Susman, "Piety, Profits and Play," in *Men, Women, and Issues in American History,* eds. Howard Quint and Milton Cantor, vol. 2 (Homewood IL: Dorsey, 1980) 221.

[613] Robert, Coover, *The Universal Baseball Association, Inc., J. Henry Waugh, Prop.* (New York: Penguin Group, 1971).

[614] Robert L. Simon, *Fair Play: Sports, Values & Society* (Boulder CO: Westview Press, 1991) 40*ff.*

[615] See Aurora Cuito, ed., *Sports Facilities* (Barcelona, Spain: Loft Publications, 2007).

[616] Rigaeur, *Sport and Work*, xvi, 33, 41, 61.

[617] Robin Vealey in Levinson and Christensen, *Encyclopedia of World Sport*, 310; John

Hoberman, *Mortal Engines: The Science of Performance and the Dehumanization of Sport* (New York: Free Press, 1992).

[618] Joann Dennett and Nancy Keogel, "Giving Athletes the Edge," in *The World & I, Washington Times*, October 1988, 163; Mark Teich and Pamela Weintraub, "Ultrasport," *Omni* 7/11 (August 1985): 42*ff.*

[619] Dennett and Keogel, "Giving Athletes the Edge," 163; Teich and Weintraub, "Ultrasport," 42, 96; Adorno quoted in Rigauer, *Sport and Work*, 38.

[620] Randy Roberts and James Olson, *Winning Is the Only Thing* (Baltimore: Johns Hopkins University Press, 1989) 18.

[621] Guttmann, *A Whole New Ball Game*, 169*ff.* See also Hoberman, *Mortal Engines.*

[622] Romanowski, *Romo*, 60–120 *passim.*

[623] See Robert A. Oppliger et al., "Grappling with Weight Cutting," *The Physician and Sportsmedicine* 23/3 (October 1995): 69–78.

[624] Teich and Weintraub, "Ultrasport," 99; Dennett and Keogel, "Giving Athletes the Edge," 167–69.

[625] Samuel N. Eisenstadt, ed., *The Protestant Ethic and Modernization* (New York: Basic Books, 1968); Michael Walzer, *The Revolution of the Saints: A Study in the Origins of Radical Politics* (Cambridge MA: Harvard University Press, 1965) 307; James A. Morone, *Hellfire Nation: The Politics of Sin in American History* (New Haven: Yale University Press, 2003) 14.

[626] See Walter T. Champion, Jr., *Sports Law in a Nutshell* (St. Paul MN: Thompson/West, 2005), for an overview; for baseball's experience, see Leonard Koppett, *Koppett's Concise History of Major League Baseball* (New York: Carroll & Graf, 2004) 135–48, 161–66.

[627] Denney, *The Astonished Muse*, 109–14.

[628] See Koppett, *Koppett's Concise History of Major League Baseball, passim.*

[629] Paul Staudohar, *The Sports Industry and Collective Bargaining* (Ithaca NY: I.L.R. Press, 1989) 133.

[630] Kendall Blanchard and Alyce Cheska, *The Anthropology of Sport: An Introduction* (Hadley MA: Bergin & Garvey, 1985) 193.

[631] Hoberman, *Mortal Engines*, 230–31.

[632] Allen Barra, "When Referee Wyatt Earp Laid Down the Law," *New York Times*, 26 November 1995, 24.

[633] Gordon Kirby, *Mario Andretti: A Driving Passion* (Phoenix AZ: David Bull Publisher, 2001) 188–93; Phil Berger, "Notebook," *New York Times*, 31 January 1990, http://query.nytimes.com/gst/fullpage.html?res=9C0CEED71E39F932A05752C0A96695826 0 (accessed 6 November 2008).

[634] Staudohar, *The Sports Industry and Collective Bargaining*, 184–85 *passim.*

[635] Ibid.

[636] Michael Novak, *The Joy of Sports* (New York: Basic Books, 1976) chapter 2.

[637] William Stern, "Play," in *A Treasury of Philosophy,* ed. Dagobert Runes, vol. 2 (New York: Grollier, 1955) 1144–46.

[638] David L. Miller, *Gods and Games: Toward a Theology of Play* (New York: World Publishing Co, 1970) 174.

[639] Mihaly Csikszentmihalyi, "The Americanization of Rock Climbing," in *Play Its*

Role in Development and Evolution, eds. Jerome Bruner, Alison Jolly, and Kathy Sylva (New York: Basic Books, 1976) 487.

[640] Heinz Meyer, "Puritanism and Physical Training: Ideological and Political Accents in the Christian Interpretation of Sport," *International Review of Sport Sociology* 8/1 (March 1973): 41, 49; Donald J. Mrozek, *Sport and American Mentality, 1880–1910* (Knoxville: University of Tennessee Press, 1983) 228.

[641] Messenger, *Sport and the Spirit of Play in American Fiction,* 134; Steven A. Riess, ed., *The American Sporting Experience: A Historical Anthology of Sport in America* (New York: Leisure Press, 1984) 58.

[642] Higginson quoted in Mrozek, *Sport and American Mentality,* 30; Homes quoted in Melvin Adelman, "The First Modern Sport in America: Harness Racing in New York City, 1825–1879," in *Sport in America,* ed. David Wiggins (Champaign IL: Human Kinetics, 1995) 95–114.

[643] Novak, *The Joy of Sports,* 152, 219.

[644] John R. Betts, *America's Sporting Heritage, 1980–1950* (Reading MA: Addison-Wesley, 1974) 194. The source of the quote (mis)attributed to the Duke of Wellington was *De l'Avenir Politique de l'Angleterre* (1856) by Charles Montalembert; see Vorin E. Whan Jr., *A Soldier Speaks: Public Papers and Speeches of General of the Army Douglas MacArthur* (New York: Praeger, 1965) 14–16; Mrozek, *Sport and American Mentality,* 51–59; Allen Guttmann, *From Ritual to Record: The Nature of Modern Sports* (New York: Columbia University Press, 1978) 72–73.

[645] Mrozek, *Sport and American Mentality,* 133–50.

[646] Ibid., 207

[647] Ibid., 72; J. Thomas Jable, "The Public Schools Athletic League of New York City: Organized Athletics for City Schoolchildren, 1903–1914," in *The American Sporting Experience: A Historical Anthology of Sport in America,* ed. Steven Riess (New York: Leisure Press, 1984) 227–33.

[648] George Santayana, *The Last Puritan: A Memoir in the Form of a Novel* (New York: Scribner, 1936) 11, 541.

[649] See Mrozek, *Sport and American Mentality,* 80–81.

[650] See Robert Merton, "Social Structure and Anomie," in *Approaches to Deviance: Theories, Concepts, and Research Findings,* eds. Mark Lefton, James Skipper, and Charles McCaghy (New York: Appleton-Century-Crofts, 1968a) 34.

[651] Paul Staudohar, *The Sports Industry and Collective Bargaining* (Ithaca NY: I.L.R. Press, 1989) 2, 73.

[652] Bero Rigauer, *Sport and Work,* trans. Allen Guttmann (New York: Columbia University Press, 1981) 20.

[653] Klaus Heinemann, "Unemployment, Personality, and Involvement in Sport," *Sociology of Sport Journal* 2/2 (June 1985): 162–63.

[654] L. G. Borisova and E. P. Podalko, "Toward Classification of Motives," *International Review of Sport Sociology* 10/3–4 (1975): 53–59.

[655] See David Greene and Mark Lepper, "How to Turn Play into Work," *Psychology Today* 8/9 (September 1974): 49–54.

[656] See Beverly L. Clark, ed., *The Adventures of Tom Sawyer,* Norton Critical Edition (New York: Norton, 2006); Kendall Blanchard and Alyce Cheska, *The Anthropology of*

Sport: An Introduction (Hadley MA: Bergin & Garvey, 1985) 44–47. See also Johan Huizinga, *Homo Ludens: A Study of the Play Element in Culture*, 7th ed. (Boston: Beacon Press, 1968).

[657] See Robert G. Osterhoudt, *The Philosophy of Sport: A Collection of Original Essays* (Springfield IL: Thomas, 1973) 78–107.

[658] Rigauer, *Sport and Work,* 9; John Carroll, *Puritan, Paranoid, Remissive: A Sociology of Modern Culture* (London: Routledge & Kegan Paul, 1977) 38; William J. Morgan, "'Radical' Social Theory of Sport: A Critique and a Conceptual Emendation," *Sociology of Sport Journal* 2/1 (March 1985): 66; Henry Thoreau, *Walden*, ed. Jeffrey Cramer (New Haven: Yale University Press, 2004) chapter 1.

[659] Arnold Beisser, *The Madness in Sports: Psychosocial Observations on Sports* (New York: Appleton-Century-Crofts, 1967) 6.

[660] Green and Lepper, "How to Turn Play into Work," 49.

[661] David Riesman, *Individualism Reconsidered* (New York: Free Press, 1954) 217; Oscar Ritchie and Marvin Koller, *Sociology of Childhood* (New York: Appleton-Century-Crofts, 1978) 151; Arnold Beisser, "Modern Man and Sports," in *Sport & Society:An Anthology*, eds. John T. Talamini and C. Page (Boston: Little, Brown and Co., 1973) 95.

[662] Beisser, *The Madness in Sports*, 7.

[663] Howard Slusher, *Man, Sport and Existence: A Critical Analysis* (Philadelphia: Lea & Febiger, 1967) 182.

[664] Seppo Iso-Ahola, *The Social Psychology of Leisure and Recreation* (Dubuque IA: Brown, 1980) 360.

[665] Rigauer, *Sport and Work*, 7–9.

[666] Quoted in Christian Messenger, *Sport and the Spirit of Play in American Fiction: Hawthorne to Faulkner* (New York: Columbia University Press, 1981) 141.

[667] Daniel T. Rodgers, *The Work Ethic in Industrial America, 1850–1920* (Chicago: University of Chicago Press, 1978) 109.

[668] Jean Marie Brohm, *Sport—A Prison of Measured Time*, trans. I. Fraser (London: Ink Links, 1978) 105.

[669] Quoted in Neil D. Isaacs, *Jock Culture, USA* (New York: Norton, 1978) 162.

[670] In Messenger, *Sport and the Spirit of Play in American Fiction*, 86–87.

[671] Howard L. Nixon, "The Commercialization and Organizational Development of Modern Sport," *International Review of Sport Sociology* 9/2 (June 1974): 110; Wiley Umphlett, *The Sporting Myth and the American Experience: Studies in Contemporary Fiction (*Lewisburg PA: Bucknell University Press, 1975) 32. See also Max Lerner, *America as a Civilization: Life and Thought in the United States Today* (New York: Simon and Schuster, 1957).

[672] Lewis Carlson and John Fogarty, *Tales of Gold: An Oral History of the Summer Olympic Games* (Chicago: Contemporary Books, 1987) 70, 78, 204.

[673] Ibid., 57.

[674] Ibid., 331, 381, 446.

[675] Donald Chu, *The Character of American Higher Education and Intercollegiate Sport* (Albany NY: S.U.N.Y. Press, 1989) 72.

[676] George Sage, "American Values and Sport: Formation of a Bureaucratic Personality," *Journal of Physical Education and Recreation* 49/8 (October 1978): 11, 36–37;

William Sadler, "Competition Out of Bounds: Sport in American Life," *Quest* 19/1 (January 1973): 124.

[677] Rigauer, *Sport and Work*, 64–74.

[678] In Susan Orlean, "Shoot the Moon," *New Yorker*, 22 March 1993, 80.

[679] D. Stanley Eitzen and George Sage, *Sociology of American Sport* (Dubuque IA: Brown, 1982) 69.

[680] Paul Borden, "SEC A.D.'s Surely Not Among 'Polk's Folks,'" *Clarion Ledger* (Jackson MS), 11 June 1985, D1.

[681] Quoted in Isaac, *Jock Culture,* 170*ff.*

[682] In Edward Epstein, *Born to Skate: The Michelle Kwan Story* (New York: Ballantine Books, 1997) 20.

[683] Carmen Salvino with Frederick Klein, *Fast Lanes* (Chicago: Bonus Books, 1988) *passim.*

[684] Bobby Riggs, *Court Hustler* (Philadelphia: J. B. Lippincott Co., 1973) 18, 150.

[685] Quoted in Steven J. Overman, "Work and Play in America: Three Centuries of Commentary," *The Physical Educator* 40/4 (December 1983): 188.

[686] Messenger, *Sport and the Spirit of Play in American Fiction*, 237–39, 294–95.

[687] See Jeff Seidel, *Baseball's Iron Man: Cal Ripken Jr., a Tribute* (Champaign IL: Sports Publishing LLC, 2007).

[688] Ralph Barton Perry, *Puritanism and Democracy* (New York: Vanguard, 1944) chapter 10.

[689] Beisser, *The Madness in Sports*, 7.

[690] George Grella "Baseball and the American Dream," in *Sport Inside Out: Readings in Literature and Philosophy,* eds. David Vanderwerken and Spencer Wertz (Fort Worth: Texas Christian University, 1985) 273.

[691] Terry Furst, "Social Change and the Commercialization of Professional Sports," *International Review of Sport Sociology* 6 (March 1971): 165; Robert Goldman and John Wilson, "The Rationalization of Leisure," *Politics & Society* 7/2 (June 1977): 172.

[692] Messenger, *Sport and the Spirit of Play in American Fiction*, 131, 141–42; Mrozek, *Sport and American Mentality*, 171.

[693] Dominick Cavallo, *Muscles and Morals: Organized Playgrounds and Urban Reform, 1880–1920* (Philadelphia: University of Pennsylvania Press, 1981) 3–4, 103, 148–50.

[694] Cavallo, *Muscles and Morals*, 8, 89–93; Messenger, *Sport and the Spirit of Play in American Fiction*, 154.

[695] Rigauer, *Sport and Work*, 54.

[696] Robert Boyle, *Sport—Mirror of American Life* (Boston: Little, Brown, 1963) 63.

[697] Debra Dagavarian, *Saying It Ain't So: American Values as Revealed in Children's Baseball Stories, 1880–1950* (New York: Peter Lang, 1987) 27, 61, 74.

[698] Leonard Koppett, *Koppett's Concise History of Major League Baseball* (New York: Carroll & Graf, 2004) 109.

[699] Jeanne Parr, *The Superwives* (New York: Coward, McCann & Geoghagen, 1976) 140.

[700] See Koppett, *Koppett's Concise History of Major League Baseball*, for professional baseball's experience.

[701] Keith Hernandez and Mike Bryan, *If at First: A Season with the Mets* (New York: McGraw Hill, 1986).

[702] Arthur Bartlett, *Baseball and Mr. Spalding* (New York: Farrar, Straus and Young, 1951) 95.

[703] Günther Lueschen, "The Interdependence of Sport and Culture," in *International Review of Sport Sociology* 2/1 (1967): 127–42.

[704] Kliever, "God and Games in Modern Culture," 570.

[705] Hans Lenk, *Social Philosophy of Athletics* (Champaign IL: Stipes, 1979) 25; Brian Sutton-Smith, John Roberts, and Robert Kozelka, "Game Involvement in Adults," in *Contemporary Readings in Sport Psychology,* ed. William Morgan (Springfield IL: Thomas, 1970) 377, 382.

[706] Quoted in Kramer, *Instant Replay*, 92.

[707] Susan Birrell, "An Analysis of the Inter-relationships among Achievement Motivation, Athletic Participation, Academic Achievement, and Educational Aspirations," *International Journal of Sport Psychology* 8/3 (1977): 178–91; Tunis, *The American Way of Sport*, 147.

[708] Jonathan Brower, "The Professionalization of Organized Youth Sport: Social Psychological Impacts and Outcomes," *Annals of the American Academy of Political and Social Science* 445/1 (September 1979): 41–43.

[709] Umphlett, *The Sporting Myth and the American Experience*, 37; Messenger, *Sport and the Spirit of Play in American Fiction*, 165.

[710] See Harry Edwards, *Sociology of Sport* (Homewood IL: Dorsey Press, 1973).

[711] In Bill Moyers, *A World of Ideas,* ed. B. S. Flowers (New York: Doubleday, 1989) 440.

[712] Novak, *The Joy of Sports*, 133.

[713] Garry Wills, *Certain Trumpets: The Call of Leaders* (New York: Simon & Schuster, 1994) 188.

[714] See Cynthia Patterson, "Athletics and the Higher Education Marketplace," in John Gerdy, *Sports in School: The Future of an Institution* (New York: Teachers College Press, 2000) 119–27.

[715] Gary Cross, *A Social History of Leisure since 1600* (State College PA: Venture Publishing, 1990) 145; Eitzen, "The Myth and Reality of Elite Amateur Sport," 551–53; Nixon, "The Commercialization and Organizational Development of Modern Sport," 112.

[716] Tunis, *The American Way of Sport*, 162; Robert Lipsyte, "Varsity Syndrome: The Unkindest Cut," *The Annals of the American Academy of Political and Social Science* 445/1 (September 1979): 15–20; Cavallo, *Muscles and Morals*, 47. See also Martha E. Ewing and Vern Seefeldt, *American Youth and Sports Participation* (West Palm Beach FL: American Footwear Association, 1990).

[717] Paul Hoch, *Rip Off the Big Game: The Exploitation of Sports by the Power Elite* (New York: Doubleday, 1972) 11.

[718] "T. Boone Pickens Makes $100 Million Gift to Oklahoma State University," *Reuters* (21 May 2008)
http://www.reuters.com/article/pressRelease/idUS177465+21-May-2008+BW20080521 (accessed 16 October 2008). See John R. Thelin, *Games Colleges Play* (Baltimore: Johns Hopkins University Press, 1994).

[719] Hollander and Zimmerman, *Football Lingo*, 15–16.

[720] Ibid., 91.

[721] Ibid., 2–3, 59.

[722] John Nef, *Cultural Foundations of Industrial Civilization* (New York: Harper & Row, 1960) 129.

[723] John Steinbeck, "Then My Arm Glassed Up," *Sports Illustrated* 23/24 (20 December 1965): 99.

[724] Betts, *America's Sporting Heritage*, 181; Jable, "The Public Schools Athletic League of New York City," 227.

[725] Donal Muir, "Club Tennis: A Case Study in Taking Leisure Very Seriously," *Sociology of Sport Journal* 8/1 (March 1991): 70–78.

[726] Brooks, *Showing Off in America*, 48–49.

[727] Christopher Nyerges, "Running to Olympus," in *Core Concepts of Health*, eds. Paul Insel and Walton Roth (Palo Alto CA: Mayfield, 1985) 302.

[728] See James D. Shaughnessy, ed., *The Roots of Ritual* (Grand Rapids MI: Eerdmans, 1973) 57; Csikszentmihalyi, "The Americanization of Rock Climbing," 484–88.

[729] Charles Krauthammer, "The Appeal of Ordeal," *Time* 123/20 (14 May 1984): 93–94.

[730] Adelman, "The First Modern Sport in America," 95–114.

[731] Tara K. Scanlon, "Antecedents of Competitiveness," in *Children in Sport: A Contemporary Anthology*, eds. Richard Magill, Michael Ash, and Frank Smoll (Champaign IL: Human Kinetics, 1978) 56–59; Rigauer, *Sport and Work*, 23.

[732] Jerry Kramer, *Instant Replay: The Green Bay Diary of Jerry Kramer*, ed. Dick Schaap (New York: New American Library, 1968) 65, 92, 159; George F. Flynn, *Vince Lombardi on Football* (New York: Van Nostrand, 1981) 14. See also Steven J. Overman, "Winning isn't everything. It's the only thing.: The Origin, Attributions, and Influence of a Famous Quote," *Football Studies* 2/2 (October 1999): 77–99.

[733] Eitzen and Sage, *Sociology of American Sport*, 67; David McClelland, *The Achieving Society* (New York: Macmillan, 1961) 324. See also Blanchard and Cheska, *The Anthropology of Sport*, and Jennifer Hargreaves, *Sporting Females: Critical Issues* (London: Routledge, 1994) 248.

[734] Grantland Rice quoted in "Alumnus Football," *The Sportlights of 1923* (New York: Putnam, 1924) 50–51. See also Zander Hollander and Paul Zimmerman, *Football Lingo* (New York: Norton, 1967).

[735] Koppett, *Koppett's Concise History of Major League Baseball*, 8–9.

[736] Quoted in E. Digby Baltzell, *The Protestant Establishment: Aristocracy and Caste in America* (London: Secker & Warburg, 1965) 13.

[737] Quoted in Mrozek, *Sport and American Mentality*, 156.

[738] Jable, "The Public Schools Athletic League of New York City," 221–24; John Brooks, *Showing Off in America* (Boston: Little, Brown, 1981) 39; Joseph Kett, *Rites of Passage: Adolescence in America 1790 to the Present* (New York: Basic Books, 1977) 226.

[739] Novak, *The Joy of Sports*, 264.

[740] Thorstein Veblen, *The Theory of the Leisure Class*, Minerva Press ed. (New York: Funk & Wagnalls, 1899) 199; Lonnie D. Kliever, "God and Games in Modern Culture," in *The World & I, Washington Times*, October 1988, 567–69.

[741] Bill Romanowski with Adam Scheffter and Phil Towle, *Romo: My Life on the Edge* (New York: William Morrow, 2005) 54–55.

[742] Kliever, "God and Games in Modern Culture," 569.

[743] Brian Atken, "Sport, Religion and Human Well-Being," in Shirl J. Hoffman, ed., *Sport and Religion* (Champaign IL: Human Kinetics, 1992) 240.

[744] Bobby Cleveland, "Sanders Must Dream a Year Before BASS Masters," *Clarion Ledger* (Jackson MS), 14 July 1985, D14.

[745] Allan Back and Daeshik Kim, "The Future Course of the Eastern Martial Arts," *Quest* 36/1 (January 1984): 7.

[746] See John R. Thelin, *Games Colleges Play* (Baltimore: Johns Hopkins Press, 1996) 81*ff.*

[747] Orlean, "Shoot the Moon," 77.

[748] See Koppett, *Koppett's Concise History of Major League Baseball,* 172–73; Barrie Houlihan, *Sport, Policy & Politics: A Comparative Analysis* (London: Routledge, 1997).

[749] See Stephen Figler, *Sport and Play in American Life* (Philadelphia: Saunders, 1981).

[750] William Fulton, "Politicians Who Chase after Sports Franchises May Get Less than They Pay For," *Governing* 1/6 (March 1988): 34–40.

[751] Boyle, *Sport—Mirror of American Life,* 56.

[752] In Messenger, *Sport and the Spirit of Play in American Fiction,* 110, 125.

[753] Mark Twain, *The Adventures of Tom Sawyer* (Berkeley: University of California Press, 2002).

[754] Robert Creamer, *Babe: The Legend Comes to Life* (New York: Viking, 1974) 24–33.

[755] Roberta Park, "Too Important to Trust to the Children: The Search for Freedom and Order in Children's Play, 1900–1917," in *The Paradoxes of Play,* ed. John Loy (West Point NY: Leisure Press, 1982) 96–104; Higginson quoted in Steven A. Riess, ed., *The American Sporting Experience: A Historical Anthology of Sport in America* (New York: Leisure Press, 1984) 86.

[756] In Michael Smith, *Life after Hockey* (Lynx CT: Codner Books, 1987) 168–69.

[757] Franklin Foer, *How Soccer Explains the World* (New York: Harper Collins, 2004) 236; Edward C. Devereux, "Backyard Versus Little League Baseball: Some Observations on the Impoverishment of Children's Games in Contemporary America," in *Sport Sociology: Contemporary Themes,* 2nd ed., ed. Andrew Yiannakis et al. (Dubuque IA: Kendall/Hunt, 1976) 63–71.

[758] Kenneth Shore, "After-School Overload," *Clarion Ledger* (Jackson MS), 3 March 1991, E5.

[759] Douglas S. Looney, "Bred to Be a Superstar," *Sports Illustrated* 68/8 (22 February 1988): 56–58.

[760] Ibid. (An adult Todd Marinovich ultimately rebelled against the structured agenda of his father and the athletic establishment.)

[761] Lewis Carlson and John Fogarty, *Tales of Gold: An Oral History of the Summer Olympic Games* (Chicago: Contemporary Books, 1987) 375–82; Lynn Hill, *Climbing Free: My Life in the Vertical World* (New York: W. W. Norton, 2002) 23; Joan Ryan, *Little Girls in Pretty Boxes* (New York: Doubleday, 1995) 34, 43, 56, 112.

[762] John Roberts and Brian Sutton-Smith, "Child Training and Game Involvement," *Ethnology* 1/2 (July 1962): 183; Tara K. Scanlon, "Antecedents of Competitiveness," in *Children in Sport: A Contemporary Anthology,* eds. Richard Magill, Michael Ash, and Frank Smoll (Champaign IL: Human Kinetics, 1978) 309.

[763] Barry McPherson, "The Child in Competitive Sport: Influence of the Social Milieu," in *Children in Sport: A Contemporary Anthology,* eds. Richard Magill, Michael Ash, and Frank Smoll (Champaign IL: Human Kinetics, 1978) 223.

[764] Robert Levine, "Culture, Personality, and Socialization: An Evolutionary View," in *Handbook of Socialization and Research,* ed. David A. Goslin (Chicago: Rand McNally, 1969) 506.

[765] Ibid., 518. See also George Sage, "Socialization and Sport," in *Sport and American Society: Selected Readings*, ed. George Sage (Reading MA: Addison-Wesley, 1974a) 133–42.

[766] Oscar Ritchie and Marvin Koller, *Sociology of Childhood* (New York: Appleton-Century-Crofts, 1978) 77; David Riesman, *The Lonely Crowd: A Study of the Changing American Character* (New Haven CT: Yale University Press, 1950) 44.

[767] Phil Berger, *Mickey Mantle* (New York: Park Lane Press, 1988) 4–15, 60.

[768] Ernest Q. Campbell, "Adolescent Socialization," in *Handbook of Socialization Theory and Research*, ed. David Goslin (Chicago: Rand McNally, 1969), 823–29; Berger, *Mickey Mantle,* 28; Robin M. Williams, *American Society: A Sociological Interpretation* (New York: Knopf, 1970) 90.

[769] Rainer Martens, *Sociology Psychology and Physical Activity* (New York: Harper & Row, 1975) 98; Arnold Beisser, *The Madness in Sports: Psychosocial Observations on Sports* (New York: Appleton-Century-Crofts, 1967) 11. See also McPherson, "The Child in Competitive Sport: Influence of the Social Milieu," 219–49.

[770] Calvin quoted in John T. McNeill, ed., *On the Christian Faith: Selections from the Institutes, Commentaries, and Tracts of John Calvin* (Indianapolis IN: Bobbs-Merrill, 1957) 43. See Thomas J. Wertenbaker, *The Puritan Oligarchy* (New York: Grosset & Dunlap, 1947) 166, 177.

[771] John Carroll, *Puritan, Paranoid, Remissive: A Sociology of Modern Culture* (London: Routledge & Kegan Paul, 1977) 5; Gerhard Lenski, *The Religious Factor: A Sociological Study of Religion's Impact on Politics, Economics, and Family Life* (Garden City NY: Doubleday, 1961) 18. See also Robert Levine, *Culture, Behavior, and Personality* (Chicago: Aldine, 1973).

[772] N. Ray Hiner, "The Cry of Sodom Enquired Into: Educational Analysis in Seventeenth-Century New England," *History of Education Quarterly* 13/1 (Spring 1973): 16–19.

[773] See Philip Greven, *The Protestant Temperament: Patterns of Child-Rearing, Religious Experience, and the Self in Early America* (New York: Knopf, 1977).

[774] See James A. Morone, *Hellfire Nation: The Politics of Sin in American History* (New Haven: Yale University Press, 2003) 16–17.

[775] Sudhir Kakar, *Frederick Taylor: A Study in Personality and Innovation* (Boston: M.I.T. Press, 1970) 23.

[776] Martha Wolfenstein, "The Emergence of Fun Morality," in *Mass Leisure*, eds. Eric

Larrabee and Rolf Meyerson (Glencoe IL: Free Press, 1958) 87–91.

[777] In T. Scott Miyakawa, *Protestants and Pioneers: Individualism and Conformity on the American Frontier* (Chicago: University of Chicago Press, 1964) 23.

[778] Michael Walzer, "Puritanism as a Revolutionary Ideology," in *The Protestant Ethic and Modernization*, ed. Samuel N. Eisenstadt (New York: Basic Books, 1968) 126; Greven, *The Protestant Temperament,* 43.

[779] Edmund S. Morgan, *Visible Saints: The History of a Puritan Idea* (Ithaca NY: Cornell University Press, 1963) 126; Kakar, *Frederick Taylor*, 16–17; Hiner, "The Cry of Sodom Enquired Into," 3–19.

[780] Levine, "Culture, Personality, and Socialization: An Evolutionary View," 515.

[781] Ibid., 515–16; Levine, *Culture, Behavior, and Personality*, 107; Dominick Cavallo, *Muscles and Morals: Organized Playgrounds and Urban Reform, 1880–1920* (Philadelphia: University of Pennsylvania Press, 1981) 50.

[782] Cavallo, *Muscles and Morals*, 49; Debra Dagavarian, *Saying It Ain't So: American Values as Revealed in Children's Baseball Stories, 1880–1950* (New York: Peter Lang, 1987) 111–12.

[783] Hans P. Dreitzel, *Childhood and Socialization* (New York: Macmillan, 1973) 8.

[784] Gary Cross, *A Social History of Leisure since 1600* (State College PA: Venture Publishing, 1990) 60–61; Daniel T. Rodgers, *The Work Ethic in Industrial America, 1850–1920* (Chicago: University of Chicago Press, 1978) 130–35. See also Joseph Kett, *Rites of Passage: Adolescence in America 1790 to the Present* (New York: Basic Books, 1977).

[785] Robin M. Williams, *American Society: A Sociological Interpretation* (New York: Knopf, 1970) 79–80; Cross, *A Social History of Leisure since 1600*, 78; Kett, *Rites of Passage*, 233; Christopher Lasch, "The Corruption of Sports," *New York Review of Books* 24/7 (April 1977): 28.

[786] Kett, *Rites of Passage*, 36, 122–29, 167.

[787] Ibid., 123; Christian Messenger, *Sport and the Spirit of Play in American Fiction: Hawthorne to Faulkner* (New York: Columbia University Press, 1981) 314.

[788] Kett, *Rites of Passage*, 243; Cavallo, *Muscles and Morals*, 86; Ernest Q. Campbell, "Adolescent Socialization," in *Handbook of Socialization Theory and Research*, ed. David Goslin (Chicago: Rand McNally, 1969) 825.

[789] See Kett, *Rites of Passage*; Cross, *A Social History of Leisure since 1600*, 112–15.

[790] Cross, *A Social History of Leisure since 1600*, 173–88.

[791] Ibid., 176–77. See also Hiner, "The Cry of Sodom Enquired Into," 16–19; Hollingshead quoted in Kett, *Rites of Passage*, 253.

[792] Thorstein Veblen, *The Theory of the Leisure Class,* Minerva Press ed. (New York: Funk & Wagnalls, 1899) 199.

[793] Kett, *Rites of Passage*, 85.

[794] Riess, *The American Sporting Experience*, 214. See also Morone, *Hellfire Nation*.

[795] Richard Swanson, "The Acceptance and Influence of Play in American Protestantism," *Quest* 11/1 (December 1968): 61; Bruce Haley, "Sports and the Victorian World," *Western Humanities Review* 22/2 (1968): 117; Dagavarian, *Saying It Ain't So*, 109; Cavallo, *Muscles and Morals*, 1–17, 59–60.

[796] Albert B. Wegener, *Church and Community Recreation* (New York: Macmillan, 1924) 40–43; Park, "Too Important to Trust to the Children," 100–101. See also Cross, *A*

Social History of Leisure since 1600.

[797] Park, "Too Important to Trust to the Children," 99–101; Wegener, *Church and Community Recreation*, 40–43; Cavallo, *Muscles and Morals*, 17, 50–51.

[798] Cavallo, *Muscles and Morals*, 2, 10–11; Park, "Too Important to Trust to the Children," 98.

[799] Riess, *The American Sporting Experience*, 214; Park, "Too Important to Trust to the Children," 96; Allen Guttmann, *A Whole New Ball Game: An Interpretation of American Sports* (Chapel Hill: The University of North Carolina Press, 1988) 82–83; Rainer Martens, *Joy and Sadness in Children's Sports* (Champaign IL: Human Kinetics, 1978) 6; J. Thomas Jable, "The Public Schools Athletic League of New York City: Organized Athletics for City Schoolchildren, 1903–1914," in *The American Sporting Experience: A Historical Anthology of Sport in America*, ed. Steven Riess (New York: Leisure Press, 1984) 234.

[800] See Cross, *A Social History of Leisure since 1600.*

[801] See Guttmann, *A Whole New Ball Game*; Susan Cahn, *Coming On Strong: Gender and Sexuality in Twentieth-Century Women's Sport* (New York: Free Press, 1994) 259–78.

[802] Martha E. Ewing et al., "Psychological Characteristics of Competitive Young Hockey Players," in *Competitive Sports for Children and Youth,* eds. Eugen Brown and Crystal Branta (Champaign IL: Human Kinetics, 1988) 49–61.

[803] Eitzen and Sage, *Sociology of American Sport*, 79.

[804] Ibid., 77.

[805] Philippe Aries, *Centuries of Childhood: A Social History of Family Life*, trans. R. Baldrick (New York: Knopf, 1962) 15*ff.* See also Harry Hendrick, "Children and Childhood," *Refresh: Recent Findings of Research in Economic and Social History,* vol. 15 (1992) http://www.ehs.org.uk/society/pdfs/Hendrick%2015a.pdf (accessed 17 January 2009), for a critical dissent.

[806] Carroll, *Puritan, Paranoid, Remissive*, 70; David McClelland, *The Achieving Society* (New York: Macmillan, 1961) 47–52.

[807] Aries, *Centuries of Childhood*, 66.

[808] Ibid., 21.

[809] See David Elkind, *The Hurried Child: Growing Up Too Fast, Too Soon* (Reading MA: Addison-Wesley, 1981); John Stravinsky, *Muhammad Ali* (New York: Park Lane Press, 1997) 5.

[810] See Raymond Moore and Dorothy Moore, *School Can Wait* (Provo UT: Brigham Young University Press, 1979).

[811] See Elkind, *The Hurried Child.*

[812] In Carlson and Fogarty, *Tales of Gold*, 42–43.

[813] Jonathan Brower, "The Professionalization of Organized Youth Sport: Social Psychological Impacts and Outcomes," *Annals of the American Academy of Political and Social Science* 445/1 (September 1979): 42.

[814] Riesman, *The Lonely Crowd*, 41; Berger, *Mickey Mantle*, 12.

[815] Melvin L. Kohn, "Social Class and Parent-Child Relationships: an Interpretation," *American Journal of Sociology* 68/1 (January 1963): 471–80; Colin C. Kelly, "Socialization into Sport among Male Adolescents from Canada, England, and the United States" (M.S. thesis, University of Wisconsin, 1970) 53.

[816] Elkind, *The Hurried Child*, 30; Jim Piersall and Al Hirshberg, *Fear Strikes Out: The*

Jim Piersall Story (New York: Grosset & Dunlap, 1955).

[817] Ritchie and Koller, *Sociology of Childhood*, 208.

[818] Dan Bickley, *No Bull: The Unauthorized Biography of Dennis Rodman* (New York: St. Martins, 1997) 2–6; Brower, "The Professionalization of Organized Youth Sport," 45; Sage, "Socialization and Sport," 166–67.

[819] McClelland, *The Achieving Society*, 127, 146, 345; Brian Sutton-Smith, John Roberts, and Robert Kozelka, "Game Involvement in Adults," in *Contemporary Readings in Sport Psychology,* ed. William Morgan (Springfield IL: Thomas, 1970) 375–82.

[820] David Riesman, *Individualism Reconsidered* (New York: Free Press, 1954) 20; McClelland, *The Achieving Society*, 415; Margaret Mead, *And Keep Your Powder Dry: An Anthropologist Looks at America* (New York: Morrow, 1965) 90–104.

[821] Mead, *And Keep Your Powder Dry*, 90.

[822] In Robert Boyle, *Sport—Mirror of American Life* (Boston: Little, Brown, 1963) 61.

[823] Sutton-Smith, Roberts, and Kozelka, "Game Involvement in Adults," 375–382; Roberts and Sutton-Smith, "Child Training and Game Involvement," 176. See also Maureen R. Weiss, V. M. Weiss, and K. A. Kline, "Head over Heels with Success: The Relationship Between Self-efficacy and Performance in Competitive Young Gymnasts," *Journal of Sport & Exercise Psychology* 11/4 (December 1989): 444–51.

[824] Roberts and Sutton-Smith, "Child Training and Game Involvement," 166–70.

[825] Ronald Woods, *Social Issues in Sport* (Champaign IL: Human Kinetics, 2006) 100.

[826] George Sage, "American Values and Sport: Formation of a Bureaucratic Personality," *Journal of Physical Education and Recreation* 49/8 (October 1978): 10.

[827] Sage, "American Values and Sport: Formation of a Bureaucratic Personality," 10.

[828] George Mead, *Mind, Self, and Society* (Chicago: University of Chicago Press, 1934) 159–60; Harvey A. Scott, "Self, Coach, and Team: A Theoretical and Empirical Application of the Social Interactionist Perspective to Teenage Sports Candidacy and Participation" (Ph.D. diss., University of Alberta, 1973) 19–22.

[829] Tim Green, *The Dark Side of the Game: My Life in the NFL* (New York: Warner Books, 1996) 22–23.

[830] Cameron Stratcher, "The Endless Summer," *Wall Street Journal*, 3 September 2004, W13; Steve Davis, "Is select soccer worth the shot?" *Dallas Morning News,* 13 June 2004, http://www.psychologyofsports. com/guest/travel.htm (accessed 17 April 2007). See also Kendall Blanchard and Alyce Cheska, *The Anthropology of Sport: An Introduction* (Hadley MA: Bergin & Garvey, 1985).

[831] Leonard Koppett, *Sports Illusion, Sports Reality: A Reporter's View of Sports, Journalism, and Society*, 2nd ed. (Champaign IL: University of Illinois Press, 1994) 258.

[832] Geoffrey Watson, "Game Interaction in Little League Baseball and Family Organization" (Ph.D. diss., University of Illinois, 1973).

[833] Eitzen and Sage, *Sociology of American Sport*, 91–92.

[834] Gary Fine, "Sport as Play," in *The World & I, Washington Times*, October 1988, 654.

[835] Phil Berger, *Mickey Mantle*, 16.

[836] Devereux, "Backyard Versus Little League Baseball," 123–24.

[837] Dagavarian, *Saying It Ain't So*, 105.

[838] Quoted in Martin Ralbovsky, *Lords of the Locker Room: The American Way of*

Coaching and Its Effect on Youth (New York: Peter H. Wyden, 1974) 86–87.

[839] George Sage, "Sports Participation as a Builder of Character," in *The World & I, Washington Times,* October 1988, 640.

[840] Harry Webb, "Professionalization of Attitudes toward Play Among Adolescents," in *Aspects of Contemporary Sport,* ed. Gerald Kenyon (Chicago: The Athletic Institute, 1969) 161–78; Jonathan Brower, "The Professionalization of Organized Youth Sport: Social Psychological Impacts and Outcomes," *Annals of the American Academy of Political and Social Science* 445/1 (September 1979): 39–46; Michael D. Smith, "Social Learning of Violence in Minor Hockey," in *Psychological Perspectives in Youth Sports,* eds. Frank Smoll and Ronald Smith (Washington: Hemisphere Publishing, 1978) 91–106.

[841] Martha E. Ewing and Vern Seefeldt, *American Youth and Sports Participation* (West Palm Beach FL: American Footwear Association, 1990); John Neulinger, *The Psychology of Leisure* (Springfield IL: Thomas, 1974) 119.

[842] Sally Friedman, *Swimming the Channel: A Memoir of Love, Loss, and Healing* (New York: Farrar, Straus and Giroux, 1996) 9.

[843] Webb, "Professionalization of Attitudes toward Play Among Adolescents," 161–78; Sutton-Smith et al., "Game Involvement in Adults," 385.

[844] Carlson and Fogarty, *Tales of Gold,* 447, 496; Sage, "Sports Participation as a Builder of Character," 640.

[845] In Sage, "Sports Participation as a Builder of Character," 639.

[846] Roberts and Sutton-Smith, "Child Training and Game Involvement," 174; Günther Lueschen, "The Interdependence of Sport and Culture," in *International Review of Sport Sociology* 2/1 (1967): 127–42; Watson, "Game Interaction in Little League Baseball and Family Organization."

[847] Sutton-Smith et al., "Game Involvement in Adults," 386. See also Elias Canetti, *Crowds and Power,* trans. C. Stewart (New York: Viking Press, 1962).

[848] Davis, "Is select soccer worth the shot?" http://www.psychologyofsports. com/guest/travel.htm.

[849] In Eitzen and Sage, *Sociology of American Sport,* 82.

[850] Green, *The Dark Side of the Game,* 191.

[851] D. Stanley Eitzen, *Fair and Foul: Beyond the Myths and Paradoxes of Sport* (Boulder CO: Rowman & Littlefield, 2003) 70–71.

[852] S. W. Pope, *Patriotic Games: Sporting Traditions in the American Imagination, 1876–1926* (New York: Oxford University Press, 1997) 22, 28; Leonard Koppett, *Sports Illusion, Sports Reality: A Reporter's View of Sports, Journalism, and Society,* 2nd ed. (Champaign IL: University of Illinois Press, 1994) 180.

[853] John R. Betts, *America's Sporting Heritage, 1980–1950* (Reading MA: Addison-Wesley, 1974) 30–43 *passim*; Koppett, *Sports Illusion, Sports Reality,* 33. See also Steven A. Riess, ed., *The American Sporting Experience: A Historical Anthology of Sport in America* (New York: Leisure Press, 1984).

[854] Howard L. Nixon, "The Commercialization and Organizational Development of Modern Sport," *International Review of Sport Sociology* 9/2 (June 1974): 116; Richard Gruneau, *Class, Sports, and Social Development* (Amherst: University of Massachusetts Press, 1983) 114–16.

[855] Ronald Smith, "Football, American," in David Levinson and Karen Christensen,

eds., *Encyclopedia of World Sport: From Ancient Times to the Present* (New York: Oxford University Press, 1999) 138.

[856] Betts, *America's Sporting Heritage,* 199.

[857] Foster R. Dulles, *A History of Recreation: America Learns to Play* (New York: Appleton-Century-Crofts, 1965) 146; Pope, *Patriotic Games,* 18–20; Gruneau, *Class, Sports, and Social Development,* 118–19.

[858] Bobby Riggs, *Court Hustler* (Philadelphia: J. B. Lippincott Co., 1973) 56–59.

[859] Pope, *Patriotic Games,* 23–25, 30–34.

[860] Barry McPherson, James Curtis, and John Loy, *The Social Significance of Sport: An Introduction to the Sociology of Sport* (Champaign IL: Human Kinetics, 1989) 138; Paul Staudohar, *The Sports Industry and Collective Bargaining* (Ithaca NY: I.L.R. Press, 1989) 190.

[861] William J. Morgan, "'Radical' Social Theory of Sport: A Critique and a Conceptual Emendation," *Sociology of Sport Journal* 2/1 (March 1985): 66; Gregory Stone, "American Sports: Play and Display," in *Sport & Society: An Anthology,* eds. John T. Talamini, and C. Page (Boston: Little, Brown, 1973) 76; Gruneau, *Class, Sports and Social Development,* 115–16.

[862] John Brooks, *Showing Off in America* (Boston: Little, Brown, 1981) 129.

[863] Raymond Callahan, *Education and the Cult of Efficiency* (Chicago: University of Chicago Press, 1962) 8, 54, quote on 152.

[864] See Laurence Veysey, *The Emergence of the American University* (Chicago: University of Chicago Press, 1970).

[865] Harry Edwards, "Desegregating Sexist Sport," *Intellectual Digest* 3/11 (November 1972): 82. See also Donald Chu, *The Character of American Higher Education and Intercollegiate Sport* (Albany NY: S.U.N.Y. Press, 1989).

[866] See Betts, *America's Sporting Heritage*; Nixon, "The Commercialization and Organizational Development of Modern Sport," 107–35.

[867] Betts, *America's Sporting Heritage,* 101–108; Nixon, "The Commercialization and Organizational Development of Modern Sport," 116–17; Chu, *The Character of American Higher Education,* 129.

[868] Nixon, "The Commercialization and Organizational Development of Modern Sport," 117; McPherson, Curtis, and Loy, *The Social Significance of Sport,* 130–31; Andrew Doyle, "Intercollegiate Athletics," in Levinson and Christensen, *Encyclopedia of World Sport* (New York: Oxford University Press, 1999) 198–99.

[869] See Reuel Denney, *The Astonished Muse* (Chicago: University of Chicago Press, 1957); Betts, *America's Sporting Heritage.*

[870] Denney, *The Astonished Muse,* 115; Betts, *America's Sporting Heritage,* 105; Chu, *The Character of American Higher Education,* 80; Doyle, "Intercollegiate Athletics," 201.

[871] Debra Blum, "Private Association's Role in Florida Athletics Prompts Changes," *Chronicle of Higher Education,* 30 September 1992, A32.

[872] D. Stanley Eitzen, "The Myth and Reality of Elite Amateur Sport," in *The World & I, Washington Times,* October 1988, 553; Allen Guttmann, *A Whole New Ball Game: An Interpretation of American Sports* (Chapel Hill: University of North Carolina Press, 1988) 106–109.

[873] See Murray A. Sperber, *College Sports Inc.* (New York: Henry Holt and Co., 1990).

[874] Chu, *The Character of American Higher Education*, 7, 139; Mike Knobler, "SEC Makes Big Bucks Off Name: Conference Slices Pie Pretty Evenly," *Clarion Ledger* (Jackson MS), 22 October 1995, D8.

[875] Nixon, "The Commercialization and Organizational Development of Modern Sport," 118; Murray A. Sperber, "The College Coach as Entrepreneur," *Academe* 73/4 (July/August 1987): 30–33.

[876] Matthew Goodman, "Bowling for Dollars," *Sports Today* (March 1989): n.p.; Betts, *America's Sporting Heritage*, 32–33.

[877] D. Stanley Eitzen, *Fair and Foul: Beyond the Myths and Paradoxes of Sport* (Boulder CO: Rowman & Littlefield, 2003) 115; Knobler, "SEC Makes Big Bucks Off Name: Conference Slices Pie Pretty Evenly," D8.

[878] Fred Milverstadt, "Colleges Courting Corporate Sponsors," *Athletic Business* 13/3 (March 1989): 22–26.

[879] McPherson, Curtis, and Loy, *The Social Significance of Sport*, 114.

[880] Chu, *The Character of American Higher Education*, 153; Sperber, "The College Coach as Entrepreneur," 30–33.

[881] Sperber, "The College Coach as Entrepreneur," 30–32.

[882] Eitzen, "The Myth and Reality of Elite Amateur Sport," 554. See also Frederick Cozens and Florence Stumpf, *Sports in American Life* (Chicago: University of Chicago Press, 1953).

[883] Betts, *America's Sporting Heritage*, 110; Nand Hart-Nibbrig, "Corporate Athleticism: An Inquiry into the Political Economy of College Sports," *Proceedings, NAPEHE* 5 (1984) 11–20; Staudohar, *The Sports Industry and Collective Bargaining*, 190–91; "More Than a Game" (telecast), narrator Frank Gifford (New York: Arts and Entertainment Network, May 1992); Allen Sack, "The Underground Economy of College Football," *Sociology of Sport Journal* 13 (1991), 1–15; Phil Schaaf, *Sports Inc: 100 Years of Sports Business* (Amherst NY: Prometheus Books, 2004) 284.

[884] Joe Drape, "High School Football, Under Prime-Time Lights," *New York Times*, 17 September 2006, http://www.nytimes.com/2006/09/17/sports/17highschool.html (accessed 11 December 2006).

[885] Susan Orlean, "Shoot the Moon," *New Yorker,* 22 March 1993, 74–80.

[886] Dave Zirin, "Varsity Ruse: High School Football Today," *Edge of Sports*, 27 August 2006,
http://www.edgeofsports.com/2006-08-27-197/index.html (accessed 6 November 2006).

[887] Gerald W. Scully, *The Business of Major League Baseball* (Chicago: University of Chicago Press, 1989) 9, 50; Nixon, "The Commercialization and Organizational Development of Modern Sport," 122.

[888] "Mammon has taken his place among the gods of the stadium."

[889] Randy Roberts and James Olson, *Winning Is the Only Thing* (Baltimore: Johns Hopkins University Press, 1989) 3, 11, 22; David Maraniss, *Rome 1960: The Olympics That Changed the World* (New York: Simon & Shuster, 2008) 331. See also John MacAloon, *The Great Symbol: Pierre de Coubertin and the Origins of the Modern Olympic Games* (Chicago: University of Chicago Press, 1984).

[890] Timothy Chandler, "Pierre de Coubertin: Le Regime Arnoldien et le Pedagogie

Sportive," paper presented at North American Society for Sport History Conference, Auburn AL, May 1996; Alan Tomlinson, "The Commercialization of the Olympics: Cities, Corporations, and the Olympic Commodity," in K. Young and K. Wamsley, eds., *The Global Olympics: Historical and Sociological Studies of the Modern Games* (London: JAI Press, 2005) 179–200.

[891] Christine Brooks, "Sponsorship: Strictly Business," *Athletic Business* 14/2 (October 1990): 59; Rober K. Barney, "Modern Olympic Games," in David Levinson and Karen Christensen, eds., *Encyclopedia of World Sport: From Ancient Times to the Present* (New York: Oxford University Press, 1999) 281; Richard Yarbrough, *And They Call Them Games* (Atlanta: Mercer University Press, 2000) 176.

[892] See John Bale and Mette Krogh Christensen, eds., *Post-Olympism? Questioning Sport in the Twenty-First Century* (Oxford, UK: Berg, 2004).

[893] Jean Marie Brohm, *Sport—A Prison of Measured Time*, trans. I. Fraser (London: Ink Links, 1978) 104; Eitzen, "The Myth and Reality of Elite Amateur Sport," 555; Roberts and Olson, *Winning Is the Only Thing*, 11. See also Maraniss, *Rome 1960*.

[894] McPherson, Curtis, and Loy, *The Social Significance of Sport*, 136–38; Lisa Delpy, "Management and Marketing," in David Levinson and Karen Christensen, eds., *Encyclopedia of World Sport: From Ancient Times to the Present* (New York: Oxford University Press, 1999) 233–34; Tomlinson, "The Commercialization of the Olympics," 179–200.

[895] McPherson, Curtis, and Loy, *The Social Significance of Sport*, 115, 136; Schaaf, *Sports Inc.*, 37.

[896] S. Woodward, "Focus, Funding Top Items on Organization's Agenda," *USA Today* (11 November 1988): C3.

[897] Yarbrough, *And They Call Them Games*, 78.

[898] Ibid., 16–17, 20, 59.

[899] McPherson, Curtis, and Loy, *The Social Significance of Sport*, 138; Staudohar, *The Sports Industry and Collective Bargaining*, 190; John Lucas, "Olympic Changes: Dollars and Sense," *Online NewsHour* (23 July 1996) http:/www.pbs.org/newshour/forum/july96/Olympics_7-23.html (accessed 1 March 2009). See also Robert K. Barney, "Olympic Games, Modern," in Levinson and Christianism, *Encyclopedia of World Sport*, 277–85 *passim*.

[900] Daniel T. Rodgers, *The Work Ethic in Industrial America, 1850–1920* (Chicago: University of Chicago Press, 1978) 108–109; Carnegie quoted in Gary Cross, *A Social History of Leisure since 1600* (State College PA: Venture Publishing, 1990) 97; David Riesman, *Individualism Reconsidered* (New York: Free Press, 1954) 203.

[901] Donald J. Mrozek, *Sport and American Mentality, 1880–1910* (Knoxville: University of Tennessee Press, 1983) 182; Lynn Hill with Greg Child, *Climbing Free: My Life in the Vertical World* (New York: W. W. Norton, 2002) 105, 139–40.

[902] Gruneau, *Class, Sports, and Social Development*, 93.

[903] Marilyn Olsen, *Women Who Risk: Profiles of Women in Extreme Sports* (New York: Hatherleigh Press, 2003) 50.

[904] John Clarke, "Pessimism Versus Populism: The Problematic Politics of Popular Culture," in *For Fun and Profit*, ed. Richard Butsch (Philadelphia: Temple University Press, 1990) 31; McPherson, Curtis, and Loy, *The Social Significance of Sport*, 115.

[905] Jay Coakley, "Beyond the Obvious: A Critical Look at Sport in the USA," in *The*

World & I, Washington Times, October 1988, 596; McPherson, Curtis, and Loy, *The Social Significance of Sport,* 114–15.

[906] See Mark Anshell, *Applied Exercise Psychology: A Practitioner's Guide to Improving Client Health and Fitness* (New York: Springer, 2005) 95.

[907] Schaaf, *Sports Inc.,* 187–88.

[908] Philippe Simonnot, *Homo Sportivus: Sport, Capitalisme et Religion* (Paris: Gallimard, 1988) 110.

[909] Foster R. Dulles, *A History of Recreation: America Learns to Play* (New York: Appleton-Century-Crofts, 1965) 209.

[910] Quoted in Arthur Bartlett, *Baseball and Mr. Spalding* (New York: Farrar, Straus and Young, 1951) 85.

[911] Jean Marie Brohm, *Sport—A Prison of Measured Time,* trans. I. Fraser (London: Ink Links, 1978) 116, 134–37, 176; William Flint and D. Stanley Eitzen, "Professional Sports Team Ownership and Entrepreneurial Capitalism," *Sociology of Sport Journal,* 4/1 (March 1987): 23.

[912] Brohm, *Sport—A Prison of Measured Time,* 176; Howard L. Nixon, "The Commercialization and Organizational Development of Modern Sport," *International Review of Sport Sociology* 9/2 (June 1974): 111. See also Bartlett, *Baseball and Mr. Spalding.*

[913] Phil Schaaf, *Sports Inc: 100 Years of Sports Business* (Amherst NY: Prometheus Books, 2004) 20–28.

[914] Allen Guttmann, *From Ritual to Record: The Nature of Modern Sports* (New York: Columbia University Press, 1978) 73; Barrie Houlihan, *Sport, Policy & Politics: A Comparative Analysis* (London: Routledge, 1997) 160–63; See N. I. Ponomaryov, *Sport and Society,* trans. James Riordan (Moscow: Izdatelstvo Fizkul'tura i Sport, 1981), for an analysis of the Soviet system; Robert Chappell, "Cuba: Before and After the Wall Came Down," *The Sport Journal* 7/1 (Winter 2004) http://www.thesportjournal.org/2004Journal/Vol7-No1/chappellCuba.asp (accessed 14 June 2007).

[915] See Mabel Lee, *A History of Physical Education and Sports in the USA* (New York: John Wiley & Sons, 1983) 241–53, 309–34.

[916] Dean Purdy, "For Whom Sport Tolls: Players, Owners and Fans," in *The World & I, Washington Times,* October 1988, 579–80; "New Yankee Stadium," http://www.ballparks. com/baseball/american/nyybpk.htm (accessed September 2007). See also Schaaf, *Sports, Inc.*

[917] Harry Webb, "Professionalization of Attitudes toward Play Among Adolescents," in *Aspects of Contemporary Sport,* ed. Gerald Kenyon (Chicago: The Athletic Institute, 1969) 161–78; Guttmann, *From Ritual to Record,* 69; John R. Betts, *America's Sporting Heritage, 1980–1950* (Reading MA: Addison-Wesley, 1974) 322; Jay Coakley, "Beyond the Obvious: A Critical Look at Sport in the USA," in *The World & I, Washington Times,* October 1988, 593.

[918] Gerald W. Scully, *The Business of Major League Baseball* (Chicago: University of Chicago Press, 1989) 1–5.

[919] Ibid. See also Betts, *America's Sporting Heritage,* 15, 30–33, 40; Leonard Koppett, *Koppett's Concise History of Major League Baseball* (New York: Carroll & Graf, 2004) 15–21.

[920] Bartlett, *Baseball and Mr. Spalding*, 31–39; David Q. Voigt, *America Through Baseball* (Chicago: Nelson Hall, 1976) 8–9; Scully, *The Business of Major League Baseball*, 1–5; Koppett, *Concise History*, 32–36.

[921] Stephen Hardy, "Adopted by All the Leading Clubs: Sporting Goods and the Shaping of Leisure, 1800–1900," in *For Fun and Profit*, ed. Richard Butsch (Philadelphia: Temple University Press, 1990) 72, 87–93; Koppett, *Concise History*, 471. See also Bartlett, *Baseball and Mr. Spalding*.

[922] Bartlett, *Baseball and Mr. Spalding*, 154; Koppett, *Concise History*, 10*ff.*

[923] Gary Cross, *A Social History of Leisure since 1600* (State College PA: Venture Publishing, 1990) 150; Bartlett, *Baseball and Mr. Spalding*, 35, 103*ff*, 210, 226–29. See also Koppett, *Concise History,* 37–53.

[924] Voigt, *America Through Baseball*, 5; Randy Roberts and James Olson, *Winning Is the Only Thing* (Baltimore: Johns Hopkins University Press, 1989) 50; Bartlett, *Baseball and Mr. Spalding*, 86, 153–54, 201; Scully, *The Business of Major League Baseball*, 32; Koppett, *Concise History*, 38.

[925] Bartlett, *Baseball and Mr. Spalding*, 201–207; Scully, *The Business of Major League Baseball*, 32.

[926] Bartlett, *Baseball and Mr. Spalding*, 268–84; Richard Gruneau, *Class, Sports and Social Development* (Amherst: University of Massachusetts Press, 1983) 117, 120; Koppett, *Concise History*, 126.

[927] Scully, *The Business of Major League Baseball*, 4; Koppett, *Concise History*, 73, 174–77, 192.

[928] See Ronald Smith, "Football, American," in David Levinson and Karen Christensen, eds., *Encyclopedia of World Sport: From Ancient Times to the Present* (New York: Oxford University Press, 1999) 137–40; William Baker and S. W. Pope, "Basketball" in Levinson and Christensen, *Encyclopedia of World Sport*, 40–45.

[929] Koppett, *Concise History*, 218–21, 133–34.

[930] Scully, *The Business of Major League Baseball*, 101, 144, 192.

[931] Barry McPherson, James Curtis, and John Loy, *The Social Significance of Sport: An Introduction to the Sociology of Sport* (Champaign IL: Human Kinetics, 1989) 119*ff.*; Scully, *The Business of Major League Baseball*, 191; Koppett, *Concise History*, 295.

[932] *Street & Smith's SportsBusiness Journal*, http://www.sportsbusinessjournal.com/ (22 September 2008); *SMG Online*, http://www.fitinfotech.com/smq/smq.tpl (22 September 2008).

[933] Flint and Eitzen, "Professional Sports Team Ownership and Entrepreneurial Capitalism," 18–22; Roberts and Olson, *Winning Is the Only Thing*, 52.

[934] Koppett, *Concise History*, 247–51, 425, 469; Roberts and Olson, *Winning Is the Only Thing*, 145–48. See also Schaff, *Sports. Inc.*

[935] Kowet, *The Rich Who Own Sports*, 52*ff.*

[936] Flint and Eitzen, "Professional Sports Team Ownership," 19–21; Jean Harvey, Alan Law, and Michael Cantelon, "North American Professional Team Sport Franchises Ownership Patterns and Global Entertainment Conglomerates," *Sociology of Sport Journal* 18/4 (December 2001): 439.

[937] Don Kowet, *The Rich Who Own Sports* (New York: Random House, 1977) 231; Harvey, Law, and Cantelon, "North American Professional Team Sport Franchises

Ownership," 436.

[938] Kowet, *The Rich Who Own Sports*, 185–86, 202.

[939] Harvey, Law, and Cantelon, "North American Professional Team Sport Franchises Ownership," 445, 448, 453.

[940] Scully, *The Business of Major League Baseball*, 133; Paul Staudohar, *The Sports Industry and Collective Bargaining* (Ithaca NY: I.L.R. Press, 1989) 22; Koppett, *Concise History*, 399.

[941] Schaaf, *Sports Inc.*, 52–54.

[942] Nixon, "The Commercialization and Organizational Development of Modern Sport," 109–13; Flint and Eitzen, "Professional Sports Team Ownership," 21–22; Roberts and Olson, *Winning Is the Only Thing*, 145–46.

[943] Flint and Eitzen, "Professional Sports Team Ownership," 21–22.

[944] Roberts and Olson, *Winning Is the Only Thing,* 53. See also Staudohar, *The Sports Industry and Collective Bargaining.*

[945] A cartel is a business combine formed to regulate production, pricing, and/or marketing by its members.

[946] McPherson, Curtis, and Loy, *The Social Significance of Sport*, 117; Roberts and Olson, *Winning Is the Only Thing,* 50, 53; Flint and Eitzen, "Professional Sports Team Ownership," 21–22.

[947] Nixon, "The Commercialization and Organizational Development of Modern Sport," 127; McPherson, Curtis, and Loy, *The Social Significance of Sport*, 119, 129; Roberts and Olson, *Winning Is the Only Thing*, 62, 68, 145; Staudohar, *The Sports Industry and Collective Bargaining,* 65, 129.

[948] Koppett, *Concise History*, 291. See also Schaaf, *Sports Inc.*

[949] Purdy, "For Whom Sport Tolls: Players, Owners and Fans," 579–80; Staudohar, *The Sports Industry and Collective Bargaining*, 64. See also Scully, *The Business of Major League Baseball.*

[950] Staudohar, *The Sports Industry and Collective Bargaining*, 16.

[951] Scully, *The Business of Major League Baseball*, 125, 128, 138.

[952] Purdy, "For Whom Sport Tolls: Players, Owners and Fans," 582; Roberts and Olson, *Winning Is the Only Thing*, 140; Staudohar, *The Sports Industry and Collective Bargaining*, 18, 63; Scully, *The Business of Major League Baseball*, 129–30.

[953] Staudohar, *The Sports Industry and Collective Bargaining*, 19, 63; Kowet, *The Rich Who Own Sports*, 214–15; Purdy, "For Whom Sport Tolls: Players, Owners and Fans," 579–80; Roberts and Olson, *Winning Is the Only Thing*, 145–46; Scully, *The Business of Major League Baseball*, 132.

[954] McPherson, Curtis, and Loy, *The Social Significance of Sport*, 126–27.

[955] Scully, *The Business of Major League Baseball*, 80, 85–87.

[956] Paul Hoch, *Rip Off the Big Game: The Exploitation of Sports by the Power Elite* (New York: Doubleday, 1972) 36; Christian Messenger, *Sport and the Spirit of Play in American Fiction: Hawthorne to Faulkner* (New York: Columbia University Press, 1981) 98; Koppett, *Concise History*, 11.

[957] Schaaf, *Sports, Inc.*, 21; Koppett, *Concise History*, 190; Bruce Evensen, *When Dempsey Fought Tunney: Heroes, Hokum, and Storytelling in the Jazz Age* (Knoxville: University of Tennessee Press, 1996) ix. See also Joan Chandler, "Media," in Levinson and

Christensen, *Encyclopedia of World Sport*, 241–46.

[958] Schaaf, *Sports, Inc.*, 22; Roberts and Olson, *Winning Is the Only Thing*, 22, 60; Gruneau, *Class, Sports, and Social Development*, 123.

[959] Koppett, *Concise History*, 492; Scully, *The Business of Major League Baseball*, 32; Staudohar, *The Sports Industry and Collective Bargaining*, 180; Christine Brooks, "Sponsorship: Strictly Business," *Athletic Business* 14/2 (October 1990): 60–61; "More Than a Game" (telecast), narrator Frank Gifford (New York: Arts and Entertainment Network, May 1992).

[960] Scully, *The Business of Major League Baseball*, 107, 139. See also Schaaf, *Sports, Inc.*

[961] Staudohar, *The Sports Industry and Collective Bargaining*, 169; Brohm, *Sport—A Prison of Measured Time*, 116; Harvey, Law, and Cantelon, "North American Professional Team Sport Franchises Ownership Patterns," 438.

[962] Scully, *The Business of Major League Baseball*, xiii, 109, 139.

[963] Staudohar, *The Sports Industry and Collective Bargaining*, 7.

[964] See Joseph L. Price, "Hallowed Ivy and Sacred Sun: The Iconic Character of Wrigley Field," in *Northsiders: Essays on the History and Culture of the Chicago Cubs*, eds. Gerald C. Wood and Andrew Hazucha (Jefferson NC: McFarland Co., 2008) 35–48.

[965] See Schaaf, *Sports, Inc.*, 220ff.

[966] Schaaf, *Sports, Inc.*, 224; "More Than a Game" (1992).

[967] Schaaf, *Sports, Inc.*, 224.

[968] Ibid., 216–18; A. Muscatine, "Tobacco Tempest: Anti-Smoking Movement Finds Deep Roots Tying Sports, Industry," *Commercial Appeal* (Memphis TN), 12 May 1991, B1.

[969] Kowet, *The Rich Who Own Sports*, 107–10; George Ritzer and Todd Stillman, "The Postmodern Ballpark as a Leisure Setting: Enchantment and Simulated De-McDonaldization," *Leisure Studies* 23/2 (April 2001): 102–103.

[970] Ritzer and Stillman, "The Postmodern Ballpark," 102–103, 111.

[971] Schaaf, *Sports, Inc.*, 208–209, 238–39; D. Stanley Eitzen, *Fair and Foul: Beyond the Myths and Paradoxes of Sport* (Boulder CO: Rowman & Littlefield, 2003) 18.

[972] Kowet, *The Rich Who Own Sports*, 94; Scully, *The Business of Major League Baseball*, 103; Kelly Smith, "Valuing Professional Sport Franchises: An Econometric Approach" (2004) *About.com:Economics*, http://economics.about.com/library/weekly/ae043004g.htm (6 June 2007); Schaaf, *Sports, Inc.*, 325.

[973] D. Stanley Eitzen, "The Myth and Reality of Elite Amateur Sport," in *The World & I, Washington Times*, October 1988, 558–59; Scully, *The Business of Major League Baseball*, 51–54, 69; Nixon, "The Commercialization and Organizational Development of Modern Sport,"125–27; David Whitson, "Sport and Hegemony: On the Construction of the Dominant Culture," *Sociology of Sport Journal* l/1 (March 1984): 73.

[974] See Schaaf, *Sports, Inc.*

[975] Koppett, *Concise History*, 451.

[976] See Bartlett, *Baseball and Mr. Spalding*.

[977] Ibid., 97, 102, 177, 229–42; Donald J. Mrozek, *Sport and American Mentality, 1880–1910* (Knoxville: University of Tennessee Press, 1983) 173.

[978] Scully, *The Business of Major League Baseball*, 2.

[979] Richard B. Cramer, *Joe DiMaggio: The Hero's Life* (New York: Simon & Schuster, 2000) 41, 56; Coakley, "Beyond the Obvious: A Critical Look at Sport in the USA," 593; Staudohar, *The Sports Industry and Collective Bargaining*, 4–5.

[980] Bartlett, *Baseball and Mr. Spalding*, 73–80; Hoch, *Rip Off the Big Game*, 45; Voigt, *America Through Baseball*, 4; Garry Whannel, *Blowing the Whistle: The Politics of Sport* (London: Pluto Press, 1983) 69.

[981] Al Stump, *Cobb: The Life and Times of the Meanest Man Who Ever Played Baseball* (Chapel Hill NC: Algonquin Books, 1994) 222–26; Purdy, "For Whom Sport Tolls: Players, Owners and Fans," 575.

[982] Koppett, *Concise History*, 231; Schaaf, *Sports, Inc.*, 91; Ben Badler, "More on Juan Duran," *Baseball America* (6 March 2008) http://www.baseballamerica.com/blog/prospects/?p=769 (30 October 2008).

[983] Koppett, *Concise History*, 310–11; Staudohar, *The Sports Industry and Collective Bargaining*, 14, 110–11, 195.

[984] Koppett, *Concise History*, 338–41; Scully, *The Business of Major League Baseball*, 37, 161; Staudohar, *The Sports Industry and Collective Bargaining*, 41–42; Schaaf, *Sports, Inc.*, 57–58.

[985] Staudohar, *The Sports Industry and Collective Bargaining*, 34–38, 88–89, 129, 152–53; Koppett, *Concise History*, 369–70.

[986] Leonard Koppett, *Sports Illusion, Sports Reality: A Reporter's View of Sports, Journalism, and Society*, 2nd ed. (Champaign IL: University of Illinois Press, 1994) x; Koppett, *Concise History*, 369, 446–67; Schaaf, *Sports, Inc.*, 350; Staudohar, *The Sports Industry and Collective Bargaining*, 57.

[987] Scully, *The Business of Major League Baseball*, 8, 35; Staudohar, *The Sports Industry and Collective Bargaining*, 28, 71, 172; "More Than a Game" (1992).

[988] Bartlett, *Baseball and Mr. Spalding,* 73; Staudohar, *The Sports Industry and Collective Bargaining*, 1.

[989] Nixon, "The Commercialization and Organizational Development of Modern Sport," 124; Roberts and Olson, *Winning Is the Only Thing*, 134–36; Staudohar, *The Sports Industry and Collective Bargaining*, 7.

[990] Scully, *The Business of Major League Baseball*, 151; Associated Press, "$10 Million-a-Year Player on Horizon," *Journal & Courier* (Lafayette IN), 26 December 1989, B3; Koppett, *Concise History*, 512.

[991] Scully, *The Business of Major League Baseball*, 193–94.

[992] Stump, *Cobb*, 284; Warren Susman, "Piety, Profits and Play," in *Men, Women, and Issues in American History,* eds. Howard Quint and Milton Cantor, vol. 2 (Homewood IL: Dorsey, 1980) 225; Patrick Hruby, "Beer and Sports, So Happy Together" *Washington Times* (17 June 2003) http://www. washtimes.com/sports/20030617-124535-9205r.htm (9 July 2008); Schaaf, Sports, Inc., 17.

[993] Judson Gooding, "The Tennis Industry," *Fortune* 87/6 (June 1973): 124–33; "More Than a Game" (1992); Schaaf, *Sports, Inc.*, 25.

[994] Cramer, *Joe DiMaggio*, 426, 446.

[995] Michael Sokolove, *Hustle: The Myth, Life, and Lies of Pete Rose* (New York: Simon & Schuster, 1990) 237–39, 281.

[996] McPherson, Curtis, and Loy, *The Social Significance of Sport*, 116; Associated Press, "Bulls Star Remains Top Earner," *Clarion Ledger* (Jackson MS), 4 December 1995, C1.

[997] Purdy, "For Whom Sport Tolls: Players, Owners and Fans," 578; "More Than a Game" (1992); Schaaf, *Sports, Inc.*, 17.

[998] Staudohar, *The Sports Industry and Collective Bargaining*, 2, 171.

[999] Allen Guttmann, *A Whole New Ball Game: An Interpretation of American Sports* (Chapel Hill: The University of North Carolina Press, 1988) 154; Roberts and Olson, *Winning Is The Only Thing*, x; Staudohar, *The Sports Industry and Collective Bargaining*, 2.

[1000] Thorstein Veblen, *The Theory of the Leisure Class,* Minerva Press ed. (New York: Funk & Wagnalls, 1899) chapter 2.

[1001] David L. Miller, *Gods and Games: Toward a Theology of Play* (New York: World Publishing Co., 1970) 174.

[1002] See Marshall McLuhan and Quentin Fiore, *The Medium Is the Massage* (Berkeley CA: Ginko Press) 2001.

[1003] See Susan Jackson and Mihaly Csikszentmihalyi, *Flow in Sports* (Champaign IL: Human Kinetics, 1999).

[1004] Richard Tawney, *Religion and the Rise of Capitalism* (Gloucester MA: Peter Smith, 1962) 284–85.

[1005] Quoted in Bill Moyers, *A World of Ideas,* ed. B. S. Flowers (New York: Doubleday, 1989) 411–25.

[1006] George S. Berkeley, *Works of George Berkeley, D.D., Bishop of Cloyne* (London: George Bell and Sons, 1897) ix.

Index